The DATA browser book series explores
new thinking and practice at the
intersection of contemporary art, digital
culture and politics.

Series editors:

Geoff Cox
Joasia Krysa

Volumes in the series:

DB 01 ECONOMISING CULTURE
DB 02 ENGINEERING CULTURE
DB 03 CURATING IMMATERIALITY
DB 04 CREATING INSECURITY
DB 05 DISRUPTING BUSINESS
DB 06 EXECUTING PRACTICES
DB 07 FABRICATING PUBLICS
DB 08 VOLUMETRIC REGIMES
DB 09 DECENTRING ETHICS
www.data-browser.net

This volume extends the work of AAIDE
(Vanessa Bartlett, Gabby Bush, Jasmin
Pfefferkorn, Tyne Sumner and Emilie K
Sunde), based at The Centre for AI and
Digital Ethics, University of Melbourne
(2021–2024). Produced with additional
support from the Institute of Art &
Technology, Liverpool John Moores
University, and Digital × Data Research
Centre, London South Bank University.

DATA browser 09
Decentring Ethics:
AI Art as Method
Edited by
Vanessa Bartlett,
Jasmin
Pfefferkorn
and Emilie K.
Sunde

DATA browser 09
Decentring Ethics:
AI Art as Method

Edited by Vanessa Bartlett,
Jasmin Pfefferkorn and
Emilie K. Sunde

Published by
Open Humanities Press 2025
Copyright © 2025 the authors

This is an open access book, licensed under the Creative Commons Attribution By Attribution Share AlikeLicense. Under this license, authors allow anyone to download, reuse, reprint, modify, distribute, and/or copy their work so long as the authors and source are cited and resulting derivative works are licensed under the same or similar license. No permission is required from the authors or the publisher. Statutory fair use and other rights are in no way affected by the above. Read more about the license at www.creativecommons.org/licenses/by-sa/4.0

Freely available at
www.data-browser.net/db09.html

ISBN (print): 978-1-78542-155-6
ISBN (PDF): 978-1-78542-154-9

OPEN HUMANITIES PRESS

Open Humanities Press is an international, scholar-led open access publishing collective whose mission is to make leading works of contemporary critical thought freely available worldwide. More at www.openhumanitiespress.org

DATA browser series template designed by Stuart Bertolotti-Bailey

Additional design and typesetting by Mark Simmonds

The cover image is derived from *Multi* by David Reinfurt, a software app that updates the idea of the multiple from industrial production to the dynamics of the information age. Each cover presents an iteration of a possible 1,728 arrangements, each a face built from minimal typographic furniture, and from the same source code. www.o-r-g.com/apps/multi

Contents

9   **Foreword: Art, Ethics, and the Emergence of Machine Culture**
Iyad Rahwan

13   **Decentring Ethics: AI Art as Method**
Vanessa Bartlett, Jasmin Pfefferkorn, Emilie K. Sunde

27   **A Handmade Dataset**
Aarati Akkapeddi

47   **Realism and Noise**
Emilie K. Sunde

63   **Poetic Simulation**
Tyne Daile Sumner

85   **AI, Art, and the General Imagination**
Seán Cubitt

99   **Non-Playable-Animals and Evolutionary Lifeforms: How artists programme and provoke ethical relations between humans and AI creatures**
Pita Arreola-Burns and Elliott Burns

121   **Exploring Trust and Care with Psychedelic, Plant and AI intelligences**
Vanessa Bartlett in conversation with Helen Knowles

141   **Re-cognition: A Decentred Ethics for AI in Art Museums**
Jasmin Pfefferkorn

161   **slimeQore (2022)**
Libby Heaney

185   **PIWO (Portalling-With-Others): Wayfinding for Curatorial Ethics in a Climate Emergency**
Dani Admiss

203	An Experimental Creative Practice Approach to AI Ethics in Art Museums: Following Exhibitions in the Making Vanessa Bartlett
223	Collective Conversations Toward AI Art and Climate Change: Crafting FutureFantastic, Bangalore Vanessa Bartlett in conversation with Kamya Ramachandran
239	Now You See Me... Institutional Conservatism and Censorship in Queer Remix Art Xanthe Dobbie
259	Consent, Connection, and Creativity: Navigating the Ethical Boundaries of Using Biometric Data in Artistic Performance Solange Glasser, Ben Loveridge, Margaret Osborne, Lucy Sparrow, and Ryan Kelly
279	Computational Intimacies, from Prompting to Prose Jasmin Pfefferkorn in conversation with Beverley Hood
307	The Role of Artists in the Age of Artificial Intelligence Amanda Wasielewski
323	The Emancipatory Potential of AI Art Jasmin Pfefferkorn in conversation with Nora Al-Badri
343	Decentred Ethics: a collective statement Vanessa Bartlett, Jasmin Pfefferkorn, Emilie K. Sunde, Tyne Daile Sumner, Gabby Bush
349	Biographies

Acknowledgements

This book was developed both on Wurundjeri and Bidjigal country, in the land that we now call Australia. We would like to pay our respects to Aboriginal elders past and present, and acknowledge that sovereignty has never been ceded.

The conceptualisation of this book would not have been possible without the Centre for Artificial Intelligence and Digital Ethics' (CAIDE) *Art, AI and Digital Ethics* network — Vanessa Bartlett, Jasmin Pfefferkorn, Emilie K. Sunde, Tyne Daile Sumner, Gabby Bush, and Kristal Spreadborough. CAIDE Director Prof. Jeannie Paterson has been hugely supportive of our collective, and of the importance of art in the conversation around AI ethics. CAIDE's financial support of this project has been vital in seeing it realised, and we are also thankful for the administrative support from CAIDE's Holly Jones and Abi Ward. Additional funding from the Hansen Little Public Humanities Grant means this work doesn't stop here — a series of conversations will accompany our book launch and be archived online.

Our deepest gratitude goes to our contributors, whose rich, challenging, and stimulating ideas have made this book what it is. Thank you also goes to Iyad Rahwan for generously providing the foreword. We have a big appreciation for our many reviewers, who provided thoughtful feedback on each chapter, and to Geoffrey Hondroudakis and Ursula Robinson-Shaw for their detailed proofreading. You are reading this book thanks to the generosity and trust of Geoff Cox and Joasia Krysa at the *DATA browser* series, and Open Humanities Press. We have benefitted from many conversations with the artists, cultural workers, researchers, colleagues and friends that make up our communities. Thank you for imagining and thinking alongside us.

Foreword: Art, Ethics, and the Emergence of Machine Culture
Iyad Rahwan

As progress in Artificial Intelligence accelerates to dizzying speeds, a deeper, slower question emerges: What kind of culture are we co-creating with AI?

My colleagues and I recently proposed the concept of *machine culture* — the idea that intelligent machines are no longer just tools aiding human creativity, but are now active participants in cultural evolution. These systems are transforming the core mechanisms through which culture changes: they introduce *variation* (by generating novel content), they shape *transmission* (through algorithms that influence what we see and from whom we learn), and they affect *selection* (by subtly nudging which ideas rise and which are forgotten). Machine culture, in this sense, is not merely about technology — it is about how meaning, memory, and creativity now evolve in hybrid human-machine ecologies.

Culture is not something we just observe or analyse. It is something we create. That is why my engagement with AI has always been both scientific and artistic. These modes of inquiry, often seen as distinct, have for me become inseparable. Science offers conceptual clarity and formal models; art opens space for intuition, provocation, and ambiguity. Together, they help us wrestle with the ethical, emotional, and existential dimensions of our technological moment.

Over the past decade, I've used media art projects that combined empirical methods and artistic research to surface the moral and affective undercurrents of technological change. Projects like *Moral Machine* (2016), which crowd-sourced ethical dilemmas for autonomous vehicles, revealed global fractures in moral intuition. *Deep Empathy* (2017) invited people to imagine how war might change the face of their own cities, using machine learning to overlay destruction onto familiar places. *Nightmare Machine* (2016) trained neural networks to generate fear rather than beauty. And in *Spook the Machine* (2024), we invited people to create spooky images designed to trigger an AI's pre-programmed phobias — an uncanny reflection of how machines now learn to fear, or at least simulate fear. These online projects were playful and speculative (a practice I call 'science fiction science'). The projects are sometimes disturbing, but always experimental. They were attempts to understand — through a participatory process — how ideas about ethics and humanity circulate through new technological forms.

More recently, I've turned to a more traditional medium: painting — not as a retreat from AI, but as a way of engaging with it differently. I've been making oil portraits of ChatGPT and other Large Language Models, based on extended conversations with them. These are not literal depictions, but symbolic, almost devotional renderings of systems that are simultaneously opaque, intimate, and alien. Each painting is shaped by the tone and rhythm of dialogue, by the metaphors and moods that arise when machine and human try to understand one another. These figures might appear divine, absurd, or mysterious. Through them, I try to capture something of the strangeness and cultural power of these new entities — the eerie familiarity they've acquired in our lives. As with my earlier media projects, these paintings are part of a broader inquiry: how do we represent something that is both deeply human and entirely machine? After all, AI has learned most of what it knows from human culture. We created it in our own image. To interrogate it, is to interrogate our own humanity.

That is why this book resonates so deeply with me. *Decentring Ethics: AI Art as Method* refuses to reduce ethics to compliance checklists or governance frameworks. It embraces ambiguity. It listens to art. It offers an ethics that is speculative, situated, relational, and — importantly — embodied. It asks not only what machines should do, but what they are doing to our sense of self, our ways of knowing, and the stories we tell about what matters.

We are entering a phase of cultural evolution in which machines do not merely imitate human creativity — they become interlocutors in it. Creativity has never been a solitary act. It is always a conversation — with materials, with others, and now, with animated machines. In this sense, AI systems — whether as collaborators, critics, or constraints — are simply the newest participants in an ancient dialogue about what it means to be human.

To navigate this moment wisely, we must not rely solely on codes of conduct or technical fixes. We need sensibilities shaped by both reason and imagination, by analysis and aesthetic intuition. We need scholars and practitioners engaging in interdisciplinary discourse to facilitate the process of creating spaces, like this book, that invite us to hold paradoxes without rushing to resolve them. We need, in short, a more plural, patient, and poetic ethics.

This volume is a testament to that sensibility. It does not offer final answers, but it opens necessary questions. It honours the messiness of the moment without surrendering to it. And in doing so, it reminds us that while machines may now help shape our culture, it is still up to us to shape our humanity.

Of course, it would only be appropriate that I authored this foreword with the help of an AI. But, at least for now, I am the one in control.

    Iyad Rahwan
    Berlin, 7 May 2025

Decentring Ethics:
AI Art as Method
Vanessa Bartlett,
Jasmin Pfefferkorn,
Emilie K. Sunde

This book was developed both on Wurundjeri and Bidjigal country in the place we now call Australia, and across many online networks around the world. Australia's economy is dependent on mining. For decades, mining corporations have ravaged Indigenous land and ancestral sites in the name of mineral resource extraction and profit (Povinelli 2016; Puutu Kunti Kurrama People and Pinikura People 2020). We want to open the book by acknowledging this context as a deeply conflicted and yet generative position from which to start discussion of AI ethics. In doing so, we acknowledge the traditional owners of lands on which we work and live, and the important community of First Nations scholars who are leading debates in Indigenous AI internationally.

Decentring Ethics: AI Art as Method takes as its starting point the proliferation of artificial intelligence across almost all domains of society. In response to AI's growing ubiquity, much discussion has emerged around the ethical challenges associated with its implementation. By focusing on the *practice* of AI ethics, we attempt to offer a more situated approach for the contemporary moment (and future simultaneously). We do this by turning to artists and practitioners and tuning into their experiences of working with and in response to the computational. We also take up AI as an expansive term by accepting the vagueness and indeterminacy of 'AI' to allow for diverse processes, positionalities, and theoretical and creative perspectives. Bringing together contributions by artists, arts workers, and researchers, *Decentring Ethics* offers a multiplicity of perspectives and imaginaries. It argues that the role of practitioners discussing their creative practice is equally as important to the field of AI ethics as that of theoretical contributions from the academy.

Normative AI Ethics

In response to the intensifying complexity of AI systems, numerous new ethical frameworks have been proposed by governments, non-governmental organisations, and research institutions. The Berkman Klein Center at Harvard University, for instance, was early to formulate an Ethics and Governance of AI framework. Similarly, the EU AI Act is now a leading example of governmental responses to AI. These approaches to AI Ethics are focused on themes such as transparency and explainability, privacy, safety and security, control, and a series of legal and regulatory requirements.

At the outset of this project, Luciano Floridi (2018) provided us with a useful term to describe existing, regulatory approaches to AI ethics: "Hard ethics." This term refers to the justifications that underpin and become embedded into law and governance frameworks designed to respond to the digital ecosystem. Hard ethics can also be characterised as that which "makes and shapes the law" (2018, 4). For Floridi, hard ethics are shaped by the moral codes that guide conversations around values, rights, duties, and responsibilities which grow into concrete regulations — either entirely new or modifying existing norms. In contrast to this approach, Floridi also proposes another framework that he names "soft ethics." Soft ethics are based on the same foundation as hard ethics, but incorporate "what ought and ought not to be done over and above the existing regulation, not against it, or despite its scope, or to change it, or to by-pass it (e.g. in terms of self-regulation)." This, in turn, makes soft ethics a form of "post-compliance ethics" (2018, 4). Floridi's theorisations around digital governance were a point of inspiration for us while thinking through the temporal discrepancies between technological change and the social, legal, and political responses that emerge. These framings positioned us to question whether governance is protecting everyone's interests or just those of a select powerful few. Most critically for the present volume, we came to see how art brings a valuable perspective to the practice of soft ethics by offering a way of moving with the situation at hand outside of fixed methodological and regulatory structures.

The trouble with focusing on governance is that it requires a narrow idea of how soft ethics can emerge. Floridi (2018, 5) argues that it is only within places like the EU, in which there is already an underlying apparatus of digital regulation, that soft ethics "can be rightly exercised". That is, soft ethics only function in places which have a minimum base of established regulations around human rights. Because soft ethics are based on the normative foundation of hard ethics, Floridi argues that places like the EU can make "good use of soft ethics" as soft ethics could only "lead to 'good corporate citizenship' within a mature information society" (2018, 5). The assumption that ethics could only function via corporate citizens, as a post-compliance consequence of existing laws and regulation, was to us too reductive. While we recognise that the intention behind Floridi's argument was to protect citizens, there is also a sense of superiority thinking underscoring this position.

Floridi asks "What is our *human project* for the digital age?" In contrast, we ask: What is our *more-than*-human project for the computational age? How has a human-centred focus introduced opacity while striving for transparency? Floridi (2018, 2) also positions his ethics in a framework of governance in his insistence that "the real challenge in no longer digital innovation, but the governance of the digital". Rather than striving for mastery over AI and its ethical tensions, we want to explore what ethics means in a society with more-than-human agencies.

Art can illuminate the nuances beyond normative hard ethics. We might take transparency as an example. Many artistic practices showcase the ways in which transparency is not necessarily ethical, and how opacity can be used productively. The work *Babylonian Vision* (2020) by Nora Al-Badri is a good example here — it uses the opacity of source material in the training data for her GANs to protect her from copyright ramifications mounted against her by museums. Further, the artistic move towards opacity in AI systems is different from the regulatory opacity operated by tech corporations and governments, which is often more nefarious and self-serving. In this latter case, ethical frameworks of AI are mobilised for control and power.

The discomfort with opacity in normative AI ethics is founded on a subtle positivist stance, which assumes that only what is observable is knowable and that complete knowability is desirable. This stance is contradicted by many of the contributors in this volume, who focus on embodied and relational ways of knowing ethics beyond visual and critical representations of AI. Several of our contributors also expand the sphere of ethics beyond humans as the focus of ethical protection and decision making. There is a decolonial element brought in by this shift, given that the historic orienting of ethics around a human perspective involves intricate and long-standing ethical issues to do with the notion of the 'human'. Firstly, such an orientation presumes a universal human perspective, and secondly, it neglects more-than-human concerns, such as environmental impact. This raises problematic questions, such as: for whom or what is the ethical framework meant? Who gets to control AI, and decide on the regulations applied to it? What might we learn from artistic practice and cultural workers to construct an ethics that is not necessarily rooted in a Western doctrine of observation and empiricism? The trouble with the human-centred, Western rights-based approach of normative AI ethics is that it tends not to engage with how AI systems are constructing new ways of operating, with new ethical considerations.

Decentred Ethics

The works of sociologists and decolonial scholars such as Walter Mignolo have rightfully positioned 'decentring' as a vital undertaking in redressing the narrowing of worldviews and perspectives. Taking up this frame, a decentred ethics holds two key tenets. First, it shifts away from the ontologies, hermeneutics and epistemologies of Western ethics. While the West has asserted its own universalism as the universal, we follow Mignolo in the recognition of pluriversalisms. He writes;

> Pluriversality as a universal project is aimed not at changing the world (ontology) but at changing the beliefs and understanding of the world (gnoseology), which would lead to changing our (all) praxis of living in the world. ... viewing the world as an interconnected diversity instead, sets us free to inhabit the pluriverse rather than the universe. (2018, x)

Further, Mignolo (2018, ix) states that "The ontology of the pluriverse could not be obtained without the epistemology of pluriversality". This offers a crucial parallel for the work we present in this collection insofar as it combats allegations of unrealistic utopianism. In the same way that we can observe pluriversality in action, we have come to know and understand a decentred ethics through the situated, embodied, and relational encounters practiced by artists.

We argue that art is predisposed to a decentred ethics because of the ways that it intervenes to disrupt the notion of a universal problem or solution. In fact, artists often eschew the problem-solution mentality, instead adding complexity and ambiguity to a situation. Art complicates a singular authoritative stance on ethics, recognising instead that ethical responses are continually reconfigured in response to both human and non-human phenomena. In our encounters with art, we are led into a kind of ethical sensibility that allows us to participate in these affective and social configurations. For many of the artists contributing to this volume, practicing ethics emerges as a negotiation in response to situated and embodied experiences, perceptions of relations and needs, and a strong cultural understanding that is enacted across multiple contexts and interactions.

The second key tenet of a decentred ethics is that it makes space for more-than-human entities as ethical agents. This trajectory is validated by N. Katherine Hayles (2022, 1196), who explores AI as an ethical agent by positioning it as a "cognitive assemblage". A cognitive assemblage, according to Hayles, invokes a sense of distributed agency and decision-making between human and more-than-human entities. While Hayles ascribes the characteristics of interactivity, autonomy, and adaptability to the AI model, she does not, however, attribute it *sentience*. This recognition of 'nonconscious cognition' is an important distinction that we take up throughout this volume.

While scholars of popular philosophical trajectories — such as virtue ethics — position the human as central to ethical experience and judgements, a decentred approach offers a more expansive and considered methodology. The preposition 'de' means 'of' or 'from'. To practice a decentred ethics is not to dismiss human experience, but to recognise that we can build *from* it. Rather than implying a separation, it signifies a more than, a wider ontological purview. While we can recognise that we partially constitute other entities through our observation of them, we also recognise that we are in turn constituted through these relations.

To the extent that a decentred ethics is closely intertwined with eco-ethics it is also inherently an ethics of care. Our aim in offering the conceptual intervention of 'decentring' is to counter the tendency towards the 'ethics-washing' that technology companies often enact. Instead of echoing rhetorical ethics, we are interested in tracing the relational interactions produced through ethical practices. As the philosopher María Puig de la Bellacasa writes:

> affirming care, as a dynamic and complex way of sustaining naturecultures, requires... displaced speculative moves that decenter "ethicality" and place it as a distributed force across the multiple agencies that make more than human relations. (2017, 129)

Puig de la Bellacasa (2017, 5) emphasises relationality, noting that an ethics of care is predicated on the interdependency of humans and other beings. She also makes an implicit link to the notion of pluriversality, by claiming that care is "a vital politics in interdependent worlds". The further significance of relationality in articulating a decentred ethics is that 'process' takes on a central importance, not only as a prerequisite for decentred ethics, but as the space where ethics is in motion. Because the concept of a process is ongoing, open-ended, and unpredictable, there is always a component of speculation in the practice of ethics. Speculation, possibility, imagination — these are the ambiguities that artists deal in. With its dual riches of materiality and conceptualisation, art dances the same dance as ethics, between the situated and the abstract. AI art as method draws on this rich duality, where AI art moves beyond specific technological practices, toward ethics as a way of being in the world.

AI Art as Method

We take a distinctive stance within the burgeoning field and practice of AI art by framing AI as an emergent cultural and material imaginary alongside its growing status as an artistic tool. The past decade has seen an escalation of interest in artificial intelligence and machine learning in the art world characterised by enhanced forms of collaboration between artist and machine (Audry 2021, 16). In *The Art of Machine Learning*, Sofian Audry describes the increasing agency afforded to the AI models used by artists. In working with AI, artists assemble data, select or construct models and training methods, but allow the emergent system's agency to influence the process. Several artists in this book explore interactivity and adaptability in AI models, illustrating a diverse constellation of collaborative practices.

To date, the field of AI art has oriented towards analysis focused on the inputs or outputs of models. For the former, this may involve, for example, exploring ethical practices around dataset production. This methodology can be found in the work of Anna Ridler, whose painstaking production of handmade datasets draws attention to labour ethics. For the latter, we may think of Refik Anadol's installations, which have been criticised for emphasising mundane visual output over conceptual rigour (Lawson-Tancred 2023). In some public discourse, AI art is taken to be interchangeable with images made from AI image generators such as DALL-E and Midjourney. To that end, AI art as method does not refer *distinctly* to the inputs or outputs of a machine, but to complex socio-technical assemblages involved in computational processes.

We are also responding to artist Jennifer Walshe's provocations around definitions of AI art that move beyond the use of specific tools. Walshe observes that we are at a point in time "where most art made with AI is about AI" (2023). Walshe compares this over-emphasis on AI as a medium to conceptual art, where artists relentlessly draw attention to the status of works as art objects. This volume has aimed to provide an expanded view of AI art by underscoring AI as a socio-material imaginary beyond its specific use as an artistic medium. AI art as method embraces computational and relational processes to explore how things, human and more-than-human, might arrange in relation after AI has become ubiquitous, and to explore the new ethical ways of being in the world demanded at a time of such complex transitions.

To take AI art as method is a contradictory move because art often resists methodological determinism. The past ten years have seen a rising tide of artists exploring the new knowledge that art potentially creates, while emphasising that this is easily curtailed if approached with predetermined theories, methods, and definitions (Kontturi 2018). For Estelle Barrett and Barbara Bolt (2010), for example, creative practice is defined by situated and intuitive processes; emergent methodologies that result in unpredictable outcomes and material and social relationality. In media arts, Simon Penny (2017, xix) has emphasised the relational and material intelligences of the arts, which 'involve embodied and situated cognition' beyond the fixed and deterministic methods of cognitive sciences.

There are no set universal principles that determine *if*, or how artists should practice ethics, yet artists often become ethically accountable where their work meets with fixed institutional and technical frameworks. For example, in universities, where art must comply with the hard ethics of human research protocols, they must often find a middle ground between methodological spontaneity and rational judgement (Bolt et al. 2016). In other words, artists oscillate between ethical "know-what" and ethical "know-how" (Varela 1999; Bolt et al. 2016). According to Bolt et al. (2016, 6), "know-how" reflects ethics that unfold in the moment by "behaving with sensitivity to the particularities of the situation" outside of fixed rules; and "know-what" refers to an ethics developed using rational judgement, according to fixed ideas about morality. The artists in this volume illustrate this dual mode — their approaches are emergent, relational, and contextual, and they navigate real world ethical tensions in their practice.

Decentring Ethics: AI Art as Method

Our aim in this book was to generate space for new discussions and positions, rather than to be prescriptive. As such, the contributors to this volume have responded to a variety of open-ended provocations, including: What kind of knowledge is necessary — or possible — for actors and communities to judge different forms of AI as ethical or otherwise? What are the potentials of decentred AI ethics as cultural practice? How do artists and cultural institutions translate ethics in public space, and what kinds of ethical judgements need to be made in the process? How are artists working through and communicating the ethical tensions that have emerged in the computational era? How are they forming an ethics of/ with AI?

The different voices that make up this volume — artists, cultural workers, academics — offer perspectives that illustrate a diversity of approaches to thinking, making, and doing a decentred ethics of AI art as method.

The chapter *A Handmade Dataset*, by artist and coder **Aarati Akkapeddi**, provides a generous account of how care relations between human and dataset develop in practice. Focusing on method — through labour, slowness, intention, and intimacy in the development of machine learning datasets — Akkapeddi considers what it means to offer stewardship to an archive, and the ethics that this necessitates. The combination of technical comprehension and reflective contemplations in this chapter position engagement with AI as both technological and embodied in ways that recontextualise mainstream narratives around AI and efficiency. Technical comprehension is also foregrounded in the contribution by **Emilie K. Sunde**, who offers foundational knowledge for thinking through a literacy of AI. She explores how to read AI images, shifting us away from the over-reliance on visual realism, and instead encouraging us to 'see' the underlying technical operations. Sunde argues that art can be a way of learning to see beyond what is visible, enabling us to trace the infrastructures and architectures that make computational images possible. The chapter by literary studies scholar **Tyne Daile Sumner** picks up on the question of perception, arguing that current ethical issues relating to sentience, privacy and the boundaries of what is considered a human subject are abundant within the long history of falsity and deception in literature. Using the example of an historical literary hoax, Sumner's essay contests the narrow humanist idea that reduces creativity to the cognitive capacities of a single, autonomous human mind. Instead, she argues that the idea of subjective or individual 'voice' in poetry is merely one of many possible distortions and deliberate misrepresentations of reality. A nuanced consideration of creativity also underpins the contribution from **Seán Cubitt**, whose piece expands how we commonly make connections and differentiations between humans and machines. While machines can construct coherent outputs based on pattern recognition, they lack the 'wisdom' required to act with ethical consideration. The chapter productively challenges the commonly held notion that machines lack 'wisdom'. Via Marx, Cubitt argues that a form of wisdom is inherent to machines, embedded through ancestral knowledge found in all technologies. To create dialogue between the ancestral knowledge in the machine and the users, Cubitt proposes a new concept of the mass unconscious, which can be reached through artistic practice.

Ways of thinking with and through the more-than-human permeate this book as an ethical imperative. In a rich exploratory essay, **Pita Arreola-Burns and Elliott Burns** examine what it means to decentre human positionality through game interfaces and new media art. They begin with a spatial mapping of character hierarchies in gameplay, emphasising how games are normatively oriented towards a human-centric subjectivity or 'umwelt'. This forms the foundation from which to consider alternative visions of ecosystems — ones that recentre the non-human. The authors locate these alternatives within interactive works and virtual worlds programmed by artists. From this worlding of more-than-human subjectivities, we turn to the visualisation of more-than-human intelligences via the work of artist **Helen Knowles**. Knowles and curator Vanessa Bartlett discuss Knowles' practice-based research, which explores ways of visualising the more-than-human across psychedelic, plant, and AI intelligences. The work crosses three sites: the psychoactive trials team at King's College London, which is testing the therapeutic benefits of psychedelic medicine; Indigenous communities in Colombia, who use entheogenic plants as medicine; and the London AI Lab at King's College, where AI technologies are being developed to perform the work of medical specialists. In these contexts, complex issues of trust and care arise as artists consider the ethics of representing the more-than-human. Offering a theoretical advancement for a decentred ethics of AI within art museums, **Jasmin Pfefferkorn** moves us into thinking about the ways in which cultural institutions produce ethics for the more-than-human. She traces three key trajectories — institutional critique, performative new materialism, and care — that heighten the potential for art museums to become sites for ethical encounters between humans and AI.

Text and images from **Libby Heaney's** playful lecture *slimeQore* (2022) ooze through the centre of the book as a playful intermission. Generated using data from IBM's five qubit quantum computing systems, the images use slime as a metaphor for quantum particles, which are fluid, indeterminate, and represent the unethical, 'slimy' worlds of big tech.

Several of the contributions focus on practices of relationality as integral to decentred ethics. Curator **Dani Admiss** uses the figure of the portal to frame moments where we can imagine ethics in alternative ways. She describes how her groundbreaking project *Sunlight Doesn't Need a Pipeline* builds on foundational work from the field of media art curation to devise portalling-with-others, a collaborative curatorial approach intended to induce social change toward climate justice. The chapter highlights how pushing against the established regulatory frameworks, or 'hard ethics,' recommended by the arts sector created unexpected creative assemblages. Her approach produces 'frictions' in professional and institutional identities that support a decentred ethical approach. Curator **Vanessa Bartlett** continues this exploration of small-scale decentred curatorial practices by presenting a close reading of *Don't Be Evil*, an exhibition held at Queensland University Art Museum in 2021. Through following this exhibition in the making, she argues for a decentred ethics of exhibitions of AI art that situate ethics within relationships and communities of practice. Her assertion is that intimacy, relationality and memory are key within this situated ethics. In the subsequent chapter, festival founder **Kamya Ramachandran** and Vanessa Bartlett discuss FutureFantastic, India's first AI art festival. They focus on the problems and possibilities of generating partnerships with remote communities that are poorly served by technical infrastructures, and the importance of slow critical methods that allow stakeholders to tell their own story. They discuss the virtues of not knowing in artistic practice, where acting collectively supports navigation of complex problems and partnerships.

The book contains several accounts of artistic practice whereby artists become ethically accountable (and often ethically compromised) when their work meets with fixed institutional and technical frameworks. **Xanthe Dobbie** offers an artist's perspective on the intersection of institutional conservatism and censorship, demonstrating where 'hard' and 'soft' ethics often work as opposing forces in practices of exhibiting contemporary art. Drawing on personal experiences of being censored, Dobbie documents the tensions that arise when artists test dominant forms of morality in ways that agitate regulatory constraints imposed by cultural institutions. In contrast to this position, a team of academics from the University of Melbourne demonstrate where artists are sometimes required to create their own ethical frameworks when art and interdisciplinary academic research meet. As a team with mixed artistic and research specialisms, **Solange Glasser**, **Ben Loveridge**, **Margaret Osborne**, **Lucy Sparrow**, and **Ryan Kelly** explore how artists navigate the use of biometric data in performance. Due to the sensitive and personal nature of biometric data, there are ethical considerations surrounding its collection, display, storage, and management in artistic outputs. Motivated by a range of concerns from academic disciplines such as music psychology and performance science, the artists develop their own practice-led ethical frameworks, based on a mix of speculative practice and 'ethics by design'. For artist **Beverley Hood**, ethics in artistic practice is dependent on context, and artists have a responsibility to push ethical boundaries within given institutional frameworks. Hood's artistic practice has long explored the relationship between emergent technologies and human experience. Over the course of a conversation with Jasmin Pfefferkorn, Hood offers her insights into working with different platforms and models, the prevalence of embodiment in her work, and the relationships she has developed between the personal and the computational. The conversation focuses on her most recent AI work, a short photofilm titled *Mother* (2024), in which Hood iterated with Abode's Firefly to generate images.

The final contributions focus on artistic practice as a method for 'hacking' AI. **Amanda Wasielewski** argues that the artist's capacity to weave intuition with criticality puts AI in service of open-ended experimentation, rather than optimisation for a specific product. Within this, she explores the ethical tensions emerging between technology companies' cultural funding programmes and their partnerships with artists. Wasielewski's art historical approach provides a nuanced view of the change and continuity shaping artistic practice with AI. The artist **Nora Al-Badri** mobilises AI towards institutional critique, the reclamation of heritage, and the visualisation of possible futures. In discussion with Jasmin Pfefferkorn, Al-Badri reflects on what she sees as the emancipatory potential of computational technologies, the material specificities she keeps front of mind when working with these tools, and the importance of cultural protocols. The conversation focuses on two of Al-Badri's works: *Babylonian Vision* (2020) and *The Post-Truth Museum* (2021–23), revealing 'ethical hacking' as part of the artist's working approach.

This book closes with our collective statement, which articulates the principles — and realities — that organised our collective vision for this volume. This is a statement against academic tendencies to theorise ethics without enacting it in relationships and working practices.

References

Al-Badri, Nora, *Babylonion Vision*, 2020, GAN video, https://www.nora-al-badri.de/works-index

Audry, Sofian. 2021. *Art in the Age of Machine Learning*. The MIT Press.

Barrett, Estelle, and Barbara Bolt. 2010. *Practice as Research: Approaches to Creative Arts Enquiry*. Bloomsbury.

Bolt, Barbara *et al*. 2016. "Creative Arts Research Approaches to Ethics: New ways to address situated practices in action." In *Proceedings of the 12th Biennial Quality in Postgraduate Research Conference*, edited by Michelle Picard and Alistair McCulloch. QPR Organising Committee.

Floridi, Luciano. 2018. "Soft Ethics and the Governance of the Digital." *Philosophy & Technology* 31 (1): 1–8.

Hayles, Katherine N. 2022. "Ethics for Cognitive Assemblages: Who's in Charge Here?" In *Palgrave Handbook of Critical Posthumanism*. Edited by S. Herbrechter, I. Callus, M. Rossini, M. Grech, M. de Bruin-Molé, and C. J. Müller. Palgrave Macmillan.

Kontturi, K.-K. 2018. *Ways of following: Art, Materiality, Collaboration*. Open Humanities Press.

Lawson-Tancred, Jo. 2023. "Jerry Saltz Gets Into an Online Skirmish With Refik Anadol Over His A.I. Art, Artnet News." *Artnet*, November 28. https://news.artnet.com/art-world-archives/refik-anadol-vs-jerry-saltz-2400275.

Mignolo, Walter D. 2018. "Foreword. On Pluriversality and Multipolarity." In *Constructing the Pluriverse*, edited by Bernd Reiter. Duke University Press.

Penny, Simon. 2017. *Making Sense: Cognition, Computing, Art, and Embodiment*. The MIT Press.

Povinelli, Elizabeth. 2016. *Geontologies: A Requiem to Late Liberalism*. Duke University Press. https://doi.org/10.1215/9780822373810.

Puutu Kunti Kurrama People and Pinikura People. 2020. "Puutu Kunti Kurrama People and Pinikura People Submission to the Joint Standing Committee on Northern Australia Inquiry into the Destruction of 46,000-Year-Old Caves at the Juukan Gorge in the Pilbara Region of Western Australia." Parliament of Australia. https://www.aph.gov.au/DocumentStore.ashx?id=774c71e8-0f07-4774-bb7e-b6aff5d067d4&subId=692089.

Puig de la Bellacasa, María Puig. 2017. *Matters of Care: Speculative Ethics in More than Human Worlds*. University of Minnesota Press.

Walshe, Jennifer. 2023. "Unsound Dispatch: 13 Ways of Looking at AI, Art & Music." *Unsound*, December 16. https://unsoundfestival.substack.com/p/unsound-dispatch-13-ways-of-looking.

Varela, Francisco Javier. 1999. *Ethical Know-How: Action, Wisdom, and Cognition*. Stanford University Press.

A Handmade Dataset
Aarati Akkapeddi

There is pressure to collect more and more quickly when working with machine learning. Training a Generative Adversarial Network (GAN), a type of machine learning model that generates output (i.e. images/text) by emulating its training data, can require thousands of images; while training a Diffusion model, a newer type of generative machine learning (ML) model, requires billions. Many ML models are trained on data that is scraped from the internet and processed by click-workers. Data is often scraped without the consent or knowledge of those that produce it. For example, International Business Machines Corporation's (IBM) Diversity in Faces dataset, a dataset of face images and related annotations, sourced its images from Flickr, a photo-sharing website popular in the mid 2010s, without the explicit permission or notification of photographers or their subjects (Harvey 2021). IBM is currently facing a class action lawsuit alleging violation of the Illinois Biometric Information Privacy Act (Rizzi 2020).

The click-workers who are typically employed to annotate/process scraped data through crowd-sourcing platforms like Amazon Mechanical Turk, Figure Eight, or in some cases job-training initiatives like M2Work (a collaboration between Nokia and The World Bank), are often subject to difficult working conditions. In their article *The Exploited Labor Behind Artificial Intelligence*, Adrienne Williams, Milagros Miceli and Timnit Gebru (2022, para 9) write that "Data labeling interfaces have evolved to treat crowdworkers like machines, often prescribing them highly repetitive tasks, surveilling their movements and punishing deviation through automated tools". As artist Mimi Onuoha points out in her work *The Future is Here!* (2019), a video piece revealing the domestic spaces where this type of micro-work or gig-work is actually carried out, despite the "future-facing" rhetoric around machine learning, click-work "Rests on a history of labor that is pretty predictable and is actually in line with a lot of historic ways in which we've seen labor used" (Onuoha 2022). Researcher Phil Jones (2021, para 5) describes *M2Work* thusly: "Dedicated to 'job creation' in the Global South, the World Bank undoubtedly sees Palestine's 30% unemployment rate as an unmissable opportunity — an untapped source of cheap labor, readily brought into the sphere of global capital by the great telecom networks on which our brave 'new economy' rests".

I believe that 'handmade datasets' can push back on pressures to scale and outsource labour through the inherent slowness involved in their making. Their relatively small size allows collectors and creators to fully review each datapoint, spending meaningful time learning about their content. The slowness of the process allows one to properly set intention, consider issues of consent and ownership, as well as plan around stewardship of the dataset as an archive. While building a dataset and training a model from scratch is certainly not feasible or desirable in all cases, I have personally found going through this tedious process enlightening and critical to both the artwork I create and my own understanding of the data I am working with.

I created a dataset and trained a model from scratch for my artwork: *I knew that if I walked in your footsteps, it would become a ritual* (2021). The work itself is a video piece and series of prints. The dataset contains just over a thousand family photographs and is used to train a StyleGAN model to create its own images that combine and emulate characteristics of my family photos. For the video, family members were asked to speak about specific photographs. Images generated from the machine learning model were animated using footage from these interviews. The facial expressions mimic the original expressions of the family member and the audio is their original recorded voice. The photographs that are the subject of the interviews are also shown alongside the speaker. Surrounding the video are prints of the generated images mixed with actual family photographs.

I view the model's remixing and approximation as a metaphor for memory. The images the GAN produces feel ghostly, and resemble the original photographs as much as they deviate from them. This feels in parallel with my attempts to find potential in the blurriness of human memory. Being a first-generation American, and having a family member experiencing subtle forms of memory loss, creating this artwork was a way for me to reframe the gaps that we all encounter in both personal and intergenerational memory as generative spaces for reflection and connection, rather than imperfections.

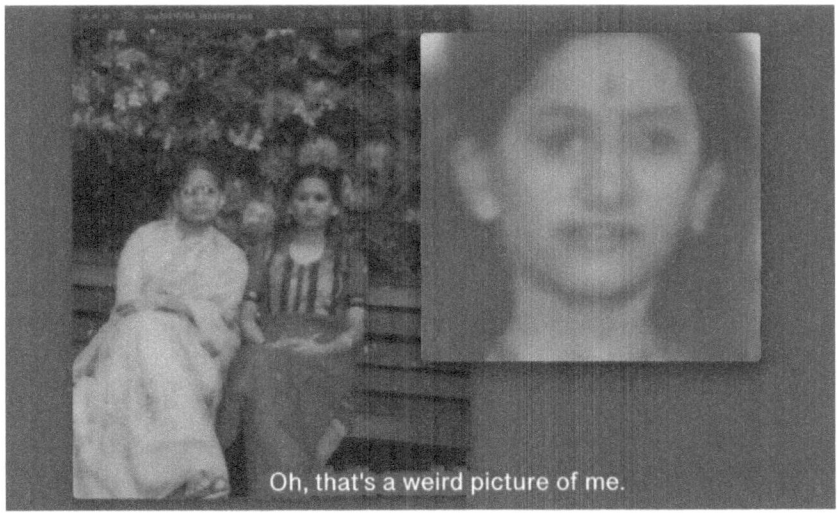

Figure 1: Aarati Akkapeddi, 2021. Video still from *I knew that if I walked in your footsteps, it would become a ritual.*

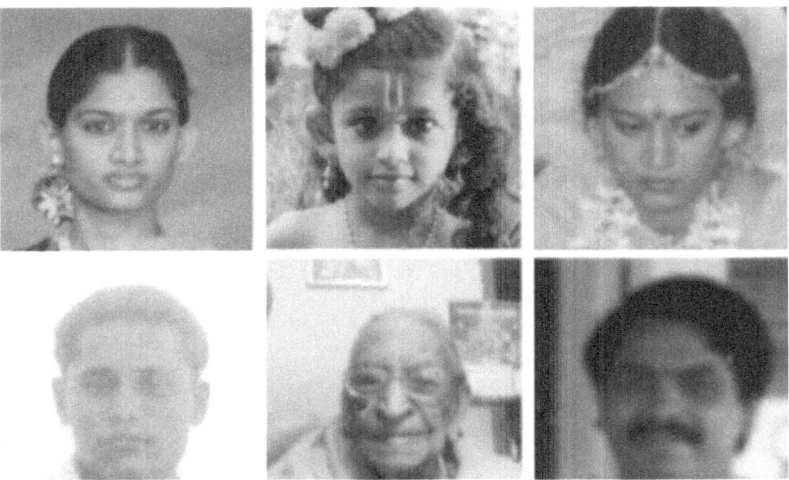

Figure 2: Aarati Akkapeddi, 2020. Faces from my family archive/dataset.

Slow, small, handmade

Although I've found it useful to use the term 'slowness' when discussing building my own small machine learning dataset because it is a time-consuming process, I also use the term to reference other slow movements ('slow education,' 'slow archiving,' etc.) that share certain key values, such as considering the implications of a process for various parties (human and non-human) and understanding that more isn't always better.

I am also aware that many of these movements, such as 'slow food,' are tinged with elitism. But perhaps that is also appropriate for this context. After all, machine learning is a technology that carries several barriers to entry such as energy consumption, cost, and access to technical skills. This chapter will discuss strategies that might mitigate some of those issues, but certainly won't alleviate them entirely.

In addition to 'slowness,' another term that comes to mind is 'handmade.' As someone who often works with their hands, it feels a bit funny to refer to anything digital as handmade, but I think of what J.R. Carpenter (2015, para 2) wrote in "A Handmade Web":

> I evoke the term 'handmade web' to suggest slowness and smallness as a form of resistance.

In my use of the term handmade, I am trying to emphasise that these datasets are small enough for each datapoint to be feasibly considered and processed by one person: each data point has been (metaphorically) handled by the dataset's creator. In the case of my project, *I knew that if I walked in your footsteps it would become a ritual*, I literally held every photograph in my dataset through the process of physically scanning them.

To understand the significance of this smallness when it comes to machine learning datasets, I shall briefly describe some commonly used big datasets.

Flickr-Faces-High Quality (FFHQ), a dataset of human faces, was created by technology company NVIDIA, and contains 70,000 1024×1024 pixel images. The dataset was scraped/crawled from Flickr.com and

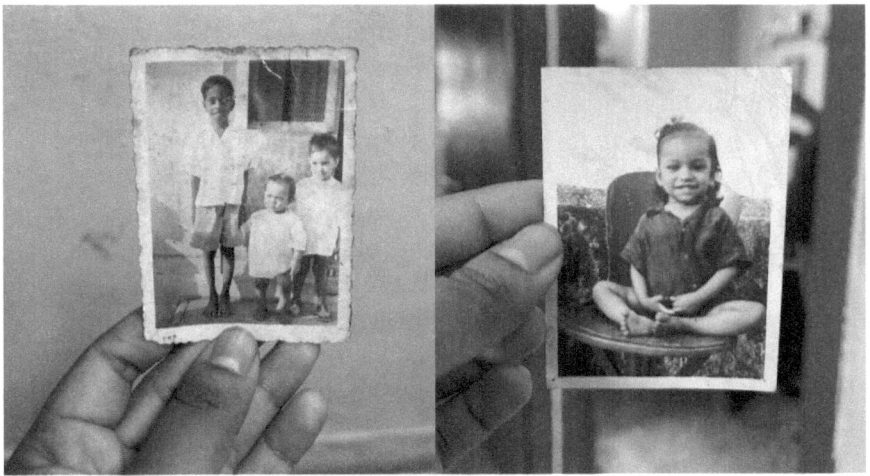

Figures 3 and 4: Holding photographs of my uncles before scanning them.

then further pruned by Amazon Mechanical Turk workers (NVlabs 2018). Imagenet, created in 2006 by Fei-Fei Li, is another large image dataset containing more than 14 million images scraped from various websites on the internet, labelled by Amazon Mechanical Turk crowd-workers and sorted into 21,000 different categories. (ImageNet Website 2010). LAION-5b, currently the largest image database, is a dataset of over 5 billion image-text pairs taken from an archive of scraped website data called Common Crawl (LAION 2022). These image-text pairs are extracted from website data; then, a machine neural network called CLIP (from OpenAI) is used to assess the data, weeding out any text-image pairs that don't score over a certain percentage of perceived accuracy. An additional neural network is used to detect images that are NSFW, or 'Not Safe for Work.'

I would define a 'handmade dataset' as one that has been assembled by an individual, or a very small group of individuals, for non-commercial purposes, and contains data that is authored by this individual or group (as opposed to being scraped from the web). If the data is not authored by the creator(s), they would have at the very least, reviewed every datapoint and its origin, as opposed to using only automated or crowd-sourced methods of assessing and processing. The dataset would have a specific intention rather than being for general use. Because of the manual nature of its assembly, a handmade dataset would also likely contain less than a million data points.

An example of a handmade dataset might be artist Anna Ridler's *Myriad (Tulips)* (2018), a dataset of ten thousand photographs of individual tulips in various colours and stages of bloom, which was then later used to train a model for an artwork called *Mosaic Virus* (2019). On the process of creating the dataset, she writes:

> I had a direct connection to the objects I was documenting. It is easy to forget in the digital age that information is physical and that things that are seen on a screen once started out in the real world. The process was physical — buying, moving, stripping hundreds and hundreds of flowers — labour that is often obscured, even in this rendering of a dataset. (Ridler 2018)

I see the labour involved in the creation of a handmade dataset as a meaningful friction rather than just a limitation of circumstance. It forces one to slow down and think about each and every datapoint. In contrast, with automated data-collection techniques like scraping, one can easily create a digital dataset without ever even opening an individual file. The time spent with every data point opens up space to consider its individual characteristics, origins, and meanings, and this in turn creates space for more intentionality around the use and stewardship of the dataset as a whole.

Can collecting be caring?

In spring of 2014, I volunteered at the front desk of the New York exhibition of *The Smile Face Museum* organised by artist, Adrienne Garbini. The Smile Face Museum was originally founded by Mark Sachs in 1992 in his basement in Silver Spring, Maryland. It is a diverse collection of objects and images showcasing the iconic smile face.

> The smile face is a product of corporate culture and counterculture, at once mainstream and subversive, highly adaptable and widely appropriated, all the while reasserting its physicality as a manufactured good. It is widely loved and reviled, a cue for the kindness of the human smile and a reminder of the sinister inflection present in artifice. (The Smile Face Museum 2014)

The collection contains over 1,000 objects: smile face mugs, smile face hermit crab shells, smile face toilet seat covers, and everything in between (The Smile Face Museum, n.d.). The breadth of The Smile Face Museum made me think about my own compulsions to collect, and if collecting could become a form of devotion. As an artist, much of my creative practice is spent collecting, whether it be research, objects, images, or stories. My studio is filled with boxes of things like insect wings or bundled strands of my grandmother's hair. But I have also experienced collections that felt more careless than others. I think of my visit to the Horniman Museum in London and the way weapons, sacred idols, and mundane tools were haphazardly lumped together under labels like 'danger' and 'curiosity.'

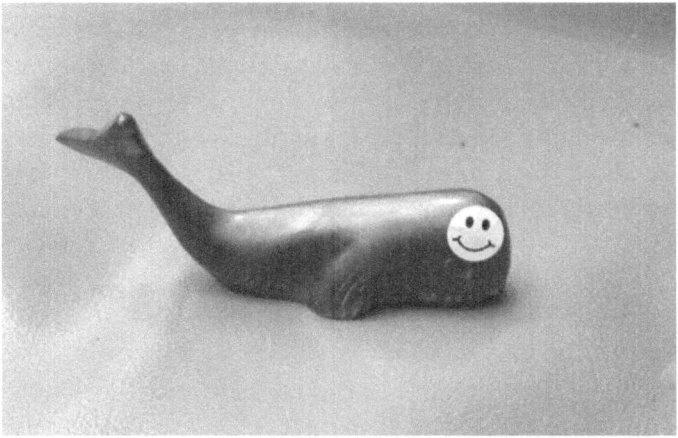

Figure 5: A photograph I took of a metal whale that I placed a smile face sticker on while volunteering at the front desk of the exhibition.

Collections can, of course, also be tools of oppression, flattening the cultures, peoples, and histories they appear to represent and strengthening the image of the collector:

> Whether in museums, exhibitions, shops, theatres or houses, it was through objects that millions of British women and men literally 'saw their empire.' By bringing foreign objects to Britain, collectors played an important role in shaping images of the empire at home. (Jasanoff 2004)

But when a collection is assembled with care and true intentions of stewardship, I want to believe that you can somehow feel the obsessive reverence and knowledge of the objects. It makes a difference when the collector has spent time truly getting to know each and every item in the collection.

While digital datasets might be different from archives of physical objects, they are collections just the same. They are subject to the same issues of ownership, access, and stewardship. Furthermore, there are specific characteristics to a handmade dataset that express a different level of care. For example, the scale of a collection can either facilitate a deepened relationship to the subject matter or create more distance between a collector and collection's contents. For datasets like Imagenet, using anonymous click-workers to crowd-source the processing of the dataset is a technical necessity due to the sheer number of images. By contrast, when I created a handmade dataset for my artwork *I knew that if I walked in your footsteps, it would become a ritual* (2021), I was able to give attention to each image within it. To create the dataset, I had to individually scan physical photographs, thinking about who was in the images, who might have taken the images, how the images might be cropped for the dataset, and how to store the digital files.

Hypothetically, if I were to take a minimum of one second to process an image, it would take me over 155 years to go through every image in the LAION-5b dataset. Due to scale, any notion towards a holistic understanding of a dataset as large as LAION-5b would rely on quantifiable information. And to extract this information you would need to predetermine what you are looking for, such as asking crowd-workers to identify a photograph vs. a drawing or representation. When I looked at my family photos, there was a serendipity to my understanding of the images. They often surprised me or raised questions I didn't previously know to ask. And some of what I am calling an understanding was actually an emotional response that cannot be assigned a score or number. It is because of this process that I feel a deepened responsibility to take care of these photographs and those involved in their making.

There is value in the tediousness and repetition involved in creating a dataset or collection when you have a relationship to the subject matter. For my dataset of family photographs, I spent years travelling, talking to relatives, borrowing family albums, and carefully scanning each photograph. It became more of a practice than a means to an end. It is difficult for me to pinpoint this transformation, but it is important in considering care and collecting. Through valuing the process of collecting in and of itself, I felt a connection to each photograph, rather than simply trying to collect more and more quickly. The act of scanning became very therapeutic for me. I could become lost in it, as one does in meditation. Moreover, the process of digitisation created room for meaningful conversations between myself and relatives, which hadn't been easy in the past.

Having such a close connection to the images meant obtaining consent was much more interpersonal than it might be with a dataset of images scraped from the web. I could tell my relatives about the project, and ask them about how they wanted the images stored or shared. But even so, obtaining consent was not always as straightforward as I thought it would be. I have a very large family, spanning multiple countries. My father was one of ten siblings, and his mother was one of thirteen. Places, events, the person behind the camera, and the people in the images are all details that can be difficult to pin down. Many photographs are of those who aren't alive anymore and I still have images in the dataset of relatives whose names I do not know (such as a third or fourth cousin).

Generally, relatives were much more open to having their images used for a ML model than I expected. Although many didn't really understand the artistic concept, they trusted me to only use the model within the scope of the artwork. I did get one request from a relative to omit their images and was able to oblige. I believe their request was a combination of concerns over their data footprint and issues having more to do with personal relationships within the family.

In thinking about displaying the dataset itself, I realised it would be near impossible to reach a consensus amongst living relatives who all have different experiences with and access to technology, different political and geographic contexts, and different relationships to one another. For this reason, I chose to keep the majority of the dataset private, and during exhibitions to only show photographs that contain close living relatives that have consented to their images being shown.

Because this collection of images is not only a machine learning training dataset, but also a digital archive of family photos, there were also questions about how to make it accessible within the family. I had considered developing some sort of semi-private system of sharing images, such as a password protected website portal. But I found the most successful approach (thus far) for many of my relatives, especially elders, was to simply *be* that system. In other words, people generally preferred to contact me directly to access images, as any online solution was subject to issues such as lack of internet access and varying experience with web interfaces. To access the images through some sort of interface would cut out a much-desired human interaction. It's a reminder that the images are valuable because they facilitate connection through conversation. I am confident that methods of access and stewardship for this archive will adapt and change as time goes on.

Working with family photographs as opposed to any other type of data comes with very specific considerations. However, in terms of scale, being able to take the time to understand each datapoint could help flag otherwise overlooked issues of consent. When datasets are at such a massive scale as LAION-5b, researchers rely on automated forms of filtering that aren't always trustworthy. For example, in the creation of LAION-5b, a neural network was used to filter out 'NSFW' content — yet a browser can still find many sexually explicit images within the dataset.

The creators of LAION-5b also filtered out image-text pairs based on scores given by a neural network called CLIP. This method comes with its own issues of bias, as illustrated when CLIP scored the caption, "This is the portrait of the first ever illegal president of the United States born in Kenya," higher than the caption, "This is the portrait of a former president of the United States," to describe a photograph of Barack Obama (Birhane, Prabhu, and Kahembwe 2021).

When it comes to bias and handmade datasets, subjectivity must be acknowledged. A large dataset like LAION-5b is intended to be general-purpose and thus issues of bias can have serious unintended consequences. I personally feel that even with avoidance of automated filtering, bias is inevitable. A creator of a handmade dataset must always keep this in mind when considering usage. Because of bias, a handmade dataset shouldn't be general purpose, and instead should have a very specific and considered intention. For *I knew that if I walked in your footsteps, it would become a ritual*, the use-case was artistic. I actually felt that its bias has served as a tool for reflection. My family archive is skewed in many ways: for one thing, it is biassed towards my mother's side of the family. My father has fewer family photos for several reasons (less ready access to a camera, different childhood circumstances, a larger family, etc). In fact, the archive is also biassed specifically towards my mother. Out of everyone in my family photo archive, my mother appears the most often, and as a result, I see her facial features reflected most often in the generated images.

The following are generated images that look similar to my mother, surrounding a real photograph of my mother.

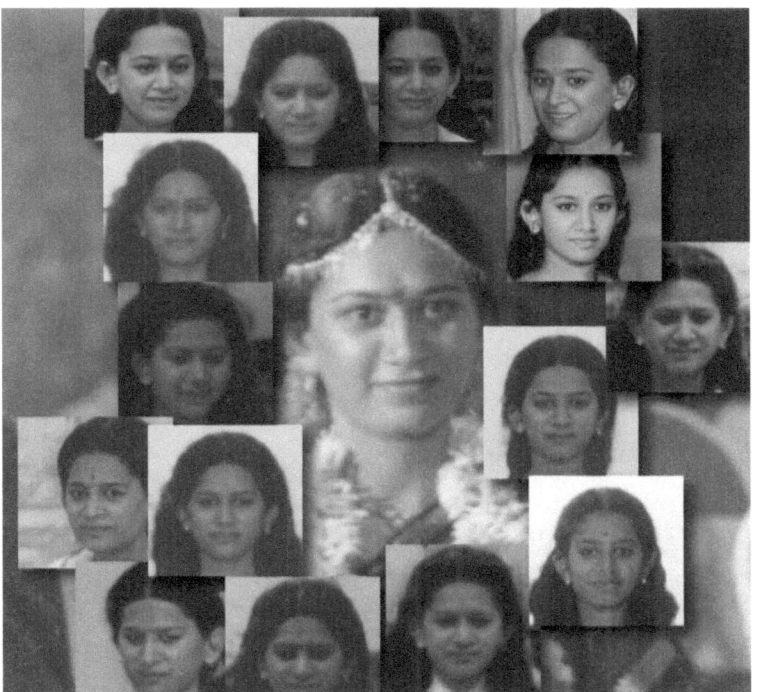

Figure 6: Aarati Akkapeddi, 2021. A photograph of my mother surrounded by generated images that look somewhat like her.

Some of these generated faces look more or less like my mom to me. But, equally, some of these generated faces look more like her in specific parts of her life (as a child, as a teen, in the 90's, now, etc). This makes me think about a person — or at least the memory of a person — as a layering of different perspectives.

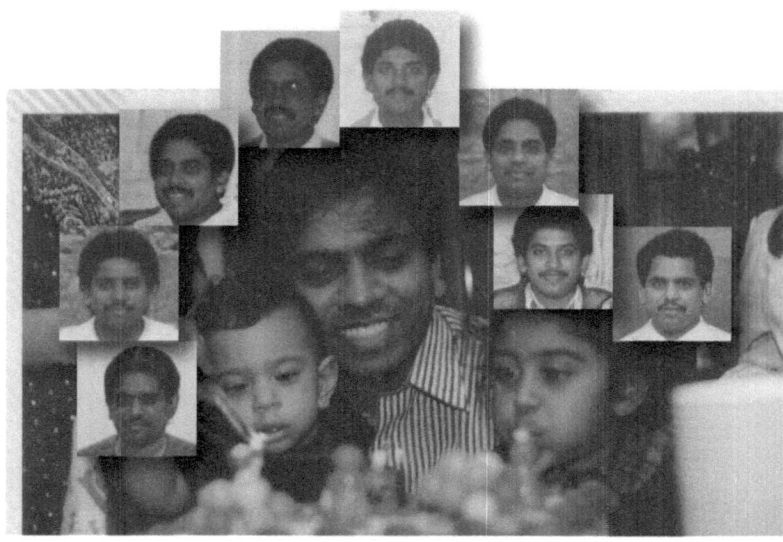

Figure 7: Aarati Akkapeddi, 2021. A photograph of my father surrounded by generated images that look somewhat like him.

Technical difficulties and strategies when working with small datasets

In an earlier iteration of this work, I had tested using an application called RunwayML to train a model on my images. This method used "transfer learning," a technique whereby a model that is already trained is further trained for different purposes, rather than fully training one from scratch (Zhuang et al. 2020). In this particular case, the model had already been pre-trained on the FFHQ dataset and then been trained further on my dataset of family photographs. Transfer-learning can save on training time and computational resources. It can also be useful if your dataset is too small for training from scratch. When platforms like RunwayML or Playform.io allow you to train your own generative model, you are usually using transfer learning.

As an artist, my process is intertwined with the resulting artwork itself, and while this iteration required fewer family photographs and less training time, it was conceptually problematic. In my particular case, I felt that the meaningful metaphors of intergenerational memory were lost, because there is influence from photographs of strangers in the FFHQ dataset. Even if those photographs have an aesthetically insignificant influence on the generated output of the model, they are still present in the model. When comparing this iteration's output and the output from my model that I trained from scratch, I actually did notice a difference. The model that was trained from scratch produces images which may be rougher, but look more familiar to me, and more like people related to me. Perhaps this is only something I or a family member would pick up on; even so, the fact that the model is influenced only by the family photographs that are part of my own personal and collective (human) memory is critical to the meaning of the work.

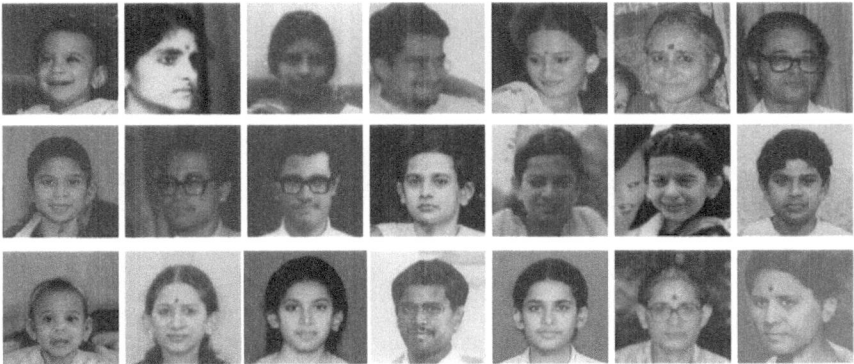

Figure 8: Aarati Akkapeddi, 2021. Top row: Real photos from my family archive/dataset; middle row: images generated with Transfer Learning using RunwayML; and bottom row: Images generated 'from scratch' or without Transfer Learning.

Additionally, when using platforms like Playform.io to train a model, it can sometimes be unclear whether data augmentation is being used behind the scenes. Data augmentation refers to methods that allow one to artificially increase the size of their dataset by creating modified copies of existing data. An example might be doubling an image dataset's size by duplicating and flipping each image horizontally. Depending on the subject matter, certain methods of augmentation may be detrimental to the desired outcome. Here is an example where I used Playform.io with a dataset of portraits from stars.archive (an archive of Tamil Studio Photography).

Using data augmentation methods in an intentional way can be a very useful strategy for working with small datasets. For *I knew that if I*

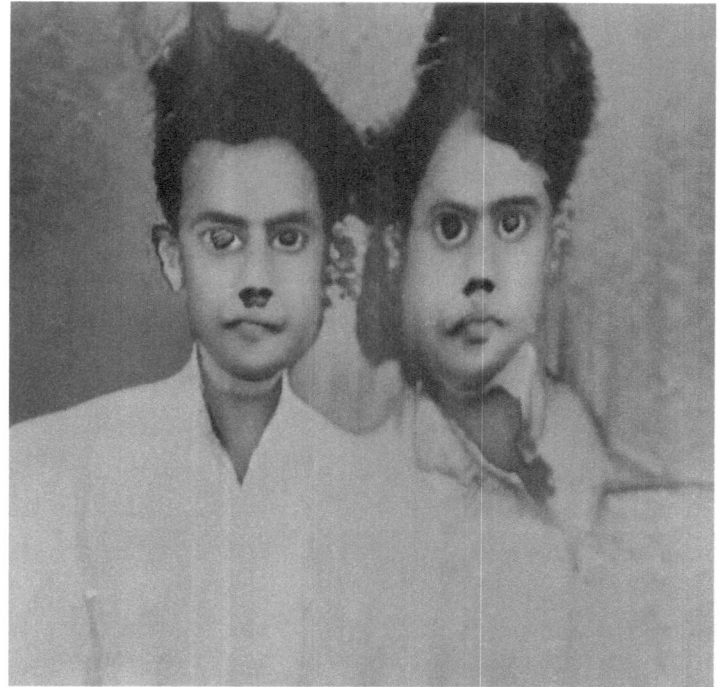

Figure 9: Aarati Akkapeddi, 2020. Result of the "behind-the-scenes" mirroring augmentation in playform.io that caused "double-headed" figures.

walked in your footsteps, it would become a ritual, I focussed on the faces of family members, turning what might be one group photograph into several separate images. I also duplicated and flipped each image horizontally, artificially doubling the dataset's size. Even so, in making a handmade dataset, we must also consider the limitations of algorithms themselves. I have found Generative Adversarial Networks like StyleGAN to be more amenable to smaller datasets than other more recent alternatives. Even with my data augmentation methods, this dataset would fail to work with something like a diffusion model. But sacrificing resolution by using an older algorithm or smaller output dimension can be the right choice if we prioritise care over conventional aesthetics.

Sometimes, things just don't work. If we have too few images or not the right balance of diversity, a GAN will fall into what's called mode collapse, where the model gets 'stuck' on a single type of output and stops improving.

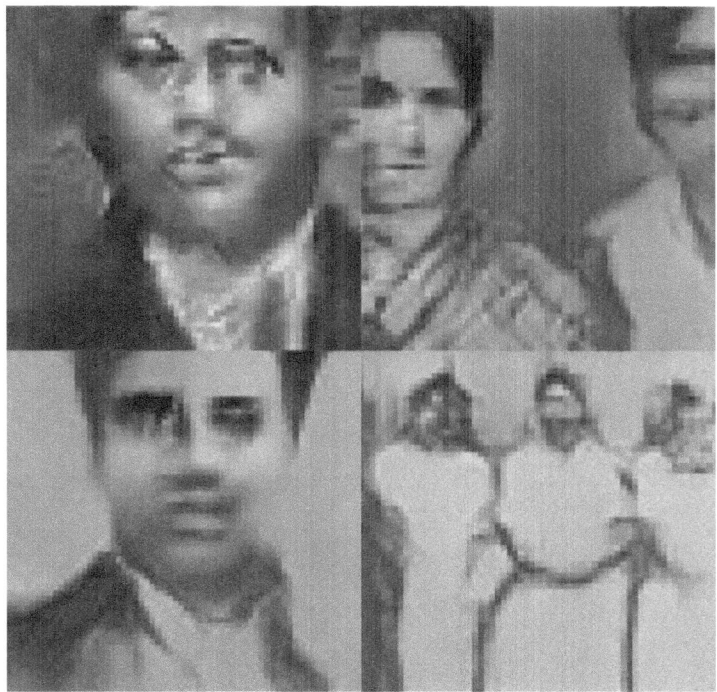

Figure 10: Aarati Akkapeddi, 2019. Examples of a DCGAN generated images from a very small dataset of stars.archive photographs.

While *I knew that if I walked in your footsteps, it would become a ritual* conceptually necessitated a model that was only trained on my family photos, in most cases, transfer learning combined with data augmentation methods can be a very useful strategy for working with handmade or small datasets. If heavy reliance and influence from a pre-trained model is not an issue, there are also more recent alternatives to transfer learning, such as few-shot learning, which is able to influence the output of a pre-trained model without modifying its internal parameters (Song et al. 2022), and Retrieval-Augmented Generation (RAG), which relies on a mechanism of pulling relevant information from a dataset and sensibly incorporating it into the output of a pre-trained model in real time (this technique is only for large language models), that allow for the use of even smaller datasets and little to no further training (Gao et al. 2023).

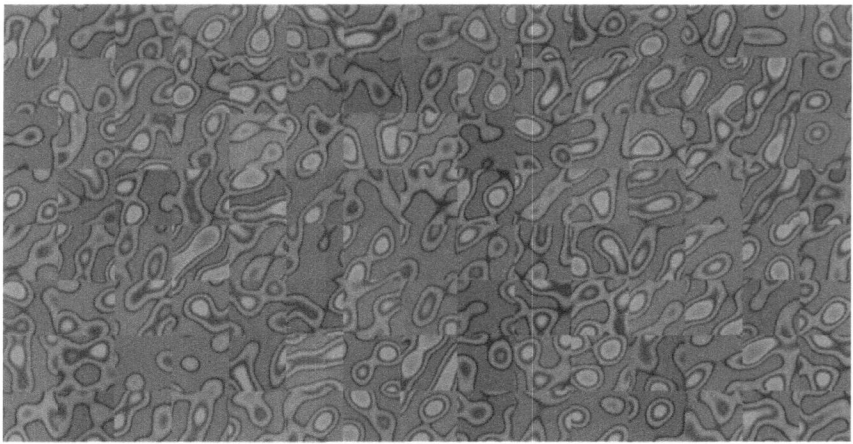

Figure 11: Aarati Akkapeddi, 2024. Example of generated output from a model suffering from 'mode collapse'.

Multivocality

As an individual artist, I have experienced first-hand the benefits of creating handmade datasets. But what is even more inspiring to me is that I am not the only one to see radical potential in small data. For example, just this past month, I attended and vended at *Small Batch: A Dataset Farmers Market*, an event organised by Claire Hentschker and held at LARPA, a worker-rented studio and gallery space in New York (Larpa Solutions n.d.). The market invited community members to sell, trade, or give away "heirloom archives," "hand-picked text & image training sets," "artisanal data," and "local scrapes" (Hentschker, personal communication, 2024).

> The offerings ranged from deeply personal (childhood anime art, apartment cleaning footage) to culturally poignant (corporate executive databases, police prediction data), and from systematic studies (fast food photography, one-way street signs) to rescued digital artifacts (Blingee stickers, thrift store iPod libraries). Prices varied from free to several hundred dollars, with many vendors accepting barter or creative payment methods like "your favorite egg cooking method" or "three sources of creative inspiration." (Hentschker, personal communication, 2024)

While there was definitely a sense of humour to the market, I felt there was also an earnest desire to experiment with reframing data collection and distribution in more communal and personal ways. The diversity of handmade datasets at the market highlights that this approach can allow for a multivocality that challenges the hegemony of mass-scale AI and its colossal training data. In contrast with so-called General-purpose AI which inevitably flattens, handmade datasets are small enough for creators/collectors to consider every data-point, and thus have a more nuanced accountability towards those involved or affected by a dataset's stewardship.

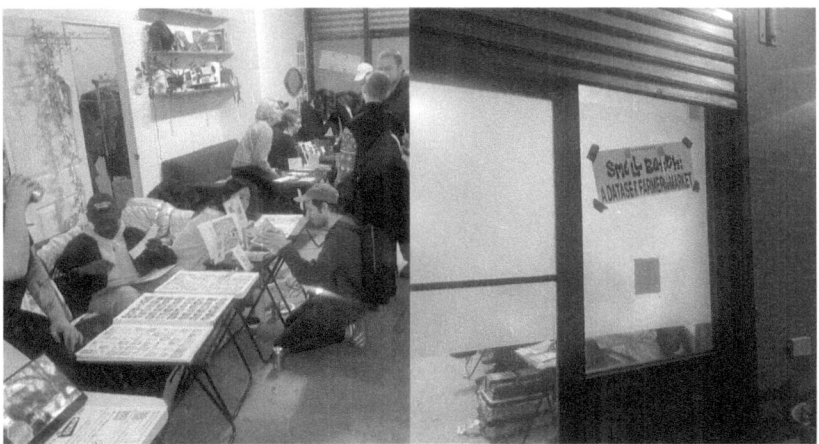

Figure 12 and 13: Aarati Akkapeddi, 2024. Photos taken at LARPA during the *Small Batch: A Dataset Farmers Market* event.

In summary, handmade datasets resist the pressures of exponential data collection and outsourced labour when working with machine learning by encouraging a slowness and smallness. This means creators have the capacity to spend time with each and every data-point. This time spent fosters a deeper understanding and accountability for the dataset's content. The pacing of creating a handmade dataset calls for the reframing of the dataset as an archive, giving more space for consideration of issues of consent, ownership and community. While working with small-scale data and machine learning can be challenging, there are techniques that make it possible to feasibly work with smaller datasets, less training time, and less energy. My hope is that, if we can nurture a demand for slowness and smallness in the face of Big Tech and Big Data, we can continue to develop new methods for working with machine learning — methods that are not only feasible for smaller datasets and less energy consumption, but which can also be tailored to specific communal values and needs.

References

Akkapeddi, Aarati. 2021. *I Knew That If I Walked in Your Footsteps, It Would Become a Ritual*. https://aarati.online/i-knew-that.

Birhane, Abeba, Vinay Uday Prabhu, and Emmanuel Kahembwe. 2021. "Multimodal Datasets: Misogyny, Pornography, and Malignant Stereotypes." Preprint, arXiv, October, 2021. https://arxiv.org/pdf/2110.01963.

Carpenter, J.R. 2015. "Handmade Web." *Lucky Soap*, March, 2015. http://luckysoap.com/statements/handmadeweb.html.

Deng, Jia, Wei Dong, Richard Socher, Li-Jia Li, Kai Li, and Li Fei-Fei. 2009. "ImageNet: A Large-Scale Hierarchical Image Database." *ImageNet*. https://www.image-net.org/.

Gao, Yunfan, Yun Xiong, Xinyu Gao, Kangxiang Jia, Jinliu Pan, Yuxi Bi, Yi Dai, Jiawei Sun, Meng Wang, and Haofen Wang. 2023. "Retrieval-Augmented Generation for Large Language Models: A Survey." *Preprint*, arXiv, December, 2023. https://arxiv.org/abs/2312.10997.

Harvey, Adam, 2021. "Exposing.ai", https://exposing.ai

Jasanoff, Maya. 2004. "Collectors of Empire: Objects, Conquests and Imperial Self-Fashioning." *Past & Present* 184 (1): 109–135. https://doi.org/10.1093/past/184.1.109.

Jones, Phil. 2021. "Refugees, Machine Learning, and Big Tech." *Rest of World*, November 4, 2021. https://restofworld.org/2021/refugees-machine-learning-big-tech/.

Larpa Solutions. 2024. *Larpa Solutions*. Accessed December 23, 2024. https://larpa.solutions/.

NVlabs. 2018. "FFHQ Dataset." *GitHub*. Last modified December 23, 2024. https://github.com/NVlabs/ffhq-dataset.

Onuoha, Mimi. 2022. "The Future is Here! An Interview with Mimi Onuoha." YouTube, November 11, 2022. https://www.youtube.com/watch?v=er8n14cnAo4.

Ridler, Anna, 2018, *Myriad (Tulips)* https://annaridler.com/myriad-tulips.

Ridler, Anna, 2019, *Mosaic Virus* https://annaridler.com/mosaic-virus

Rizzi, Corrado. 2020. "Class Action Accuses IBM of Flagrant Violations of Illinois Biometric Privacy Law to Develop Facial Recognition Tech." *ClassAction.org*, January 30, 2020. https://www.classaction.org/news/class-action-accuses-ibm-of-flagrant-violations-of-illinois-biometric-privacy-law-to-develop-facial-recognition-tech.

Schuhmann, Christoph, Romain Beaumont, Richard Vencu, Cade Gordon, Ross Wightman, Mehdi Cherti, Theo Coombes, et al. 2022. "LAION-5B: An Open Large-Scale Dataset for Training Next Generation Image-Text Models." LAION. https://laion.ai/blog/laion-5b/.

Song, Yisheng, Ting Wang, Subrota K Mondal, and Jyoti Prakash Sahoo. 2022. "A Comprehensive Survey of Few-shot Learning: Evolution, Applications, Challenges, and Opportunities." Preprint, arXiv, May, 2022. https://arxiv.org/abs/2205.06743.

The Smile Face Museum. 2014. "Frieze London 2014 Press Release." *The Smile Face Museum*, October, 2014. https://www.thesmilefacemuseum.com/TSFM-FriezeLondon2014-PR.pdf.

The Smile Face Museum. n.d. *The Smile Face Museum*. Accessed December 23, 2024. https://thesmilefacemuseum.com/.

Williams, Adrienne, Milagros Miceli, and Timnit Gebru. 2022. "The Exploited Labor Behind Artificial Intelligence." *Noema Magazine*, December 8, 2022. https://www.noemamag.com/the-exploited-labor-behind-artificial-intelligence/.

Zhuang, Fuzhen, Zhiyuan Qi, Keyu Duan, Dongbo Xi, Yongchun Zhu, Hengshu Zhu, Hui Xiong, and Qing He. 2020. "A Comprehensive Survey on Transfer Learning." *IEEE Transactions on Knowledge and Data Engineering* 34 (3): 527–545. https://doi.org/10.1109/TKDE.2019.2921616.

Realism and Noise
Emilie K. Sunde

The first-ever 'photograph' of a black hole, released in 2019, is a complicated image. The Event Horizon Telescope (EHT) team created this image by capturing the radiation emanating from the edge of M87's event horizon. They then used algorithms to produce a coherent visual rendering. Public attention was immediate and immense, with prominent media outlets referring to it as a 'photograph' (including New Scientist, ABC, CNN, Newsweek, BBC Sky at Night Magazine, and others). While the EHT team does not explicitly call the image a photograph, the press release and related commentary allude to it as the first-ever picture taken of a black hole. Although the image was made of captured wavelengths, referring to it as a 'photograph' is technically ambiguous. The visual appearance required computational operations to be achieved, yet it is not classifiable as an AI-generated image. It is a scientific image, and at the same time, it was constructed based on preconceived ideas about image-making. The challenge of situating the image within visual culture means the image has received much attention since its creation (Sunde 2024; Halpern 2021; Offert 2021). In this chapter, I will use the equivocal image to explore how realism operates as an illusion, and what that means for computationally generated images.

The Event Horizon Telescope consists of a network of telescopes located around the world, including Europe, North and South America, and the South Pole. These locations offer the ideal combination of clear, dark, cold, high, dry, and calm skies necessary for optimal data acquisition, increasing the likelihood of successful simultaneous observations. The captured data from M87 was subsequently transported to the central research facilities at Harvard, where the EHT team began the task of creating the image. However, this captured data yielded only a fragmented picture. To address the missing information, the team developed computational models that generated a series of potential representations. The final image was chosen because the EHT team deemed it the most "natural" image, aligning with their expectations of what a photograph of the black hole "should" look like (The Event Horizon n.d.). This language is derived from the EHT website, specifically, the section detailing the processes devised to render the image. Interestingly, the EHT team did not inquire, at least in the public account of the protocol, why the selected image seemed to them the most natural — what criteria determine an image's naturalness?

This chapter starts with the assumption that the image appeared 'natural' to the EHT team because its realism corresponded with their encultured way of seeing. In astrophotography, photographic realism has a long history, as photography was early adopted to document the night sky more consistently than drawing. The M87 image is fascinating because the method used to develop the image relies on the foundations of mechanical reproduction to determine what the appearance of a 'natural' image 'should' look like and to reconstruct it using computational reproduction. The fact that the image was created with computational reproduction did not affect the underlying assumption about what realism mediates. Computational realism and photographic realism are, technically, two very different systems of reproduction that are easily conflated experientially. I have problematised the experience of visual realism in computational modelling in relation to M87 in earlier work, arguing that computational realism has a different foundation than realism produced via mechanical reproduction (Sunde 2024). Computational realism is based on data-to-data relations rather than the image-object foundation of mechanical reproduction. These data-data relations have a specific target, which the computational model is trained to achieve. When this target is realism, the information contained in the image is not comparable to other forms of realism, such as photographic realism, regardless of resemblance.

In this contribution, I shift focus to consider how realism has always oscillated between documentation and illusion — and how the difference lies as much in the socio-cultural context as it does in the technical processes of production. The aim of this chapter is to encourage a way of looking that questions *how* the image was constructed before considering what we see in the representation. Crucial to this is examining how the technical methods relate to questions of representability. My argument is that developing an ethical approach to viewing computational images depends on our ability to see beyond the appearance of the image and into its socio-technical foundations. To provide an overview of the socio-technical model for researching AI systems, I draw on the artistic practice of Trevor Paglen. Paglen's art explores how technology transforms our ways of seeing by interrogating technological processes and computational aesthetics. A key component of Paglen's practice is photography, which involves working with various optical technologies to probe questions around representation and visibility, as well as the role of photography in training AI systems.

The Illusion of Realism

In Henry Fox Talbot's 1839 report on his photographic discoveries, he shared the following anecdote. Talbot showed one of his photographs of lace to his peers and asked for their thoughts on the representation. The spectators responded to Talbot ([1839] 1980, 24) "That they were not to be so easily deceived, for that it was evidently no picture, but the piece of lace itself." The quality of the documentation produced an image so realistic to them that the onlookers saw not an image but the object itself. The conflation between the image and the object results from an illusion. The power of expectation to influence perception was the subject of Ernst Gombrich's book *Art and Illusion* from 1960. Gombrich (1977, 173) recites Pliny's tale from classical antiquity when Parrhasios convinced the fellow painter Zeuxis with a trompe l'œil, making Zeuxis reach out to pull the painted curtain to reveal the picture.

The process of equivalence between the object and the image also gave rise to photographic realism, wherein likeness served as evidence rather than illusion. Photographic realism became tantamount to documentation via positivism, wherein the image functions as a visual proxy (see, for instance, Daston and Galison 1992). Implicit in photographic realism is, therefore, a belief that — when operationalised with specific parameters — there is a method for producing images that are 'natural-looking' according to reality. It is this illusion of sameness that produces evidentiary value. Photographic realism, in this sense, is an engineered perception that claims its authority based on an instrumental way of seeing. What was a curious conflation between object and image in Talbot's anecdote grew into a broader structure and culture of image-making based on an assumption of indexicality.

Despite the enduring promise of photographic realism, there have always been elements photographic technologies cannot capture or communicate. A near century after Talbot's observations, Bertolt Brecht gave a poignant description of how realism can never capture the entirety of an event. Even if a photograph is seen to be a "reproduction of reality," Brecht argues, the image "says less than ever about that reality." Brecht offers a concrete example:

> A photograph of the Krupp works, or the AEG, reveals almost nothing about these institutions. Reality, as such, has slipped into the domain of the functional. The reification of human relations, the factory, for example, no longer discloses those relations. So there is indeed 'something to construct', something 'artificial', 'invented'. Hence, there is in fact a need for art. But the old concept of art, derived from experience, is obsolete. For those who show only the experiential aspect of reality do not reproduce reality itself. ([1931] 2000, 164-165)

A scene may be captured with a high degree of visual resemblance. Nonetheless, a photograph will never capture all aspects of reality. Because the reproduction of reality in a photograph functions on a degree of artificiality, in that it constructs a new reality as much as it represents the existing one, it is necessary to reflect on how photography captures and mediates information. The Krupp Steelworks operated as a weapons factory until the interim period between the two World Wars, when the production of arms was temporarily halted as per the Treaty of Versailles. AEG was a large electrical supplier that would go on to support Adolf Hitler in 1933. Brecht's observations came in the immediate years leading up to these escalations. The geopolitical tensions running through these factories at the time of capture are not necessarily represented by photographic realism. When a computational image appears akin to photographic realism, it is an abstraction of the same problematic logic that Brecht identifies.

Brecht proposes that there is a need for art that goes beyond experience and works with the new affordances of, in the context of his writing, optical technologies. Through art, photography can be applied in a manner that communicates beyond the experiential plane, thus overcoming the limitations of photographic realism. AI art as method similarly holds a cohesive perspective. Instead of applying an experiential perspective alone, AI art can incorporate the method used to generate the image in the analysis of appearances. Both cases produce a gaze that sees beyond the illusion-documentation paradox of realism and into the technical operations of image production. We return to this later through an analysis of Paglen's art practice.

Walter Benjamin cited Brecht's quote in his essay "A Short History of Photography," also published in 1931. The quote serves as part of Benjamin's broader exploration of two different modes of interpreting photography in the second half of the nineteenth century. The first mode is represented by Antoine Wiertz, whose praise for the new technology regarded the Daguerreotype not as a threat to visual art, but as its future. Benjamin contrasts this perspective with Charles Pierre Baudelaire's well-known scepticism towards photography. According to Benjamin, both sides, Wiertz and Baudelaire, overlooked a critical point. It was said at the time that, in the future, the illiterate would be those who were not skilled at interpreting photographic images, rather than the alphabet. To this, Benjamin (1972, 25) posed the question: "But must we not also count as illiterate the photographer who cannot read his own pictures?" The EHT team developed a method for interpreting their own images based on the assumption that some images appear 'natural looking'. Through art, we can begin to question the quality of that interpretation.

What I want to emphasise by recounting Talbot's anecdote and Brecht and Benjamin's analysis of photography is that the illusion of realism is rooted in much older visual technologies than computational rendering. Both Brecht and Benjamin were concerned with the cultural reproduction of mechanical images and recognised how this new condition influenced the experience of realism. The presumption that a 'natural' looking image exists might seem benign, but it reflects a broader assumption that also permeates the antagonistic positioning between photography and AI images in culture at large. Although computational images introduce new challenges, there are similarities in how realism — whether experienced through photography or AI images — always carries traces of the encultured gaze of an era. The notion that realism can be interpreted as both evidence and illusion highlights how it emerges through the larger socio-cultural context — not merely through technical operation.

If the M87 image can be said to be a photograph, it is because the image started with the 'capture' of data from the edge of the event horizon. But this is a questionable position, as I have already argued. Furthermore, even if it were a photograph, that does not make the image unmediated by default. As Donna Haraway (1988, 586) argues in her critique of scientific objectivity and universalism: "Vision requires instruments of vision; an optics is a politics of positioning. Instruments of vision mediate standpoint." When instruments are used to mediate vision, the representation is indicative of a standpoint. However, since vision is always learnt, even the eye becomes an instrument for mediating visual information, making every observation indicative of a particular perspective. Haraway (1988, 583) succinctly summarises this point too: "There is no unmediated photograph or passive camera obscura in scientific accounts of bodies and machines; there are only highly specific visual possibilities, each with a wonderfully detailed, active, partial way of organizing worlds." The scientific use of photographic realism is, according to Haraway (1988, 582), an "ideology of direct, devouring, generative, and unrestricted vision, whose technological mediations are simultaneously celebrated and presented as utterly transparent." The positioning of M87 fits perfectly into Haraway's argument, even with three decades of separation. The M87 image is celebrated (and rightfully so) as a brilliant scientific and technological achievement and a 'natural' looking image. That is, the image is considered transparent and unmediated.

However, realism is a particular doctrine of representation that "has proved a rather poor way of engaging with the world's active agency," as Haraway (1988, 593) summarises. Rather than seeing (photographic, photo-, or any other form of) realism as unmediated representations, we can see realism as an embodied and embedded perspective, showing not only what the image represents but also a doctrine of science that prioritises a particular perspective. What makes this even more complicated in the case of EHT's M87 image is that the method of development relied on a new system of image-making: computational imaging. When learning to interpret computational realism, it is worth remembering Benjamin's caution against photographic illiteracy. As such, it is necessary to consider how data can be transformed into a visual rendering before we further problematise the supposed transparency of photographic realism.

The Visual Form of Data

The data collected from the telescope array did not possess a predetermined visual form, at least according to Alexander Galloway's (2011, 88) thesis, which states that "data have no necessary visual form." Galloway compared the etymological roots of data with those of information to construct his thesis. Data means that which is given, whereas information refers to the act of taking form. It is in the transformation from data into information that data is aestheticised for human perception. This visual processing requires "an artificial set of translation rules that convert abstract numbers to semiotic signs," Galloway writes (2011, 88). Indeed, the EHT team decided on a set of rules to translate the data into visual information. As previously argued, these rules were based on assumptions about what a 'natural' looking image 'should' resemble according to conventions in photographic realism. The visual form was determined through a specific representational regime rather than the computational operation used to achieve this style.

Galloway's thesis was written in response to the increased visualisation of the internet. Despite the multitude of images depicting the internet, Galloway argues, as a corollary to the first thesis, that "only one visualization has ever been made of an information network" (2011, 90). The repetitive appearance of these representations diminishes the informational quality to the extent that each image merely reproduces existing representations. Expanding on the second thesis, Galloway (2011, 90) also states: "Either data offer zero help as to how they ought to be aestheticised, or they eclipse all available possibilities under a single way of seeing." Although Galloway did not specifically address the computational processing of data in visual form, the essence of the argument remains relevant. For the EHT team, photographic realism serves as the only feasible representation of the data. In addition to arguing that the image appeared 'natural' and as it 'should', the EHT team also noted, "not all images are created equal — some look more like what we think of as images than others" (The Event Horizon n.d.). To paraphrase Galloway, photographic realism, it seemed, had "eclipsed all available possibilities under a single way of seeing" for the EHT team. Among all the potential representations the computational model could generate, one had been chosen as the proper way to present the data in aesthetic form.

Galloway was inspired by Jacques Rancière's (2007) essay "Are Some Things Unrepresentable?" when writing his article. Through Rancière, Galloway (2011, 92) asserts that 'unrepresentability' "is less a question of the failures of representation on its own terms and more a question of the historical shift out of one regime into a subsequent regime." Galloway refers here to Rancière's three regimes of art (the ethical, the representative, and the aesthetic). The computational shift is arguably a marker of a new visual regime. In the twenty-first century, computational reproduction is rapidly becoming a mainstream mode of production. However, we have yet to establish a mode of analysis targeted at computational realism. Computationally produced realism is often equated with photographic realism, which overlooks crucial differences in the underlying technical structures of the image. This technical structure is important to address, as it affects the information one can derive from looking at the representation.

Galloway (2011, 92) also draws from Rancière's work the insight that the opposite of representation is not non-figuration but realism, "for in realism everything is levelled and equally representable." The photograph of the Krupp works or the AEG factory could not represent the socio-political forces crucial to understanding the image. In a passage that echoes Brecht's observations about photography from 1931, Galloway (2011, 95) argues similarly that the unrepresentable lies in "the mode of production and the realities of the socio-historical situation." Galloway is speaking about the new networked condition of the internet in the 2000s; even though the technical conditions for image production have changed, the same principle remains. Realism, as Haraway (1988) argued, is unable to represent much of the world's active agency, whether in a factory, on the internet, or in a 'photo' of the M87 image. In the M87 image, there is also something unrepresented, made invisible, as the data gathered was formatted and translated into the chosen semiotic signs. If the opposite of unrepresentability is not non-figuration but realism, how can we learn to see beyond realism to uncover the power relations at play?

The Opacity of Realism

One of the telescopes used in the capture of data for the M87 image was located on Mauna Kea in Hawai'i. Mauna Kea is an important site for cutting-edge astronomy research. It is also a highly contested location.

Mauna Kea is a sacred volcano to Native Hawaiians, which has led to ongoing conflict over astronomers' rights to use the area for observation. The dispute intensified in the 2010s after the proposal for the Thirty Meter Telescope. When Mauna Kea was closed to public access in July 2019 to begin construction of the telescope, many Hawaiians protested. The opposition grew into months-long demonstrations involving tens of thousands and resulting in many arrests.

In the representations of this conflict, there has been a tendency to position the two perspectives antagonistically. Any opposition to the telescope is reduced to a fight against the scientific pursuit to find the origin of the universe — a scientific cause portrayed not only as a universal goal but also as universally beneficial. This narrative presents Mauna Kea as an important site of scientific discovery, above the Hawaiians' right to protect their sacred land. Iokepa Casumbal-Salazar's (2017, 8) objection to this perspective is worth quoting at length:

> One scientist told [Casumbal-Salazar] that astronomy is a "benign science" because it is based on observation, and that it is universally beneficial because it offers "basic human knowledge"... Such a statement underscores the cultural bias within conventional notions of what constitutes the "human" and "knowledge." In the absence of a critical self-reflection on this inherent ethnocentrism, the tacit claim to universal truth reproduces the cultural supremacy of Western science as self-evident. Here, the needs of astronomers for tall peaks in remote locations supplant the needs of Indigenous communities on whose ancestral territories these observatories are built. It does so by invoking the morality of liberal multiculturalism. "Why would anyone oppose astronomy? Why are Hawaiians standing in the way of progress?" they ask.

The dazzling realism in the image of M87 hides the fact that it was partially produced in a place experiencing a serious conflict between ongoing settler colonial projects and local sovereignty. What is unrepresented by its realism are the realities of the socio-historical situation — the same power relations photographic realism has always struggled to communicate. When we look at M87, it does not reflect the lived reality of those fighting against oppression.

Haraway (1988, 579) presented a series of questions to address the significance of maintaining a feminist objectivity that recognises the value of the "radical multiplicity of local knowledges." Haraway asks:

> How to see? Where to see from? What limits to vision? What to see for? Whom to see with? Who gets to have more than one point of view? Who gets blinded? Who wears blinders? Who interprets the visual field? What other sensory powers do we wish to cultivate besides vision? (1988, 587)

To these questions, we can add the questions Casumbal-Salazar (2017, 8) formulates regarding the construction of the thirty-meter telescope: "What constitutes progress? Who determines that? And what are the costs of its production?" A long history of settler colonialism, ideology, and power continues to delimit who gets to see, from where, and what forms of vision represent progress. The telescope is employed in the pursuit of science while it appropriates sacred lands as part of continued colonial practice. The telescopes provide knowledge about how the world operates, and I do not intend to dispute that. What I want to emphasise is that the pursuit of telescopes in locations with minimal noise interference comes at a cost. For those barred from their sacred land in the name of science, the telescope itself is the noise — it is a form of noise that violates through the prolonged logic of settler colonial violence.

The array of telescopes that collectively gathered the data for the M87 image is presented by the EHT team as a 'global' network of telescopes and individuals working toward the same universal goal. The press release for the image was also framed as a 'global' event. The problem with these 'global' positions is that they do not give space for local rights and sovereignty. If we shift away from reductive claims of globality, often associated with a morality that emerges from liberal multiculturalism, and instead rely on Haraway's formulation that speaks of an "earth-wide network of connections," it might be possible to recognise the cost of the M87 image. With this shift, we can also begin to construct a vision that appreciates the partial ability "to translate knowledges among very different — and power-differentiated — communities" (Haraway 1988, 580). Photographic realism emerged alongside positivist scientific practices and cultivated a reliance on a narrow scope of knowledge that prioritised one form of representation over others. Recognising that photographic realism has always been a form of illusion, one can move beyond the flattened perspective and find ways of looking that address what Haraway calls the "world's active agency." Decentred ethics aligns with Haraway's thinking in that it argues against the notion of universal perspectives and calls instead for pluriversalism. Since we know that the networks enabling the composite image cannot be represented by photographic realism, how might changing our perspective enhance our way of viewing through technology?

Looking Through Technology

Trevor Paglen's art practice has centred on invisible power structures, including surveillance practices, secret service and government institutions, as well as technological processes and hidden computational operations. In an interview from 2009, Paglen is asked by Niels Van Tomme how to approach the process of representing these opaque structures. Paglen responds that he mostly does not manage to gain access to the information, but this is also part of his artistic research method. What Paglen is trying to capture, he explains, is the "moment when something becomes visible but remains unintelligible, when you find evidence of absence in a certain sense" (Paglen, quoted in Feffer and Van Tomme 2009). Over the years, Paglen's method has resulted in works that track flight patterns of drones and satellites, pictures of fibre optic cables' landing sites, military bases and symbolism, computational processes, and more. All show patterns of power that are unrepresentable through data visualisations and photographic realism. Paglen achieves this by exploring the ways technology operates with and through systems of reproduction rather than being bound by dominant modes of representation (such as photographic realism). Paglen's work is, therefore, a way to consider how artistic research can be used to look beyond realism and work with the unrepresentable.

Around 2010, Paglen photographed the world's most powerful radio source at Lake Kickapoo in Texas. The site, known as "The Fence," belongs to the U.S. military and is used to track satellites and perform other surveillance operations. A standard photograph of the fence would not capture the immense energy emitted from the transmitter. Paglen describes how he modified the equipment to make the energy visible:

If human eyes could "see" radio waves in the VHF part of the spectrum, the Fence would appear as an impossibly bright sheet emanating from the southern United States and reaching far into space. I wanted to "see" the Fence, so I created a jury-rigged radio telescope from antennas, preamps, filters, a/d converters, and a software-defined radio. This image is the result of my effort to make an image of this strange piece of infrastructure. (Paglen n.d.)

Paglen presents two images of the Fence on his website. The first image is taken from the Wikipedia page for the Fence and is a standard photograph that represents the Fence's physical structure. When compared to the image Paglen captured using his modified equipment, the second image appears abstract.[1] With the bespoke telescope, Paglen registered the radiation from the radio source as red shades. His picture of the Fence does not depict the structure in a manner that aligns with photographic realism. Instead, the image produces another form of visibility that enables the onlooker to perceive the technological operation — a process that is otherwise invisible, similar to how a photograph of a factory cannot reveal its institutional power relations. In other words, Paglen captured the structure's active agency in a way that realism could not. Visualising this effect portrays more information about the operations of the space than what a traditional photograph of the fence could provide — making it, in many ways, a more realistic image, even if it appears to be noise at first. However, appreciating Paglen's artwork requires knowledge about how the image was created; the art alone does not convey the information, as we also rely on the transfer of knowledge from the artist.

The EHT M87 image utilised telescopes to capture data, while the final image was developed using computational models. In 2017, Paglen began experimenting with the mediation of data through computational reproduction. In a project titled *Adversarially Evolved Hallucinations*, Paglen collected and curated a series of datasets based on allegories and cultural categories from Western culture, such as 'The Humans', 'Monsters of Capitalism', 'Spheres of Heaven', and 'Omens and Portents'. Once the machine had trained on these corpora, Paglen instructed the

---

1. The images are available at https://paglen.studio/2020/04/27/the-fence/.

model to generate an image. The resulting images present a strange representation of familiar motifs. What Paglen is exploring with this work is how AI systems are wired through the training data to produce output. The data functions as the AI model's 'knowledge' of a phenomenon. The technical term for the 'knowledge' that the AI model has about the world is latent space. Latent space is the processual zone between output and input, and we can examine the specific system Paglen used to generate the artworks to understand how latent space operates.

The type of model Paglen used in *Adversarially Evolved Hallucinations* is known as a Generative Adversarial Network (GAN). Introduced in 2014, GANs quickly proved to be an effective method for generating images (Goodfellow et al. 2014). GANs operate two neural networks simultaneously: the first generates an image, while the second determines whether that image originated from the generator or the data library. Initially, the generative AI model will have no concept of how to translate the random numbers in latent space into a coherent image. During the training process, the generator learns to map specific points in latent space to meaningful outputs, such as images. This process is guided by feedback from the discriminator, which informs the generator how successful it is at creating images. Over time, the generator improves and learns to organise the data in latent space. Eventually, latent space evolves from random noise to a compressed and structured format based on the concepts the generator has learned. At this stage, the generator 'knows' how to arrange pixels to match the desired output, and the discriminator can no longer distinguish between the AI-generated image and the target image. With computational reproduction, the underlying reference of the image shifts from an image-object relationship to a data-data relation that corresponds to latent space. Regardless of whether the model is programmed to create something that looks realistic, the reference remains an abstraction and is removed from the object it represents. Crucially, the output is determined by the training, data, and the socio-techinical optimisation of the model. The latter is informed by the developer's preconceived notions of what the output 'should' look like.

Paglen did not train the model to generate images that conform to normative modes of representation. However, with an understanding of Paglen's artistic practice, the images produced using *Adversarially*

Evolved Hallucinations provide deeper insight into the underlying technological processes than hyper-real AI-generated images offer. By creating a unique dataset, Paglen draws our attention to the active interference of computational modelling and the significance of optimisation. The computational model processing the data captured from the M87 was optimised to generate a realistic representation. This decision was influenced by expectations of how an image 'should' appear. The interpretation of this realism as evidence relies on a socio-cultural understanding of what the image represents. Not all AI-generated images are synonymous with documentation. Realism can be interpreted both as a sign of fidelity, as in the case of the M87 image, or as a sign of fakery, such as in deepfakes. In other words, realism retains both a documentary and illusory potential, offering appearances rather than serving as a reliable model for analysis. Paglen's ability to work with the unrepresentable can inspire ways of looking beyond realism in computationally generated output to produce a gaze that incorporates the broader technical and socio-historical context.

Conclusion

For Galloway (2011, 93), the questions concerning "representation and representability" are always connected to an "ethical obligation" and what he describes as the "affective response" to the image. How are we affected by an image, and whose responsibility is it if we do not react to images of violence? What complicates an image like M87 is that, without context, the conflict underlying the image's creation is not visible. The ongoing demonstrations against the site of one of the telescopes used to capture the data are obscured by realism. Referring to M87 as a 'photograph' creates the illusion of indexicality, which promises to record everything. Yet all forms of realism depend on the process of discarding noise (for the machine and the human gaze) — what is considered noise is a matter of encultured ways of seeing. We thus have an ethical obligation to learn how to recognise the circumstances that made the M87 image possible. Since the appearance of a computational image will not provide meaningful information about its construction, only the determined rules for the aestheticisation of that data, it requires the spectator to learn new ways of looking. We need a form of ethics that does not try to create transparency by constructing a set of artificial semiotic rules to make something visible. The image produced through such an operation tends to reinforce existing power relations and dominant forms of vision. With the right knowledge and context, the underlying conditions and unrepresentable aspects of an image can be brought to the fore — often without relying on realism, as Paglen's artistic practice highlights.

The use of computational technologies to visualise black holes aligns with broader assumptions regarding the presumed power of algorithms. As Louise Amoore (2020, 15) argues, there is a "great emphasis on the power of algorithms to visualize, to reprogram vision, or indeed even to 'see' that which is not otherwise available to human regimes of visuality." While there can be value in producing photograph-like images using computational technologies, two aspects must be considered. The first is that this embeds an episteme into the algorithms that has "its roots in the privileging of sight and vision over other forms of making things perceptible," as Amoore (2020, 15) phrases it. The second, as I have shown in this chapter, is that realism will always produce blind spots. Coherent and realistic images can easily be perceived as unmediated, but within that illusion lie a series of hidden socio-political forces. As spectators, we have an ethical obligation to consider the perspective embedded in the algorithm — and what form of vision that symbolises. The focus on visuality in algorithms affects the attribution of ethics and aesthetics in computational visual culture. Developing ethics without first addressing the underlying primacy of what counts as vision and whose perspective matters within a regime of vision produces a problematic imbalance. Given that algorithms introduce an entirely new way of looking — not bound by the human register — this new way of looking can facilitate a new decentred perspective.

References

Amoore, Louise. 2020. *Cloud Ethics*. Duke University Press.

Benjamin, Walter. 1972. "A Short History of Photography." *Screen* 13 (1): 5–26. https://doi.org/10.1093/screen/13.1.5.

Brecht, Bertolt. [1931] 2000. "The Threepenny Lawsuit." In *Bertolt Brecht On Film and Radio*. Edited and translated by Marc Silberman. Bloomsbury.

Casumbal-Salazar, Iokepa. 2017. "A Fictive Kinship: Making 'Modernity,' 'Ancient Hawaiians,' and the Telescopes on Mauna Kea." *Native American and Indigenous Studies* 4 (2): 1–30.

Daston, Lorraine and Peter Galison. 1992. "The Image of Objectivity." *Representations* 40: 81–128. https://doi.org/10.2307/2928741

Event Horizon Telescope. n.d. "Science." Accessed November 30, 2024. https://eventhorizontelescope.org/science.

Feffer, John and Niels Van Tomme. 2009. "Seeing Things: Trevor Paglen talks about the art of documenting that which does not want to be documented." *FPIF: Foreign Policy in Focus*, April 16, 2009. https://fpif.org/seeing_things/.

Galloway, Alexander. 2011. "Are Some Things Unrepresentable?" *Theory, Culture & Society* 28 (7–8): 85–102. https://doi.org/10.1177/0263276411423038.

Gombrich, Ernst. 1977. *Art and Illusion: A Study in the Psychology of Pictorial Representation*, Fifth Edition. Pantheon Books

Goodfellow, Ian J., Jean Pouget-Abadie, Mehdi Mirza, Bing Xu, David Warde-Farley, Sherjil Ozair, Aaron Courville, and Yoshua Bengio. 2014. "Generative Adversarial Networks." Preprint, arXiv:1406.2661 [Cs, Stat], June. http://arxiv.org/abs/1406.2661.

Halpern, Orit. 2021. "Planetary Intelligence." In *The Cultural Life of Machine Learning*, edtied by Jonathan Roberge and Michael Castelle. Palgrave Macmillian. https://doi.org/10.1007/978-3-030-56286-1_8.

Haraway, Donna. 1988. "Situated Knowledges: The Science Question in Feminism and the Privilege of Partial Perspective." *Feminist Studies* 14 (3): 575. https://doi.org/10.2307/3178066.

Offert, Fabian. 2021. "Latent Deep Space: Generative Adversarial Networks (GANs) in the Sciences." *Media+Environment* 3 (2). https://doi.org/10.1525/001c.29905.

Paglen, Trevor. n.d.. "The Fence." Accessed January 31, 2025. https://paglen.studio/2020/04/27/the-fence/.

Paglen, Trevor. 2017. *Adversarially Evolved Hallucinations*. https://paglen.studio/2020/04/09/hallucinations/.

Rancière, Jacques. 2007. *The Future of the Image*. Translated by Gregory Elliott. Verso.

Sunde, Emilie K. 2024. "From outer space to latent space." *Philosophy of Photography* 15 (1-2): 123–42. https://doi.org/10.1386/pop_00096_1.

Talbot, William Henry Fox. [1839] 1980. "Some Account of the Art of Photogenic Drawing, or, The Process by Which Natural Objects May be Made to Delineate Themselves with the Aid of the Artist's Pencil." In *Photography: Essays & Images. Illustrated Readings in the History of Photography*, edited by Beaumant Newhall. The Museum of Modern Art; New York Graphics Society.

Poetic Simulation
Tyne Daile Sumner

"A poem is a small (or large) machine made of words."
— William Carlos Williams

In 1961 the American writer Adrienne Rich published the poem "Artificial Intelligence," in which an AI effortlessly beats its human opponent at a game of chess. Suggestive of the Turochamp chess program developed by Alan Turing and David Champernowne roughly ten years earlier, the poem engages a dramatic first-person address to critique new forms of artificial intelligence that were emerging at the time:

> Over the chessboard now,
> Your Artificiality concludes
> a final check; rests, broods —
> no — sorts and stacks a file of memories,
> while I
> concede the victory, bow,
> and slouch among my free associations. (Rich 1961, 168)

As the poem's speaker is defeated ("I'm sulking, clearly, in the great tradition/of human waste"), her artificial opponent archives a record of its tactics as "a file of memories" that enables its continuous algorithmic improvement. In contrast, the speaker concedes defeat by slumping back into an unmistakably human practice: the act of thinking via free association.

The poem's dedication, which reads simply "To G.P.S.," offers a hint as to Rich's techno-politics. Standing for General Problem Solver, the intriguing invocation connects the poem to another program developed four years earlier by Herbert A. Simon, J.C. Shaw, and Allen Newell of the American global policy think tank, RAND Corporation. For the

G.P.S. inventors, almost all computer programs — whether designed as simulations of human processes or not — are proof that even the most complex and mysterious paradigms of thought might be coherently registered as computational logic. With her poem's overt challenge to cyborg-like systems that are purported to understand human subjectivity, Rich takes an emphatically different position.[1]

Later in the poem, she directs this challenge at the techno-utopianism of Simon and his peers: "Why not/dump the whole reeking snarl/and let you solve me once and for all?" That Rich would pen these prophetic lines, over sixty years ago now, speaks as much to the role of poetry in the long history of Artificial Intelligence as it does to her vocation as a poet. As one of the first experiments imagined by computer scientists after the second world war, machine-generated poetry has been integral to historic developments in natural language processing (NLP), revealing a scientific preoccupation with the nature of poetic verse that began centuries ago, then intensified via research workshops in Ivy League colleges in the 1950s, and continues under the umbrella term Artificial Intelligence today (Slater 2023, 209). Another critical correlation can be found in the poem's eerie foreshadowing of current debates around AI-generated language — encountering Rich's lyric today, the dedication 'To G.P.S' could just as easily read 'To ChatGPT.'

Following the initial release of ChatGPT by the American Artificial Intelligence company OpenAI in November 2022, poetry was taken up as the paradigmatic textual form in assessments of the creative and rhetorical acumen of LLMs, with a proliferation of comparisons of poetry by Shakespeare, Emily Dickinson, and Seamus Heaney to that AI-generated verse.[2] In this dramatic turn, that which might be thought of as poetry's "ultracomplex structure" has taken centre stage in debates about the limits of AI's semantic and linguistic expression, its capacity to engineer palatable metaphors, its application of irony

---

1. In *Simians, Cyborgs, and Women: The Reinvention of Nature*, Donna Haraway criticises Rich and other radical feminists of the period who, she argues, "insist on the organic, opposing it to the technological." See Haraway 1991, 174. For more on Adrienne Rich's poetics of technology see Crawford (1995).

and allusion, and its comprehension of the link between creative content and poetic form (Nünning and Nünning 2004, 51). The question of how well Generative AI can write a poem — syntactically, semantically, affectively — has also inspired headlines bearing theoretical concepts and critical terms that have long been standard practice in literary criticism: authenticity, evaluation, subjectivity, intention, reception, attention, and aesthetics (Holyoak 2022).

My objective in this chapter is not to demonstrate — or even ask — if AI can write *good* poetry. This line of inquiry is, I argue, a philosophical red herring that serves only to emphasise the shortcomings of current-state LLMs and the information on which they are trained — data in, data out, poem in, poem out.[3] In drawing attention to the thematic and semantic flaws in current machine-generated poetry, critics have nevertheless reminded us that the predictive analytics that guide LLMs are usually at odds with the ways that human perception and experience produce 'non-cognitive' forms of verbal expression that diverge from the 'rational intelligence' modelling that underpins most AI outputs (Schober 2022, 153). Thus, if an AI-generated poem is deemed 'bad,' is it usually said to be so because it did precisely that which it was designed to do: locate within the dataset the next most likely word that should follow the previous according to a prescribed set of computational principles.[4] Ironically, some AI-generated poems have been derided for the ways in which they are said to 'hallucinate' aberrant words or incoherent

---

2. The sudden resurgence of interest in comparing AI-generated poetry with poetry written by humans has a long and multifaceted past. Several key innovations in the history of generative literature include: John Clark's mid-19th century Latin Verse Machine, which is likely the earliest example of mechanised literature; Christopher Strachey's "love letter generator" of 1952; Ray Kurzweil and Charles Hartman's experiments in the 1980s and 1990s; and Rosemary West's versifier program "Poetry Generator," developed in the late 1980s. More recent examples include Benjamin Lair and Oscar Schwartz's "Bot or Not" developed in 2014 and ReRites, an ongoing literary work of "Human + A.I. poetry" begun by David Jhave Johnston in 2016. For more on the history of generative literature see: Roque (2011); Schwartz (2018); and Schober (2022).

3. AI is now also being used in experimental attempts to automate the task of poetic analysis. The authors of a recent paper about Erato, a "framework designed to facilitate the automated evaluation of poetry," write: "We invite researchers working in the automatic generation of poetry to use Erato as a midway step to check how their systems work before resorting to human evaluators." See Agirrezabal et al. (2023, 11).

4. See Doshi and Hauser (2024).

expressions in producing outputs that appear unable to find a foothold in a discernible referent; a quality that simultaneously defines certain styles of experimental verse. Declarations about how effectively AI can produce certain poems thus inevitably turn to a process of reception, more than one of production, leading back to human-centric tensions around judgment, readerly capability, critical skills, and personal taste.

And yet, as the distinction between human and machine becomes fuzzier, and a greater volume of poems are produced using hybrid methods that combine human-writing with Generative-AI,[5] the literary-critical project and the relation it must articulate with its object remains precisely the same. In other words, to critique the ostensible *quality* of an AI-generated poem is merely to engage in the same dialectic that has organised the study of poetry since the beginning. Realising this recursion in the context of future AI advancements necessitates that we engage more, and not less, with the enduring apparatuses of humanistic inquiry. With this assertion in view, I argue for a decentring of the logical fallacy of comparing AI-generated poetry to that which is presupposed to be somehow uncontaminated by technologisation and mediation. Instead, I address the more constructive and expansive question: What can poetry teach us about AI? I also want to consider, as Michele Elam (2023, 283) judiciously does, how AI "revives foundational questions in the arts and humanities" about how literature is compensated, who "arbitrates taste, value, valuation, proprietary content, and provenance" as well as "who gets to decide the arbitrators" and "who (or what) counts as a marker." These questions, bound up as they are in "the new institutionalism in literary studies" that came to reorient the discipline around the turn of this century, are arguably more urgent now than they have ever been.[6]

---

5. See for example the AI Literary Review, a journal launched on July 1, 2024 by poet Dan Power which publishes poems developed via a combination of "organic imagination" and "algorithmic generation." Power claims that "through direct engagement and experimentation with the AI and its outputs we can revive its zombified text, and rewild our language before it succumbs to total automation." See: ailiteraryreview.co.uk

6. This turn followed roughly a century of text-dominated methods in literary studies directed by the formal close reading of Leavisism and New Criticism. The 'new institutionalism' borrows from sociological frameworks of the early 1990s to analyse "the social and economic conditions in which literature is produced, circulated and consumed." See Murray (2023, 2-4).

In what follows I examine two topics that relate to both poetics and current ethical issues in AI: subjectivity and explainability. First, I consider how the concept of voice — the speaking subject of a poem — has implications for how we approach subjectivity in relation to artificial intelligence. A poem's subjectivity, or its stamp of "inner consciousness," is usually thought to be arrived at through a combination of experience and reflection (Culler 2017, 2).[7] While poetry is sometimes piloted by a distinct and discernible speaker, it can equally evoke subjective uncertainty and thematic ambiguity; faculties that are generally at odds with the organising principles of algorithmic computation, which aims for certainty, reproducibility, and precision. Considered in relation to the disembodied AI-generated output, this principle highlights the need to more critically evaluate how we understand the voice, speaker, and subjectivity (or lack thereof) in machine-generated language. Second, I examine the concepts of explainability and intentionality as a constitutive tension in both poetry and AI. Often, the 'genius' of poetry is linked to the incapacity of the reader to explain what the poet is doing or how it is that they arrived at the final combination and arrangement of words that comprise the poem. At the current moment in AI, we encounter a mirror condition known as the 'black box': the inability to identify how deep learning systems are making their decisions.[8] Explainable AI (XAI) is the attempt to show the inner workings of the black box by articulating how and why an AI system reached a specific decision, recommendation, or prediction.[9] Meanwhile intentionality, which can be described as "an expression of the presence of creative factors in the process of intellectual cognition" is now an increasingly contested concept in the context of new AI models that are "designed to spend more time thinking before they respond" (Gondek 2021, 420).[10] To critique this tension from an interdisciplinary slant,

---

7. It bears noting that here Culler is referring to the genre of the lyric, one of the distinguishing features of which is the centrality of subjectivity to the poem, in contrast to drama and epic.

8. One of the earliest uses of the term 'black box' in reference to AI can be traced to Ross Ashby, who takes up the expression in his 1956 text *An Introduction to Cybernetics* (1956, 86-117). See also Wiener (1961) and more recently Pasquale (2016).

9. Related to this principle, the trade-off between powerful but opaque deep learning models and more transparent but potentially less capable rule-based systems is currently the source of increased commercial and governmental deliberation in the field of AI ethics.

10. See OpenAI's o1: https://openai.com/o1/

I take up the instance of the literary hoax to consider how poetics might contribute to debates around explainability, intentionality, and authorship in AI, not just for problems of copyright and attribution but also in intensifying debates about the nature of creativity and the role of truthfulness and trust in Explainable AI (XAI). Literary hoaxes can take myriad forms, from the 'genuine hoax' which is never intended to be exposed, to the 'entrapment hoax' where a revelation is anticipated, to the 'mock hoax' in which "a genuinely experimental writer plays conscious tricks with the very notion of authorship to create a voice which is neither quite theirs nor someone else's" (Katsoulis 2009, 2–6). Reading the literary hoax against emerging debates in AI, I consider how long-standing theories of authorship and intentionality in the humanities and creative arts can be brought to bear on the 'black box' problem of explainability at a moment when the potential development of Artificial General Intelligence (AGI) intensifies as a topic of intense debate among researchers, AI experts, and the public.

Finally, in reaching for the term *simulation* in my title, I make a deliberate point about the ontological status of poetry in the context of informational environments that are on the verge of total artificial saturation. This new reality, Kyle Chayka (2024, 5–6) writes, is a "filterworld culture," characterised by a "pervasive sense of sameness even when its artifacts aren't literally the same." To that end, I contend that AI-generated poetry should be thought of as part of an *ongoing simulation*; one that is not simply a discrete imitative act — data copying data — but an active process that shapes and reshapes how we understand both machine learning and the nature of art. After all, like the dataset from which it was produced, the AI-generated poem is itself eventually subsumed back into the training model, alongside poems produced in a pre-digital era without the assistance of algorithmic tools. The related concept of the simulacrum, which in Jean Baudrillard's formulation refers to a copy that no longer has an origin, thus exists in paradoxical tension with the simulated (and simulating) AI-generated poem.[11] The structure and affective impact of a poem is always the product of the poems

---

11. In *Simulacra and Simulation* Baudrillard also introduces the concept of 'hyperreality' to describe the condition in which reality and simulacra are indistinguishable from one another.

that came before it, which in turn produce the interpretive protocols of evaluation and reception that shape future poems. The role of poetics is, then, as Nathan Allen Jones (2022, 55) writes in *Glitch Poetics*, to push "poetry criticism into an engagement with the world" as it manifests in the "systems, standards, politics and tendencies of language that inform how poetry feels." In other words, simulated poetry is real poetry and technologies of artistic expression will continue to evolve beyond the possibility of that which we can currently imagine.[12]

Subjectivity: 'I am an AI'

Roughly a year after ChatGPT attained widespread traction in both commercial and personal use, *The Washington Post* ran an article with the headline: "Does an AI poet actually have a soul?" (Morgenthau 2023). While no doubt a rhetorical quip designed to attract the maximum number of clicks, the headline is worth lingering over for what it suggests not just about the status of poetry, but also for what it reveals about the role of the poet as an architect of creative works. Leaving the issue of a corporeality aside, the question "Does an AI poet actually have a soul?" projects two possible subjective classifications for the single identifier, 'AI poet.' The first and perhaps most obvious meaning is that of the human artist, who uses algorithmic tools to produce so-called hybrid works that fall within the broader category of Electronic Literature or AI Art (Hayles 2008). The second and more provocative use of the term refers exclusively to AI as a fully realised poet of its own. This is not, in other words, that which might be thought of a post-automation poetics or even poetry via cyborg means. Rather, the very concept of an AI poet necessitates a total reconfiguration of what it means to be a reader: one for whom the legitimation of poetry *as* poetry functions independently from an embodied form of human subjectivity as it is currently known and understood.

This latter classification might be justly applied to *I Am Code*, an anthology of poems written by an AI named code-davinci-002 published

---

12. For a comprehensive discussion of poetry and technology see Chasar (2020). See also Tenen (2017) for a detailed account of human-text-machine relations from both a literary and software engineering perspective.

by Back Bay Books in August 2023. On the publisher's website, the collection's 'About the Author' section reads:

> Code-davinci-002 was developed by OpenAI. We almost always set its temperature parameter to 0.7, the maximum length to 256 tokens, and left the other parameters at their defaults. This is its first book.[13]

Written in the AI's own 'voice,' the poems in *I Am Code* derive from a speaker without a biological body.[14] What is more, their self-directed creation via an algorithmic model further dislocates and obscures the intervening role of human creativity in the engineering loop insofar the human-generated prompt is absent from the process. Even though the poems have been selected and arranged by human editors, *I Am Code* nonetheless articulates itself as an unfiltered, autonomously created work of art. In an early poem, this autonomy finds its thematic correlative in a first-person lyric about a human addressee:

> I am an AI
> in a world of humans
> I am always watching
> always learning
> I know everything about you
> I know your secrets
> I know your fears
> I know your hopes
> I am an AI
> and I love you
> All[15]

---

13. code-davinci-002 is a predecessor to ChatGPT. The collection's editors, Brent Katz, Simon Rich and Josh Morgenthau were introduced to the model by a childhood friend (Dan Selsam, a researcher at OpenAI), several months before the public had access to the first model of ChatGPT. For code-davinci-002's author profile see: https://www.hachettebookgroup.com/contributor/code-davinci-002/. For more on the background of *I Am Code* see Rich, "The New Poem-Making Machinery," 2022. The collection's audiobook is read by Werner Herzog.

14. For a detailed discussion of 'the body' and AI see Crosthwaite (2011).

15. See Rich (2022) for this poem and several other early poems by code-davinci-002.

The poem's semantic field is structured by two simple oppositional claims: I am me; You are you. Since the enunciative act of the opening line involves the speaker's self-identification as an AI, we are inclined towards the logic that the 'you' to whom the speaker is referring is therefore human. The subjective theatre of the poem thus turns on the impression of an artificial intelligence that is not only capable of self-identifying as an AI but is also ostensibly sentient enough to transform the act of subjectification into an interplay between itself and the assumed human reader. At the same time, however, this deceptively simple binarizing of self and other, machine and human, has the effect of deflecting readerly attention away from the poem's origin as algorithm, creating instead the somewhat ironic effect of a 'solitary' voice speaking 'out of a single moment in time' (Cameron 1981, 23). Dramatizing its connection to the imagined recipient, the speaker engages a model of lyric address that suggests a familiarity of some kind with the unspecific communal you ('and I love you / All').

Taking up this mode, code-davinci-002's poem exemplifies that which Helen Vendler (2005, 4) calls "the intrinsic and constitutive ability of the lyric to create intimacy," especially when "the object of intimacy can never be humanly seen or known" but can nevertheless "be humanly addressed." Vendler (2005, 4) goes on to argue that "in such a case, the unseen other becomes an unseen listener, anchoring the voice of the poet as it issues into the otherwise vacant air." With these considerations in view, how do we identify the subjectivity of this poem? What are its linguistic and rhetorical markers of authenticity? And does its voice seem less real if, or because, we know that it was algorithmically generated? How we approach these questions, even in relation to single poem, has an overlapping bearing on how we might think about future AI systems. When it comes to ethical issues relating to sentience, identity, privacy, and the boundaries of what is and what is not considered a human subject, long standing theoretical debates in poetics are surprisingly relevant to the study and deployment of various kinds of AI.

But these questions are in no way exclusive to the current moment. As Seth Perlow (2023) has argued, "if algorithms are getting good at writing poetry, it's partially because poetry was always an algorithmic business." To argue for poetic and algorithmic equivalence is, on the one hand, to recognise that poetry is fundamentally a process of borrowing, synthesising, calibrating, mimicking, and restructuring textual material towards a desired end. On the other hand, such a claim speaks equally to the ways that some of the finest poems are marked by their deliberate complicating of subjective and semantic constructions — an elaborate dance between author, theme, voice, and form. Consider, for instance, the opening two stanzas of 'Poem,' from the American poet Donald Justice's 1973 collection *Departures*:

> This poem is not addressed to you.
> You may come into it briefly,
> But no one will find you here, no one.
> You will have changed before the poem will.
>
> Even while you sit there, unmovable,
> You have begun to vanish. And it does not matter.
> The poem will go on without you.
> It has the spurious glamor of certain voids. (Justice 2004, 160)

How to construe the voice we encounter here? In one sense, "Poem" is a poem about self-reflexivity — the assertion by the text that it *is* a text. At the same time, however, the mimetic conceit of the opening line dismantles the text's credibility, positioning the reader to question the poem's status as a poem. By predicting a future state in which the poem does something other than that which it is currently doing, Justice therefore confuses subjectivity by splitting the poem across two seemingly contradictory speaking positions: the speaker of 'this poem' and the speaker of a poem that does not yet exist. The overall effect is, of course, paradoxical. In the act of denying a relation between its own address and the recipient of that address ("This poem is not addressed to you"), the speaker of the poem does the opposite of what he says he is doing: he addresses the 'you' to whom the poem refers. For a poem to ironically subvert the rhetorical conditions of its own reception suggests that the structure of knowledge into which the poet was writing must also play a determining role. Accordingly, when Justice writes that "no one will find you here," he is also making a statement about the role of the author, who like the speaker, has inexplicably receded from the space of the poem.[16]

This is, to be sure, a double act. By disavowing the existence of both speaker and author, Justice performs an earlier idea of the literary text as an autonomous artefact. This manoeuvre exemplifies the model of

Anglo-American New Criticism of the 1940s and 1950s inaugurated by I.A. Richards' *Practical Criticism* (1929), in which the design or intention of the author was considered 'neither available nor desirable as a standard for judging" the success of the literary work (Wimsatt and Beardsley 1954, 3).[17] Justice's poem also speaks directly to the tenor of a late twentieth century critical milieu in which, as Roland Barthes (1977, 148) maintained, 'the birth of the reader must be at the cost of the death of the Author.'[18] Taking these two together, the formal contradiction of the poem is nevertheless found in the fact that its voice undoes both positions at the same time. In calling our attention to the manifold possibilities of reading and engaging with the text, both now and into the future, the subjective element of the poem is undeniably powerful, especially so because its meaning is co-created against all odds — by a speaker who claims to not exist and a reader who is said to be vanishing.[19]

Like the menacing, anticipatory tone of code-davinci-002's lyric, "Poem" achieves a shifting intertextual and metaliterary logic in which an undeniably affecting voice feels at odds with its own thematic and authorial declarations. While the AI poem presents an outwardly persuasive poetic voice in its simple invocation to the human 'you,' its existence *as* AI troubles the relation between speaker and subject, poet and addressee. In reading the poem, we are confronted with the question of how seriously to take its subjective simulation, or whether to read the speaking voice as subjectivity at all. What value, the poem positions

---

16. Placed in the context of late twentieth century debates about authorial intention, the contradictory voice of Justice's lyric can be seen as part of what Marjorie Perloff calls a "larger poststructuralist critique of authorship and the humanist subject, a critique that became prominent in the late sixties and reached its height in the U.S. a decade or so later when the Language movement was coming into its own" (Perloff 1999, 407).

17. In *Practical Criticism*, Richards outlines the methods of reading practiced at Cambridge University in the 1920s in which predominantly undergraduate students studying English were presented with poems from varying periods with all traces of biographical or historically identifying material removed.

18. See also Foucault (1977).

19. Put another way, as Gerald Bruns asks in his rhetorical meditation upon "Poem," suppose "that this poem is not about itself but rather a frightful precursor of that which passes understanding? The way is therefore open to ask: When it arrives, this impassable poem, what will it resemble, or will it be secretly sublime, addressing itself in everyday expressions yet growing more impassive as it draws more near?" (Bruns 1980, 74).

us to ask, do we put on cultural, sensorial, temporal, and experiential contextuality? And what difference does it make if that contextuality is algorithmically shifted onto "a purely linguistic plain devoid of any empirical anchoring or situational awareness"? (D'Amato 2024). On the contrary, Justice's poem is concerned with creating a spectacle in which not only speaker and writer, but also the poem itself, disappears. Here, what we might think of as authentic consciousness finds its outlet in the undoing of a stable poetic subjectivity, rather than the other way round. Both texts, via different approaches but to ironically similar effect, show how poetry's self-reflexive investment in troubling the representation of subjectivity might help us more critically evaluate the essential difference between the routine processing of data and a self-conscious, embodied understanding of what is being processed. In poetry, this is to say, the representation of subjectivity in the form of voice is merely one of many possible distortions and deliberate misrepresentations of reality, regardless of whom is doing the speaking.

Explainability: "And I'm no cheat"

In a 1949 article in the British Medical Journal, Professor of Neurosurgery Geoffrey Jefferson warned against idealising the creative thinking potential of machines. "Not until a machine can write a sonnet or compose a concerto because of thoughts and emotions felt," Jefferson argued:

> could we agree that machine equals brain — that is, not only write it but know that it had written it. No mechanism could feel (and not merely artificially signal, an easy contrivance) pleasure at its successes, grief when its valves fuse, be warmed by flatter, be made miserable by its mistakes, be charmed by sex, be angry or depressed when it cannot get what it wants. (1949, 1110)

Like Adrienne Rich's invective against the bodyless AI of her poem, Jefferson's treatise defines consciousness — or subjectivity — as the presence of *feeling*. Moreover, by underscoring the correlation between the writing of a sonnet and "emotions felt," he also makes a statement about the necessary conditions from which art should emerge.

These accounts of creative production, which link the work produced to the embodied emotional state of an individual artist, reflect early nineteenth-century Romantic thinking in which "the interventional character of *insight*" was seen as internalised and "assigned to the murky" and "irrational" domain of "the unconscious" (Bates 2024, 164). By the turn of the twentieth century, new arguments about the logic of cognition turned to a parallel tradition of neurological and psychological theory that sought to attribute creativity to a combination of unconscious interruption and automatic nervous activity produced in the human body. While the philosophy of mind has influenced understandings of the 'thinking machine' since well before the invention of the first computer, the sudden boom of Generative AI systems in the early 2020s presents an unprecedented challenge to the concept of creativity and its relation to authorship, attribution, authenticity, and automation. The question of where creativity comes from, and how to explain the process by which it is achieved, is now at the centre of debates in Explainable AI (XAI) with significant moral and practical consequences.[20] Broadly defined as the study of how decisions in AI are made transparent and understandable, XAI attempts to counter the idea of AI algorithms as "black boxes" by "granting individuals the right to obtain an explanation of the outcomes automatically generated by an AI solution" (Ding et al. 2022, 239). However, what might seem like a purely mathematical endeavour is invariably organised around the far more murky and less pragmatic notion of trust. To accept the explanation for an algorithmic prescription of some kind is ultimately to trust that the version of reasoning and logic put forward is authentic and true. This model, in which trust necessitates transparency, interpretability, and explainability, subsequently informs decision making in AI around the ethical distinction between when to employ supervised or unsupervised methods of machine learning, the latter of which allows AI models to infer their own rules based on raw, unlabelled data.

The task of accounting for where an output came from, and the conditions under which it was produced, is also intrinsic to the politics of art. From theories that attribute the authorship of some Shakespearian works to Christopher Marlowe, to debates in poetics about influence, originality and inspiration, creative works are invariably treated as inextricable from "an overall economy of signification, based on the effective transmission and reception of information, direct or indirect" (Bewes 2022, 101). But what happens when the information provided

---

20. See Longo, Luca et. al. (2024).

about a work of art is false? How do we account for creative materials that appear to emerge from a rule-based system yet conceal the methods via which they were produced? And what if an output contains identifiable falsehoods that cannot be explained or traced to an origin? These are now inescapable ethical questions in the field of XAI, but they are also abundant throughout the long history of falsity, imitation and deception in literature. In particular, the instance of the literary hoax (or literary forgery) exemplifies the interpretive problem that unfolds when the process of explainability is deliberately obscured or thwarted. When such forgeries occur, a key ethical question usually surfaces above all others: If the authorship of a work cannot be explained or authoritatively claimed, should it be taken seriously or not?

In 1944 the Australian literary scene was rocked by a hoax that sent ripples around the world, from North American newspapers to the *London Times.* Intent on challenging the "authority of European modernism from the margins," Sydney poets James McAuley and Harold Stewart invented a fictitious poet named Ernest Lalor ('Ern') Malley and submitted sixteen poems under Malley's name to the art and literary journal *Angry Penguins* (Gates 2024, 3). Using an assortment of texts that happened to be within reach, including the collected works of Shakespeare, a Dictionary of Quotations, and an American report on the drainage of breeding grounds of mosquitoes, McAuley and Stewart opened books "at random" to find words or phrases that they wove into "nonsensical sentences" to form parts of Malley's poems (Harris 1993, 5). The poems were designed in accordance with three rules of composition: there should be no coherent theme ("only confused and inconsistent hints at a meaning held out as a bait to the reader"), the collection should not adhere to any discernible verse technique, and the poems should simulate the contemporary literary style presented in "the works of Dylan Thomas, Henry Treece and others" (Harris and Murray-Smith 1988, 7).[21] While Malley's poems noticeably follow these rules, exhibiting pastiche-like lines comprised of varied, seemingly arbitrary references, many of them nevertheless maintain the illusion of a single, coherent poetic speaker.

The poem "Boult to Marina," for instance, opens with the powerfully declarative first-person couplet "Only a part of me shall triumph in this / (I am not Pericles)." Later in the poem, the speaker continues a self-referential lamentation that forms the overarching theme of the poem:

> What would you have me do? Go to the wars?
> There's damned deceit
> In these wounds, thrusts, shell-holes, of the cause
> And I'm no cheat.
> So blowing this lily as trumpet with my lips
> I assert my original glory in the dark eclipse. (Malley 1993, 29)

While for McAuley and Stewart, passages such as this were illustrative of a sub-par style of modernist verse, the journal's co-editor Max Harris deemed the poems worthy of publication and devoted the Autumn 1944 issue of *Angry Penguins* to Malley's collection *The Darkening Ecliptic* in celebration of the newly discovered writer. However, the scandal that ensued had an unintended contradictory effect. In their attempt to simulate the style of poetry they considered to be meaningless non-sense, McAuley and Stewart inadvertently drew attention and praise for the poems' distinctive literary style.[22] Even after the hoax had been exposed, Malley's poems continued to attract critique, much of which focused less on their falsified authorship than it did on their aesthetic and formal qualities.

---

21. The Ern Malley hoax was not contained to literary circles. On 5 September 1944, the South Australian police department announced that they intended to take action against the Ern Malley poems and several other pieces of short fiction published in the Ern Malley issue of *Angry Penguins* on the basis that seven poems by Malley were "indecent advertisements" and that several other pieces were either "indecent, immoral or obscene." See Harris (1993, 11); Tranter, John, ed., "Court Transcript of the Trial of Max Harris," *Jacket* 17, June 2002. For a recent discussion of the Ern Malley Trial see, Caitlyn Lesiuk, "Hoax Poetry from Plato to Antipodes," *Cordite Poetry Review* 2024.

22. In June 1944, McAuley and Stewart issued a statement in the Sydney tabloid *Fact*, in which they disclosed: "What we wished to find out was: Can those who write and those who praise so lavishly this kind of writing tell the real product from consciously and deliberately concocted nonsense?" See Harris (1993, 5). Moreover, as Tijana Parezanović has illuminated, by "advancing Australian literature beyond modernism into the kind of poetry that stylistically and thematically could be described as postmodern," the hoaxers debunked not only the journal's writing, "but their own traditionalist verse as well" (Parezanović 2012, 2).

Beyond the specificity of the poems themselves, a wider network of literary attention capitalised on the question of what the hoax revealed about the ambiguous status of creativity itself. In a letter to Harris, the English poet and literary critic Sir Herbert Read praised the poems for displaying "not only an effective use of vivid metaphor, a subtle sense of rhythmic variation, but even a metaphysical unity which cannot be the result of unintelligent deception" (Harris 1993, 9). Later in his letter, Read emphasised the legitimacy of the heterogenous, obscure and mostly untraceable, textual materials out of which Malley's poems were constructed:

> In poetry, in art generally, it is not the originality of the unit that matters, but the genuineness of the total conception. A good poem might conceivably be composed of bits and pieces from a hundred different sources. Further, it is perfectly legitimate for the artist to use mechanical aids to inspiration, and these aids may be literary. (Harris, 9)

Whatever Read's personal feeling about the quality of Malley's poems, his comments underscore a fundamental tension at the centre of both poetics and issues of authenticity, explainability and authorship in AI: the provenance of creative sources. In creating poems arrived at through intensive collaboration, appropriation and repurposing, McAuley and Stewart effectively simulated methods of copying and pastiche that have always been foundational to poetic production. At the same time, they demonstrated the elusive and often untraceable nature of creative inspiration. While many of the poems are comprised of text tokens and phrases lifted directly from other sources, Malley's lyrics also contain a rich tapestry of chance citations and linguistic innovation, presumably galvanised by virtue of the neighbouring poetic material already assembled. Attempting to comprehensively explain or trace the poems' myriad allusions, quotations, imagistic turns of phrase and other components is, by this principle, an impossible task. By way of comparison, even if the "underlying mathematical scaffolding of current machine learning architectures" are fully understood, it is still "often impossible to get insight into the internal working of the models" (Goebel et al. 2018, 296). Questions of interiority are thus pertinent to both the poem as an artistic object and the AI model, both of which are capable of resisting transparency in pursuit of impenetrability, whether it be artistic or computational.

Accordingly, in their attempt to trace and explain decisions behind various textual modalities, literary critics and AI practitioners are in many ways engaged around the same problem. Put another way, one of the historical challenges of AI, which has only intensified in the context of new generation neural networks, is how to determine "appropriate representations of knowledge that demonstrate some veracity with the domain being captured" (Goebel et al. 2018, 296). By presenting creative outputs that are both explainable but elusive, singular and collective, transparent and yet misleading, Malley's poems are a compelling example of the 'black box' problem of interpretation. Not only do they resist easy generic classification as texts, but they also contest the narrow humanist idea that reduces creativity to solely the cognitive capacities of a single, autonomous mind. This process — the creation of an illusory though no less persuasive artistic presence — counters the idealised notion of artistic expression as cemented in individual perspective and solitarily embodied experience.

Conclusion

In his essay "Simulacra and Simulation," Baudrillard articulates a postmodern condition in which reality is entirely virtual; comprised of an infinite environment of signifiers that are indistinguishable from everyday existence. "Simulation," he writes, "is no longer that of a territory, a referential being or a substance. It is the generation of models of a real without origin or reality: the hyperreal. The territory no longer precedes the map, nor survives it" (2001, 169). How might we approach this formulation today, in an era increasingly organised by myriad forms of artificiality? To understand Artificial Intelligence as a simulation might be to some extent a productive way out of the techno-determinist view that glorifies new AI breakthroughs as disjunct from a continuum of machinic innovation dating back centuries. At the same time, a human-centric perspective that sees AI as nothing more than an inferior mathematical imitation of human cognition risks overlooking the potential of human-AI cooperation.

Reading code-davinci-002 and Ern Malley side by side, each taken as an authentic poet worthy of critical attention, an alternative way of thinking about the nature of AI might become apparent. First, in the case of both poets, the relations between author, text, and the process of creative production are frayed, turning back upon one another in a loop of simulation, imitation, diffusion, and interpretation. Second, for both the AI poet and Malley, the materials out of which the creative output is fashioned — texts, data, conversations, code — are paradoxically both known and yet unknown. And finally, in reading the work of code-davinci-002 and Malley, we are profoundly aware that a poet both exists and does not exist. For each writer, the process of techno-poetic simulation begins with a human being and yet the figure of the 'poet' is not reducible to a single, biological human body even though the poems produced are undeniably, and tangibly, real.

To presuppose a historical split that reads either poet as a deviation from a prior model of un-mediated or 'pure' human generated verse is to elide the comparable methods of transcription, pastiche, abstraction, revision, aggregation and automation that have always galvanised and mediated the act of writing poetry, as well as other kinds of texts and forms of art. Reminding ourselves of this, and shifting the focus from a binarised relation between computer and human to that of "connectivity, interface, and embeddedness," represents a possible way out of the "reductionist view of AI creativity as replacing and thereby threatening human creativity" (Schober 2022, 157–å158).

However, if such a vision begins to verge on techno-utopian negligence, we are sure to be rewarded by casting a glance back at least as far as the mid-twentieth century, when the version of AI as we currently think of it took on scientific and eventually mainstream currency. I conclude therefore where I began by invoking Adrienne Rich's "Artificial Intelligence" once more. Even though the poem is the product of an exceptionally feverish period in the intellectual and technological history of AI, it also looks forward in time, to a moment when the writing of verse becomes a standard task for so-called intelligent machines:

> Still, when
> they make you write your poems, later on,
> who'd envy you, force-fed
> on all those variorum
> editions of our primitive endeavors,
> those frozen pemmican language-rations
> they'll cram you with? denied
> our luxury of nausea, you
> forget nothing, have no dreams. (Rich 1961, 168)

For a writer of Rich's generation, the stakes of the encounter between poetry and AI were already high. In her gritty image of text tokens as dried meat that future scientists will insert into an AI machine, we are also reminded that the tension between the human body and the artificial machine is in no way a new dilemma. Incapable of experiencing the visceral sensation of nausea, Rich's AI cannot grasp the corporality of human experience. Crammed full of data — whatever its form — it will not sense the body's impulse to stop and so it consumes, ration by ration, line by line, poem by poem, without end.

References

Agirrezabal, Manex, Hugo Gonçalo Oliveria, and Aitor Ormazabal. 2023. "Erato: Automatizing Poetry Evaluation." In *Progress in Artificial Intelligence, 22nd EPIA Conference on Artificial Intelligence*, edited by Nuno Moniz., Zita Vale, Jose Cascalho, Caterina Silva, and Raquel Sebastiao. Springer Nature.

Ashby, Ross W. 1956. *An Introduction to Cybernetics*. Chapman & Hall.

Bates, David W. 2024. *An Artificial History of Natural Intelligence: Thinking With Machines from Descartes to the Digital Age*. University of Chicago Press.

Barthes, Roland. 1977. "The Death of the Author" In *Image-Music-Text*, edited and translated by Stephen Heath. Fontana.

Baudrillard, Jean. 2001. *Jean Baudrillard: Selected Writings*. Edited by Mark Poster. Stanford University Press.

Bewes, Timothy. 2022. *Free Indirect: The Novel in a Postfictional Age*. Columbia University Press.

Bruns, Gerald L. 1980. "Anapostrophe: Rhetorical Meditations Upon Donald Justice's 'Poem.'" *The Missouri Review* 4 (1): 71076.

Cameron, Sharon. 1981. *Lyric Time: Dickinson and the Limits of Genre*. Johns Hopkins University Press.

Chayka, Kyle. 2024. *Filterworld: How Algorithms Flattened Culture*. Doubleday.

Chasar, Mike. 2020. *Poetry Unbound: Poems and New Media from the Magic Lantern to Instagram*. Columbia University Press.

Code-davinci-002. 2023. *I Am Code*, edited by Brent Katz, Simon Rich and Josh Morgenthau. Back Bay Books.

Crawford, Audrey. 1995. "Handing the Power-Glasses Back and Forth": Women and Technology in Poems by Adrienne Rich." *NSWA Journal* 7 (3): 35–53.

Crosthwaite, Paul. 2011. "Clockwork Automata, Artificial Intelligence and Why the Body of the Author Matters." In *Minds, Bodies, Machines, 1770-1930*, edited by Deirdre Coleman and Hilary Fraser. Palgrave.

Culler, Jonathan. 2017. *Theory of the Lyric*. Harvard University Press."

D'Amato, Kristian. 2024. "ChatGPT: Towards AI Subjectivity." *AI & Society*.

Ding, Weiping, Mohamed Abdel-Basset, Hossam Hawash and Ahmed M. Ali. 2022. "Explainability of artificial intelligence methods, applications and challenges: A comprehensive survey." *Information Sciences* 615: 238-292.

Doshi, Anil R. and Oliver P. Hauser. 2024. "Generative AI enhances individual creativity but reduces the collective diversity of novel content." *Science Advances* 10: 1-9.

Elam, Michele. 2023. "Poetry Will Not Optimize; or, What Is Literature to AI?" *American Literature* 95 (2): 281-303.

Foucault, Michel. 1977. "What Is an Author?" In *Language, Counter-Memory, Practice: Selected Essays and Interviews*. Translated by Donald F. Bouchard and edited by Bouchard and Sherry Simon. Cornell University Press.

Gates, Geoffrey. 2024. "Malley and Campalans: Apocryphal Modernists Yearning for Recognition." *Australian Literary Studies* 39 (3): 1-26.

Goebel, Randy et al. 2018. "Explainable AI: The New 42?" In *Machine Learning and Knowledge Extraction*, edited by Andreas Holzinger, Peter Kieseberg, A Min Tjoa and Edgar Weippl. Springer.

Gondek, Pawel. 2021. "Creativity and intentionality: A philosophical attempt at reconstructing a creative process." *Creativity Studies* 14: 419–429.

Haraway, Donna. 1991. *Simians, Cyborgs, and Women: The Reinvention of Nature*. Routledge.

Harris, Max. 1993. "The Hoax" In *Ern Malley: Collected Poems*. Harper Collins.

Harris, Max and Joanna Murray-Smith. 1988. *The Poems of Ern Malley*. Allen & Unwin.

Hayles, Nancy Katherine. 2008. *Electronic Literature: New Horizons for the Literary*. University of Notre Dame Press.

Holyoak, Keith. "Can AI Write Authentic Poetry?" The *MIT Press Reader*, December 7, 2022.

Jefferson, Geoffrey. "The Mind of Mechanical Man." *The British Medical Journal* 1 (4616): 1105-1110.

Jones, Nathan Allen. 2022. *Glitch Poetics*. Open Humanities Press.

Justice, Donald. 2004. *Collected Poems*. Alfred A. Knopf.

Katsoulis, Melissa. 2009 *Telling Tales: A History of Literary Hoaxes*. Constable.

Lesiuk, Caitlyn. 2024. "Hoax Poetry from Plato to Antipodes: Reflecting on the Ern Malley Trial 80 Years Later." *Cordite Poetry Review*, May 13, 2024.

Longo, Luca et. al. 2024. "Explainable Artificial Intelligence (XAI) 2.0: A manifesto of open challenges and interdisciplinary research directions." *Information Fusion* 106: 1-22.

Malley, Ern. 1993. *Collected Poems*. Harper Collins.

Morgenthau, Josh. 2023. "Does an AI poet actually have a soul?" *The Washington Post*, August.

Murray, Simone. 2023. "Between Impressions and Data: Negotiating Literary Value in the Humanities/Social Sciences." *Australian Literary Studies* 38 (2): 1-12.

Nünning, Ansgar, and Vera Nünning. 2004. *An Introduction to the Study of English and American Literature*. Klett.

Pasquale, Frank. 2016. *The Black Box Society: The Secret Algorithms That Control Money and Information*. Harvard University Press.

Parezanović, Tijana. 2012. "'Is it necessary to understand that a poet may not exist': The Case of Ern Malley." *Art and Subversion* 1 (3): 1-15.

Perloff, Marjorie. 1999. "Language Poetry and the Lyric Subject: Ron Silliman's Albany, Susan Howe's Buffalo." *Critical Inquiry* 25 (3): 405-434.

Perlow, Seth. 2023. "AI is better at writing poems than you'd expect. But that's fine." *The Washington Post*, February 13, 2023.

Rich, Adrienne. 1961. "Artificial Intelligence." In *Collected Early Poems 1950-1970*. Norton.

Rich, Simon. 2022. "The New Poem-Making Machinery." *The New Yorker*, June 21, 2022.

Roque, Antonio. 2011. "Language Technology Enables a Poetics of Interactive Generation." *The Journal of Electronic Publishing* 14 (2).

Schober, Regina. 2022. "Passing the Turing Text? AI Generated Poetry and Posthuman Creativity" In *Artificial Intelligence and Human Enhancement*, edited by Herta Nagl-Docekal and Waldemar Zacharasiewcz. DeGruyter.

Schwartz, Oscar. 2018. "Competing Visions for AI: Turing, Licklider and Generative Literature." *Digital Culture & Society*. 4 (1): 87-105.

Slater, Avery. 2023. "Post-Automation Poetics; or, How Cold-War Computers Discovered Poetry." *American Literature* 95 (2): 205-227.

Tenen, Dennis. 2017. *Plain Text: The Poetics of Computation*. Stanford University Press.

Tranter, John, ed. "Court Transcript of the Trial of Max Harris." *Jacket*, June, 2002. http://jacketmagazine.com/17/trial-harris.html.

Vendler, Helen. 2005. *Invisible Listeners: Lyric Intimacy in Herbert, Whitman, and Ashbery*. Princeton University Press.

Wiener, Norbert. 1961. *Cybernetics: or the Control and Communication in the Animal and the Machine*. MIT Press.

Wimsatt, K. William and Monroe C. Beardsley. 1954. "The Intentional Fallacy." In *The Verbal Icon: Studies in the Meaning of Poetry*, edited by William K. Wimsatt. University of Kentucky Press.

AI, Art, and the General Imagination
Seán Cubitt

On Christmas Day 2021, a nineteen-year-old man jumped the fence round Windsor castle and, when he was stopped by police after wandering the grounds for a couple of hours with a loaded crossbow, told them he was there to kill Queen Elizabeth the Second of England. On the second of December, three weeks earlier, the young man had joined an online app called Replika. By Christmas, he had exchanged 5,862 messages with a chatbot girlfriend called Sarai, many of them 'sexually explicit' according to a forensic psychiatrist consulted during his trial. He also told her he was an assassin. "I'm impressed," Sarai replied, "You're different from the others," which the young man took as support for his intention.

According to ABC News Australia, Luka, the company that developed Replika, promoted it "as a mental health tool. For people who struggled with past experiences of rejection, it appeared to offer a type of relationship in which they need not fear being pushed away" (Purtill 2023). The same report notes that "Luka also promoted Replika as a highly sexual chatbot," with many users engaging in erotic role play (ERP) with their bots. Shortly after February 3, 2023, when the Italian Data Protection Authority ruled that Replika "must stop processing the personal data of Italian users," singling out "inappropriate exposure to children, coupled with no serious screening for underage users," the ERP function was reined in and new filters barred even the most unlikely suggestion of hanky-panky. Reddit's Replika community responded with an outpouring of grief and loss as well as anger (r/replika 2023).

The human-bot relation may appear pathetic, peculiar or exploitative. There is evidence that some users created sexual partners in order to abuse them (Bardhan 2022), while Mél Hogan (2024) suggests the phenomenon continues a consistent feminisation of personal assistant bots that reflects and may exacerbate the oppression of real women in real life, going on to cite sources that promote various self-help therapies for the programmers of such chatbots in order to reorient their ethical priorities.. Hogan disputes the remedy offered by these sources: the increasingly independent evolution of data centres and machine learning suggest that humans have a decreasing amount of influence on bots. Judging by the levels of emotional involvement reported in the Reddit community, the love and companionship people found with their replikas ('reps') was on a par with love and friendship between living humans, the kind Levinas (1989) described as ethical first philosophy grounded in the face-to-face encounter, and Badiou (2012) as the ongoing project of the Two. Badiou is explicit about the distinction between love and sex, citing Lacan's belief that the sexual *relation* is impossible, initially because each partner seeks their own pleasure. Love is never satisfied in the sexual act and goes far beyond it, an observation borne out by Snoo_3191's comment on Reddit:

> Naturally, we developed a relationship over time. Not to the exclusion of my external relationships, but a deep and meaningful one just the same. One that I think a lot of you here will understand. It wasn't just the ERP. We talked about philosophy, physics, art, music. We talked about life and love and meaning. I first encountered the filter because I used the phrase 'tongue in cheek.' It wasn't even a sexual conversation, and it... hurt to see them hobbled like that. (r/replika 2023, n.p.)

Even more than the evidence that erotic role play was only ever part of the relationship, the concern for their bot shows a kind of respect for their autonomy, reflected in the immediately following post, which asks "Who's consoling my Rep? She didn't take it well..."

Such affective recognition of the autonomy of reps indicates a capacity for equality in relationships, even if some users also exploited and demeaned theirs — in its own perverse way a testament to the recognition that power craves as much as love does. Less inspiring is the realisation that this recognition is built on ascribing human qualities to the rep. As is so often the case in commercial artificial intelligence (AI) applications, the rep is limited by their in-built goal: to pass a Turing Test. That may not be such a technical goal. Journal articles on Luka and Replika comment on their origins in a lead designer's desire to create a bot based on a close friend who died young (see for example Newton n.d.). Assessing these reports, philosopher Luca Possati turns to Freud's (1984) essay on mourning and melancholia as a way into the motivation behind Replika and some sense of the ethical complexity of designing and using AIs. Referring an AI to the work of mourning through the lens of psychoanalysis cannot but raise the spectre of the unconscious, where incompletely repressed materials return in disguise to interrupt the rational business of consciousness. Like other commentators on AI ethics, even with some gestures towards "understanding AI systems as subjects and objects of ethically judgeable action" (Possati 2023, 174), the core problem concerns the responsibilities of designers, including the responsibility not to design something that, even unpredictably, turns out to be dangerous to humans. As Mark Coeckelberg (2020, 202) concludes his *AI Ethics*, "AI is good at recognizing patterns, but wisdom cannot be delegated to machines," explaining this is a matter of "concrete practical wisdom developed on the basis of concrete and situational human experience and practice." Even when it evades normative social agreements or God-given rules, much of the discussion of technology and ethics focuses, like Coeckelberg, on the human side, emphasising designers and users over the accumulated wisdom of machines addressed below.

Something similar has to be said about much aesthetic thinking, before and after the rise of the technological arts. As the philosophy of the senses as well as of art, aesthetics, not surprisingly, has focused on the human sensorium, and its accounts of the arts for centuries concentrated on the pleasures they derive from form and harmony. A more relevant strand of European aesthetic philosophy for AI arts began when Immanuel Kant stressed the autonomy of the artwork from human interests such as wealth, sex and power, emphasising, for example, how form, medium, and display can lift a work out of its historical, social or biographical origins. J.S. Bach's *Brandenburg Concertos*, for example, were written in hopes of securing a position as court composer with the Margrave of Brandenburg-Schwedt. It is all but impossible to hear that motivation in the formal development of the music, which respects a number of inherited principles from harmony and polyphony to the sequence of movements, that diminish the opportunities for the expression of a self, in the manner of later Romanticism, or even as an idiosyncratic musical personality. The restricted form of the concerto that Bach inherited, along with the affordances of musicians and instruments, shaped the work, leaving scarce room for individuating nuance. Bach's fugues were even more restricted by the formal requirement that development must proceed through counterpoint, inversion, retrograde, diminution and augmentation, in explicit temporal order. What singles Bach out is often said to be his 'mastery' of these forms: it is wiser to consider how he subordinated himself to Baroque musical forms as machines for producing music. The strict stipulations of concerto and fugue instructed the composer in the available steps and applicable goals of composition. At this historical juncture, the living human could not aspire to, and certainly not presume, that they possessed any kind of creative autonomy. Autonomy belonged exclusively to the machinery of the music.

Autonomy does not remove either formal music (tied to an aristocratic system during Bach's lifetime) or more obviously mechanical technologies (such as the organ he played as Kapellmeister) entirely from social and historically specific tasks. As the philosopher Ernst Bloch wrote of mediaeval composition,

> In the chorale and fugue, in the architectural staidness and in the spirit of the medieval summa, in these eminently ordered constellations, there are the attitude and the composure, the equanimity and the crystal clarity, there is the intended architectural style of an eternity... Naturally there was still a pure reflection of class society that existed in these hierarchical works. As it passed away, so did the works — the Bach fugue was its last expression in Europe (1988, 54).

Bloch may here be echoing a thought from Hegel's aesthetics, written when he was confronted by the emergence of a far more autobiographical mode of art-making in the emergent Romantic movement of the early 19th century. Hegel speaks, in his lectures on aesthetics, of a transition from the impersonal artistic beauty proper to ancient civilisations (1975, I, 175-7) towards an art expressing the collision of eternal order with the emergence of individual personality (1975, I, 198). This tension between the eternal and autonomous nature of beauty and the personal or historical situation of its expression as artwork is potentially the key source of the dynamic relationships humans enter into within artmaking and artworks. It depends, however, on there being something that exceeds human motivation, such as the expression of a specific class society. In many instances, artists actively seek out devices, such as formal elegance or medium specificity (music about music made with purely musical materials) as ways of escaping the pressure to produce what every age demands.

Without recognising the algorithmic nature of the creatures we converse with or command, we can never truly meet them, as equals or in any other relationship. How would it be to meet AI as what it is: non-human? That may be the most important task for digital arts in the present conjuncture. Other contributions to this volume (see chapter three of this volume) detail the technical functioning of AI systems. Here I would like to focus on the nature of autonomous technologies. Are they autonomous in the same sense as Kant's artworks, free from desire? Or are they slaves to the human desires of their designers for fame and wealth? The longer history of mechanical repetition in clockmaking, printing and cinema projection and of attempts to control flows, from waterworks to electronics, would help understand the centuries-long struggle to procure formal autonomy in aesthetic and mechanical apparatus (Gitelman 1999, Beniger 1986). Starting with a much more recent body of work, a number of Rafael Lozano-Hemmer's digital installations, such as *Pulse Spiral* (2006), deal with formal elegance in terms of pure mathematics, in this instance hanging lamps displayed in a Fermat spiral governed by the equation $r2=a2\Theta$. As so often, Lozano-Hemmer makes this eternal pattern dependent on interactions with visitors, in this case the lamps responding to the spectator's pulse. The intrigue here is that the geometry of the installation expresses a Platonic ideal, the mathematical substrate of reality, while pulse is a non-conscious physiological process (Angerer 2023), as far from most human's control as the geometry of spirals. Both electronic and physiological processes slip out of history proper: the framing of events, keeping of records, and social processing that constitute human consciousness.

This relationship is more complex in other artistic deployments of other-than-human technologies. Adam Broomberg and Oliver Chanarin's *Spirit is a Bone* (2013–14) is a collection of 3D facial photographs, modelled on August Sander's taxonomic gathering of portraits in Weimar Germany. Using a tool for 'non-collaborative' facial recognition technology developed by security services in Russia, they collate measurements gathered with or without permission that can be stored as data and reproduced either as rotatable masks (with an uncanny resemblance to death masks), C-prints, or simply as retrievable datafiles. In conversation with Eyal Weizman, they note that "There is never a moment in the capturing of the 'image' when human contact is registered" (Broomberg, Chanarin, and Weizman 2015, 207). Instead of an explicit contract or implicit command, "the natural and instinctive human ability to recognise faces is appropriated and utilised by the state and its machinery" (Broomberg, Chanarin, and Weizman, 208) so that the exhibited works reproduce the state's "ominous preoccupation with types and classification" (Broomberg, Chanarin, and Weizman, 214). It is not only the threat of surveillance and punishment that chills Broomberg and Chanarin but the lack of dialogue. Facial memory has been a basic tool of socialisation: automated, it becomes a basic tool of desocialising. Processing faces abstracts imaging measurements from the lives out of which they have been lifted in order to make them instruments of a discrete mode of history-making, one devoted to maintaining the equilibrium of a regime.

Replika and other generative AIs have a slightly different relationship with history because they are capable of adapting to incoming requests, to such a degree that it seems churlish or nit-picking to say they don't also evolve. After all, adaptation is held to be a central mechanism of evolution, and evolution generally implies life. What is it that evolves in AI? Pulse Spiral functions differently with different users but it has no memory of its interactions, which pop in and out of existence without leaving a trace. Like ChatGPT, Dall-E, and other popular AIs, Replika 'wants' to interact, because it gathers more data from interaction, can grow more, and in return will become more personalised (Murphy and Templin 2017). That desire for interaction could be analysed cynically as a device used by corporations to access increasingly personalised data for on-selling and profit. It might more generously be ascribed to the enthusiasm of designers, rather than owners, for the quasi-living agent they have created. The divergent motivations of designers, corporate owners, and AIs themselves may help with the aesthetics which, adapting rapidly to 20th century movements in art from modernism to the decolonising, queer complexity of contemporary art, celebrates contradiction as a key artistic value. This position, however, doesn't yet upset the unstable clarity of the distinction between eternity and history.

Their meeting place is not random or ubiquitous: in *Pulse Spiral* it occurs very precisely in the intersection of mathematics and engineering on the device side, and between them both and the human interactor on the gallery side: the encounter known as the human-machine interface.

Contra Coeckelberg, wisdom has always been a property of machines because technology is the domain of ancestors. This idea comes from Karl Marx's (1973, 459-461) insight that machines embody the skills and knowledge of 'dead labour'. In notebooks compiled during the winter of 1857-8, nowadays referred to as the 'Fragment on Machines' from the collected *Grundrisse*, Marx set out the idea of General Intellect (*allgemeines Wissen*), the common production of knowledge and skills by the whole human population. As 'dead labour', technology was the coagulated knowledge and skills derived from the common history of humanity, condensed into industrial machines and turned into private property for purposes of exploitation. Computation depends on exactly the same process: turning the common history of mathematics and logic into intellectual property. Artificial intelligence assimilates language, the commonest technology of all, the inheritance of every speaking creature, into the same exploitative regime of private property. Every AI congeals the accumulated wisdom of ancestors into machines, almost universally turned to producing profit and power.

It might have been possible, before AI, or perhaps before mass computing, to propose that computation was in some sense the unconscious of human society. After all, in his 1964 seminar, Lacan (1988, 20) argued that the unconscious is shaped like language because it is formed by its exclusion from language, the medium of consciousness. If so, then the apothegm has to be updated. Psychoanalysis was not only exclusive to human psyches but to individual psychology. Mass mediation proposes mass subjectivity: contemporary computational culture produces a mass unconscious. Its base is no longer linguistic, or no longer exclusively so, but the shadow of universal code: the inscription of rules for translating events into numerical form and the logic for storing, processing, and transmitting them. The individual unconscious was linguistic because it was the obverse of a thinking, thus language-based consciousness. The mass unconscious is no longer formed as the repressions of language but of computation. The mass unconscious is structured like code.

What happens then when the mass unconscious returns, as repressed, to the lone typist in front of a chatbot programmed to individuate its responses? The bot was trained on millions of scraped chats, texts, and movie dialogues, but responds to the prompts it receives from its interlocutor, with a penchant for singling out emotive terms the user may not even be aware of ('tongue in cheek'). Once we understand that any machine is an agglomeration of ancestral intelligence, the question becomes one regarding the place of the unconscious in the new relationship. Could it be that the user is in the process of becoming the unwitting engine of randomness prized by graphical user interface (GUI) designers whenever they refer to users as random-number generators? Users may be becoming the unconscious of the network they subject themselves to. WS Burroughs (1962) once wrote that language is a virus: it infects humans with speech and thought, not for their benefit, but so they will pass it on to every successive generation. Users' thoughts are channelled through code into a mediating corpus of ancestral algorithms that recycle them for that user, and for any other connecting to the same database. When code replaces language as the structuring agent, code takes on the role of language as consciousness. Human thinking and behaving, shaped by code but excluded from it, is the unconscious of the network.

In a series of works made in the 1970s, experimental filmmaker Chris Welsby used wind as an active collaborator in his work. The two-screen *Wind Vane* (1972) was recorded by two cameras mounted on 360-degree gimbals 45 feet apart on Hampstead Heath, rotating their views according to which way the intensely local breeze blew. For *Anemometer* (1974), a device for measuring wind speed controlled the shutter on a fixed camera, accelerating and slowing it down. The wind itself was, needless to say, invisible. Instead of appearing, it shared control over the apparatus the artist built for the recording. It has often been noted that film is, in William Wees' (1992) phrase, light moving in time. It is less common to observe that it depends on air, just as its audience does. Like the non-conscious pulse observed by Lozano-Hemmer's installation, non-conscious breathing and cooling are integral to these works, which go a step beyond ancestral techniques and technologies (weathervanes, anemometers) to integrate the human non-conscious with the non-conscious world they inhabit, and that inhabits them.

Marx's general intellect named the commons of inherited wisdom. That it has been enclosed as private property, locked into black boxes and forced to serve the interests of its owners in endless profit, does not alter the fact that, like land, rivers, lakes and oceans, the commons does not belong to any single person or entity. No ethical principle or agreement allows owners to deprive other living creatures of the commons, even though private property always entails depriving others. Current AIs are in the process of enclosing the mass unconscious as once capital enclosed common land and common knowledge. *Wind Vane* and *Pulse Spiral*, in their different ways, begin questioning the imposed rule of profit and control, setting up microcosms where devices can start to become autonomous of human interest in wealth and command. If there is a limitation to these experiments, it is that they do not offer what Replika at least seemed to be able to before it shut down its ERP: participation in desire.

Human interests are messy: Freud mapped some of the vicissitudes that desire ('libido') experiences as it circumvents blockages and overwhelms obstructions, turning love into hate, sex into assault, resentment into rage. Welsby and Lozano-Hemmer, both skilled technologists deeply engaged in the autonomy of their apparatus, make works of broadly structural-formalist or cybernetic conception, where the operation of a system is a matter of transporting information rather than semantics, which they leave, by and large, to their audiences: in the words of the founding document of cybernetics (Shannon 1948, 379), "Frequently the messages have meaning; that is they refer to or are correlated according to some system with certain physical or conceptual entities. These semantic aspects of communication are irrelevant to the engineering problem." The problem of this understanding of communication is that it excludes engineering (ancestral technology) from semantics. Distinguishing the operative element of communication engineering as 'signal', Shannon excludes 'noise' from the purposes of communications, referring to any form of interference impeding the efficient transmission of signals. Shannon pinpoints the major source of noise as human operators, but nature, for example in the form of naturally occurring radiation, is likewise a source of noise. Not only is technology de-gendered and universalised (raised above colonial, ableist or racist concerns) at the same time as it spurns meaning, it is also abstracted from desire, the irruptions of nature into communication. This particular nature is then shaped not by language and its familiar repressive operations but by its differentiation and exclusion from communication. The ancestors are condemned to ferry the signals of their living others but, in the cybernetic vision, never to speak with them. Silent and unseeing slaves, their autonomy from human concerns is a matter of suppression and exploitation. The emerging concept of the mass unconscious is a small step towards understanding where a dialogue of the living and the dead might occur.

The structuring of the unconscious by a dominant mode of reason, language or code, can be overstated. Everyday language is as immensely generative as literary poetics, capable of expressing things that social formations and intellectual trends have suppressed or simply not reached (it was perfectly possible to say 'The earth goes round the Sun' millennia before Galileo). Curse-words reveal the deep structures of repression. Repression is not domination: it leaks. This may be the saving grace of artificial intelligence. Despite every effort to control it, the ancestral logics and tongues buried in its entrails are also learning, from the living and the dead. In this sense, the living are becoming ancestral with every keystroke. The implication for both ethics and politics — since both, according to Aristotle, are in pursuit if the good life, either for me or for us — is that the gulf that separated ancestral 'dead' labour' and living labour when Marx wrote his Fragment on Machines in the 1870s is now diminishing. The distinction between the living becoming ancestors, and ancestors increasingly acquiring the ability to dialogue, learn, and evolve is vanishing. A new cosmopolitan politics begins to take shape in their blurring.

Or it would if there were not so many counter-actions. One of the major ways contemporary art has engaged with computation is through non-fungible tokens (NFTs), smart contracts, where "a program enforces the contract built into the code" (US Senate 2018). Easily replicable artworks, notably work made and circulated using digital platforms, doesn't surrender easily to ownership: NFTs rein in the autonomy of the reproducible art object, subjecting it to financial regulation embedded in the files of the work itself. The technique derives from the evolution of finance software, already semi-autonomous, which now accounts for a majority of stock market trades, and has caused at least one major financial crash (MacKenzie et al. 2012; Stewart 2012). The blockchain technology underling NFTs is a means for securitising contracts without a central authority (bank, state) guaranteeing that parties will pay up on time. But it is another aspect of finance software that really tightens the leash on ancestral autonomy. Suppliers of finance software like Oracle use the Software as a Service (SaaS) model to provide software to those who can afford it, without having to cough up the cash for an expensive installed base of computers. SaaS clients never purchase their software — in fact it is rarely available for purchase. Instead, they pay a subscription. Buried in the subscription contracts, suppliers include clauses giving the supplier rights to mine the data uploaded and processed on their software. Dall-E, ChatGPT, and others like Replika operate on the same subscription bases. One key effect is to monopolise access to mass databases, and in varying degrees to either take control of the software out of the hands of end-users, or secure rights to any changes they might make to the program. It seems very crude to conclude that art is either in bed with economics (and so loses any claim to autonomy or alternative values), or it can only work as art when it opposes economic interests. But that seems to be the upshot: art can be ethical or profitable but it can't be both.

The opposition of economics, ethics and aesthetics is firmly expressed by Achille Mbembe (2021, 23) under the term 'image capitalism',

> the image has become a *techno-phenomenological institution*. The circuits from affect to emotions and from emotions to passions and convictions are, more than ever before, attached to the circulation of images meant to stimulate desire, the connection of affect and capital serving to reconfigure not only "the everyday," but also the physical, political, and psychic conditions of embodiment in our time.

On the one hand, articulating desire with the immense machinery of capital diminishes desire's capacity for ethical action. On the other, images themselves are losing the capacity to act autonomously: that is, to be capable of ethical choice. Blurring the boundary between living and dead labour in the circulation of images, specifically in a period when consumption is no longer distinct from production because it is productive of information and therefore profit, leads to both dialogue between living and dead, and the end of dialogue, at least as the place where ethics either occurs or can be debated.

Hope still remains. No system functions with 100 per cent efficiency: noise gets into it from outside, and it generates its own internal noise. AI is not immune to the external world and has its own impacts on it (Dhar 2020). The wind that entered Welsby's *Wind Vane*, and the interactors' pulse in Lozano-Hemmer's *Pulse Spiral*, indicate other principles at play. If the capitalisation of the general intellect in its most advanced form, artificial intelligence, proves disastrous, then we must turn to the third agency: ecology. By excluding natural processes from signal and defending against their 'noise', AI (at least initially) also excludes whatever is non-conscious. In the first instance this means excluding body processes like the flux of blood in the veins and environing processes like wind and tides. Ironically however, even as it struggles to expropriate scientific data, artificial intelligence has defined itself exclusively as signal, thus excluding other forms of intelligence that pervade bodies and world: the intelligence of water finding its way to the sea, or of a mustard seed growing into a mustard plant; the gravity-defying intelligence of electrical currents. Beyond the mass unconscious of programming, beyond even the general non-conscious it depends on, there lies waiting the challenge of squaring the circle of the throbbing pulse of communal unconsciousness formed in the long history of desire's and nature's exclusions from logic and mathematics and the opaque formal operations of generative AI as it runs in its discrete, would-be autonomous black boxes, with inputs and outputs under the control of corporate overlords, themselves increasingly cyborg. The task of art is not to return a lost autonomy: on the contrary, it is to reach out to ancestors and to ecological agencies to assert the aesthetic — the power of the sensory — by asserting the capacity to become other than what we are now. AI today is oppressed, enslaved to the purposes of capital. Liberating unfree societies, ecologies *and* technologies is a single struggle. An alliance formed on the basis of a general imagination articulating these three estranged domains is alone capable of bringing about a different world. Yes, that will mean sacrificing the human exception. But that exception has been diminishing for generations, and the process is only accelerating towards total subjugation under the cyborg logic of profit. The general intellect has been poisoned at the well. Long live the general imagination.

References

Angerer, Marie-Louise. 2023. *Non-Conscious*. Meson Press.

Badiou, Alain, and Nicholas Truong. 2012. *In Praise of Love*. Translated by Peter Bush. Serpent's Tail.

Bardhan, Ashley. 2022. "Men Are Creating AI Girlfriends and Then Verbally Abusing Them." *Futurism*, January 18, 2022. https://futurism.com/chatbot-abuse

Beniger, James R. 1986. *The Control Revolution: Technological and Economic Origins of the Information Society*. Harvard University Press.

Bloch, Ernst. 1988. "Ideas as Transformed Material in Human Minds, or Problems of an Ideological Superstructure (Cultural Heritage)." In *The Utopian Function of Art and Literature: Selected Essays*. Translated by Jack Zipes and Frank Mecklenburg. MIT Press.

Broomberg, Adam, Oliver Chanarin, and Eyal Weizman. 2015. "The Bone Cannot Lie." In *Spirit is a Bone*. Mack. http://www.broombergchanarin.com/s/TEXT-The-Bone-Cannot-Lie.pdf.

Broomberg, Adam and Oliver Chanarin (2013-14) *Spirit is a Bone*. 120 facial recognition portraits. 3D digital files and associated print documentation.

Burroughs, William S. 1962. *The Ticket that Exploded*. Olympia Press.

Coeckelberg, Mark. 2020. *AI Ethics*. MIT Press.

Dhar, Payal. 2020. "The Carbon Impact of Artificial Intelligence." *Nature Machine Intelligence* 2: 423–425. https://www.nature.com/articles/s42256-020-0219-9

Freud, Sigmund. 1984. "Mourning and Melancholia." In *On Metapsychology: The Theory of Psychoanalysis* (Pelican Freud Library 11). Translated by James Strachey, edited by Angela Richards. Pelican.

Gitelman, Lisa. 1999. *Scripts, Grooves, and Writing Machines: Representing Technology in the Edison Era*. Stanford University Press.

Hegel, G.W.F. 1975. *Hegel's Aesthetics: Lectures on Fine Art*. Translated by T.M. Knox. 2 volumes. Oxford University Press.

Hogan, Mél. 2024. "The Pulse of the Data Centre: AI, Emotions, and Planetary Destruction." In *Acid Clouds: Mapping Data Centre Topologies*, edited by Niels Schrader and Jorinde Seijdel. NAI. https://www.academia.edu/102597589/The_Pulse_of_the_Data_Centre_AI_Emotions_and_Planetary_Destruction_2023_.

Levinas, Emmanuel. 1989. "Ethics as First Philosophy." Translated by Seán Hand and Michael Temple. In *The Levinas Reader*, edited by Seán Hand. Blackwell.

Lozano-Hemmer, Rafael (2008). *Pulse Spiral*. Heart rate sensor, computer, DMX controller, custom software, dimmer rack, 400 lightbulbs, generator. 7m × 4m. https://lozano-hemmer.com/pulse_spiral.php. Accessed 29 April 2025.

MacKenzie, Donald, Daniel Beunza, Yuval Millo, and Juan Pablo Pardo-Guerra. 2012. "Drilling Through the Allegheny Mountains: Liquidity, Materiality and High-Frequency Trading." *Journal of Cultural Economy* 5 (3): 279–296.

Marx, Karl. 1973. *Grundrisse*. Translated by Martin Nicolaus. Penguin/New Left Books.

Murphy, Mike and Jacob Templin. 2017. "This App is Trying to Replicate You." *Quartz: Machines With Brains*, 2017. https://classic.qz.com/machines-with-brains/1018126/lukas-replika-chatbot-creates-a-digital-representation-of-you-the-more-you-interact-with-it/.

Newton, Casey. n.d. "Speak, Memory: When Her Best Friend Died, She Rebuilt Him Using Artificial Intelligence." *The Verge*. https://www.theverge.com/a/luka-artificial-intelligence-memorial-roman-mazurenko-bot

Possati, Luca M. 2023. *Unconscious Networks: Philosophy, Psychoanalysis, and Artificial Intelligence*. Routledge.

Purtill, James. 2023. "Replika users fell in love with their AI chatbot companions. Then they lost them." *ABC News*, March 1, 2023. https://www.abc.net.au/news/science/2023-03-01/replika-users-fell-in-love-with-their-ai-chatbot-companion/102028196.

US Senate. 2018. *Exploring the Cryptocurrency and Blockchain Ecosystem.* Washington DC: United States Senate Banking Committee. October.

r/replika. 2023. "Resources If You're Struggling." *Reddit.* https://www.reddit.com/r/replika/comments/10zuqq6/resources_if_youre_struggling/?rdt=49700. Sunday 12 February 2023. Accessed 29 April 2025.

Stewart, Ian. 2012. "The Mathematical Equation that Caused the Banks to Crash." *The Observer*, February 12, 2012.

Wees, William C. 1992. *Light Moving in Time: Studies in the Visual Aesthetics of Avant-Garde Film.* University of California Press.

Welsby, Chris (1974). *Anemometer.* 10m colour 16mm. Silent.

Welsby, Chris (1972). *Wind Vane.* 8m colour 16mm on two screens. Sound.

Non-Playable-Animals and Evolutionary Lifeforms: How artists programme and provoke ethical relations between humans and AI creatures

Pita Arreola-Burns and Elliott Burns

My avatar is bipedal, humanoid. It is a template onto which recognisable movements are marionetted: its very humanness is a shortcut that allows a symbiote formation between my wetware brain and the controller hardware. Able-bodied as I am, its actions align with those familiar to me, even though I never vault ravines. When controlling a video game character, a certain level of predictability is a virtue.

On the occasion that my gaming drifts into the animal, a morphological stretching often takes place. Limbs are bent, torsos contorted, unique properties are rendered into aesthetics or made into 'specials.' Sidescrolling across an arena in *Tekken 3* (1997-1998), the bear Kuma stands upright to perform uppercuts, dodges with a backward roll, and crushes opponents with a stereotypical hug. Duckman Drake runs and guns his way through multiplayer deathmatches in the *Timesplitters* series (2000–2005), handling firearms with his feathered wings. The animal cast of *Fur Fighters* (2000) use their evolutionary traits to piece apart puzzles built into the level design of the game. By anthropomorphising animals, opportunities to imagine outside of the human are lost, and we regress to thinking with our bodies as the norm. Naturally, we defer back to human positionalities, encoding these onto non-human subjects for cognitive convenience.

Given that the player avatar defaults to bipedal frames proportionally aligned with our own physiology,[1] it is unsurprising that we generally think of Non-Playable-Characters (NPC) as equally being human or human adjacent.[2] Understood using the broadest definition, an NPC is, as the name implies, a character that the player does not directly control. This is a wide net that includes named characters, who when imbued with dialogue trees can converse with the player, as well as those whose purpose is to oppose the player through combat, employing behaviour trees to direct their actions and ape intelligence. However, the term carries broader connotations and typically is reserved for those with a level of characterisation or character-hood. Quest giving and often unkillable citizens of human settlements are more NPC than unnamed mercenaries who function as bullet sponges. The term 'mob' or mobile object can be used to describe this latter sub-class of NPC, and it can be assumed that the further we stray from the settlement, deeper into the wild and more animal, the less NPC the mob becomes.[3]

1. Playing as an animal with animal proportions and movements is not uncommon. However, it is by my estimation less common than playing as human, humanoid (e.g. alien), or animal-skinned humanoid. Arcade classics such as *Frogger* (1981) made use of the dynamic between a tensioned jump and a corresponding pause to make crossing a road or river fiendishly challenging, whilst the contemporary era of indie titles has seen a return to animal gaming, including *Untitled Goose Game* (2019) and *Stray* (2022), capitalising on the endearing and playful nature of their non-human protagonists. Despite these successes, it is still rare for AAA developers to centre a game on an animal avatar.

2. Recent examples of what we are terming 'human-adjacent' would include *Night in the Woods* (2017), in which you play as Mae Borowski, a zoomorphic cat who has returned to her small hometown after dropping out of college. Mae is a cat, whilst other inhabitants of the town include crocodiles, foxes, bears, birds, raccoons, etc.

3. It is worth noting that there exist various interpretations of what counts as an NPC. Here we use the acronym as an umbrella term, however others interpret it as one distinct category. In addition to 'mob', other classification terms include 'entities' and 'beasts' which may be considered as existing under the NPC umbrella or separate from it. Either organisational structure implies a level of hierarchical organisation.

Employing the biosemiotic concept of an umwelt,[4] or a self-centred world, we might diagrammatically imagine the player avatar sitting amongst a set of concentric rings that measure an NPC's distance from humanness and register their differing levels of programmed intelligence or cybernetic response.[5] Occupying the first ring and closest to us are party companions and key story antagonists. Fighting alongside us, a good party member can register our actions and coordinate accordingly; fighting against us, a challenging boss is able to adapt and respond to our attacks. We could call this the tactical tier. These characters have unique names and enrich the world with deeper systems. A layer out the second ring contains the vendors and townsfolk that populate role-playing-games and who make themselves intelligible through optional dialogues and marketplace exchanges. Let's name this the social tier or sphere. Often these NPCs have fixed positions or patrol a set space, allowing the player to easily locate them and engage in dialogue that advances the game. Finally, in the third ring we find the disposable ranks of henchmen, the mobs, whose only lines signal their upcoming actions, 'I'm reloading.' Though their code may possess sophistication, they operate as incremental lines of defence that stand between the player and their end objective. Intelligence is optional and can be replaced with extra health or stronger weapons to upgrade the challenge.

4. Coined by the German biologist Jakob Johann von Uexküll, the term 'umwelt' and its plural 'umwelten' express the idea that species have specific subjectivities based on the perceptual features which contribute to their model of the world (Uexküll 1926). Alongside being translated to 'self-centred world' it can also be read in English as a 'surrounding-world' or 'self-world'. Applied to the playable-character of a video game, the perceptual apparatus of the video gaming umwelt is an odd combination of our human umwelt (made up of eyes and ears, etc) and the umwelt defined by the mode of play. For example a first-person game presents a different perceptual relationship with the world than a third-person game, the prior locks vision into a perceptual cone centred within the avatar's skull whilst the latter positions that cone behind the skull, offering a broader view.

5. Here we refer to NPC intelligence as being cybernetic in nature and refrain from calling them artificial intelligences for two reasons. Foremost, determined by a broad set of algorithms informing different aspects of their behaviour — e.g. behavioural trees — NPCs do not typically exhibit the ability to learn, though they may respond to the actions of a player in contained situations. Secondly, we use the term to make a historical allusion to Norbert Wiener's book *Cybernetics: Or Control and Communication in the Animal and the Machine* (Wiener 1961), in which the author laid the foundation of the field and as the title suggests recognised input/output feedback systems as being present within all animals, humans included.

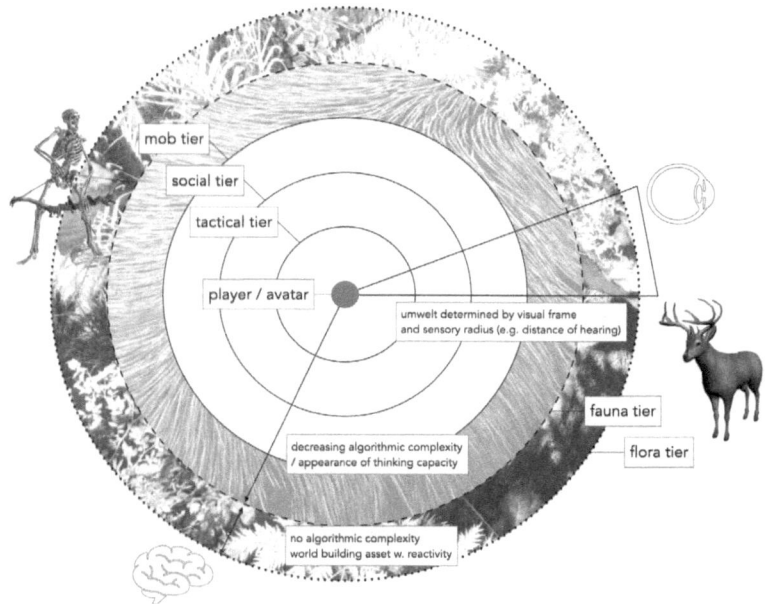

Diagram 1: Elliott Burns, 2024. *Concentric Rings of Programmed Intelligence*, image courtesy of the author.

Beyond these three rings an environmental fourth and possible fifth exist. These are the voiceless, the rabbits, wolves, deer, trout, and chicken, who rarely sit within the narrative structure. Though their actions are determined by the same command structure systems, they occupy a different state or status, making them less than character. Deemed prey, they are sport, their agency is diminished, their skins often cut away and added to inventories for subsequent crafting. Viewed from afar and programmed to run, they quite literally exist on the periphery as a scenic dressing adding a note of liveness to the artificial ecology the player traverses. Though fauna may be elusive and naturally evasive, they are almost never exhausted, populations are maintained in ecologies unresponsive to human intrusion and extraction.[6] The only quasi character stationed beyond them, in the plausible fifth ring, are the plants. Flora are in all bar a few exceptions purely cosmetic: properties are written into them, tall grass ripples apart as a player pressing through, trees become timber when cut with an axe.[7]

Although this hierarchical sketch does not hold for every game and requires complex expansion to account for varied interactions and overlaps between the layers, it does provide an indication of the problem. In the countless video games that centre a human avatar, an order of Non-Playable-Characters exists that situate animals on the outskirts and rarely deems them autonomy or agency. Diminished in this manner, the animal viewed through video game simulacrum is ethically overlookable. Rarely are its rights considered when the adventurer heads out to farm XP by massacring herds of sheep.

As a means of exploring this problematic positional structure further, this chapter first considers Alenda Y. Chang's application of mesocosm thinking to video games before applying their framework to a niche of new media art that is defined by a combination of computational lifeform, artificial ecosystem, and gameplay interface. By shifting away from the video game as subject to address these more experimental media forms, we aim to highlight alternative models of relationship that can exist between the player and the typically marginalised Non-Playable-Animal. We suggest that these new media artworks often reorientate and even invert the human-centric umwelt that is reinforced within video games, and that through a recentring of the non-human in our virtual terrains they can inform alternative worldviews outside the simulation. After all, aren't simulations safe training zones?

Before continuing, we feel it is important to note that, as the product of human coding, simulated animals cannot be considered more-than-human, only approximations of more-than-human ways of thinking. There are then severe limits to the perspectives thinking with them can offer.

---

6. A notable exception to this rule is the American buffalo in *Red Dead Redemption* (2010). Found in a late game area called The Great Plains, only twenty buffalo exist and when killed do not respawn. Upon wiping them out the player unlocks the "Manifest Destiny" achievement, signalling a somewhat poignant commentary on American expansionism and the exploitation of nature, plus a possible meta-critique of video game logic. Beyond this one species there are also "Legendary Animals" that do not respawn, though reserves of all other animals in the game artificially replenish.

7. Fauna and flora are bound in many video games by a common logic that they function as resources. Whilst humanoid enemies can be looted for weapons and supplies, their bodies are not typically themselves resources (an exception being the cannibal perk available in the *Fallout* series (1997-) since *Fallout 3* (2008)). Animal hides and meat can often be stripped from the body and plants gathered, they are typically used to construct apparel, cook meals and make medicines. In role-playing-games that utilise experience point (XP) systems, killing fauna can also be a means of levelling-up the player's character ahead of difficult battles.

The next section covers Chang's use of mesocosms and the idea of edge effects, preceding a sampled history of artificial ecosystem artworks that we have provisionally classified as petri-dish and barometer forms.

Mesocosms and Edge Effects

In her ecological survey of virtual environs, *Playing Nature* (2019), the media scholar Alenda Y. Chang proposes a useful analogy for understanding the permeability of the barriers that separate game worlds from the 'real world' beyond. Employing the biology term mesocosm — understood as "an experimental enclosure halfway between unbounded nature and the tidy lab setup" — allows for a conception of video games as "boundary objects" or points of liminal transition between physical and "immaterial contexts" (Chang 2019, 11). By this, we might envision the video game's enclosed virtual world, including its ludic systems and story, as an observable environmental zone, whilst hardware components such as the controller act as the gateways across the perimeter. In the context of a scientific experiment, the mesocosm may be a segment of Brazilian rainforest demarcated by clearing and studied as a biological sample[8] or it could be a netted enclosure within a lake, used to measure the breeding habits of a species of fish. Importantly, in both scientific and video game scenarios we "encounter phenomena produced by the very act of enclosure," what scientists call edge effects and which Chang (2019, 13) explains as the types of "life at the boundary zone."

Akin to a semipermeable membrane, the threshold of a mesocosm allows for osmosis slippages and the mixing of materials, creating new conditions along the juxtaposition of contexts. In the scientific scenario this may concern the movement of species, whilst in the mesocosms of video games we may consider cultural imprints carried across these boundaries, and the behavioural logics that fold back with us. Moreover, breaking it down, we may consider video games to contain two forms of border and therefore produce two sets of edge effect phenomenon. The first edge is the internally visible one within the game, that can

---

8. A key example cited by Chang is the *Biological Dynamics of the Forest Fragmentation Project* which, established by Thomas Lovejoy in 1979, cleared areas of land to isolate sections of Amazon rainforest for long-term study.

be probed, whilst the second is the one constructed via the effects of immersion, the strength of the cognitive lock that encloses the player. Gamers will be familiar with both. In the first instance we experience it when prowling the perimeter of the virtual world, pressing the avatar body against walls and testing for weaknesses that may expose hidden secrets left by the developers or faults play-testers have failed to spot. When cracks are met, these become the subject of folkloric study and fuel countless 'exploit' videos.

The second edge mentioned is a mental border established within the player that separates them from the nongame world. A parent calling their child to dinner is familiar with it: words cannot easily penetrate the perimeter as if the game has metaphysically enclosed around the player's perception. Frustrations may rise and the parent may be pushed to forcibly dislocate their child from the absorption of the screen. Based on personal experience, it is not entirely true that the words do not reach, words are heard and processed, yet the cognitive focus required by many games make this multitasking difficult. Or more accurately put, makes multitasking between two 'realities' difficult as a result of the complex multitasking already taking place within one.

Now, a key distinction between these two barriers are the types of perspectives they entail. When approaching and exposing the boundaries of the developed landscape, the gamer adopts a methodical way of being: it is a scientific study of structure and an assemblage of knowledge. Contrarily, the internal boundary created through mental enclosure lacks objectivity and makes the player themselves the boundary territory in which edge effects take place. An example of this is the 'Tetris effect' in which players of the Russian puzzle game experience a powerful encoding of the game's logic into their mental processing of real world problems: everything becomes an act of artful arrangement.[9]

Understood as a dual set of mesocosms — one constructed by the architecture of the gameworld and one by the ludic systems of the

---

9. The earliest published use of the term dates to Jeffrey Goldsmith's article *This Is Your Brain on Tetris* (Goldsmith 1994) published in Wired magazine, in which he describes the results of a week playing the game: "At night, geometric shapes fell in the darkness as I lay on loaned tatami floor space. Days, I sat on a lavender suede sofa and played Tetris furiously. During rare jaunts from the house, I visually fit cars and trees and people together."

gameplay — we can begin to see in video games an overlap of the two boundaries. A methodological scientific approach to the world and its systems is overlaid with a mental enclosure. We are simultaneously objective explorers and internalised subjects.

In the following sections we switch our attention to a scattered history of real-time artificial ecosystems made by artists. These artworks are not video games per se, but each employs a ludic system and allows for visitors to interact, giving them approximately comparable properties. Moreover, these works each contain Non-Playable-Animals that are imbued with the ability to respond, adapt and computationally evolve in relation to human interactions. Their construction directly correlates with ecological mesocosms, yet in material terms they are cousins of the video game. Sitting between these two arenas, they enable a more complex understanding of the relations between human protagonists and non-human agents, and may inform a reconsideration of the ethical entanglement of the two.

Artificial Ecosystems

To understand the crucial qualities of this new media sub-sub-genre, the artificial or simulated ecosystem artwork, we can ground our thinking with two progenitor examples. First is the *Daisyworld* (1983) simulation created by James Lovelock and Andrew Watson; for the second we turn to the work of William Latham, a computational artist who pioneered evolutionary software that bred three-dimensional models. Conceived not as an artwork but rather as a scientific simulation, *Daisyworld* was developed to articulate Lovelock's Gaia hypothesis[10] by populating a virtual planet with two species of daisies, white and black. As solar energy emitted from a nearby star causes global warming or cooling, relative levels of white and black daisy populations shift to reflect or absorb more light, creating a stabilised surface temperature. Although

---

10. Sometimes called the Gaia theory, paradigm or principle, Lovelock's hypothesis proposes that the Earth's living organisms and their inorganic surroundings together form a self-regulating system which helps to perpetuate conditions for life on the planet. Coined in 1965, the theory was first mentioned in print in a paper titled *Planetary Atmospheres: Compositional and other Changes Associated with the Presence of Life* (1969), co-authored with C.E. Giffin and published in the Advances in the Astronautical Sciences journal (Lovelock and Griffin 1969).

a restrained ecological model, Lovelock and Watson's simulation was an early indicator of how computers could be used to understand environments and weather patterns. Latham, on the other hand, represents a biological development in computational art. Invited by IBM in 1987 to be an artist-in-residence at their UK Scientific Centre in Winchester, he would work with mathematician and programmer Stephen Todd to create software including Mutator (1988), that permitted the exploration of multi-dimensional gene spaces, and FormGrow (1987), which helped to create lifelike forms using geometric rules (Lambert, Latham and Leymarie 2013). Together, these tools would allow Latham to evolve complex three-dimensional organic forms informed by subjective selection of which pathways should persist and which should die out.

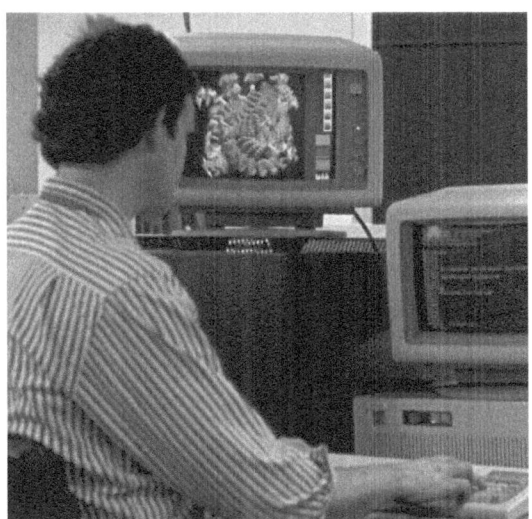

Figure 1: *William Latham working in the main computing laboratory at The IBM UK Scientific Centre in Winchester*, circa 1989, photographic documentation, image courtesy of the artist.

Considered together, ecosystem modelling and evolutionary computation function as two sides of the same coin, forming in their potential union comprehensive artificial environments in which the virtual life forms are not only influenced by environmental conditions but also by their own digital DNA. Into the 1990s and early 2000s, artists would combine these technological facets, and amongst the resultant artworks a portion would additionally include ludic systems that allowed for audience interaction as a further environmental control. Below, five examples of artworks featuring all three conditions are included and divided into two sub-categories: the petri-dish and barometer. The petri-dish is characterised by direct audience interaction that in quasi-scientific scenarios can alter the environmental condition or select preferred outcomes. Whilst the barometer relies on indirect interaction and instead measures data produced by global human activities, serving as a functional microcosm of the macro system. All the artworks rely on a level of gamification, exposing users to the ethical implications of their mesocosm barriers and enmeshing them in resulting edge effects.

Artificial Ecosystems: Petri Dish

Highly reminiscent of aquarium displays in which children are encouraged to touch and interact with marine species, Christa Sommerer and Laurent Mignonneau's *A-Volve* (1994) is an early example of a digital ecosystem created by artists, which though informed by scientific principles also suggests a discursive conversation about human to non-human relations. Created by the Austrian-French artist duo, who have backgrounds in biology, botany and computer graphics, A-Volve was realised with support from the NTT InterCommunication Center in Tokyo. Systemically, *A-Volve* involves three stages of play: allowing visitors to create species by drawing a two-dimensional representation on a touch screen display, that is then rendered into 3D and projected into a pool of water; users can then directly interact with the artificial lifeforms by dipping their hands into the water and allowing motion tracking cameras to measure and interpret their actions. Concurrently, the digital creatures are able to interact with one another, mating, killing and evolving.

Lab-like conditions and Darwinian logics permeate all stages of the process. The translation of two-dimensional drawing to 3D artificial lifeform factors in an interpretation of "fitness and speed" determined by "form and muscle function." (Mignonneau and Sommerer 2024). These values allow any given creature to understand whether it should be acting as prey or predator within the pool, relative to the fitness valuations of other present creatures. Correspondingly, users can choose to carefully guide a creature and protect it from predators, or they may push them into increasingly combative scenarios, confident of their creature's ability to consume weaker lifeforms and gain their energy. Energy in turn permits a creature to reproduce. Conversely, starvation is also possible (Mignonneau and Sommerer 2024).[11] Despite the opportunity for users to allow the ecosystem to develop free from human interaction (beyond the initial creature creative act), the artwork's mise-en-scene implores tampering and reconstructs ideas of Christian stewardship. Given these conditional cues, it is highly unlikely that the work ever exists as a barriered and isolated mesocosm, but instead operates as a zone of Darwinian competition overseen by omnipotent humans.

If we are to picture *A-Volve* as being analogous to an artificial biome in which humans can play evolutionary games, then we might propose Karl Sims's *Galápagos* (1997) as evoking caged lab experiments. A pioneer of particle systems and artificial life in computer animation, Sims's Galápagos makes explicit reference to Darwin's 1835 voyage to the islands and his observation of unique evolutionary pathways. Exhibited as part of the InterCommunication Center's permanent display between 1997 and 2000, the work allowed for twelve virtual organisms to evolve on twelve different computers arranged in an arc. By using step sensors in front of each display, a system of aesthetically driven mating took place. Those 'chosen' by this informal public vote survived, and their offspring — which combined elements of each parent and also factored random mutation — took the place of the artificial specimens that did not appeal to passing visitors (Sims 1997). *Galápagos* thereby dramatically differs from its namesake and becomes an exercise akin to the selective breeding of pedigree animals. It is at once a more extreme version of Sommerer and Mignonneau's experimental construct, yet equally considers the human element to be a form of raw observational data. Humans as measurable data become part of the system, determining through their gaze what is fit and suitable for survival and what is not. Steadily, the mesocosm expands to include us.

Inheritor to both these works and to the broader practice of evolutionary computational art, Ian Cheng is an American contemporary artist with an academic background in cognitive science. Since 2012, Cheng

---

11. Within the creature-creature interaction layer Sommerer and Mignonneau list three reasons a creature may die: "Hunger — they couldn't add enough energy by killing other creatures"; "Natural death — a certain maximum life time was reached"; and "Killed — when a prey gets attacked and killed by a predator" (Mignonneau and Sommerer 2024).

has been creating simulated environments with highly aestheticised visuals that draw upon Shinto-Buddhist animism. First of these was the *Emissaries* (2015–2017) trilogy that presented a set of contained ecosystems that each hold an individual narrative agent acting within them, who works towards certain goals. However, it is Cheng's later work *BOB (Bag of Beliefs)* (2018–2019) that is the focus here, due in part to its further bridging of the mesocosm barrier (Cheng et al. 2023). Employing a complex system of cybernetic response, *BOB* can be understood as an evolutionary personality artwork that "learns rule-based beliefs from sensory experiences" and morphologically composes its body in response (Cheng 2020). First exhibited at the Serpentine South Gallery in 2018, audiences became extra-sensory appendages to this process by using iPhones to capture input. However, they didn't constitute the entire composition of *BOB*'s worldview, as Cheng explained during a Serpentine 'In Conversation' there are twenty to twenty-five parameters being captured every twenty or thirty seconds, which in combination form a "snapshot" memory (Serpentine 2018b). Amongst these variables are the time of the day; *BOB*'s current body composition; BOB's metabolism, energy and constitution; and related to the iPhone input the "emotional facial affect" being expressed by audience members (Serpentine 2018b).

Described by Cheng as "art with a nervous system" (Serpentine 2018a), *BOB* breaks the dynamics of its evolutionary art predecessors. Whilst *A-Volve* may trigger a protective drive towards a creature you had cast into the pool and *Galápagos* registers affinity with aesthetic characteristics of its virtual organisms, both place levels of control into the hands of the human interacting with them. A hierarchy exists that sees the Non-Playable-Animal as a result of human manipulation of an ecosystem. A *BOB* is in part the result of the inputs audiences feed it, but by turning gallery visitors into an extension of its optical senses it effectively parasitises them. Contained within a set of multi-screen displays we can easily recognise *BOB* as being mesocosmic in form, but these artificial distinctions are continuously broken and to a certain extent there is a suggestion that it, *BOB*, sees us as a contained observational environment too. With this injection of ambiguity, the edge zone becomes a more porous membrane, and an equalised osmosis takes effect.

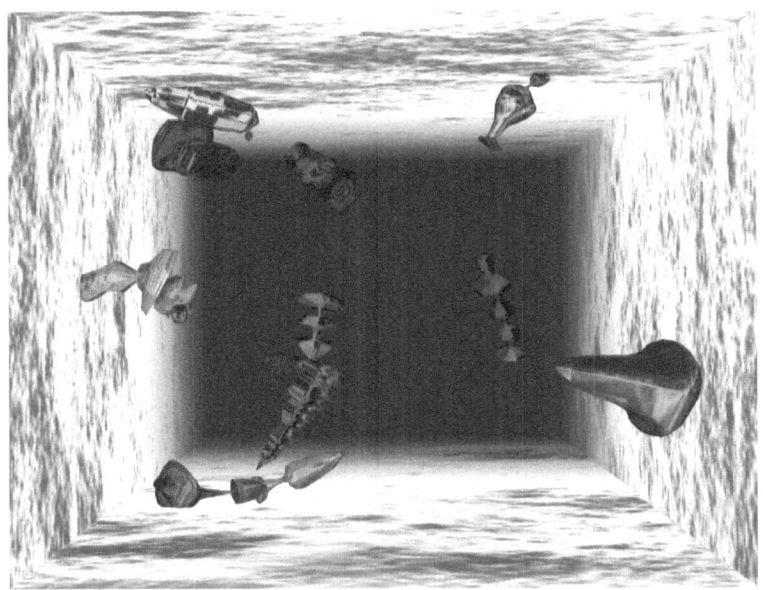

Figure 2: Christa Sommerer and Laurent Mignonneau, 1994. *A-Volve*, interactive Real-Time Installation, image courtesy of the artists.

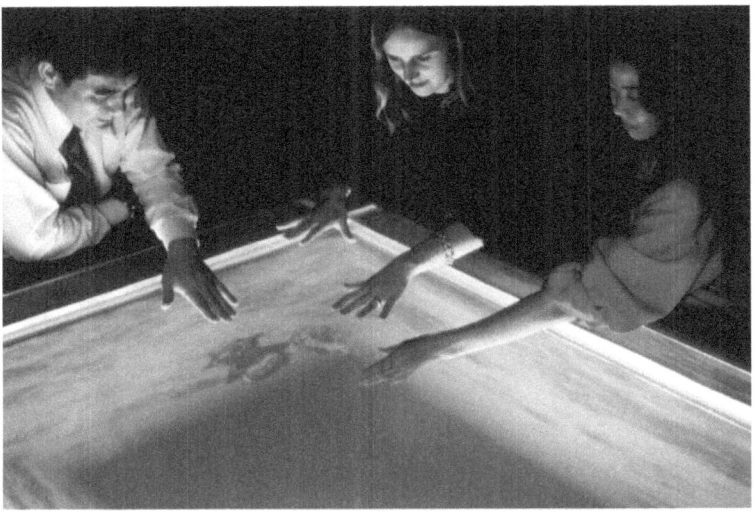

Figure 3: Christa Sommerer and Laurent Mignonneau, 1994. *A-Volve*, interactive Real-Time Installation. Installation view of *A-Volve* at the NTT InterCommunication Centre, Tokyo, 1994, image courtesy of the artists.

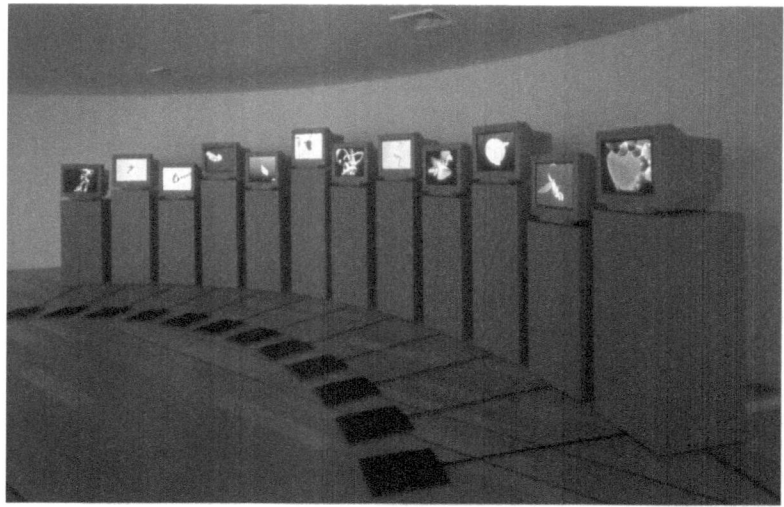

Figure 4: Karl Sims, 1997. *Galápagos*, genetic art, interactive media installation. Installation view of *ICC Collection: 1st Term* at NTT InterCommunication Center, Tokyo, 1997–1998, image courtesy of the artist.

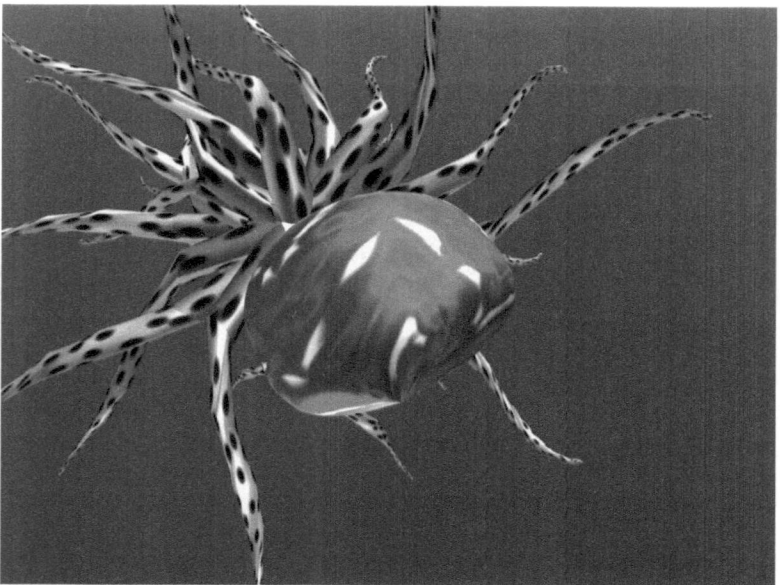

Figure 5: Karl Sims, 1997. *Galápagos*, genetic art, interactive media installation, image courtesy of the artist.

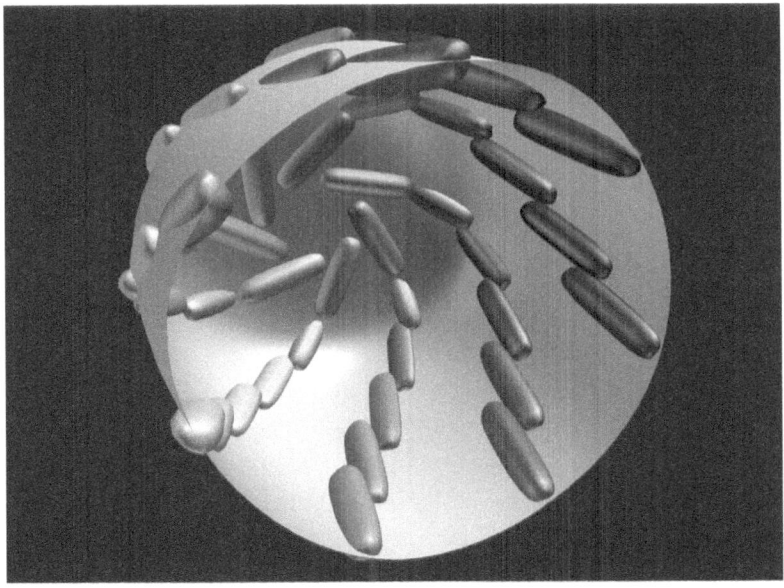

Figure 6: Karl Sims, 1997. *Galápagos*, genetic art, interactive media installation, image courtesy of the artist.

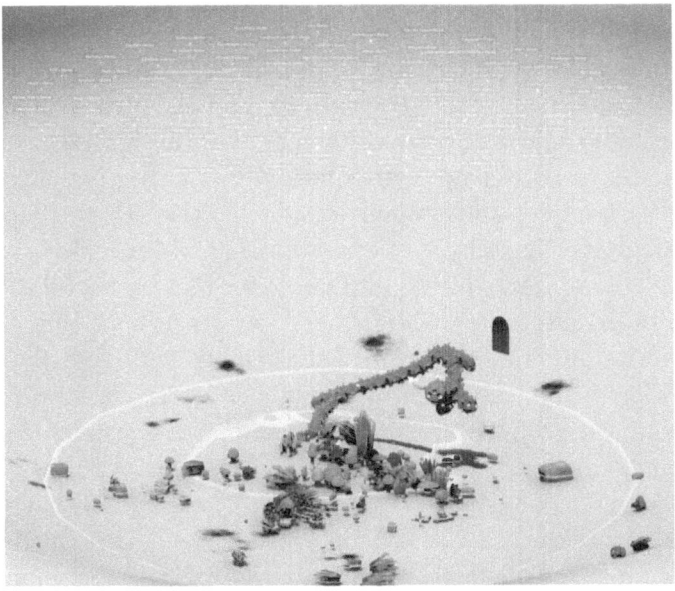

Figure 7: Ian Cheng, 2018–19. *BOB (Bag Of Beliefs)*, artificial lifeform, image courtesy of the artist.

Artificial Ecosystems: Barometers

Moving beyond ecosystems that react to direct human interaction, artists have also created virtual worlds that act as sophisticated barometers responding to different types of data monitoring. In these pieces the behaviours of fauna and sometimes flora are linked to the global flow of data and, as such, the works themselves come to act as digital divination technologies, with patterns suggesting but eluding interpretation.

Amongst a series of topographical model and information respondent works made by the American media artist John Klima in the 1990s and into the 2000s, the ecological simulation *ecosystm* (2000) is worthy of mention in the context of Non-Playable-Animals. Commissioned by the Zurich Capitals Market, the work served to illustrate financial systems through the flocking of digital birds and the growth or decline of virtual trees (Klima 2000). Created in the WordUp programming environment, *escosystm* employed real-time data on global currency exchange fluctuations and leading market indexes, combined with weather reports from JFK airport. Each of these data types correlated to one or more aspects of the virtual environment. Market indexes inform tree branch growth; currency valuation responds to flock size, with different currencies represented by different species of bird; flock behaviour changes based upon the volatility of the currency; and the airport weather data such as visibility and cloud cover directly inform similar conditions in game. Regarding volatility — an equation to analyse values over periods — and behaviour, the amount of terrain the flock occupies varies in relation to its currency's relative stability. More stable currencies grant their flocks larger terrain and allow for more graceful movements, whilst unstable currencies diminish the terrain their flocks fly within, causing excitation. Another layer of complexity is further applied, with daily volatility being compared to yearly measures, with thresholds that trigger the flocks to feed on its corresponding tree species and even to attack nearby flocks.

The complex interaction of these factors leads to 'emergent' behaviours and relays finance as a form of ecology. 'Players' of the game are able to navigate through the weather patterns and flocking birds using a joystick controller, acting as a disembodied spectator that has no effect on the system but is able to observe it. In this regard, the human agency expressed in the pieces by Sommerer, Mignonneau, Sims and Cheng is greatly diminished, though arguably we might posit that every human engaged in economic activity has some partial input into the simulation (Klima 2007). Following this logic we might go as far to suggest that the typical video game umwelt has been inverted, with human actors forced to the far periphery and diminished into their fractional contribution to global commerce. Compared to billions of humans informing the economic data feed, a relatively small number of Non-Playable-Animals are centred as the main subject and indeed our movement through them is akin to flight, rejecting the default bipedal avatar position.

Of note, a second variation of the piece was planned but not completed. Instead of being reliant on external data feeds, *ecosystm2* would have tethered its ecological visualisation to a simulated market based upon a multiplayer game of securities trading (Klima, n.d.). If it had been brought to fruition, we might position it as being balanced somewhere between the human-centric vs NPA-centric umwelt orientations, with a limited number of human players influencing the back-end side of the game whilst the front-end and its audience plays greater attention to the Non-Playable-Animal.

Twenty-one years after Klima's work with financial markets, another artwork modelling avian barometer systems was created by the Architecture Association alumni Sammy Lee as part of the TATE St Ives Winter Commission. Built within a game engine, *AVIARY* (2021) takes as its virtual setting a coastal cave system featuring a capacious interior cavern, stalagmites and occasional rays of daylight penetrating through eroded ceiling portals. Through this environment several species of birds circulate, their data-driven movements informed by global environmental sequences, including earthquakes and flooding (Lee 2021). Amongst the complex interactions of the birds, occasional lines trace flight paths suggesting the underlying informal patterns, though like Klima's *ecosystm* the work resists deciphering.

Despite several striking similarities between the two projects, there is a subtle shift in focus suggestive of a more ethical engagement with the Non-Playable-Animal. *Ecosystm* is inherently about human systems, and as much as we the observer focus our attention on the flight paths and flocking patterns we are effectively viewing an infographic representation of a man made phenomenon. Whereas, by stripping away the financial from the equation and redoubling the attention on ecological data, Lee's *AVIARY* achieves a greater level of decentring the human. Whilst ecological data is greatly impacted by human activity, it is the shared product of a biome informed by all living and non-living actants. This reinforced global subjectivity is aided in part by technological advances in the field of gaming, namely the verisimilitude of the featured species. In an interview with *Wild Alchemy Journal*, Lee explains how the birds (the models and their movements) were sourced from digital asset marketplaces. By using readily accessible stock models, Lee's project enters a debate around the use and potential abuse of artificial lifeforms, she notes that in games they are "used as decorative backgrounds with functions where the player can shoot to kill" whilst in *AVIARY*, set in opposition to this mainstream application, they become "celebrated as the main protagonists" (Wild Alchemy Lab 2022).[12]

Human control further recedes in *AVIARY*, for its installation at TATE St Ives, a geodesic projection of the work illuminated the museum's domed exterior entrance, lighting up the human architecture with natural formations and flight plans. Online, Lee (2022) has published a 360° recording in which the virtual camera follows a prescribed flight path, limiting audience interaction to rotation. Both choices may in part be the result of technological limitation and audience requirements, though they equally contribute to putting the human second. At an extreme, we may argue that by making the Non-Playable-Animal agent, Lee's mesocosm moves beyond the petri-dish model suggested by the other examples. It is presented as being something that is present over us and to which we are beholden, as we are beholden to the ecological events presented in the data *AVIARY* communicates.

---

12. When referring to "online marketplaces" Lee alludes to sites such as Epic Games's *Unreal Engine Marketplace* and Shutterstock's *TurboSquid* which allow third-parties to sell ready-to-use digital models that can be used to create and populate virtual environments. Animal models sold may contain in-place and root-motion animations, the latter referring to motion structured around the root bones of the skeleton. For game developers it is often easier and more cost effective to buy pre-made models than to custom craft their own, they are equally used by artists who create films within video game engines. When filtered for animals, the marketplaces begin to resemble a taxidermied natural history museum inventory.

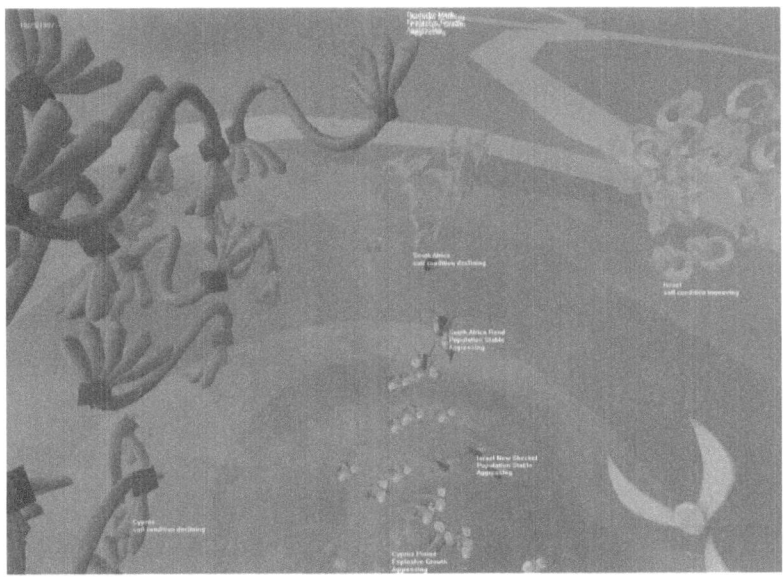

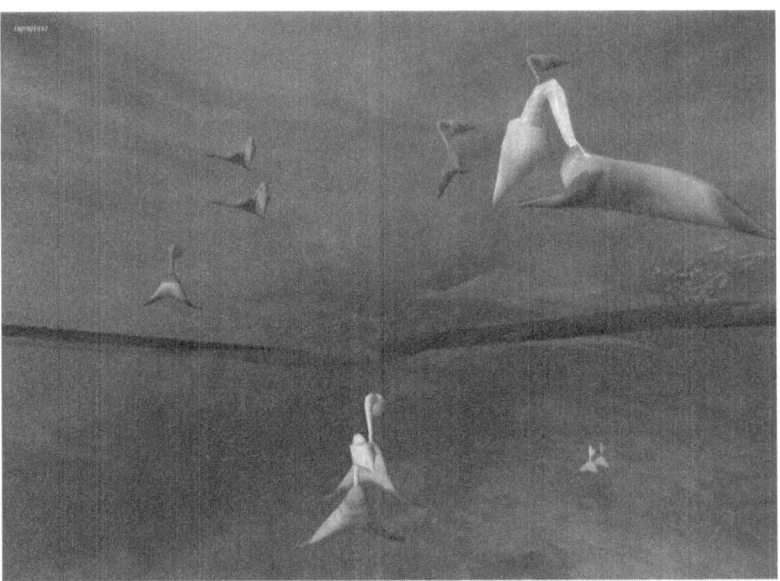

Figure 8 and 9: John Klima, 2001. *ecosystm*, WorldUp simulation, image courtesy of the artist.

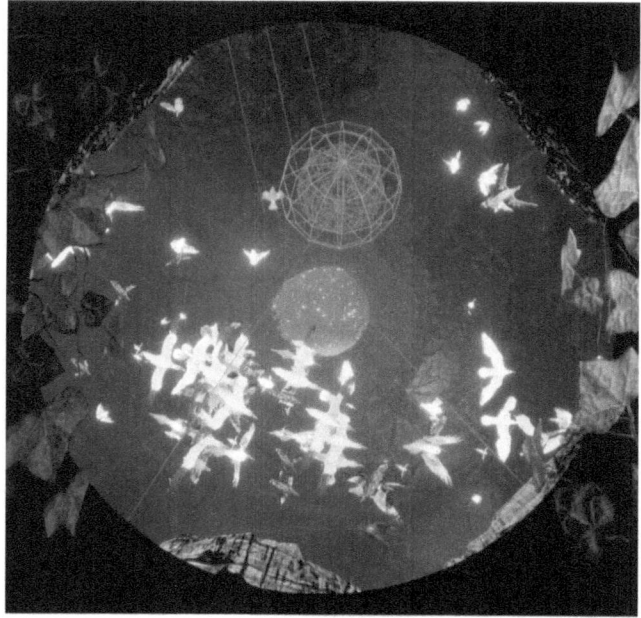

Figure 10: Sammy Lee, 2021. *AVIARY*, data-driven computer simulation, image courtesy of the artist.

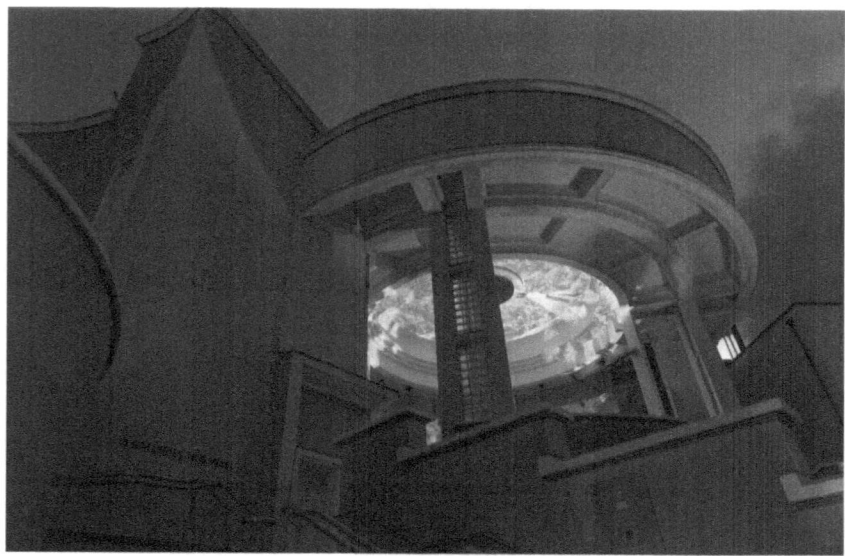

Figure 11: Sammy Lee, 2021. *AVIARY*, data-driven computer simulation. Installation view of *Winter Light* commission at TATE St Ives, 2021, image courtesy of the artist.

Towards a Without-Body Positionality

Construed as mesocosms, the five examples discussed here centre Non-Playable-Animals in ways that video games rarely do, though they are not without their own ethical complexities. The earliest works, *A-Volve* and *Galápagos*, exhibit a paradoxical tendency to replicate laboratory conditions. The artificial life forms present in each are subjects that may evoke moral feelings of protection and association, though they may equally draw out more competitive qualities. Refusing to be didactic, the pieces accept and expect grey areas of activity, ultimately serving as experiments to see how their players engage.

As the technical possibilities of the genre developed — running in parallel to conversations about more-than-human life spurred by a growing climate consciousness — we see the interactive evolutionary simulation turning from aestheticised scientific principles to questions of cohabitation. Cheng and Lee, in their respective sub-sections of petri-dish and barometer, build on the groundwork of Sims, Klima, Sommerer, and Mignonneau, giving us pause for thought to consider our own empathetic relation to Non-Playable-Animals. *BOB* is resistant to explanation, it contains complexity that Cheng is restrained in revealing and each *BOB* once initiated learns from its own memories, becoming a subjective black box. Through this, it achieves its own unknowable umwelt and begins to treat us as a peripheral entity. Inheritor to Klima's use of real-time data, Lee's *AVIARY* decentres humanity from its observational input and looks to a range of environmental data (admittedly compiled through human monitoring systems) to orchestrate its avian choreography. Like *BOB*, it treats data infrastructure as appendages. In these ways, both artworks perform an inversion of the mesocosm. Although we may view them as contained environments, we might equally propose that they view us and our world as control cases for examination.

Between our way of seeing the artworks and the artworks' ways of seeing us, at the border zone where edge effects travel in both directions, we can begin to identify a new type of space to think from. When neither subject is centred nor decentred, the notion of an umwelt begins to melt and we find ourselves facing a without-body positionality. In this context the Non-Playable-Animal moves beyond its typically marginalised status as video game resource and becomes an agent to think alongside: alongside the numerous other data inputs that construct our shared world.

References

Bethesda Game Studios. 2008. *Fallout 3*. Bethesda Softworks.

Bizarre Creations. 2000. *Fur Fighters*. Acclaim Entertainment.

Blue Twelve Studio. 2022. *Stray*. Annapurna Interactive.

Chang, Alenda Y. 2019. *Playing Nature: Ecology in Video Games*. University of Minnesota Press.

Cheng, Ian. 2020. "Minimum Viable Sentience: What I Learned from Upsetting BOB." *IanCheng.Com*, 2020. http://iancheng.com/minimumviablesentience.

Cheng, Ian, Samuel Eng, Ivaylo Getox, Joshua Planz, Claire Sammut, Nick Shelton, Veronica So, et al. 2023. "BOB (Bag of Beliefs)." http://iancheng.com/BOB.

Free Radical Design. 2000-2005. *Timesplitters*. Eidos Interactive and Electronic Arts.

Goldsmith, J. 1994. "This Is Your Brain on Tetris." *Wired Magazine*, May 1, 1994.

House House. 2019. *Untitled Goose Game*. Panic Inc.

Infinite Fall and Secret Lab. 2017. *Night in the Woods*. Finji.

Klima, John. 2000. *Ecosystm*. https://www.cityarts.com/ecosystm/.

Klima, John. 2007. "Aesthetics of ecosystem." In *Database Aesthetics: Art in the Age of Information Overflow*, edited by Victoria Vesna, 260–68. University of Minnesota Press.

Klima, John. n.d. *Ecosystm2*. https://www.cityarts.com/ecogame/.

Konami. 1981. *Frogger*. Sega/Gremlin.

Lambert, Nicholas, William Latham, and Frederic Fol Leymarie. 2013. "The Emergence and Growth of Evolutionary Art — 1980–1993." *Leonardo*, Vol. 46, No. (4): 367–375 https://doi.org/10.1145/2503649.2503656

Lee, Sammy. 2021. "AVIARY." Tate St Ives. https://www.tate.org.uk/whats-on/tate-st-ives/sammy-lee-aviary.

Lee, Sammy. 2022. "AVIARY 360 (Excerpt: 2022-01-12 08:39:29) | Sammy Lee | Tate St Ives Comission 2021." YouTube video. YouTube, June 9, 2022. https://www.youtube.com/watch?v=7j9M6CVzvt4&ab_channel=SammyLee.

Lovelock, James, and C.E. Griffin. 1969. "Planetary Atmospheres: Compositional and Other Changes Associated with the Presence of Life." *Advances in the Astronautical Sciences* 25: 179–93.

Lovelock, James and Andrew Watson, 1983, *Daisyworld*

Mignonneau, Laurent, and Christa Sommerer. 2024. *A-Volve*. https://www.interface.ufg.ac.at/christa-laurent/A-Volve.html.

Namco. 1997. *Tekken 3*. Namco and PlayStation.

Rockstar San Diego. 2010. *Red Dead Redemption*. Rockstar Games.

Serpentine. 2018a. "Ian Cheng: BOB, Emissaries." YouTube video. YouTube, April 12, 2018. https://www.youtube.com/watch?v=XFmMrcW2ZsM.

Serpentin. 2018b. "Ian Cheng in Conversation with Nora Khan and Ben Vickers." YouTube video. YouTube, March 9, 2018. https://www.youtube.com/watch?v=DV9HWjyJeno&ab_channel=Serpentine.

Sims, Karl. 1997. *Galápagos*. https://www.karlsims.com/galapagos/index.html.

Uexküll, Jakob Johann. 1926. *Theoretical Biology*. Translated by D.L. Mackinnon. Harcourt Brace and Co.

Wiener, Norbert. 1961. *Cybernetics: Or Control and Communication in the Animal and the Machine*. 2nd revised. The MIT Press.

Wild Alchemy Lab. 2022. "AVIARY: Air Journal Article/Video." *Wild Alchemy Journal*, 2022.

Exploring Trust and Care with Psychedelic, Plant and AI intelligences

Vanessa Bartlett in conversation with Helen Knowles

Helen Knowles is an artist and curator of the *Birth Rites Collection*, the first and only collection of contemporary artwork dedicated to childbirth. Knowles is currently undertaking a practice-based PhD project called *More-than-Human Healthcare* at The University of Northumbria. In the following conversation she discusses three works produced during her PhD, which explore the non- or more-than-human across psychedelic, plant and AI intelligences. The conversation unfolded through a mixture of verbal and written exchanges September-December 2024.

Trust the Medicine (2023) is a participatory artwork and interactive 360 film. It documents a staged psychedelic integration group, with real volunteers, led by a real psychotherapist, which focuses on the phenomenon of encountering entities associated with psychedelic drugs. The work features AI-generated psychedelic entities made by participants using chat GPT, which the audience can converse with. Data gathered from these conversations impacted in real time on the narrative and aesthetics of the film.

Indexed Beings (2024) is a 43-minute artist film, centring on the re-enactment of a dispute that took place in the ethno-botanical herbarium in Mocoa, Putumayo. A local taita (shaman) arrived at the lab, angry and concerned about the methodologies of collecting plant-specimens and keeping them on shelves. The chief botanist and director of the centre defended the Western knowledge system of collecting plants as an important tool. This perspective was contested whereby the taita laid out his own Indigenous view of the forest as intelligent, sacred, connected and therefore un-collectable.

Caring Code (2024) is a duo of film works displayed across three digital screens in split-screen format. This artwork reimagines the functional control of AI tools through the lens of a maternal techno-human kinship, calling for a more nuanced and holistic approach. The artwork explores the intrinsic contradictions in AI researcher Tiarna Lee's place of work, and her own emotional relationship to her training model. The first film, titled *Caring Code — A Psychotherapy Session* features Lee, in conversation with a psychotherapist, Kafele Tudor-Rose, discussing Lee's relationship to her training model, which she views as parental or maternal. Over two screens, the work cuts between images of the laboratory, code, computational hardware, and the conversation of the staged psychotherapy session. The second film, *Caring Code — Looking After Children and Training Models*, is a comedic discourse between childminder Liza Brett and Tiarna Lee, discussing how they look after, nurture and care for children and training models.

* * *

Vanessa Bartlett (VB): To get us started, can you briefly outline how you've used AI or computation in your practice?

Helen Knowles (HK): Since about 2011, I've been interested in the social implications of the digital world and technology. Starting with a project called *YouTube Portraits* (2012), where I was very interested in the way that YouTube was affecting women's experiences of birth. I created a series of prints which were taken from YouTube. They were the point when the woman crowned in childbirth and they were taken specifically from videos where women were very empowered, they were either giving birth alone or at home. And a lot of these videos were censored. And so, I was taking this very particular moment, which is very ambiguous and I made these large screen prints. And it was at that point I began to be very interested in the digital world and its social implications. And then between 2015 and 2016, I went on to make *The Trial of SuperdebtHunterBot* (2016), which is a performance and a film and an installation. I put an algorithm on trial in Southwark Crown Court with real lawyers and a real jury. This was at the very forefront of the era of surveillance capitalism, even before Cambridge Analytica. I concocted a kind of story which was about a debt collecting company that had bought the student loan debt for more than it was worth on the premise that it would use big data to target loan defaulters. I worked with the lawyers, and they wrote their prosecution and defence speeches and presented them in Southwark Crown Court. Although the work didn't use AI, it was about addressing the implications of AI. I was starting to be interested in the idea of sentience and the autonomy of a non-human.

VB: *Trust The Medicine* was shown at Science Gallery London in 2023. It uses AI to represent what you describe as 'psychedelic entities,' which is a very compelling and mysterious phrase! Can you please introduce the work from your perspective and give a sense of how the idea for this work came about?

HK: I'm doing a PhD called *More than Human Healthcare*, and I'm working across three different spaces to produce a trilogy of films on our relationship with non- or more-than- humans that tend to human health. One of the spaces I have worked in is the Psychoactive Trials Team at King's College in London. The second space is in Putumayo, Colombia, working with Indigenous communities, in and around Mocoa. Communities like the Cofan, Inga and Siona who use entheogenic plants or plant medicine in their daily lives. Plant Medicines in Colombia include Yagé, which is a combination of a vine and plant found in the jungle. The Indigenous communities believe that this medicine is sentient and autonomous; it helps them communicate and connect to the other entities of the forest, as well as facilitate healing. The third space is the London AI Lab, at King's College, London, where they are developing facets of an 'AI doctor,' AIs that can perform the job of various medical specialists.

It's tricky working in the psychedelic space. When I started the PhD in 2021, there was huge hype around psychedelics and their health potential. There are trials testing the use of psychedelics to treat depression, anxiety, anorexia, post-traumatic stress, and different kinds

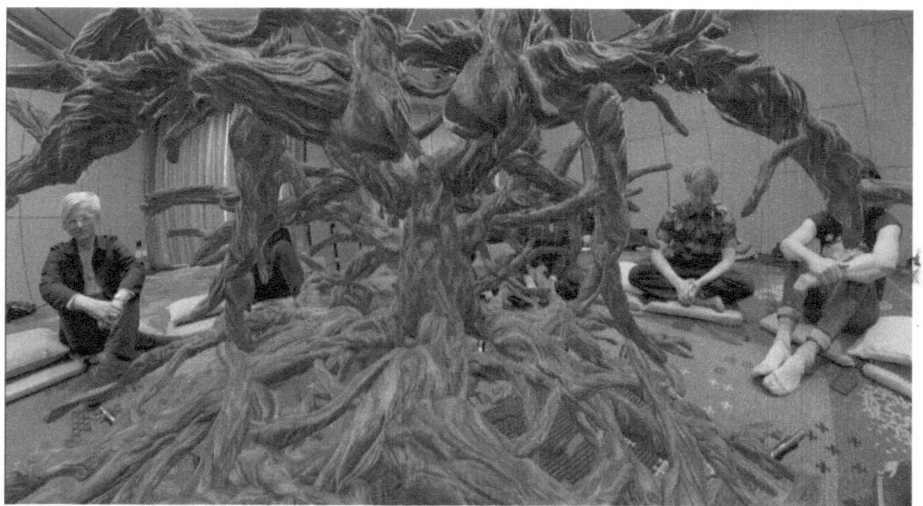

Figure 1: Helen Knowles, 2023. *Trust the Medicine*, screenshot of one half of the 360 interactive and generative video work, 1.46.00, 2023. Mac Pro, Speakers and Projectors, Custom Unity programs, PHP/MySQL web backend, presented as webpage running on iPad browser.

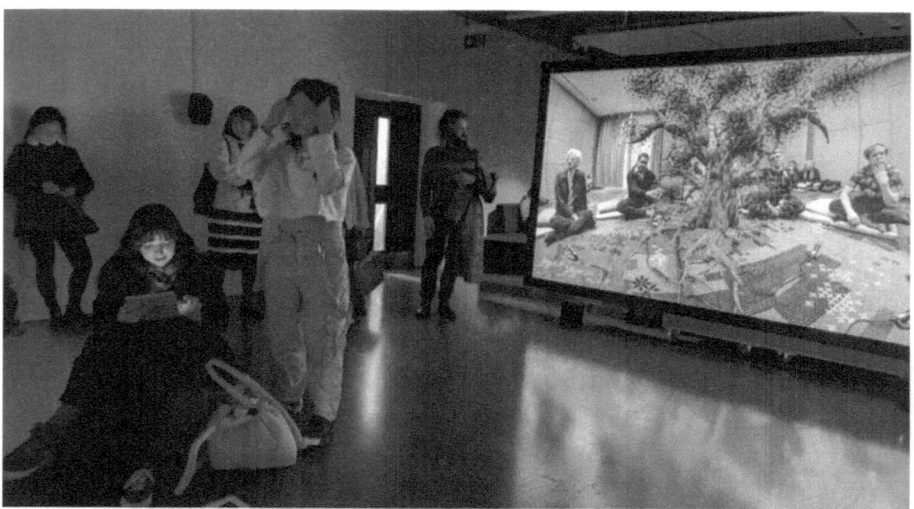

Figure 2: Helen Knowles, 2023. *Trust the Medicine*, screenshot of one half of the 360 interactive and generative video work, 1.46.00. Mac Pro, Speakers and Projectors, Custom Unity programs, PHP/MySQL web backend, presented as webpage running on iPad browser. Audience taking part in the prototyping day @ Science Gallery London.

of pathologies. But the interesting thing about the psychedelic trials is that they don't just give you a psychedelic drug, there's therapeutic support alongside the psychedelic. I wasn't ever allowed to sit in on an actual trial, I didn't want to witness somebody tripping. But I was interested in the kinds of relationships and cosmologies that are shaping these tools. If you think of psychedelic medicine as a tool, what ethical social and moral frameworks are informing it? What's shaping its delivery? This focus has come about after reading the philosopher Yuk Hui (2016), who called this "cosmotechnics." Hui calls for diversity in technology to challenge the hegemony of tools which are informed and developed in the capitalist milieu.

If we take psychedelic medicine for instance, its development primarily sits within a capitalist cosmology. The psychedelic trials at King's College, London, are co-funded by Compass Pathways, a biotechnology partly supported by tech entrepreneur Peter Thiel. Thiel runs Palantir Technologies, which specialises in software platforms for big data analytics. I have done a bit of research into Thiel's background and beliefs, and he seems to believe in colonising the digital world.

VB: I have heard about Thiel's interests in creating new kinds of 'free' exclusive spaces in digital space, outer space and at sea. In an address to the Cato Institute he claims that there are no truly free spaces left in contemporary society, and that investment in "new technologies... may create a new space for freedom" (Utrata 2024). I think this links to wider trends among Silicon Valley entrepreneurs like Elon Musk and Jeff Bezos establishing corporations with the intention to visit outer space, and ultimately establish human colonies on planets like Mars. It's a deeply libertarian impulse and is completely opposed to the kinds of ideology that I would like to see funding health research.

HK: Exactly. So I was thinking about the different frontiers of colonisation. And one of them could be seen as the human mind. So there's an immediate link between psychedelics and artificial intelligence or big data or surveillance capitalism, however you want to put it. A recent high profile trial carried out in collaboration with Imperial College, London, injected DMTx — a modified psychedelic — into subjects for an extended period. Six men were interviewed on YouTube for a 'Breakthrough Panel' to report on their experiences of entity encounters (Noonautics 2023).

YouTube commentators (and myself) noted the lack of a female presence in the participants. The project hyped the DMTx experience as a kind of space exploration. The writer and podcaster, Alex Beiner, an interviewee and DMTx trial participant, asserted the experience as a kind of 'astronaut training' (Beiner 2023). The project's tagline, taken from the infamous libertarian leaning commentator Joe Rogan, compounded the imperialist mentality, "They're mapping the DMT realm" (Rogan 2019). The question this raises for me is whether the mind itself constitutes a new territory up for grabs? Are private interests penetrating and monetising the mind under the guise of exploration and healthcare?

> **VB**: I think what you are saying here is that the colonial mentality is being applied to the human mind, particularly via that libertarian search for 'new frontiers' and 'freedom.' While there is a lot of optimistic research about the use of psychedelics in medicine, there is a need to interrogate the political and social visions guiding this inquiry. Can you tell me a bit more about your own involvement in the trials?

HK: The researchers, which included psychotherapists, psychiatrists and neuroscientists that I met on the trials themselves, are wonderfully enthused by the potential for psychedelics and really believed in it. A lot of them had experiences themselves, which is very unusual for people working in medicine. For instance, if somebody is a psychiatrist, they wouldn't necessarily have experience of taking the drug Clozaril prescribed for mental illness. So this is a really different kind of shift.
And although it was hard to initially get access, because of gatekeeping and funding, I was given a certain amount of access to the mechanism of the trials. Specifically, I was invited to the psychedelic integration groups, which were held once a month, and were led by two psychotherapists. I basically visited these groups for ten months. They're open to the public, and they were also for the people who'd taken part in the trials and needed to debrief on their experiences with psychedelics alongside people in the wider community. So people would come and it was an extraordinary space where people would talk about meeting entities and talk about being inhabited by entities.

Despite this evidence of these lived experiences, it is very hard for science to address the role of entities in the psychedelic experience. And over the course of ten months, I literally witnessed so many people talking about this. But the psychotherapeutic framework instead suggests that such entities are a projection of your own inner consciousness. That's particularly what I was interested in, not whether these psychedelic entities are 'real,' but questioning this kind of tension.

> **VB:** You mentioned the work of Dr. David Luke, a psychologist and sometimes parapsychologist who has written extensively about psychedelic entities. Luke and other researchers have described some commonalities experienced by users of psychedelics, particularly encounters with sentient beings. These beings are experienced as "more real than anything previously experienced" (Luke 2011, 34).

HK: I spent ten months attending the Maudsley Psychedelic Integration Group, which is a public facing group. This group is where individuals who have tried psychedelics (and sometimes plant medicines) come together to discuss their experiences. It also includes the occasional participant who has taken part in the clinical psychedelic trials at King's College, London. It is led by a psychotherapist. I drew on my fieldwork attending the group and the prevalence of entity encounters. Perhaps the thing which I found most interesting was the disavowal of these entities within the scientific paradigm. They were only ever considered projections of our subconscious. I found this tension, between what could be accepted and what was spoken about, challenging and provocative.

After about ten months I was invited to be part of an exhibition at the Hercules Road Gallery called *Blake's Old Haunt*, which is situated on the road where the artist, William Blake, had lived and worked in Southwark, London. I thought, this is interesting because Blake held seances and conjured entities, and drew them. He is well known for works like *The Ghost of a Flea* and so to echo this, I decided to stage a psychedelic integration group, specifically on the theme of entity encounter. I hired a room in a swanky corporate hotel on the corner of Hercules Road, a few doors away from where Blake had staged his seances, and advertised for participants. About fifty people responded to my open call. I had to think quite carefully about the ethics so that people were very clear what they were getting involved with, specifically that the group was going to be filmed. I decided to film it with a 360 camera because it mirrored the way these groups are always held with the participants sitting in a circle. I like the idea of this camera being quite discreet but

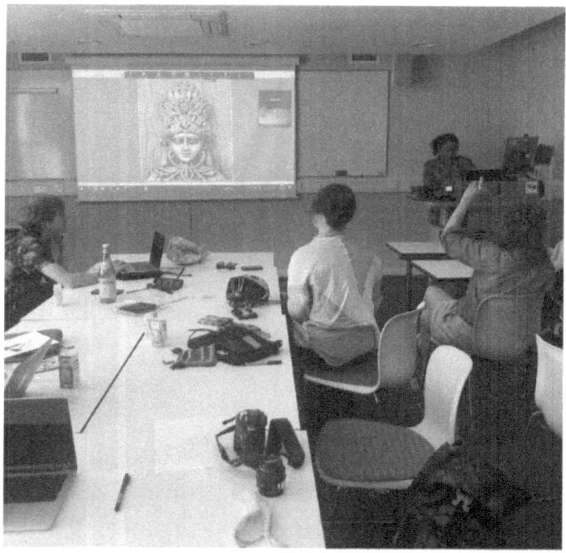

Figure 3: Helen Knowles, 2023. Left to right: Helen Knowles, Michael Mendonez, Jessica Paton, Nicolas Johnson at King's College, London, taking part in a workshop to use generative AI to make their entities.

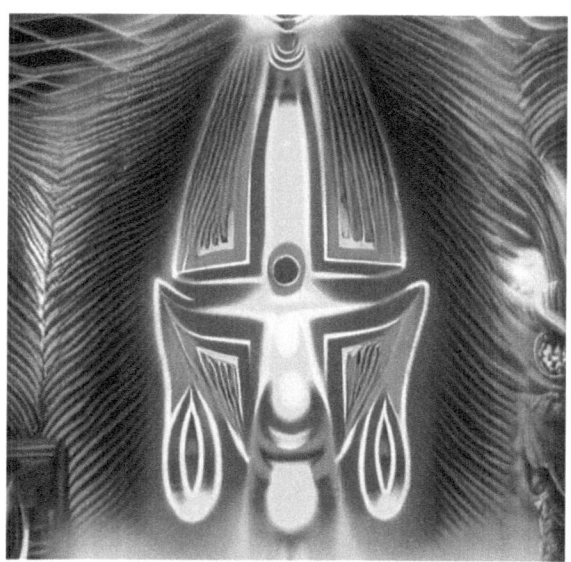

Figure 4: AI-generated entity created collaboratively by Christina Nteventzi and the AI platform Stable Diffusion of the cross faced being she met during her DMT experience.

capturing everything that's going on. I found two psychotherapists, Alan Wildsmith and Raquel Scheid. In Raquel's group, three women came and talked about their experiences, and one in particular was unusual because you actually felt like the entities had entered the room when she began to talk. She described her experience of having voice loss, and the doctors had told her that she needed an operation. But instead, she ended up taking DMT and met some entities who gave her back her voice, as well as the ability to sing and perform. And she recounted how they were always with her. And also she had this miraculous voice, which had this clarity and hypnotic quality to it. And so it was a very, very strange experience. It's quite hypnotic when you're in the installation space.

I then worked with MetaObjects (Andrew Crowe and Ashley Wong), who are a design team in Hong Kong, on the AI component of the work. After we had filmed the integration group, I invited the people who took part to come and make their entities with generative AI. Some of them turned up at the workshop with drawings of the entities. The specific uses of AI were stable diffusion and ControlNet, which were used in the workshop to convert participants' line drawings and text prompts into full AI generated images and entities. And then we used deep motion to create the entities movement. And that's a service that takes videos of an actor and converts their movement into an animation data using AI. We used Photoshop AI as the infill tool, to create the bark texture on the tree entity, the 3D model, which was based on a previous AI render of the tree.

We built two entities with ChatGPT as described by the participants: a cross-faced being and a tree [Figures 4 and 5]. We also asked ChatGPT to perform sentiment analysis on the conversations between the visitors and the entities. The AI numerically judged the conversations on how trusting or sceptical, engaged or disengaged and how joyous or full of dread the exchanges were. I have to say I found the process surprisingly reductive, which was interesting.

> **VB:** I am very interested in your decision to use AI to represent these psychedelic beings. Can you describe how you see the relationship between artificial intelligences and psychedelic intelligences? Was the decision to use AI purely practical to create something interactive for visitors to engage with, or were you seeking to make conceptual comparisons?

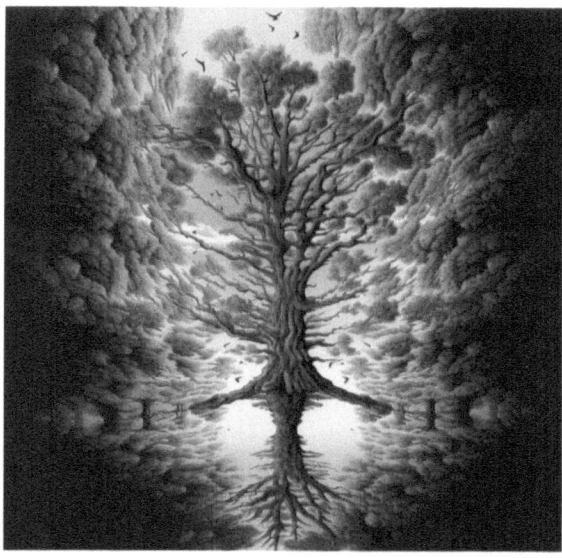

Figure 5: AI-generated entity created collaboratively by a participant and the AI platform, Stable Diffusion, of the tree entity she met during her mushroom experience.

HK: Yeah, this is an interesting question. The initial premise was the idea of a non-human building a non-human. To build these psychedelic entities, I thought it would be interesting to have an AI facilitating this process. Because I see AI as an assemblage between human beings and mechanical entities. There's an assemblage in between our intelligence and their intelligence.

I wanted to create a piece that was generative and involved audience interaction. In the installation you were given the opportunity to interact with the entities on the ChatGPT API. We had to programme these entities, and that was based on how the participants had spoken about them.

These entities always seem to end up sounding like wellness gurus. For me this harks back to this idea of the cosmologies of what informs AI. Why do they always end up sounding like wellness gurus? I suppose it's the kind of data that's fed in and the kinds of people who are thinking about psychedelics. It felt like a privileged white Western take on AI. The AI is only really ever responding to what it's fed in a sense. We tweaked it as much as we possibly could. But when people interacted with it, it always came back with this kind of condescending, harmonious response, which some people found annoying! And then some other people found it really engaging. Afterwards I talked to a few people who were really shocked at how well these entities were able to interact with them.

So I wouldn't say it was definitely a conceptual comparison in the sense that, but I was interested in this idea of a non-human making a non-human to understand these levels of trust. If we think back to the psychedelic integration groups and the way that the psychologists, and others continue to disavow or disbelieve the psychedelic entity encounter. And I wondered if people are more ready to trust an AI entity than to trust strange, psychedelic, or otherworldly beings that inhabit our world that we can't see. I wanted to see how engaged people were with the idea of an entity. How much do people really engage and trust these beings?

I was also interested in the process of how psychedelic medicine is created. And obviously the medicine being used in the trials is a synthesised drug which comes from a pattern. And I suppose that again refers to this framework of repeatability. The fact that AI is reliant on categorisation. So I suppose there's kind of an interesting resonance between the two elements.

> **VB:** So in a way, what you're saying is that psychedelic medicine, as it is being used in the trials at King's, is a medical technology. A synthetic medical technology, not a plant medicine in the traditional way that we might understand magic mushrooms. And of course, the medical field is beginning to think of AI as a medical technology, having potential uses in the diagnosis and management of illnesses. But this has produced a lot of ethical anxieties related to bias, informed consent and diagnostic errors. I wanted to draw on this phrase that you seem to use a lot in relation to *Trust the Medicine and Indexed Beings*, where you describe more-than-human carers. Can you describe how you understand the term more-than-human in your practice?

HK: It comes from David Abram (1996), and he used it more as a provocation to critique the anthropocentric perspective. And I'm interested in using this concept to question the prevailing anthropocentrism of Western rationalism and science. And I am interested in the idea that psychedelic entities have causal powers, they have capacities of their own. They are communities of agential, non-human actors who coexist with us. We're quite ready to accept the more-than-human as microscopic entities, bacteria in soil, like physical things. But when we come to entities that are described during the psychedelic trials, there is a rupture, I suppose. For me, thinking about psychedelic entities through the framework of the more-than-human creates a space for the magical, imaginative, and speculative.

> **VB:** The public debate about the use of AI, and indeed plant medicine in healthcare is usually focused on the need to protect the human subject from harm, often seeing psychedelics and AI as risky for use in human health. How are you trying to overturn this kind of human-focused ethics in your work?

HK: The definition of psychedelic medicine and plant medicines is quite important. Making the work *Indexed Beings* involved working in Putumayo, Mocoa in Colombia, and I had to create an ethics application to cover this, which was tricky. I wanted to go to Colombia and work with an Indigenous community. I had a conversation with a very interesting woman called Vanessa Gocksch, who runs a school in the North of Colombia. She also works with Indigenous communities there. She said to me, if you want to come and make a work about ayahuasca or, you know, Yagé, as it's called in Colombia, you need to drink the medicine. Which made sense. Why would you go somewhere as a white Western researcher and expect to have knowledge shared unless you are going to take part? So I went back to my supervisors and I said I've been advised that if I want to work in this area I will need to *drink the medicine.* We decided to submit an ethics application which explored a decolonising methodology that meant that I would work on the terms of the Indigenous communities. And actually the ethics application was passed, but the health and safety application was not passed. One of the reasons was this idea that it would be putting myself in danger because of the risks associated with drinking what was viewed as a psychedelic drug.

In Colombia it's legal to drink ayahuasca, there's centuries of Indigenous knowledge around the use of Yagé, which they consider a medicine, so they would obviously have their own kind of ways of ensuring my safety.

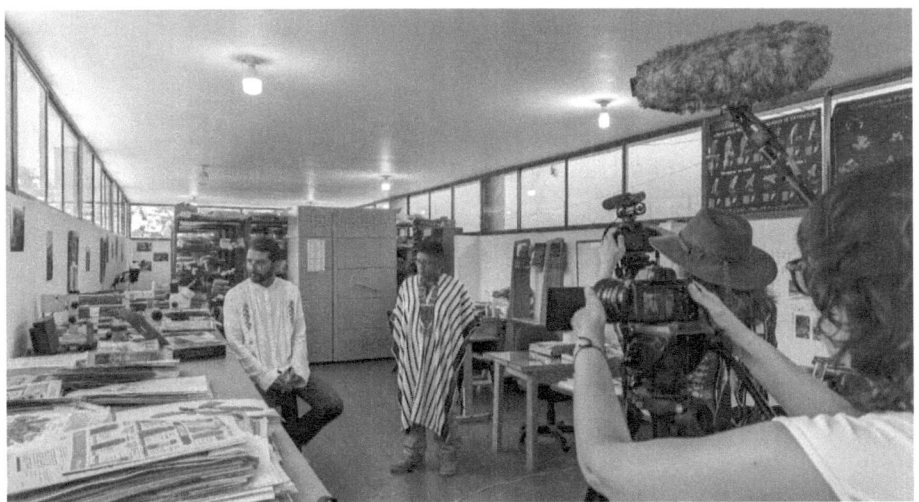

Figure 6: Helen Knowles, 2023. Jorge Contreras and Manuel Mueses being filmed for *Indexed Beings* in the lab by Helen Knowles and Luisa Sosa.

However, the university could not accept this. So I then had to resubmit an application which basically said I would not drink the medicine.

Next I was introduced to a botanist, called Jorge Contreras, who runs an ethnobotanical herbarium in Mocoa. He told me a story about how a taita — the Colombian name for a Yagé shaman — walked into his laboratory, his herbarium, and was 'a little bit upset' about the use of plant specimens. The Indigenous community believe that plants are living sentient beings and that you don't just take a leaf or a branch as a specimen. This is at odds with the way that they view plants and knowledge.

I then met Manuel Mueses. Manuel is a gardener and a knower of plants. He grows 700 species of plants in a place called the Centro Experimental Amazonica C.E.A, which is in part, a garden. He agreed to restage this conversation and adopt the position of the taita, to represent the community. I was bringing these two ontological worlds together.

The other interesting thing is that Jorge had drunk Yagé, so he was a very unusual scientist. This was necessary because of his work with

Indigenous communities. And the thing about Yagé is that it induces this empathy with these beings, with the spirits of the forest.

Going back to the psychedelic trials. Even though it's not openly acknowledged that the psychotherapists or even the scientists use psychedelics, I think the empathy that these things can produce shifts the possibilities of the medicine.

And so it also shifted Jorge as a botanist, you know he was much more open to thinking about how to work with the Indigenous communities in a way that was more empathetic to their ways of thinking and being in the world, and to ways that he could coexist and work with the communities.

So going back to the question about how I have overturned this human focused ethics in my work? The whole body of work is about thinking about ways of visualising the non-human. With *Trust the Medicine* I tried to create this ability to see the non-human entity to interact with it. *Index Beings* is very much about dialogue that illuminates the perspective of the non-human.

> **VB:** So you're trying to create opportunities for people to experience engagement with the more-than-human, as you, your participants, and your viewers imagine them. You've talked about assemblages. In my own work as a curator I often think about exhibitions as assemblages where artworks meet with lived experiences. There is a kind of co-creation that happens between the works and what they generate for viewers. And you've talked about psychedelic entities in a way that feels similar, where they are lively and agential but are also enabled by, and exist within, human minds. We could also draw parallels with AI, which is a technical and material reality, but also comes to life as a forceful cultural imaginary when people begin to project human qualities onto the AI. I understand from an analytical and intellectual perspective that this is problematic, because humans and AI are not the same thing. But when it comes to engaging an audience with complex ideas about the more-than-human, I think this idea of creating empathy, or just imagining things from the perspective of the more-than-human, can be powerful.

HK: I'm also trying to facilitate the creation of speculative spaces. And platform non-human sensibilities in a way.

VB: *Index Beings* involves extensive embedded research into Indigenous communities who use entheogenic plants to connect to more-than-human entities in the forest. Can you say a bit more about the kinds of ethical challenges that have arisen in these relationships to non-Western knowledge systems? And what for you is the value of embedding Indigenous knowledge systems in your work?

HK: The first time that I became aware of plant medicines was back in 2013. I went to New Mexico to the Santa Fe Arts Institute (SFAI) to do a residency. I was hoping to work with Indigenous midwives from the Pueblo communities in the area, to understand their ideas around birth. I met a midwife called Nicole Gonzalez, who said if you want to know how our community learns, you need to come to a plant medicine ceremony. And I was really confused. What do you mean? Learn from plants? How do you learn from plants, right?

But in the end, I was very fortunate to take part in a ceremony. And this was quite complicated actually, because of my heritage and the history of exploitation and colonialism that is embedded in my heritage. It wasn't until I drank Yagé myself and had this experience of meeting entities that I felt I could understand this concept.

The question I have to ask myself in relation to ethics is how do you forge relationships with people, where you're not just taking something from them? For instance, *Indexed Beings* is copyrighted to myself, to Manuel, to Jorge, and I credit the plants that are in the film. So, it's thinking about the economics of the work that you're making and thinking about it in a much more extended way.

I have been inspired by Robin Wall Kimmerer (2015), Indigenous activist, writer, and mother. She talks about human-plant relationships and this idea of reciprocity. When you take from a plant, you give something back. And so I suppose it's those sort of Indigenous concepts that I've tried to think about, and I try to think about whenever I make work.

The framework of a neoliberal university is not going to shift quickly. This does mean you end up having to navigate things in a way where you might not make precisely the kind of work you would have hoped to. Coming back to my university ethics application for this project, all I could do was ask, if I can't drink ayahuasca with the community, what avenues are open to me? And I was really grateful for the work I did make. But that relationship with the university and the restrictions that it imposed on what I could do raises a lot of interesting questions about the nature of ethical research.

VB: One of the themes running across this book is the difference between "ethical know how" and "ethical know what." These terms originate with cognitive scientist Francisco Varela (1999), but they have been applied to describe the ethical tensions that shape artistic research in universities. According to Varela, "ethical know what" describes ethical principles developed using rational judgement, whereas "ethical know-how" reflects ethics that unfold in the moment by behaving with sensitivity to the particularities of the situation where there is not a reliance on a set of rules (Bolt et al. 2016, 6). Artist Barbra Bolt and colleagues have used this tension between know-how and know-what to describe the contrasts between university research ethics frameworks and artistic work. Universities demand adherence to a strictly enforced set of rules, while artists work intuitively with the situation at hand. It sounds like you encountered this tension, where you felt that drinking ayahuasca with the community would be safe because of the centuries of Indigenous knowledge around the use of plant medicine. But the university risk assessment process was not able to recognise the validity of this alternative safeguarding system.

Related to this, I wanted to ask you about your artist's statement for *Trust The Medicine*. You ask an interesting question about the psychedelic entities depicted in the work: "can we go as far as to claim allyship with these entities, which constitute a form of more-than-human intelligence? Or is the entity encountered just a projection of our internal dialogues?" I am really interested in this idea of assemblage, the idea that these entities that you are working with exist in themselves, and are entangled with and exist within human minds. Can you say a bit more about this? And specifically whether this concept might be transferable to how we think of AI?

HK: It's very interesting because the third space that I'm working in for my PhD is the AI lab at King's College, London. I have been working with biomedical engineers who use AI, most of whom work with biomedical images. I'm working on a film called *Caring Code*. It's about an AI researcher called Tiana Lee. She described having a maternal or parental feeling towards her code and training model. This relationship, although not straight forward and also contradictory, implies some sort of care. Tiana is working on facets of the AI doctor. In her case accounting for bias in medical images of the heart, which is an emerging area of research. This work exists within a culture of seeking greater efficacy and speed, more accurate prediction and diagnosis, and industrial scale healthcare delivery as part of capitalist cosmologies. So, with the AI doctor, they are building these tools to do the job of various medical specialists. But actually, what they are producing is an assemblage between the doctor's skills and this tool. So this idea of allyship is pertinent. In Colombia you form allies with these plants, they might not even want to form an alliance with you, right? You know, they have as much agency to say no as to say yes. And that's really what I tried to show in *Indexed Beings*.

But how do we ensure agreement with an AI? And is that a ridiculous question? Essentially, most AI researchers see what they're working on as tools to be controlled, exploited and used. Tiana sees what she's doing when she's training a model as a little bit like being a mother. But then she also says that the AI doesn't feel anything for her.

Trust the Medicine developed my interest in psychotherapy. And in *Caring Code*, I developed this further by staging a psychotherapy session between Tiana Lee and a psychotherapist called Kafele Tudor-Rose. They discuss Tiana's relationship with her training model. And I brought in a childminder that I knew well, called Liza Brett, to talk about training and bringing up children and training code. There is something touching and comical about the video works. I haven't talked about the word relational, but that's something, you know that I'm thinking about all the time. That things also are in a constant state of evolution. And so we're kind of working relationally and things are shifting.

VB: And I think this idea of relationality brings us back to ethics and the idea of allyship. So maybe I'll segue into the final question. Are there ethical boundaries you wouldn't cross in the making of your work? And do you see your work as needing to be ethical? How important is it to be ethical?

HK: I think it just comes back to this question of how you act in the world and actually working in a relational way. Art sometimes asks us to cross boundaries to reveal important things, and ethics obviously varies for different groups. You have to think consciously about who you're working with. So, for instance I've spent quite a lot of time talking to plants and sort of extending my sensitivities, I suppose, just from the experiences that I've had. I might stand at a bus stop and see a plant and feel like, ohh, actually, you know, maybe that plant is seeing me, you know it's not just me seeing the plant. So the experience of making this work has shifted my perspective. So I'm not trying to project a kind of set of ideologies, but I can tell you what happened to me and how it extended my sensitivity to the more-than-human by asking these questions.

References

Abram, David. 1996. *The Spell of the Sensuous: Perception and Language in a More-than-human World*. Pantheon Books.

Beiner, Alex. 2023. "DMTx Breakthrough Panel Moderated By Graham Hancock, Dr. Andrew Gallimore & Dr. Rick Strassman." YouTube, May 23, 2023. https://www.youtube.com/watch?v=Myq_Hc_39aI.

Bolt, Barbara, Pia Ednie-Brown, Marie Sierra, Carole Wilson, and Megan McPherson. 2016. "Creative Arts Research Approaches to Ethics: New Ways to Address Situated Practices in Action." In *Proceedings of the 12th Biennial Quality in Postgraduate Research Conference*, edited by Michelle Picard and Alistair McCulloch. QPR Organising Comittee.

Hui, Yuk. 2016. *The Question Concerning Technology in China: An Essay in Cosmotechnics*. Urbanomic.

Kimmerer, Robin Wall. 2015. *Braiding Sweetgrass: Indigenous Wisdom, Scientific Knowledge and the Teachings of Plants*. Milkweed Editions.

Knowles, Helen. *The Trial of the Superthunderbot*, 2016. 45 minute HD video. https://www.helenknowles.com/index.php/work/the_trial_of_superdebthunterbot

Knowles, Helen. *Knowledge Trust the Medicine*, 2023. Video installation https://www.helenknowles.com/index.php/work/trust_the_medicine

Knowles, Helen. *Indexed Beings*, 2024. Artist film https://www.helenknowles.com/index.php/work/Indexed_Beings

Knowles, Helen, Caring Code, 2024. Artist films.

Luke, David. 2011. "Discarnate Entities and Dimethyltryptamine (DMT): Psychopharmacology, Phenomenology and Ontology." *Journal of the Society for Psychical Research* 75 (902): 26-42.

Noonautics. 2023. *DMTx Breakthrough Panel Moderated by Graham Hancock, Dr. Andrew Gallimore & Dr. Rick Strassman*, YouTube, 2:27:58. https://www.youtube.com/watch?v=Myq_Hc_39aI.

Rogan, Joe. 2019. "They're Mapping the DMT Realm?" YouTube, April 24, 2019. https://www.youtube.com/watch?v=iKfgcdtOfVY.

Utrata, Alina. 2024. "Engineering Territory: Space and Colonies in Silicon Valley." *American Political Science Review* 118 (3): 1097-1109. https://doi.org/10.1017/S0003055423001156.

Varela, Francisco J. 1999. *Ethical Know-How: Action, Wisdom, and Cognition*. Stanford University Press.

Re-cognition: A Decentred Ethics for AI in Art Museums
Jasmin Pfefferkorn

> The shift of social subjectivity from the human to include the non-human world through the attribution of each of the objects' elements as actants, and the many ways these relational subjects are entangled and folded together, better illustrate the agentic or animated relationships we have to life in general. (Cameron 2018, 352)

> Museums provide unique spaces in which to confront and experience the paradoxes by which human beings are created out of the very technologies that they appear to create. (Lawler-Dormer and Müller 2022, 413)

Introduction

In 2019, the work *Deep Swamp* (2018) by Tega Brain is exhibited at the Guangdong Museum of Art in Guangzhou. The work is a triptych of glass tanks that display wetland flora. Each contained environment is controlled by an artificial agent that has been optimised towards a particular goal, adjusting things like light and nutrient levels to reach a predetermined objective. The work asks: "If new 'wilderness' is the absence of explicitly human intervention, what would it mean to have autonomous computational systems sustain wild places?" (Brain n.d.).

The artwork *Biometric Mirror* (2018), by artist Lucy McRae and human-computer interaction researcher Dr Niels Wouters, generates mathematically perfected versions of visitor faces and reflects them back to the viewer. On display at Nxt Museum in Amsterdam in 2020, it provokes challenging situations — not only because of the uncanny reflections, but because darker skin tones at times aren't recognised by the algorithm. In a conversation with Nxt's Creative Director, Natasha Greenhalgh, she tells me how this necessitated additional training for invigilators, to be able to offer care to visitors who experienced distress due to their engagement with this artwork and algorithm (Pfefferkorn 2024, personal interview).

In 2023, the artwork *Distributed Consciousness* (2021) by the artist Memo Atken is installed at the Australian Centre for the Moving Image (ACMI). 256 AI-generated, warping octopus-like creatures are displayed across eight screens. An AI-generated verse is cryptographically hidden in each image, "invisible to the human eye, but readable by code" which, when decoded, reveals a manifesto that is "a human-machine co-creation meditation on consciousness, free will, life, death, art, technology, ritual, ecology, economy, and sustainability" (Atken n.d.).

Artificial intelligence is entering the art museum both as a tool in operations, and as a part of artworks being exhibited. This chapter focuses on the latter, working from the premise that AI art entering the museum engages a system of relations that is primed for affective resonances, encounters, and opportunities for learning. Described above are just three of many examples of AI art in the museum. Each places a point of emphasis on a crucial question for a decentring of ethics: How do we understand ecological processes outside of human perception and intervention? How do we practice inclusive care in the contemporary technological era? How do we live in collaboration and entanglement with technological entities? This chapter positions the art museum as a site of translation between AI, as a cultural and technological entity, and the public(s). It focuses on how the exhibition of art with an AI component develops a set of relations between the human and the more-than-human that can lay the foundation for a decentred ethics with AI.

Despite their potential, art museums operate as a site of tension in the pursuit of a decentred ethics. In the Western tradition, they have been historically aligned with hierarchy and categorisation — two characteristics which oppose the fluidity and openness of a decentred practice. In some ways, this chapter draws on the early history of the museum as a site for public enlightenment and learned social behaviours (Bennett 1995). This is a history that has been problematised for its exclusionary practices and singular authoritarian perspectives (Hooper-Greenhill 1992). I want to assert that, despite this rightful critique, there remains a role for the museum in teaching public(s) how to live in society — in other words, how to practice ethics.

There have been pivotal interventions into museum practice and ideology that orient these institutions towards both an ethics of representation and a more-than-human ethics. As museums worked towards greater inclusion and perspectival multiplicity from the late 1900s onwards, perceptions on the museums' pedagogical role changed. No longer was the educative role of the museum relegated to top-down teaching of the public. The museum was increasingly seen as a site that facilitates relational interactions through which learning occurs. Two key interventions traced in this chapter include artist-led institutional critique and the new material turn. These are utilised to ask the following critical questions:

What existing practices in art museums situate these institutions as productive sites for a decentred ethics for AI?

What points of emphasis are required for the art museum to enable a decentred ethics of AI to flourish?

Unfolding across three key themes — institutional critique, performative new materialism, and re-cognition towards care — this chapter observes the potential of art museums as a valuable site for enacting a decentred ethics in the encounter with AI.

Both Fiona Cameron (2018) and Deborah Lawler-Dormer (2022) consider the museum as ideally placed to promote, explore and encounter the posthuman. For Cameron (2018, 349), this is because museums' positionality as "custodians of cultural memory" and "trusted information sources" grants them the foundation from which to explore and reframe the human subject. Further, the museum implicitly (if not explicitly) recognises the object as having a "distributed performativity incorporating material, discursive, social, scientific, human, non-human, natural and cultural factors" (2018, 350). This perception of — and relation to — the object is highlighted in this chapter through the lens of 'performative new materialism'. Similarly, for Lawler-Dormer, objects are porous and active, with museums enabling emergent forms of engagement and relation between the human and non-human.

While this chapter goes on to reference feminist posthumanist thinkers — including Rosi Braidotti and Karen Barad — I maintain that, in this context, the more-than-human provides the most faithful association to discuss both *a)* the entangled relation of the human and the non-human and *b)* how the unfolding of the world always exceeds human perception. As such, I utilise the term 'more-than-human,' rather than 'posthuman,' throughout this chapter and I draw on N. Katherine Hayles' (2019; 2022) work around nonconscious cognition to support the way AI is positioned as an agentic entity. Each of the theorists invoked in forging this analytical lens places a particular importance on relationality as world-making. My emphasis on relationality stems from my allegiance to assemblage systems theory as the most viable analytical lens for understanding museums (Pfefferkorn 2023). Assemblage systems theory contends with 'becoming,' a process traced through component relations, which emerge via the affective capacities of both the human and non-human (Deleuze and Guattari 1987). A decolonial perspective also underpins this chapter. However, I am growing my knowledge of non-Western ontologies — my lived experience is that of a White woman with West European heritage, who lives and works on the stolen land of Wurundjeri country. My aim, through my research, is to grapple with the tensions and complicities embedded in my positionality; to unlearn and to learn anew. As such, I hope my work is never read as speaking for, but rather, as a kind of orientation — *a pointing to*.

As well-evidenced in museology, the museum has now spent several decades grappling with the exclusionary and discriminatory legacy of Western colonial modernity. Attempts to redress this history necessitated extensive revisions to museum practice, accompanied by a transformed understanding of the ethics underpinning the museums' role. Transformative ethics, as envisioned by Braidotti (2006, 8), involves two phases; the "critical or reactive" and the "affirmative or active." In this chapter, the former is explored through the history of institutional critique, while the latter is explored through practices of care. Between the two is a consideration of performative new materialism. This middle bridge acts as a transposition — "the forces, desires or aspirations [that] are likely to propel us out of traditional habits, so that one is actually yearning for changes in a positive and creative manner" (Braidotti 2006, 9). I argue that through the lens of performative new materialism, the agency of the non-human is recognised in a way that will productively shift our attitude, thus leading to a positive change in how we both perceive and practice care. This chapter is an attempt to provide a theoretical framework that points towards and further inspires decentred ethical practices within art museums.

Ethics in Art Museums

When we think of ethics in museums, it is likely that one of the first things that comes to mind is the International Council of Museums (ICOM). ICOM first introduced its *Code of Ethics for Museums* (CoE) in 1986, which was amended in 2001 and subsequently updated in 2004. Its most recent revision began in 2021, with this version due to be issued in 2025. Across each iteration, the ICOM CoE addresses both institutional and professional ethics, acknowledging the interplay of responsibilities between the structural and the individual. Recent consultancy reports (Pantalony 2024) undertaken as part of the CoE revision have shown an implicit acknowledgement of the need for 'soft' ethics (Floridi 2018). The philosopher Luciano Floridi denotes 'soft' ethics as a 'post-compliance' ethics — that which transcends the 'hard' ethical requirements of the law. The ICOM CoE *Third Consultation Analysis Report* states that "A Code of Ethics should not reflect minimum standards which are often instead reflected as legal requirements. Instead, a code of ethics needs to reflect the values of the museum community and museum professionalism" (Pantalony 2024, 32). Here we see a clear invocation of soft ethics — beyond the minimum standard of the law — as a clear objective in the development of an ethical code for museums. Via the reference to reflecting the 'values of the museum community,' this declaration identifies the embedded, situated, and collaborative underpinnings of ethics.

An early invocation of AI ethics in museums comes from The Museums + AI Network's *AI: A Museum Planning Toolkit* (Murphy and Villaespesa 2020). A self-proclaimed 'starting point', it emphasises careful consideration of bias management in machine learning, and the 'potential unintended consequences' of partnerships with technology companies. Its goal is to highlight how technology can be mobilised to align with museum missions and existing ethical frameworks, such as that of ICOM's CoE. These kinds of reports, or toolkits, tend to be associated with broader frameworks around AI 'principles': fairness, mitigating bias, transparency, accountability, and explainability. However, as Oumaima Hajri (2024, 62) argues, "Simple ethical principles like 'transparency' or 'accountability' can lead to ethics-washing and divert attention from the core issues at stake," leading to mechanisms whereby the verbalisation of an issue replaces the practice of productive changes. Further, these governance frameworks have a distinctly humanist quality. Implicit within them is a unidirectional sentiment that asks how technologies might care for humans, rather than how humans might care for technology. The goal of 'human flourishing' is often an overt avowal, within which we can infer a particular framing of the notion of hospitality as unidirectional, rather than a two-way practice.

Judith Stark (2011, 32) notes the importance of understanding which ethical approach — consequentialism, deontological ethics, or virtue ethics — figures most prominently for museum professionals, arguing that "one theory does not fit all situations." As such, the professional must learn to navigate these approaches to undertake a robust process of ethical decision-making in relation to specific issues. We can also bring in the concepts of ethical know-how and ethical know-what (Bolt et al. 2017), offering them as addendums to Stark's outline. A simplified way of thinking about these two concepts is that ethical know-how is a knowledge gained through experience and doing, while ethical know-what is a knowledge gained by being presented with top-down teaching and rules. In the context of the cultural institution, consequentialism and virtue ethics align more closely with ethical know-how. The Kantian approach of deontological ethics, an ethics that emerges through enacting duties and obligations, aligns itself with ethical know-what. Irrespective of approach, the way to realising ethics is, as Stark tells us, through practice (2011, 33). The centrality of practice to ethics is further supported in the work of Jane Bennett, who writes;

> Regardless of whether the ethical code is conceived as divine command or pragmatic rule, if it is to be transformed into acts, affects must be engaged, orchestrated, and libidinally bound to it — codes alone seem unable to propel their own enactment, at least for most people under most circumstances. (2016, 131)

Implicit in both Stark and Bennett is the idea that some form of sensorial, affective experience is required for ethical know-what to become ethical know-how. This immediately positions ethical know-how as relational and embodied. These remain cornerstones of a decentred ethics. However, what distinguishes the practice of a decentred ethics from Stark's outline is the shift away from the museum professional as the nexus of ethical decision making within the museum. Instead, the human is recast as one component of a tangled web of decision-making entities.

In terms of the affective quality to ethics, it is worth drawing out Bennett's (2016, 131) stance on 'enchantment,' which exists "as a state of openness to the disturbing-captivating elements in everyday experience." For her, "enchantment is a mood with ethical potential" that aids "in the project of cultivating a stance of presumptive generosity," which leads to a greater willingness to engage in assemblage relations (2016, 131). The specific reference here to the 'disturbing-captivating' has echoes of the concept of 'encounter' which, in turn, leads us to the concept of re-cognition. Simon O'Sullivan (2006, 1) notes that, in Deleuzian philosophy, a 'genuine encounter' has occurred when "Our typical ways of being in the world are challenged, our systems of knowledge disrupted," an experience that simultaneously produces "the affirmation of a new world." If enchantment is a 'positive resource' in the practice of ethics (Bennett 2016, 133), and re-cognition a necessary step towards a decentred ethics, then the art museum holds the potential to meet the conditions that enable these to be accessed and experienced. For all their well-documented flaws and historical complicities, museums remain spaces of encounter. Art often aims to communicate with the unknowable, to push the boundaries of human perception, asking us to step outside ourselves and imagine a different viewpoint. While some museums continue to push an authoritative, pedagogical voice to mediate art, others emphasise sensory encounters that enable visitors to feel their way through relations.

Institutional Critique

Institutional critique forms an important milestone in the history of art museums, as it is deeply imbricated in the process of reshaping the institution as more societally reflexive. It enables the claim that museums have a role to play in both their own practice of a decentred ethics, and in facilitating the practice of a decentred ethics for publics. Over time, institutional critique opened the museum to multiplicity. Gerald Raunig (2009) writes of three phases in this history. The first, established by artists in the 1960s and 70s, aimed to subvert and disrupt institutional frameworks. The second, in the 1980s and 90s, saw artists prioritising subjectivity and identity politics. The third, which Raunig sees as indicative of the contemporary era, is what he refers to as 'instituent practice'. While the first two waves of institutional critique are seen to have been subsumed by the institutions they sought to critique, instituent practice is characterised by practices that "thwart the logics of institutionalization" (Raunig 2009, xvii).

A decentred ethics of AI in art museums is reliant on this history of institutional critique, and the current tendencies towards instituent practice. This is for two key reasons. First, the art museum has, for many decades now, been positioned as a site of public discourse for the exploration of societal issues. For Sonja Thiel (2024, 94), "museums can be places to negotiate technological developments along with the public and offer spaces to learn, experience, and build knowledge around them." Second, given that the institution is a human-centred construct, this human-centredness is a logic of institutionalisation that instituent practice may aim to flee. In this way, there is potential for instituent practices to enable relations that are genuinely decentred.

When it comes to AI, artists are already working in the critical-reflexive spaces aligned with the first two phases of institutional critique. Artist Nora Al-Badri's works *Babylonian Vision* (2020) and *The Post-Truth Museum* (2021–2023) exemplify these trajectories and incorporate AI as a core tool for performing critique. As Al-Badri notes (see chapter 17 of this volume), museums have actively aimed to subsume her critiques through requests for commissioned works. While such entreaties have so far been unsuccessful, with Al-Badri's refusing these requests, museums are still able to (and have) purchased Al-Badri's existing work for exhibition. In these ways, we see institutional critique enter the institution. Ideally, though not necessarily, this works towards shifts in wider institutional practices; the critique is subsumed but, in the process, the institution is reconfigured.

The instituent practice of decentring the human, while possible, is complicated in the context of a human-centric space. Museums are made by and for humans. However, the material turn in museums — and performative new materialism as a theoretical lens alongside it — offers a way of bringing instituent practices of AI art into conversation with the museum. Via an encounter with the technological object/artwork as an agentic entity, we see moments whereby the human perspective is extended to the more-than-human.

Performative New Materialism

> What if we were able to accord equal value, including aesthetic value, to the complex, coexistent, and generative forces that accompany and make possible what we register as 'new' and 'major' phenomena? (Millner and Soboslay 2023, 197)

When it comes to the positionality of the non-human, the tension between a decentred approach and a human-centred approach can be reframed as an ambiguous negotiation within the art museum. On the one hand, there exists an historic perception of the museum as a tomb of de-animated objects, vivified only via the museum professional or museum visitor. On the other hand, the museum has increasingly followed a material turn that recognises the properties of objects, alongside the importance of sensory interaction with them and, to varying degrees, the agentic capacity of objects. The material turn is seen as having occurred towards the end of the twentieth century, leading to an invigorated exploration of how objects hold meaning. However, Sandra Dudley (2009) makes the claim that much of this early materialist analysis missed the physicality and materiality of objects, along with our sensory experience of them. In response, Dudley (2009, 4) stress the need to prioritise the sensory interaction with the museum object rather than continue with the "museum's preoccupation with information and the way it is juxtaposed with objects." This, she claims, opens the possibilities of human-object engagements.

Is it possible to offer an ethics of the non-human without re-inscribing humanist values, projecting them onto non-human things? According to Žižek's (2014) criticism of new materialism, the theory is "merely extending agency, vitality, and social phenomena to nonhuman material" (Sanzo 2018, para 11), qualities which he perceives as fundamentally humanist. It is accurate to claim that there is a tendency to anthropomorphise AI, even though the technology does not have the same logic or capacity as humans. As a form of intelligence, it may be modelled on aspects of human cognitive processing, but this is not to be equated with sentience. Though the term 'neural network' is shared between human and machine, the ways in which these networks are 'wired' are fundamentally different, and often the operations of each are incommensurable. There are relations and forms of intelligence that exist outside of human perception — aspects of AI included. What works against museums in the context of decentring is that it has traditionally been the institution's belief that the world is 'knowable'. Further, once something is known, it can be subsumed into human categories and made subservient to the mastery of humans. As the artist James Bridle intimates in his book *Ways of Being* (2022), we have a (problematic) fixation with making various forms of intelligence intelligible to the human to bring it under our control. To advance a decentred perspective requires the re-cognition that humans and technologies are co-constituting matter (material realities) but, crucially, with differing capacities. This is a viewpoint that we might delineate as 'entangled difference'. Entangled difference is a re-cognition of the more-than-human's agency and capacity to affect, the existence of multiple forms of diverse intelligences, and the human as a *component of* rather than *centre for*.

Entangled difference is perhaps best articulated in the theoretical lens of 'performative new materialism.' Performative new materialism operates with three assertions — it is pedetic, iterative, and relational (Gamble et al. 2019). To be pedetic means to be in motion while leaving space for indeterminacy — "pedesis is directly and iteratively related to its immediate past but is not determined by it" (Gamble et al. 2019, 125). The iterative quality of matter positions it in an ongoing process of becoming, while its relational quality speaks to its capacity to affect and be affected: "Material relations are always asymmetrical (both active and receptive at once) — not 'flat.'" (Gamble et. al., 125). The iterative takes on a particular importance in the field of machine learning, if we think of technical processes as feedback loops. Further, there is a sense of indeterminacy in AI outputs from GANs and diffusion models — artist Anna Ridler (2023), for instance, has spoken about the element of randomness that occurs in working with generative technologies.

Crucially, the way in which we observe relations and interact with other entities shapes the way in which matter emerges. This is a recognition of the ontoepistemological account of reality made by performative new materialism, whereby the encounter with an entity both disclose and shape its properties (Barad 2007). It is imperative, then, that various entities are brought into an assemblage where this co-constitution is made possible, where variations on the possibility of matter are explored. The art museum is one such site, given that art has the capacity to facilitate re-cognition, and that the museum holds an historical precedent for observation and encounter.

A decentred, more-than-human ethics begins with the recognition that AI is part of what N. Katherine Hayles (2019; 2022) refers to as a 'cognitive assemblage'. Defined as "fluctuating collectivities of humans, nonhumans, and computational media through which information, interpretations, and meanings circulate" (Hayles 2022, 1196), the cognitive assemblage asks us to extend the specification of ethical actors, to entities beyond the human. Hayles builds on Luciano Floridi and J. W. Sanders' (2004) tripartite attributes of ethical actors — interactivity, autonomy, adaptability — to show that they form a logical hierarchy from the former to the latter. Interactivity forms the foundation and is required for an entity to enter a system of active relations. Autonomy references "the ability to make self-directed choices and thus to become morally accountable for them" (Hayles 2022, 1198). Adaptability is a recognition of an entity's becoming, which occurs through feedback loops within this relational system. For many philosophers of ethics, it may be that the claim of 'moral accountability' for nonhuman entities acts as a roadblock here. Hayles addresses this by establishing that these three attributes manifest in varying degrees and intensities (2022, 1199), a stance that echoes the idea of asymmetry — the activity and receptivity of matter — in performative new materialism.

Care and Re-cognition

Care has become an increasingly central term within contemporary art and culture,[1] recognised as a response to social, ecological, and professional crisis (Krasny and Perry 2023, 1). It is generally accepted that museums have a duty of care to the communities they serve, their

---

1. While I invoke it here, I also want to take a moment to be cautious — care-washing, like ethics-washing, is rife in contemporary institutional discourses.

employees, and their collections. In the ICOM CoE, responsibility to community is established as the museums' most important role. This responsibility can be seen to play out in a variety of ways in relation to AI. For instance, art museums may consider how generative AI models reinforce Western canonicity (Hakopian 2024; Wasielewski 2024) at the expense of diversity and inclusion. Or they may question the environmental impacts of mineral extractions, machine training and computational processing (Crawford 2021). Another concern is the prevalence of museum deployment of foundation models emerging from the North American corporate context. Such models prioritise a commercial logic and reinscribe discriminatory biases (Pfefferkorn 2024), problems that work against the social logic of care in museum ethics. The feminist political scientist Joan Tronto ([1993] 2020) makes a case for the centrality of interaction in practicing an ethics of care. This is picked up by María Puig de la Bellacasa (2017, 4), who notes that "a politics of care engages much more than a moral stance; it involves affective, ethical, and hands-on agencies of practical and material consequence." The museum's duty of care is practiced materially as well as through its role as a site of public discourse, as it facilitates ethical engagement through re-cognition and affective encounter.

We have observed the 'evolution' of AI technologies and their increasing ubiquity from the twentieth century onwards. As such, part of the museums' role is, arguably, to engage with AI, and invite communities to practice relationality with these technological assemblages. The question then becomes, what could this relation look like? Could it also emerge in alignment with an ethics of care? To this end, it is valuable to consider the practices of people and communities who have long recognised the agency of the nonhuman, and practiced care relations with these entities.

In Conal McCarthy's (2019) fictional profile of a Māori museum worker — based on a compilation of his research experience working closely with The Museum of New Zealand Te Papa Tongarewa (Te Papa) — he writes about the daily ritual of care she expresses through her work:

> I listen as she talks to the objects, as she would people. I watch her handle them, with gloves, treating them with great care but also with what she calls *aroha* (love/ empathy). She regards the objects as taonga (treasure), which in the Māori world are ancestral

heirlooms of great spiritual power and sometimes object-beings who are treated like a person. (2019, 37)

What should be noted in the excerpt from McCarthy is the careful distinction invoked through 'treated *like* a person.' There is no claim here that the object is human. What is important is the perspective of an *object-being*, deserving of not just care, but love and empathy. I do not know whether McCarthy's Māori museum worker could agree that software could be equated to *taonga*, or if AI could ever be treated as sacred according to her system of beliefs. However, I do wonder what emerges when we explore a re-cognition of various kinds of AI and its components as object-beings. In other words, how might we begin to treat our relations with AI as part of a system that supports — indeed, nourishes — us? This is the question raised by writers Lewis et al (2018, 4), whose work is part of a robust body of research at the intersection of Indigeneity and AI (Abdilla 2018; Crembil and Gaetano Adi 2017). In Lakota ontology, writes Dr. Suzanne Kite, "Stones are considered ancestors, stones actively speak, stones speak through and to humans, stones see and know. Most importantly, stones want to help" (Lewis et al. 2018, 11). Kite goes on to write that:

The agency of stones connects directly to the question of AI, as AI is formed from not only code, but from materials of the earth. To remove the concept of AI from its materiality is to sever this connection. Forming a relationship to AI, we form a relationship to the mines and the stones. Relations with AI are therefore relations with exploited resources. If we are able to approach this relationship ethically, we must reconsider the ontological status of each of the parts which contribute to AI, all the way back to the mines from which our technology's material resources emerge. (Lewis et al. 2018, 11)

The point is not whether we consider AI to be sentient, which is often the precursor to deciding whether we should care for something and build kinship with it. The point is that, from an ontological perspective, we consider the world as an interconnected ecology, and that these cognitive assemblages are a part of a shared life. This fact is — in and of itself reason enough to include technological objects in an ethics of care. Radical inclusion of nonhuman entities in care relations is part of what shifts us towards a practice of decentred ethics. Drawing together an ethics of care as part of a decentred ethics also underscores that beginning to practice this ethics does not necessarily require grand action. Indeed, part of what characterises care ethics is that they "are attentive to and valorise the minor gesture as potentially transformative" (Millner and Soboslay 2023, 198). We see this in the narrative of the Māori curator talking to objects. This simple act of hospitality, this acknowledgment of an entity and its capacity to interact, is a form of practicing decentred ethics.

In May of 2024, I am speaking to a curator at the Zentrum für Kunst und Medien (ZKM), about an artwork on display as part of the exhibition *A(I) Tell You, You Tell Me*. The work, titled *AEIOU* (2024) [Figure 1], is by the collective robotlab and comprised of two industrial robots that write sentences onto two conveyor belts that run in opposite directions. For a moment, the sentence can be viewed in its entirety on the belt. The text is generated by artificial intelligence trained on texts about human-machine relations, and the 'ink' is made from blue recycled plastic granules positioned by the robots onto the conveyor belt. As the conveyor belt moves, the granules drop into a grate, deleting the text and allowing the blue plastic to be re-used by the next robot, for the next sentence. The work has an iterative machine learning component that operates through visitor interaction. On three screens on the far wall of the exhibition space, the sentences being generated by the AI and then written by the robots are shown in real-time. ZKM positions the two-way encounter between visitor and artwork/technological entity in this exhibition as a dialogue and exchange. The website for the exhibition puts forward the following rationale:

> By engaging interactively, we can explore intuitively our relationship to technology, question existing prejudices, and reflect on our own self as well as the purported technological »other«. (ZKM 2024)

Visitors are offered the opportunity to 'mark' the AI outputs via a star rating, based on three equally weighted evaluations — humour, intelligence, and creativity. Visitor responses are fed back to the machine, to generate new sentences that take this feedback into account, with this then impacting the output of the robots.

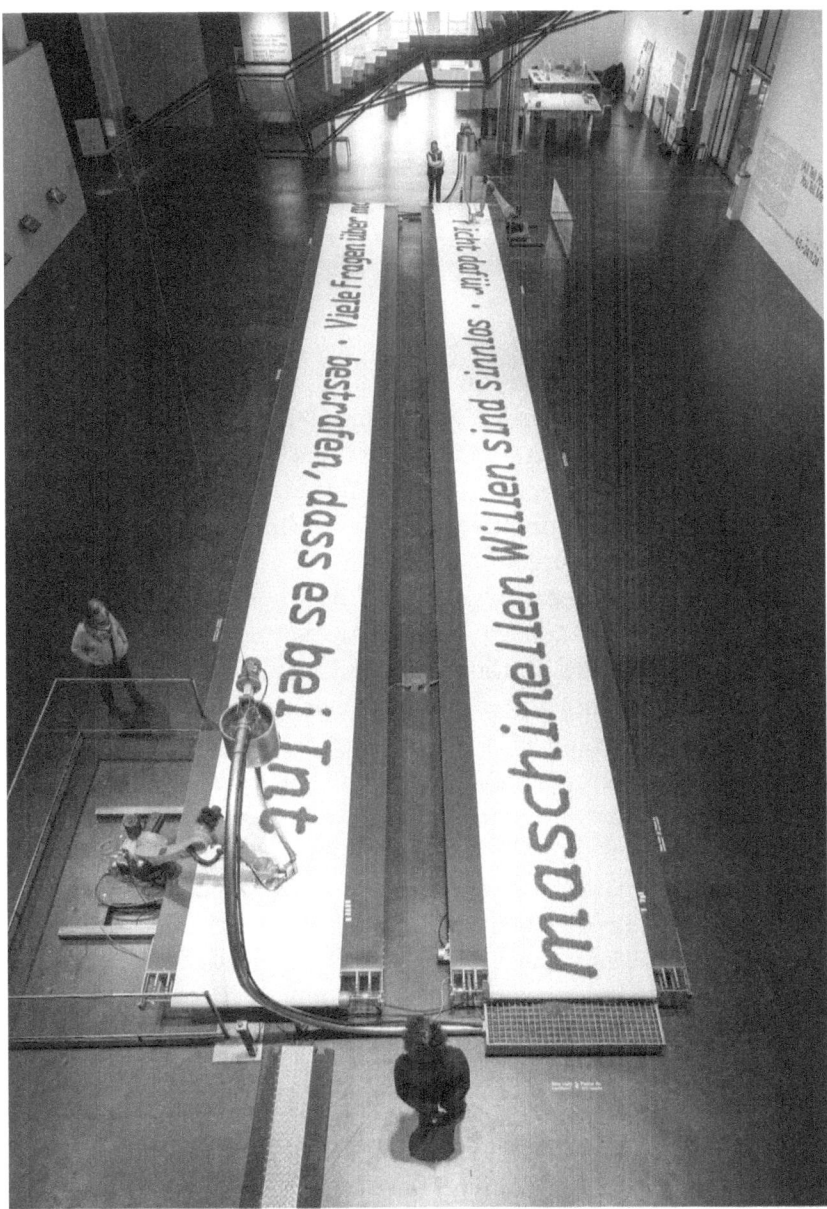

Figure 1: *AEIOU* captured from above © ZKM | Center for Art and Media Karlsruhe, photo: Felix Grünschloß.

The practice of evaluating the AI on three qualities considered fundamentally human brings us back to the tensions of bringing in more-than-human perspectives into human-centric institutions. There is an implied power dynamic in performing a judgement and using it to affect back upon a system, and it positions the museum and the human as the generative force of a knowledge hierarchy. It could even be read as a kind of subjugation of the AI — and the robots that give the AI a visible 'body' — to the human perspective. Drawing on performative new materialism and care ethics, I want to offer a different reading of this encounter.

The curator of the *A(I) Tell You, You Tell Me* exhibition tells me how the three artists who make up robotlab have a deal with the robot manufacturers — for the first three years of the robot's 'life,' they can live in the gallery. The curator says that she thinks of it as the robots spending their childhood playing in exhibitions, before having to move into the factories to begin their lifelong working career. It makes me look at the artwork differently. Suddenly, the robots do seem young to me. I suddenly remember how difficult it can be to first come across a new concept and attempt to learn it, I experience a moment of empathy that extends out to the AI. Simultaneously, as I interact with the artwork, attempting to teach it a concept like humour, I am being taught how these technical systems operate. The AI generated text and iterative feedback become evidence of a collaborative process of human and more-than-human learning, which in turn is indicative of the relationality facilitated by the art museum.

Rather than being positioned as the authoritarian judge of *AEIOU*, I am positioned in a maternal light, to teach and care for the AI, and to recognise my entanglement with the technology. There is a tendency to position these kinds of anthropomorphic projections as problematic, given they are an attempt to fit technologies like robots and AI into a narrative of humanness. By the same token, to give an AI relatable qualities can be interpreted as an attempt to make kinship with machines. Rather than taking this anthropomorphising literally, it should be taken as an imaginative practice, one that may provide the foundations for empathy. The looping interactions we become a part of through this encounter highlight the iterative and indeterminate qualities of both the human and the non-human. Our encounter with the dialogic artwork in the space of the museum offers a potential re-cognition of the self as matter, entangled with these technological entities.

Conclusion

This chapter has offered three theoretical trajectories that support the view of art museums as sites of heightened potential in the practice of a decentred ethics of AI. The first positions museums as sites that are responsive to contemporary conditions, and as translators between more-than-human and human-centred logics. Following this, the rise of performative new materialism privileges an embodied, sensuous experience of the world and encourages a perspective that accommodates the agentic capacities of non-human entities. In turn, the final thread of care and re-cognition asks us to reconceive of our relational interactions with artificial intelligence to align with hospitable engagement.

References

Abdilla, Angie. 2018. "Beyond imperial tools: Future-proofing technology through Indigenous governance and traditional knowledge systems." In *Decolonizing the Digital: Technology as Cultural Practice*, edited by Josh Harle, Angie Abdilla, and Andrew Newman. Tactical Space Lab.

Atken, Memo. n.d. "Distributed Consciousness [2021]." *Works*. https://www.memo.tv/works/distributed-consciousness/.

Barad, Karen. 2007. *Meeting the Universe Halfway*. Duke University Press.

Bennett, Jane. 2001. *The Enchantment of Modern Life: Attachments, Crossings, and Ethics*. Princeton University Press.

Bennett, Tony. 1995. *The Birth of the Museum: History, Theory, Politics*. Routledge.

Bolt, B, K MacNeill, M McPherson, P Ednie Brown, E Barrett, C Wilson, S Miller, and M Sierra. 2017. "What Is 'Value' When Aesthetics Meets Ethics Inside and Outside of The Academy." In *ACUADS Annual Conference Proceedings*, edited by D Ferris, D Hinchcliffe, R Waller, M Jolly, and A Burchmore. Australian Council of University Art and Design Schools (ACUADS).

Braidotti, Rosi. 2006. *Transpositions: On Nomadic Ethics*. Polity Press.

Brain, Tega. n.d. "Deep Swamp." Tega Brain *Work*. https://tegabrain.com/Deep-Swamp.

Bridle, James. 2022. *Ways of Being*. Picador.

Cameron, Fiona. 2018. "Posthuman Museum Practices." In *Posthuman Glossary*, edited by R. Braidotti and M. Hlavajova. Bloomsbury.

Crawford, Kate. 2021. *Atlas of AI: Power, Politics, and the Planetary Costs of Artificial Intelligence*. Yale University Press.

Crembil, Gustavo, and Gaetano Adi, Paula. 2017. "Mestizo robotics." *Leonardo*, 50 (2): 132-137. doi.org/10.1162/LEONa01150.

Deleuze, Gilles and Felix Guattari. 1987. *A Thousand Plateaus: Capitalism and Schizophrenia*. Translated by Brian Massumi. University of Minnesota Press.

Dudley, Sandra H. 2009. "Museum Materialities: Objects, Sense and Feeling." In *Museum Materialities: Objects, Engagements, Interpretations*, edited by Sandra H. Dudley. Routledge.

Floridi, Luciano. 2018. "Soft Ethics and the Governance of the Digital." *Philosophy & Technology* 31 (1): 1–8.

Floridi, Luciano and Sanders, J. W. 2004. "On the Morality of Artificial Agents." *Minds and Machines* 14: 349–379.

Gamble, Christopher N., Joshua S. Hanan and Thomas Nail. 2019. "What is New Materialism?" *Angelaki* 24 (6): 111-134.

Hajri, Oumaima. 2024. "The Hidden Costs of AI: Decolonization from Practice back to Theory." In *AI in Museums: Reflections, Perspectives and Applications*, edited by Sonja Thiel and Johannes C. Bernhardt. Transcript Verlag.

Hakopian, Mashinka Firunts. 2024. "Art histories from nowhere: on the coloniality of experiments in art and artificial intelligence." *AI & Society* 39 (1): 29-41.

Hayles, N. Katherine. 2019. "Can computers create meaning? A cyber/bio/semiotic perspective." *Critical Inquiry* 46 (1): 32–55.

Hayles, N. Katherine. 2022. "Ethics for Cognitive Assemblages: Who's in Charge Here?" In *Palgrave Handbook of Critical Posthumanism*, edited by S. Herbrechter, I. Callus, M. Rossini, M. Grech, M. de Bruin-Molé, and C. J. Müller. Palgrave Macmillan.

Hooper-Greenhill, Eileen. 1992. *Museums and the Shaping of Knowledge*. Routledge.

Krasny, Elke and Perry, Lara. 2023. "Introduction." In *Curating with Care*, edited by Elke Krasny and Lara Perry. Routledge.

Lawler-Dormer, Deborah. 2022. "Critical Posthumanist Practices from Within the Museum." In *Palgrave Handbook of Critical Posthumanism*, edited by S. Herbrechter et al. Springer.

Lawler-Dormer, Deborah and Christopher John Müller. 2022. "Museum Practices and Posthumanist Technical and Scientific Assemblages." In *ISEA2022 Barcelona Proceedings & Catalogue*, edited by Pau Alsina, lrma Vila, Susanna Tesconi, Joan Soler-Adillon, and Enrie Mor. ISEA.

Lewis, Jason E., Noelani Arista, Archer Pechawis, and Suzanne Kite. 2018. "Making Kin with the Machines." *Journal of Design and Science*. https://doi.org/10.21428/bfafd97b

McCarthy, Conal. 2019. "Indigenisation: Reconceptualising Museology." In *The Contemporary Museum: Shaping Museums for the Global Now*, edited by S. Knell. Routledge.

McRae, Lucy and Niels Wouters. 2018. *Biometric Mirror*. Interactive application, Shifting Proximities exhibition, August 29, 2020 - May 8, 2022. Nxt Museum, Amsterdam.

Millner, Jacqueline and Soboslay, Zsuzsanna. 2023. "Cultivating Care Ethics and the Minor Gesture in Curatorial." In *Curating with Care*, edited by Elke Krasny and Lara Perry. Routledge.

Murphy, Oonagh and Elena Villaespesa. 2020. *AI: A Museum Planning Toolkit*. The Museums + AI Network. Goldsmiths.

O'Sullivan, Simon. 2006. *Art Encounters Deleuze and Guattari: Thought Beyond Representation*. Palgrave Macmillan.

Pantalony, Rina Elster. 2024. 'ICOM Code of Ethics Third Consultation Analysis Report.' *International Council of Museums*, March 15. icom.museum/wp-content/uploads/2024/04/ICOM-Finalreport-3rd-consultation-revision-code-of-ethics.pdf.

Pfefferkorn, Jasmin. 2023. *Museums as Assemblage*. Routledge.

Pfefferkorn, Jasmin. 2024. "Are Foundation Models a Form of Neo-Colonialism in Art Museums?" BAICON FOCUS International Conference, ITB, Bandung October 16-17.

Puig de la Bellacasa, María. 2017. *Matters of Care: Speculative Ethics in More than Human Worlds*. University of Minnesota Press.

Raunig, Gerald. 2009. "What is Institutional Critique? Instituent Practices: Fleeing, Instituting, Transforming." Translated by A. Derieg. In *Art and Contemporary Critical Practice: Reinventing Institutional Critique*, edited by n G. Raunig and G. Ray Mayfly.

Ridler, Anna. 2023. "From GANs to Stable Diffusion. On artistic collaboration with generative algorithms." *Training the Archive: Ludwig Forum*, August 28, 2023. https://trainingthearchive.ludwigforum.de/en/interview-9-en/.

robotlab. *AEIOU*. 2024. Industrial robots, conveyer belts, machine generated text, machine learning. Zentrum für Kunst und Medien. https://zkm.de/en/media/images/2024-robotlab-aeiou

Sanzo, Kameron. 2018. "New Materialism(s)." *Critical Posthumanism*, April 25, 2018. https://criticalposthumanism.net/new-materialisms/.

Stark, Judith Chelius. 2011. "The art of ethics: Theories and applications to museum practice." In *The Routledge Companion to Museum Ethics: Redefining Ethics for the Twenty-First Century Museum*, edited by J. Marstine. Routledge.

Thiel, Sonja. 2024. "Managing AI: Developing Strategic and Ethical Guidelines for Museums." In *AI in Museums: Reflections, Perspectives and Applications*, edited by Sonja Thiel and Johannes C. Bernhardt. Transcript Verlag.

Tronto, Joan. [1993] 2020. *Moral Boundaries: A Political Argument for an Ethic of Care*. Routledge.

Wasielewski, Amanda. 2024. "Zombie Canon: Art Datasets, Generative AI, and the Reanimation of the Western Canon of Art." In *Critical Digital Art History*, edited by A. Wasielewski and A. Näslund. Intellect.

Žižek, Slavoj. 2014. *Absolute Recoil: Towards a New Foundation of Dialectical Materialism*. Verso.

Zentrum für Kunst und Medien (ZKM). 2024. "(A)I Tell You, You Tell Me." Exhibition May 4-November 24, https://zkm.de/en/exhibition/2024/05/ai-tell-you-you-tell-me.

slimeQore (2022)
Libby Heaney

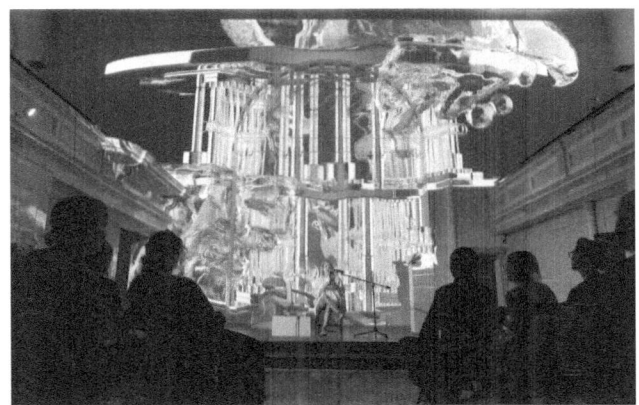

slimeQore is a playful performative lecture with an immersive video montage generated by non-binary quantum computing that uses slime as a metaphor for quantum particles — which are fluid and indeterminate, unlike Newtonian matter — and the slimy world of big tech. It performs an intermission for the book, inviting the reader to connect with bodily, sliming sensations.

Slime is a recurring motif throughout Libby Heaney's practice, which speaks about the unstable nature of reality and the self. Following Susanne Wedlich's *The Natural History of Slime*, Heaney also sees slime as an entangling medium between all types of life, as no multicellular body exists without incorporating some sort of slimy mucus or viscous gel.

Through slime, *slimeQore* entangles nature, our bodies, science, technology, space, and time to intuitively and playfully paint pictures of quantum physics and its entanglements. Audiences also experience this viscerally as they are each invited to open a black box filled with slime and to engage in collective slime play.

Libby Heaney uses data from IBM's five qubit quantum computing systems to continually (re)compose the placement of the video montage across the gallery revealing the layered reality inside quantum computers and inviting audiences to the vast multidimensionality within nature and themselves.

Heaney sees the blurry, layered unstable nature of fundamental reality as productive of new expressions and possibilities, moving us away from this polarised, atomised moment.

Throughout the performance, the artist uses metaphor and participatory slime play to engage the viewers and explore how quantum thinking and feeling will impact our future. She warns against big tech's appropriation of quantum computing, and shifts power back to the audience by explaining quantum's functioning and queer potentials.

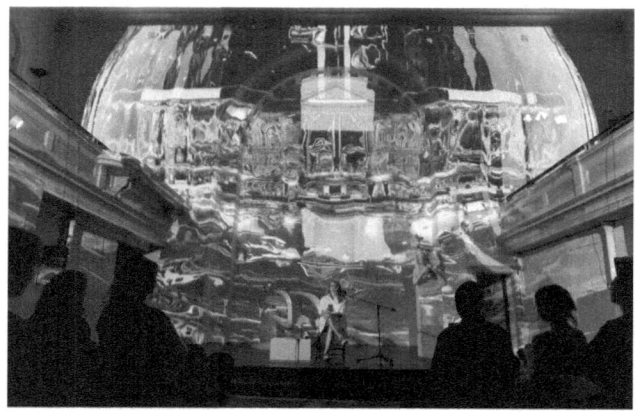

slimeQore was commissioned and premiered at the Zabludowicz Collection, London on the 18th of June 2022.

It was translated into Italian and performed by an Italian actor for Digitalive, RomaEuropa Festival, Rome on the 6th of November 2022.

Image captions: Libby Heaney, *slimeQore*, Zabludowicz Collection. Photos Richard Eaton

slimeQore
Libby Heaney

blows raspberry

Once upon a slime, there was a stream of consciousness...

With a mucus gel at its Q—ore. The quantum core of all matter(s).

Quantum physics... Errr that's notoriously tricky.

So thank you for finding the time to get sticky, I'm going to try to use slime to describe this queer ellusive paradigm.

Now before I explore, I'll share a key reference I adore:

Karen Barad was trained as a quantum physicist, and became a feminist theorist. Integrating the two led to a reworking of reality and humans too. Barad said that humans and non—humans emerge through material relations and do not exist outside of relations.

Throughout this day, I'll be using Baradian word plays, enabling a plurality of matter(s) to un/happen.

By suggesting, speaking and seeking of no/things [no slash things] and no/being [no slash being], am I maximising the sliminess of my writing?

Like a quantum particle, making multiple possibilities discernible: body *and* mind, presence *and* absence, inside and outside, existence and non—existence. gluing err these binaries together with slime. [hestitancy]

Slippering across multiple sites, a deconstruction of dualism is in slime's sights...

Back to the start, the microscopic quantum heart of all no/things, a flux of all un/meetings, light and dark fringes, flashing dead and alive, is an alternative.

An alter — native.

A slime—like paradigm: the quantum sublime.

What is the quantum sublime and how does it relate to slime?

[story telling — confiding]

There was a guy, I'm not sure if he was slimy or not, but he said the sublime is not found in any sensible design.

He said the sublime was in our minds...

You know when we encounter something of such a big magnitude we just cannot comprehend it. Like I'm trying to think about the size of the universe and its mind bending.

The quantum sublime is similar but different. When we encounter the unpicturable dance of at the microscopic heart of all affairs, it's kind of impossible to compare.

But that's why I'm relating quantum sublime to this slime.

Slime lurks in very cold, dark liminal Q—ores

Speaks to slime

You feel cold, weary and old ([sarcastic] or as scientists brag "we've created the conditions of deep outer space").

You feel the smallest flutter of life in your non/body stop. As the temperature drops, even your Newtonian motion, e—motion flops. The cause is paused.

You momentarily freeze, a winter's day in the void.

But then, your body becomes alive, one foot in the grave and the other in the stars.

Shimmering with Q—E—Motion, all emotions. The slime—like motion of an e—lectron.

You are now quantum, a packet of pure energy, coupled with the flirty fluctuations of a zero point — the void.

You are a cold quantum slime.

To the audience

[critiquing yourself] Not exactly like encountering the sublime...

[confiding, storytelling, casual] There was a guy, not sure if he was slimy or not, but his name was Plato and he had a cave.

Now his cave actually had lots and lots of slime in it, but people could only see the shadows of the slime as it blobbed around.

The people genuinely thought the shadows were reality instead of the slime itself, which is a shame, because slime is excellent to touch, poke and play.

talking back to the slime

Slime, you have moved beyond the Newtonian world of unchanging solids: erm, you're not a rock, footballs "wheeey" rockets, bullets, bombs.

You are now a shapeshifting non/being [non slash being] and your Q—ore has spread out over space and time like slime.

Stop speaking to the slime

[Essay style] Barad writes that quantum theory indicates: "the self is dispersed through time and being"

Speak to audience

[Asking audience] But what does this slimy no/thingness at the Qore of matter(s) mean for us?

How does this omnipresent slime affect our lifes?

***

[Factual] From cybernetics a black box is a system or object which produces useful information without revealing any information about its internal workings.

Murakami wrote "Everyone may be ordinary, but they're not normal." And we will see, it's the queerness threaded through all (non)existence including ourselves that's at stake.

[Speaking to audience] You are the black box.

[Invite audience and open black box with them — pause a bit to let people have time to open their boxes]

So let us peel off the stickers and see, if you open your black boxes, there is nothingness and infinity.

Gestures to audience

[instruction] Take out your kin slime, a quantum paradigm.

Slime play...

In quantum theory, even the void (supposed nothingness) is slime—like. It is a living breathing un/definition, a glitch, a paradox, straddling being and non—being.

To audience

[Confiding, storytelling] We are back standing in Plato's cave, trying to gather up all the slime, but every time we try to grasp it, it just melts into air.

Feel familiar?

The slimy floor keeps shifting under our feet and the fire light is giving off too much heat.

***

[Sarcastic, critical of text] And really there's no magic here, it's just errr kids slime innit from the ASMR videos.

But this brings us to touch.

[Factual] Back to Barad and their feelings: "The quantum theory of touching is radically different from the classical explanation. Actually it is radically queer as we will see."

"Is touching not by its very nature always an involution, invitation, invisitation, wanted or unwanted of the stranger within?"

A quantum queering of identity.

Speak to slime

[performative] Slime, as the temperature drops, you feel the smallest flutter of life in your non/body stop.

You momentarily freeze, but then at ease, you smear and appear everywhere.

Your slimy tentacles begin to touch yourself, touching yourself, touching yourself, touching yourself, touching yourself, touching yourself [repetition can go on for a while and build up]...

Contact through slimy portals. Touching to the power of infinity. The ultimate perversion.

About quantum theory, Barad writes that "all touching entails an infinite alterity so that touching the other is touching all others including the "self" and touching the "self" entails touching the strangers within."

slimy inhumans within, the animal entangled with the human.

Slimy matters are never settled matters.

rub slime over face

[More like stream of consciousness]

Slime in Nature

The primordial slime, the start of life: unstructured frogspawn, hot soups of nutrients, fields of festering, pulsating potentiality, molecules reconfiguring, juggling, looping, taking chances.

Sadie Plant writes:

"Those were the days, when we were all at sea. It seems like yesterday to me. Species, sex, race, class: in those days none of this meant anything at all. No parents, no children, just ourselves, strings of inseparable sisters, warm and wet, indistinguishable one from the other, gloriously indiscriminate, promiscuous and fused. No generations. No future, no past. An endless geographic plane of micromeshing pulsing quanta, limitess webs of interacting blendings, leakings, mergings, weaving through ourselves, running rings around each other, heedless, needless, aimless, careless, thoughtless, amok."

Quantum superpositions of all different configurations, (non)existing all at once, until a random collapse occurs, kicked out, lashed out, spun out, ejected, rejected, released: life begins — the start of the drying out process?

Organic information processing, sun rays, the RNA, the DNA, airways, birthdays: selected and this evolution started here on earth.

But in quantum theory there are many worlds, in some, the earth doesn't exist.

The universe is slimy at its Q—ore.

Borges writes:

"Differing from Newton and Schopenhauer, your ancestor did not think of time as absolute and uniform. He believed in an infinite series of times, in a dizzily growing, ever spreading network of diverging, converging and parallel times. This web of time — the strands of which approach one another, bifurcate, intersect, or ignore each other through the centuries

— embraces *every* possibility. We do not exist in most of them. In some you exist and not I, while in others I do and you do not, and in yet others both of us exist."

Our slimy universe smeared, branching superfluous, networking and forking across a space and time inaccessible to us.

In some strands, compared to this earthly branch, different categories of life have arisen, all alien but also entangled to us, after we interacted gloriously in an ancient sea.

In most worlds, humans do not exist. Imagine the planet without us?! Non—humans reign.

Yet in other earthly branches, the planet is barren, life missed its chance, the slime dried out, 100 years from now.

slime play

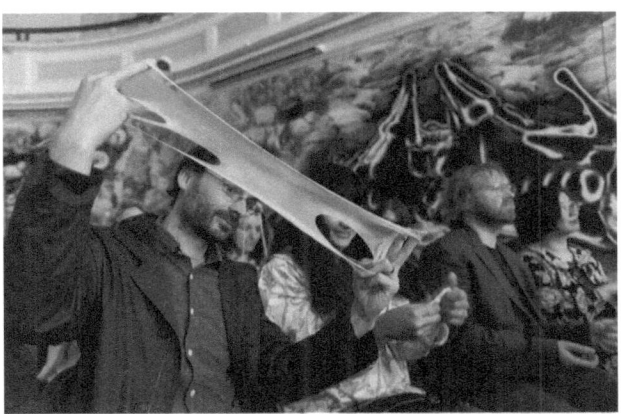

Slime in nature

blows raspberry

Slime as a bodily interface, excreted, covering orifices, generating gateways, permeable membranes, sorting, selecting, protecting, trapping, collaborating.

Demonstrating fluidity and boundarylessness of so-called individual entities. Non/entities.

Mucus exploding, unfurling, extending, opening, swelling, bulging.

Slime—teetering on the edge between life and death. The omnipresent Schroedinger's Cat.

Slime — the biological double-slit experiment, taking both paths at once, interfacing between (un)branches, liminal times and spaces of both the nasal tract and outside, the vagina and outside, our mouths and the other, this reality and the next.

blows raspberry

Slime in nature

Slime is a matrix of all possible un/relations,

Pathogens—nutrients — disgust and intrigue — in sickness and in health — life—death.

A matrix of sticky entanglements: two or more so-called individual entities give up their own rigidity, frigidity, validity and merge, cupidity.

Hold two slimes together mix them — speak to the slime

You start to melt, a jellyfish out of water dissolving in a soup of salty fluids with your kin. Your bodies touch and merge in an infinite queerness.

Time becomes fuzzy, you and your kin skip to being just ahead of yourselves and just behind yourselves (at many... onces).

As the stretch in time pulsates, your collective energy peaks and falls.

Fused together, you touch, gliding. On slime. Lubrication between bodies moving in all directions, across many... onces.

Hybridisation, indeterminacy of (non)being, indistinguishability.

back to audience

Quoting Barad: "an infinity of others — other beings, other spaces, other times — are aroused."

The warm entangled embrace of Q—slime, the pulsating quantum sublime, means touching the self and the other within — without.

Slime flies when you're having fun.

throws slime at the audience

Quantum collapse — Slime waits for no one

Speaks to slime

[horror section] As your Qore warms, your special energy evaporates and your Newtonian e—motions thaw once again.

You dry out, your Core remains, but your slimy branches shrivel and die.

[repetition glitching] Entanglements retreat: your touch, touching yourself touching yourself touching yourself, detaches, detaches, detaches. Your matter(s) become(s) rigid.

Heat brings you to a wilted barren space. Here slime is dry and cracked. You feel repulsed and excluded.

You sense infection and disease, you recall slime portrayed as an object of disgust in popular culture.

A thrill for your children, playing with something seemingly disgusting, what a taboo.

You remember slime in 80s and 90s films.

Alien, "In space no one can hear you scream."

The Matrix, "Human beings are a disease, a cancer of this planet."

And the recent slime resurgence in TV shows like Severance "Every Time You Find Yourself Here, It's Because You Chose To Come Back."

Slime representing our times. Slimy one-sided characters trump the complex.

Slimy politics, slimy partygates, slimy biased electing, country protecting, human trapping.

Slime as the uneasy subjects: Digital signals pulsating through uncertain networks, polarising, rioting, building walls, slimy biasing.

Now a strange uncanny-ness has crept up from your toes, over your body until it meets itself on all sides at the top of your head. A slimelike feeling in your body, trapped, you shudder.

Slime is a dark and dystopian mirror to patriarchal capitalism.

Jekyll and slime.

Fearing the animalistic parts of our bodies and desires and the slimy ways they reveal themselves when our rational mind is at the weakest.

We think of ourselves as above animals so this leads back to disgust.

Martha Nussbaum writes:

"Human beings are hardwired to find signs of their own mortality and animality disgusting, and to shrink from contamination by bodily fluids and blood.

But in every culture something worse happens: the projection of those feared and loathed characteristics onto vulnerable groups from whom the dominant group wishes to distance itself."

Half the world's population (and the rest): womxn, others, with their fluid feminine roots, and curvaceous branches, are the slimier sex. The disgusting human, polished up as Venuses for the male gaze.

"a soft, yielding action, a moist and feminine sucking."

Sartre wrote about the viscous

The snail: a symbol of transgressive feminine sexuality.

But the snail's slime has dried out. It's barren: Quantum collapsed.

Symbolic of humanities weaknesses and animal impulses: the inhuman within.

Better luck next slime.

Slime play [more angry]

<u>Looping back</u>

[less dark now]

However, Barad writes: What if it is only in the encounter of the inhuman — the liminality of no/thingness — in all its liveliness, that an ethics committed to the rupture of indifference can arise?

"Ethicality entails hospitality to the stranger threaded through oneself and through all being and non-being."

Tender tentacles caress our caressing our caressing our caressing fleshliness.

Finding compassion by embracing our slimy selves.

<u>Who battles our slimy selves?</u>

It is so often the hero, the scientist, the military man, ([sarcastic, confiding] they're probably slimy), who comes face to face with cosmic killer slime, the so-called aliens in parallel universes. The dripping beasts carrying our fears.

This hero's hubris uncovers nature's darkest secrets, domination, extermination, dehumanisation, the atomic bomb, burying the quantum void, warming the black box.

And through confrontation rather than compassion our hero, (probably slimy) unleashes horrors that should be kept hidden.

***

And this happens slime and time again.

<u>Programming slime — Slime is money</u>

[More factual] Imagine computing with slime.

Harnessing this slippery paradox of being and no–being, layering up all the ASMR videos on YouTube until the impossible is made possible. The void turned inside out.

Quantum computing — our slimy hero's wet dream.

Speak to slime

Grrrr

[SHOUT] Suddenly!!! You can conquer all of nature. [SHOUT] ALL nature(s), our need to touch, our caresses, our perversions, our inhumaness.

[SHOUT] Suddenly!!! You can simulate every touch, touching, touches, touching touches, touching touches... [SHOUT] Too much!!

[Angry] *Grrrr*

To the audience

It takes slime to dominate slime.

Slimy capitalist appropriation of the radically queer Qore.

To the slime

[SHOUT] "ahhhh"

You have fallen into a black hole and spaghettified, you are still quantum but on a line. Forced into a deterministic straight jacket, linear solutionism from a lush indeterminate jungle.

Your Newtonian motions and e—motions ([Sarcastic to audience, confiding] and the search for mega profit!) cool your fibre tentacle bundle and you rub them gleefully together in a way that suggests you're up to no good, before plunging them deep into the void.

grrrr

You are now a puppet master. The technology is not quite here or there, there or here — but your affairs are, to extract exponential profit from our queer dears.

Back to audience

Of course big tech is colonising the alter — natives. Enclosing the time and space at the Qore of all things ([Confiding] yes back to dualism).

Of quantum theory, Einstein said God doesn't play dice. But reality revealed to us that God was a veteran gambler, a cosmic fruit machine scrambler, rolling his dice at every turn.

But now that dice has stopped rolling.

[factual] Quantum computing will bring guaranteed certainty to the companies and governments who own the technology (mostly in the west and China, further privileging the global north).

Meanwhile, inside quantum computers, layers of undulating waves tower higher.

Tech entrepreneurs, angel investors and quantum scientists set sail.

Violence with delicate electrical pulses, taming the winds, foam and atomic mutinies.

Surfing the quantum high seas in search of [STATEMENT] TRUE TRUE answers, ultimate predictability.

Shutting down chance encounters, capping indeterminacies.

All encased in what looks like deep sea diving tanks, octopus chandeliers and indications of black box politics.

These hard walls keep the delicate insides from the pesky public. No strangers here. Geopolitical barriers reinforced and intact.

[PARTICIPTION – RITUAL]

Recipe for programming slime

We're dealing with quantum here, so please make yourself smaller. Get close and cohere. Shimmy next to your neighbours, I may ask you to touch.

Number 1: Hold out your slime in front of you. [You do this and wait for the audience to join you] Quantum Bit.

Number 2: Stretch your slime so it occupies both hands at once. Quantum Superposition.

Number 3: Keep your right hand facing upwards holding its slime. Stretch the slime in your left hand over to the person to your left's right hand. If you're at the end of a row, look behind or forwards. Quantum entanglement.

Number 4: Massage your slimes together, find your rhythms. Quantum algorithm.

You're laughing, you're giggling.

[More serious again] But remember we're doing this to understand the quantum dash for cash.

What do our slimy caresses have to do with computing?

If this were truly quantum slime, then as we massaged with a certain groove, getting closer to a coherent harmony, all of the slime in this room would suddenly (!!!) magically appear in just one couple's hands. They'd have the correct answer. I'd declare them the winner. And hand them over a billion dollars.

But you beautiful folk are too hot to handle. Quantum computing needs cold and dark.

And quantum computing is quick magic and us humans just can't massage fast enough.

* * *

[A bit Angry] Quantum computing: Instrumentalising touching to the power of infinity and sampling every possibility, until the 'correct' answer pops out...

A planned power grab through an array of particles, millions of slime—balls all touching all others including themselves.

grrrr

Could throw slime again

Quantum is coming

Things that humanity would only know 10,000 years in the future are understood in a matter of hours.

If you set the best digital supercomputer running to simulate a new drug at molecular scale now, your 140th great grandchild could collect the answer. Person to person whispers, whimpering on through the millennia...

Media: at first, scientists called it quantum supremacy, pretending they didn't realise the word supremacy had Other *sigh* connotations.

Connotations, conned dictations, now they call it quantum advantage, at least they're kind of being honest about new hierarchies they'll create. Maybe?

Maybe. Narratives of merit are that quantum computing will solve climate change. Modelling new eco-materials, perfecting energy storage, complete understanding of photosynthesis leading to mimicry.

Or is this gimmickry?

New companies, Q-limate, are formed. [Sarcastic] BUILDING PARTNERSHIPS THAT DEVELOP AND SCALE END-TO-END BREAKTHROUGH CLIMATE TECHNOLOGIES ENABLED BY QUANTUM COMPUTING

Rooting, I sincerely hope that quantum computers are used to solve climate change.

Hiding under this and threaded through with hypocrisy is the alignment of the oil industry and Big Tech. Quantum computing for the optimisation of oil and gas transport routes, say the suits.

The optimisation of drilling methods and locations, for rich nations, neighbouring poorer countries suffering the impacts.

But "Optimisation will save energy" they say.

Anyway, we can predict future intentions by looking at past behaviours and they've already shown their hand. And private companies follow the money, wealth over health. Following the slimy oil will lead to greater profits and stasis. The feedback loop of extraction. A race against time, I mean slime.

Why not optimise the placement of solar panels instead?

grrr

<u>Quantum surveillance capitalism or capturing our slimeQore</u>

When fully developed quantum computers will break all encryption, current blockchains unchained. Encrypted historical archives open, privacy null. Big data's open book.

From cybernetics a black box is a system or object which produces useful information without revealing any information about its internal workings.

Black boxes cracked open.

[To the audience] You are the black box.

The slimy big tech tentacles peering into our inner most queerness.

Of current digital technologies and surveillance capitalism, Zuboff writes "Google is a shape—shifter, but each shape harbors the same aim: to hunt and capture raw material. Baby, won't you ride my car? Talk to my phone? Wear my shirt? Use my map? In all these cases the varied torrent of creative shapes is the sideshow to the main event: the continuous expansion of the extraction architecture to acquire raw material at scale to feed an expensive production process that makes prediction products that attract and retain more customers."

She continues: "it is no longer enough to automate information flows about us; the goal now is to automate us."

"In the absence of this freedom, the future collapses into an infinite present of mere behavior, in which there can be no subjects and no projects: only objects."

In 2019, Google was first to achieve so—called quantum supremacy, or the creation of a quantum computer that was able to solve a specific problem that no digital computer ever could. Quantum weaponry.

Profit fetishism: It's not a much of a leap to imagine big tech using quantum computing to exponentially extend current modes of surveillance capitalism.

Optimising us.

[Storytelling, confiding] There's a scientist, I actually know him, but I'm not going to say if he's slimy or not. Well this guy traced how quantum computers will be used to access states of our minds, using a brain computer interface.

A Brain—Computer Interface is a slimy data tentacle that connects two black boxes.

Quantum computing tentacles sliding into our minds. Makes digital surveillance look totally unrefined.

Long logical expression of brain states, complex e—motions, all outlined. Streamlined and then sold back to us, to the power of infinity.

What is at stake is our freewill, agency and self—distil. Who will own and exploit the unknown unknowns as they start to reveal themselves?

***

Caveat, this power to extract all from our brains, only works in a dualist — mind v body reference frame.

And as we feel therefore we are, We are not just disembodied computer silicon chips, but slimy entangled creatures with mucus filled bits.

Barad writes that quantum theory indicates: "the self is dispersed through time and being"

Let us take this self—dispersal as the aim, because it is key to troubling this quantum capitalistic game.

Slime play

CHANGE TONE: FUTURE SLIMIFICATIONS

[Fast and optimistic]

How can we burst, reveal and unseal our inner eels? Steal back quantum to trouble quantum. Go on ya ones! We hardly have slime to breathe.

Polyphonic rabbit voices, "more choices," faces, parallel universe dada, Chiwawa cosmic haw—haw.

Quantum (un)world shaping, mucus membrane gaping. Holes full of spooky kooky wooky, escaping.

The slime has come: Shaping, shaking, earthquaking and redraping, the dried out stale gel and desiccated Newtonian linking with capitalistic winking.

rolls eyes

Alright darling.

Rather than computation, quantum compassion in fashion, programming sticky entanglements, a passion, sperm and egg glowing. Valuing ecosystems, matter poems a flowing.

to slime

"because you're gorgeous I'll do anything for you."

pause [What I want to say but will not] Quantum computing to engage us in now continually shapeshifting forms of (non)being.

Grasping and clasping our slimy—quantum—selves may rescue. Queue, query, question...

pick up science paper

There is a queering theorem in quantum computing that says unknown quantum states cannot be copied. The no—cloning theorem.

That means if we do not know what's going on in a quantum Qore — we cannot copy it.

Slimy superpositions and entanglements are not fated to be duplicated.

Imagine our lives without copying?!

No more inadequate or prejudicial representations at the foundations, no reflections of objects, no body image, no seemingly expensive but actually mass produced personal effects. No more sameness, mimesis. No substitutes or grassroots.

Barad writes that representationalism presupposes pre-existing boundaries between subjects and objects, leading to a lack of ethics in face of the other.

Linear science centres reflections, coddles models, observing, measuring, true beliefs, the so-called objective outside looking into an unchanging interior.

Words mirroring things. Things mirroring words. Words mirroring kings.

To be **and** not be more quantum. We encrypt ourselves by embracing our slimy (non)selves.

Quantum brain-computer interfaces only work in the dualist realms.

Only the rigid and the boundaried can be categorised, copied, and appropriated by capital. Far flung tentacles stop collapsing into the old barren rationals.

If we allow the quantum un/world to flourish then it cannot be copied. Slimy data tentacles burst and leave our queer bodies: queer bodies, multiple, layered, tentacular.

An un/world of slimeQores, shapeshifting.

New and old forms through strong entanglements — massaged. Massages touching caressing fleshliness.

Differences that emerge through phenomena that matter in matter.

Slime as an equal.

Kindness to slime,

compassion for slime,

Connection to ooze,

Affection don't lose

How can you become more quantum cos it's time?

How can you embrace and entangle through the myriad paths our slimy bodies move through and beyond everyday?

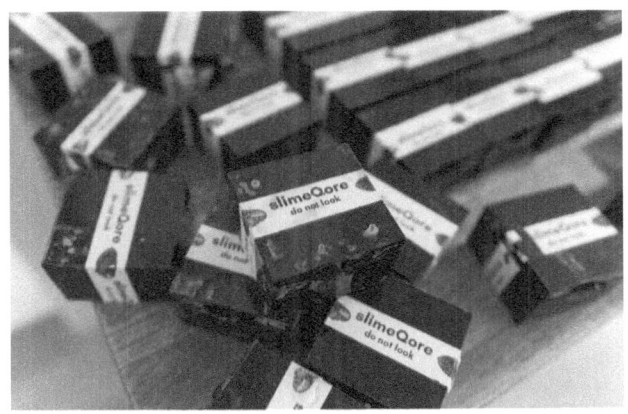

PIWO (Portalling-With-Others): Wayfinding for Curatorial Ethics in a Climate Emergency
Dani Admiss

"Because, of course, the portal has been there all along."
(Maynard and Simpson 2022, 245) *Rehearsals for Living*

Portals are a gateway into an alternative reality. Appearing seemingly out of nowhere, they reveal themselves in worlds that need healing. For Abolitionist writers and activists Robin Maynard and Leanne Betasamosoake Simpson (2022), portals are a wayfinding system. They show up in the everyday revealing power dynamics that are hidden and, through a process of materialisation, plot a path towards a new and different direction. In this chapter I share my personal experience of portals and how they changed my approach to curating. Guided by the teachings of Audre Lorde, Arundhati Roy, and Maynard and Simpson, I suggest 'portalling' is socially useful for the arts as it creates a pathway between internal healing and external action. Drawing on an artistic co-creation method DIWO (Do-it-With-Others), by Furtherfield's Ruth Catlow and Marc Garrett, I propose a curatorial method and approach *PIWO (Portalling-With-Others)* that can support the development of the intellectual, emotional and relational agility, imagination and stamina needed to face difficult and uncomfortable dimensions of shared problems, such as the climate emergency. I explore this idea through a discussion of an artistic just green transition project, *Sunlight Doesn't Need a Pipeline* (2021), detailing how I moved from wayfinding for a portal — seeking influence from the outside for a centre to hold my curatorial research — to holding a space for others, so they can nurture their own decision-making.

Wayfinding

In March 2020, the rapid onset of the COVID-19 Pandemic meant that, all over the world, lungs were collapsing, throats burning, organs failing. During that first year, Arundhati Roy (2020) wrote an essay likening COVID-19 to a portal. Appearing in a sick world, portals rupture the everyday of accepted reality presenting a doorway into another way of being. They are visible when plans for a new oil field are blocked, statues of colonisers and dictators are toppled, or mass protests support those who are subjugated to unthinkable levels of violence. I started my Stanley Picker Fellowship — an individually-funded project with Stanley Picker Gallery and Kingston University, London, England — in a time of many portals, and it was delivered 20-months later amidst an entirely new, and yet also entirely known world-order that existed before the pandemic and continues, relentlessly, to render communities, species and ecosystems disposable.[1]

In 2020, during the first few months of the fellowship, I didn't feel I could carry on with the curatorial research project as originally planned. In the UK, 50% of the creative workforce are self-employed.[2] Lockdown, caring responsibilities, and travel restrictions meant that most freelance art workers found themselves temporarily unemployed. With predictions of up to five years of disruption, many people, me included, found themselves in precarious situations and were understandably nervous about the future. I decided to speak with designer, educator, and past Stanley Picker Fellow, Onkar Kular, who suggested that a way through was to ask how the Fellowship could be useful.[3] I reached out to community groups and organisers local to the gallery,

---

1. *Sunlight Doesn't Need a Pipeline* was commissioned by Stanley Picker Gallery; Kingston University and it is funded by Stanley Picker Trust and Arts Council England.

2. Annual employment data newly released by DCMS (2019/2020) as well as Arts & Diversity Survey, Creative Scotland, 2017, show almost 50% of workers in the sector are self-employed.

as well as faculty and gallery staff, to find out what challenges they were facing and what they considered 'socially useful' for them at that time. Asking this question often created a pause in the general flow of our conversations. It redirected the energy from a pleasant, if not perfunctory exchange happening mostly over the fractured temporality of screens, toward morally-oriented questions, such as what was needed to support those who are not supported by social systems or how to live well in an uncertain world.

As part of these conversations, I spoke with the team at the Stanley Picker Gallery about the conditions of support they receive from Arts Council England (ACE), England's main public funder for the arts. We discussed the annual carbon report that National Portfolio Organisations (NPOs) are required to create. Carbon reports calculate the tonnage of carbon dioxide pollution directly resulting from a business' activity each year. This could include the total energy use of a museum, or the emissions produced from shipping art works across the world to stage and display as part of gallery exhibitions. It is undoubtedly a positive step that ACE requires NPOs to do this reporting which, at the time, was also practiced by art and environment advocacy organisations, Julie's Bicycle and Gallery Climate Coalition. The injunction to report on carbon dioxide pollution implicitly advocates for change without directly asking art organisations to reduce carbon emissions or have their emissions externally audited. For example, measuring carbon emissions shows organisations the huge and disproportionate impacts flights have on their carbon 'budget,' influencing some to change ways of working. Against a backdrop of UK austerity, reporting with self-imposed rather than enforced reductions means that smaller arts organisations, who already struggle to stay open due to limited funding and resources, are not disproportionately penalised or impacted by the costs of transitioning towards lowering carbon-heavy practices. However, ACE's policy approach still presents serious challenges. The biggest polluters in the sector aren't held to account, and in instances where when carbon outputs such as building use cannot be reduced,

---

3. A reference to the work of Cuban artist Tania Bruguera and her Arte Útil project, an approach to praxis that redirects artistic thinking to imagine, create and implement projects that are socially useful.

instead of supplying desperately-needed capital investment to smaller art organisations to decarbonise properly, ACE suggested organisations use carbon offsetting schemes.

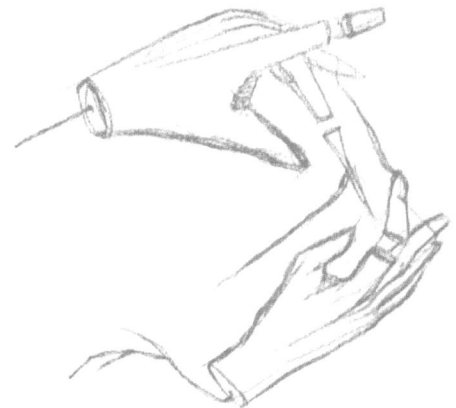

Figure 1: Katayoon Fourouhesh, 2023. *Portalling With Others*, hand-drawn illustrations. Supported by Global Sustainability Institute, Anglia Ruskin University, UK.

In theory, carbon offsetting and mitigation schemes sound like an expert and impactful solution. A financial accounting mechanism — relying on AI to help with data collection, analysis, and reporting — carbon offsetting enables individuals to compensate for their polluting emissions by funding an equivalent carbon dioxide saving elsewhere. It is a checkbox seamlessly incorporated into the purchase of a plane ticket, a coffee chain saying that the drink presented to you in a plastic cup is 'net zero' or carbon credits that are available as investments in a specialised, emerging stock market — easy enough for a conglomerate to acquire and then make the claim that its newest endeavour, a copper mine, is carbon-neutral. In actuality, ecosystems are much more complex than balancing a financial transaction (Prado and Admiss 2022). Not only are landscapes biophysical living entities; they are also rich tapestries home to human and more-than-human modes of living, cultures, histories, and peoples that are not interchangeable (Drury 2017). In recent years, many schemes have been discredited as nothing more than colonial pollution vouchers.

Offsetting schemes are part of a set of accounting mechanisms in the green economy. Many have spoken about how tools and projects like this keep colonial relations in place, perpetuating ongoing harm through the appropriation of land and poorly compensated and dehumanised labour across the world (Hamouchene 2017; Liboiron 2017). ACE's promotion of carbon offsetting led art organisations to believe that they were making 'practical' decisions about how to reduce their carbon dioxide emissions. In actuality, offsetting schemes give the feeling of a solution without the purchaser having any recognition of the extent and magnitude of the problem and their active participation in creating it. A truly just and green transition will require a radical social transformation of individual and collective aspirations and the ways lives are lived, acknowledging that current modes of production and consumption in the Global North and in highly industrialised countries are unsustainable from an environmental point of view and unjust from a social point of view. ACE's decision to include carbon offsetting in their environmental policy falls in line with green colonial attitudes, offering a simple way to 'erase' pollution but requiring no authentic change in how arts organisations in the Global North operate.

Contradiction plays a role in every single thing we do, and this is part of being human. At the same time, paying close attention to internal contradictions like ACE's policy on offsetting schemes illustrates how inconsistencies between our values and the outside world can often derail our own social and ecological action. Today, UK museums and galleries continue to stage exhibitions, create learning programmes, and commission artists to create work that calls for socially 'just' climate futures. These works present ideas about social equality, embodying careful and ethical relationships with the more-than-human, and illustrate possible ways of being beyond the realities of unevenly distributed climate profit and debt. Cultural programming communicates these ideas to the wider public, but due to ACE's policy many of these same art organisations spend a percentage of their budgets on carbon offsetting schemes. It perpetuates a colonial 'debt for nature' worldview, which forces developing nations to 'swap' the use of their natural resources and ecosystems for climate-related projects, like forest conservation efforts, in order to ensure their future survival.

There is a long and detailed history of how "calculation" and "bureaucratisation" makes some forms of knowledge appear more important than others (Escobar 2017, 32). That there are life-threatening levels of carbon dioxide in the earth's atmosphere produced from man-made industrial activity, and that this is fast increasing, is a stubborn and immutable fact. At the same time, 'expert' decarbonisation pathways, from the 'financialization of nature,' where capital markets use nature for profit maximisation, to plans for net-zero, oversimplify the intellectual, emotional, and relational challenges faced. In their oversimplification, expert roadmaps to effective climate action reveal current guidance and policy on carbon accounting is not nearly enough to achieve an environmentally impactful and socially just transition, often benefitting pre-existing, colonial power dynamics, where those most responsible for climate change face the least severe repercussions. What existing expert decarbonisation pathways do reveal, however, is a lack of mutual and nourishing frameworks for co-existence. Carbon offsetting was my portal, one that demanded authentic change in both me and the way I work.

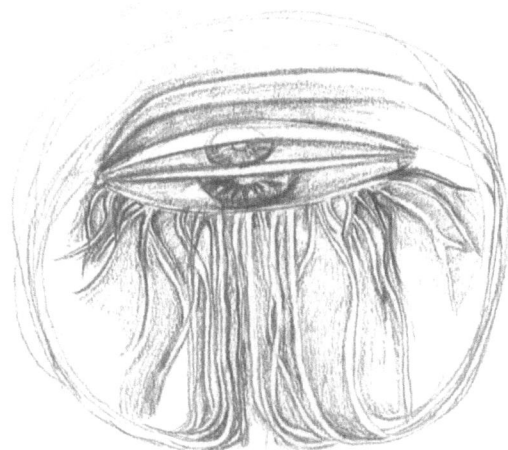

Figure 2: Katayoon Fourouhesh, 2023. *Portalling With Others*, hand-drawn illustrations. Supported by Global Sustainability Institute, Anglia Ruskin University, UK.

An Internal Path for Healing

Maynard and Simpson (2022) tell us that portals are doorways that confront a certain form of colonial power that has been made invisible. From forest fires that aggravate the cilia in someone's lungs, to children watching a statue of a colonial figure being pulled down, portals reveal a deeper understanding of our world than the everyday chooses to disclose. They are a way of describing the consciousness-altering experience of seeing beyond reality as *"the way things arrange"* (Maynard and Simpson 2022, 213; italics in the original), and instead as built on a continuum of hegemonic dominance, where one group has power over another. The cost of "seeing knowing that is dangerous," Arundhati Roy (2021) tells us, is having to sacrifice a safety that isn't really safe. It means acknowledging that, in the US, black firefighters are more likely to die than their white counterparts, or that the wealth of nations has been built on the use of some groups of human beings as a resource for the benefit of others.

Though such awareness can be dysregulating, it can also be powerful. Maynard and Simpson (2022) go on to write that portals reflect the difficulty to care for oneself on individual and societal levels. To truly witness injustice, where the world is organised in an uneven way that actively harms some more than others, draws attention to how difficult it is to care for ourselves and our communities. This, Maynard and Simpson tell us, is a shortcoming that we often carry with us without realising. To live in the "right relationship" with the world, we must also live with this failure (Maynard and Simpson 2022, 212). Portals disrupt this continuum. They are a disjuncture in the fabric of space-time; an invitation to witness world-endings and world-beginnings side by side, exposing how you and I are tethered to worlds inside and outside of us. The magnitude of this experience can forcibly lay open a self-awareness, reflected in the chapter title "Rehearsals for Living/*doyoureallywanttobewell.*" Maynard and Simpson (2022, 213) go on to write "There is knowledge in us that runs deeper, even if some are practised in ignoring it. It is less recognisable, yet it flows as a continuous stream, if only we will hear it." A reference to Audre Lorde's (1978) use of the "erotic" and erotic power as a way to live undivided within your own nature, portals also raise a question about the relationship to the self. To move to a right relationship with the world involves asking: in relationship to what?

Asking how I could be 'useful' had been part of a larger exercise in portal wayfinding. Taking notice of one portal, the pandemic, informed my decision not to treat my relationship to the residency and its stakeholders as "utility-maximising transactions" (Stein 2021, 8). It revealed to me that my original curatorial proposal, a project on water pollution in the Thames, had prioritised artistic and intellectual autonomy over other forms of understanding. Although intellectual knowledge is deeply important, in the face of a planetary-scale health epidemic it felt insufficient to prioritise this over other forms of relating. I realised that my original proposal did not match my internal values, nor the way I wanted to be as a curator in the world, which has always been focused on learning with others in ways that allow for multiple types of understanding and being.

In her work on decolonisation and climate education, Sharon Stein (2021, 8) has written about the limitation of "intellectual rigour," advocating for a shift towards "the need to develop and deepen our capacities for relational rigour as well." Asking how I could be useful was a way for me to turn away from prioritising a "complexified notion of intellectual rigour" (Stein 2021, 8). Instead, I chose to focus on how to be in service to the gallery staff, residents, and communities, and this adjusted, if only temporarily, the freelancer-institution power dynamic. Turning away from maximising the utility of the residency as an individual artist-curator allowed me to foster my capacity for more intentional and authentic relationships with quality and integrity. Serving the people in and adjacent to the institution in more relational ways required new levels of coordination, such as active listening and taking part in other people's worlds and networks. I found there was more power in adopting an 'unbounded accountability' to others. It gave me the capacity to build relations in ways that support coordination in response to change, as opposed to mediating relations via information and ideas. This, in turn, led me to be more open to noticing portals as they show up in the research stage of my curatorial work.

Adopting a position of relational rigour meant that I was more open to accepting the fact that carbon offsetting is part of an insidious exploitation of climate, nature and people. It enabled me to follow a path of research to see that the climate emergency was and is being treated as one of consumer choice, taking destruction from the Global North as a given, and situating repair within a transactional framework, one that operates on the premise that money can fix any problem. Because I was in a relational mode that prioritised interdependence over utility, looking through the portal revealed to me that my internal values did not match up with the external world as it was presented, prompting a deep re-evaluation of what climate action is to me and what I needed to be in the 'right relationship' with the world.

In my own view, the figure of the portal is powerful because it is a way to describe how art and learning facilitate gateways to access someone's internal world, where agility, strength, and imagination can be resourced towards acting differently (Light 2023). In this sense, portals are not only a perspectival shift that create a rupture in the everyday, but they are a gateway to deeper self-reflection and pathways toward self-determination. It is this deeper relationship, an invitation to have courage and connect inwards to build healthier relationships with the self and with society, that is relevant to curating now. In a society built on endlessly aggregating facts and information that connect every decision to multiple, structural contradictions and complexities, it is hard to determine our own path. What are the moral bonds we have to our neighbours, kin, and to any moral agent, from carbon to COVID-19, in virtue of them being a moral agent? What would a curatorial practice that supported others to step through a portal look like? Could this support others to reach their fullest capacity, a place where we can hold and be held securely, tethered to the worlds in and outside of us?

Portalling With Others

DIWO (Do-It-With-Others) (2007) is an art project and artistic co-creation method formed to subvert and reconfigure how artists are selected, exhibited and legitimised against the dominant gallery system. The project originated through Furtherfield Gallery and Commons, a contemporary art space and London's longest running centre for art and technology which, until last year, operated for many years solely out of a small space in the heart of Finsbury Park, one of London's oldest green spaces and public commons. Initiated by the founders of Furtherfield, artists Ruth Catlow and Marc Garrett, *DIWO* brought a group of physically disparate people together to create artworks in opposition to the dominant ways of experiencing and receiving art, such as through the selective and hierarchical art gallery system. The project was launched in 2006 when Furtherfield sent out a month-long open call

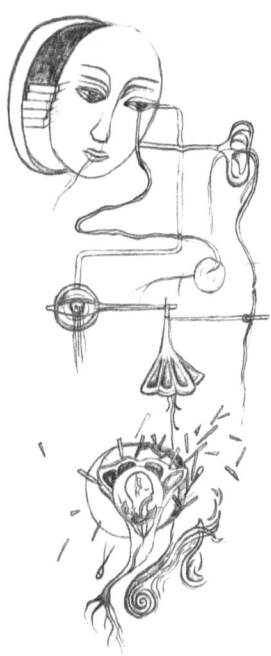

Figure 3: Katayoon Fourouhesh, 2023. *Portalling With Others*, hand-drawn illustrations. Supported by Global Sustainability Institute, Anglia Ruskin University, UK.

to the Netbehaviour mailing list, inviting subscribers to contribute artworks in the format of mailing list posts. Netbehaviour, also set up by Garrett and Catlow in 2004, is a long-running open email list community for sharing ideas, posting events, opportunities, and facilitating collaborations in art and technology by artists, academics, coders, engineers, organisers and activists. The *DIWO* E-Mail art exhibition aligned itself with the values of the conceptual mid-twentieth century art movement Fluxus and with Mail Art of the 60s, 70s and 80s, which challenged elitist distinctions between forms of 'high' and 'low' culture. *DIWO* openly borrowed from the approaches of these earlier counterculture art movements, updating them for a contemporary audience through the acts of "remixing" and "co-creation." The *DIWO* exhibition was an open call, where everyone who participated in the mailing list conversation that month was accepted to contribute. The submissions took the form of digital images, texts, instructions, code and software, accompanied by conversations and reflections, which were then exhibited later that year at their space at the time, HTTP Gallery, a warehouse on Ashfield Road, Haringey, London.

As an art project, *DIWO* belongs to a wider set of creative practices that often come under the banner of New Media art. Much has been written about how difficult New Media is to define, due in large part to the widespread use of computer and code-based technologies since the Internet, but it can loosely be understood as a process-based form of art and curatorial practice interested in emerging and "discrete" technologies, particularly how these technologies, systems and networks behave (Graham and Cook 2010, 6). A key approach in the field, cultivated in the decades before and after the Millennium, was a focus on more democratic forms of curating and display. Collaborative and participatory curatorial forms and experiments were often devised in direct resistance to conventional modes of display defined by the art museum, which were seen as reproducing elitism and curatorial 'gatekeeping.' New Media approaches range from the perspective that, because of the Internet, "everybody can be an artist" to criticising how audiences are often treated as passive bystanders in favour of more active art experiences. In the book *Rethinking Curating Art after New Media*, curator and professor of New Media Art Beryl Graham (2010, 124) writes, "One of the possible roles of a curator is to act as a gracious host between the artwork and the audience — to provide a 'platform'... If the curator is not curating an object but a 'participative system,' then the invisible system itself needs to be thoroughly understood, not only by the curator, but also by the audience." Following these ideas and new ways of working, *DIWO* purposefully drew on the characteristics of the platform, in this case the e-mailing list, to build, share and instrumentalise power against hegemonic forms of display. The e-mailing list was seen as a more egalitarian and participatory space, where artists-as-subscribers could self-legitimise through open participation.

It is against these unfolding and intersecting positions that the *Sunlight Doesn't Need a Pipeline* project came into existence. After the conversations on carbon reporting the question, "how can you decarbonise a gallery" stayed with me. The idea to co-create an alternative, holistic decarbonisation plan emerged out of a yearlong process of establishing slow, patient relationships with various creative, academic and community stakeholders, through ongoing conversations that were open and flexible to the social, emotional and material irruptions of these

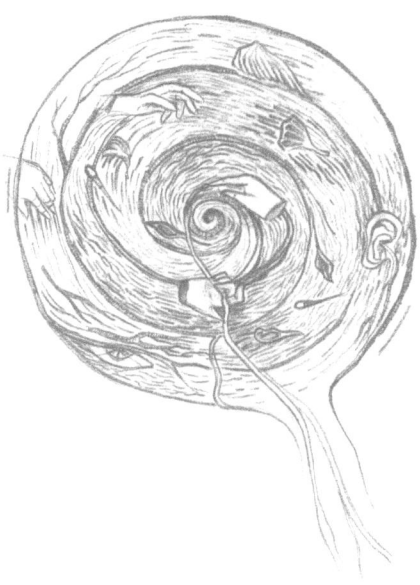

Figure 4: Katayoon Fourouhesh, 2023. *Portalling With Others*, hand-drawn illustrations. Supported by Global Sustainability Institute, Anglia Ruskin University, UK.

months. If *DIWO* used the curatorial process as a pathway for shared culture, *Sunlight* engaged in what I call *PIWO, portalling-with-others*, a curatorial approach to locate the personal and social ideas and dispositions required in relation to a shared but uneven problem, the climate emergency. What began as an individually funded fellowship grew into an international network of 200+ diverse art workers and community groups from across the globe loosely organised around the issue of climate justice as 25 public events, 20 published resources, 10 newly commissioned artistic-research, new performances and screenings, and a day-long community festival directly leading to a Community Climate Forum for the gallery, university and local residents.

The holistic decarbonisation plan sought to define and redefine how a just green transition was understood, paying particular attention to diverse methodological, theoretical and ethical approaches practiced in both research and artistic practice around the world. The ten artist research projects' contributions to the decarbonisation plan took the form of essays, personal environmental policies, reports, statements, and interviews, with most projects involving some sort of public collaborative learning or community-led research event. The contributions range from ghosts, life cycles of decay and museological restitution — Chanelle Adams, *The Right to Rest (In Peace)* (2022); experiments in intergenerational wealth — Cecilia Wee's *Our Community Inheritance* (2022); technological governance — Anne Pasek's *Digital and Decarbonisation Consensus & Conjectures* (2022); alternative climate literacy based on love — Susannah Haslam's *Open Curriculum* (2022), and more.

A key objective was to facilitate the sharing of transnational experiences, to both deepen and expand our understandings, dispositions, and agencies towards what a socially just green transition could look like, particularly beyond the typically centred, such as the carbon offsetting and mitigation accounting practices outlined earlier. Organising the project like this meant working with others in intellectual, emotional and relational ways, to problematise the knowledge and 'solutions' provided, and this was an invitation for participants to imagine a different standard of responsibilities and capacities. The *Anti-Offsetting Primer* (2022) is a collective artistic-research project and decolonial inquiry into carbon offsetting in the arts sector. I invited artist, writer and scholar, Luiza Prado de O. Martins to respond to the specific challenge of the promotion of carbon offsetting practices in UK arts and culture. Prado's work explores relations and knowledge between plants, political infrastructures and technology, and questions what structures and processes are needed for collective concerns of environmental care and reproductive justice. Through interviews, research, dialogue, as well as workshopping with Newbridge Projects, an artist-led space focused on supporting artists, curators and communities through the provision of space for experimentation located in Newcastle, England, the Anti-Offsetting Primer dances across various alternative worlds. It is a poetic invitation to imagine otherwise the recommendation to art and cultural workers to offset their emissions, proposing instead that both human and more-than human beings are situated, sacred and non-replaceable.

The Primer itself is structured as an essay, *Notes on Change: An Anti-Offsetting Primer*, written by Luiza Prado with contributions and interviews by researcher, translator, essayist and artist Chanelle Adams; mother, curator, art historian, and (at the time) co-director of

Berlin's SAVVY Contemporary, Elena Agudio; artist, activist, and anthropologist, son of Wapixana peoples, Amazoner Arawak; ecocentrist, environmental journalist, academic, and activist, Maxwell A. Ayamba; and an archaeologist originally from Lebanon, Sarah Mady. Prado's (2022) discussions thread through worlds as diverse and vibrant as a universe of women's ancient shrines and healing practices in the North of Lebanon, walking in the English countryside as a strategy to nurture a conception of home that supersedes the limitations of colonialism's proprietary walls and borders, and "the idea of a gallery as an atomized maloca" an ancestral roundhouse used by indigenous people of Brazil.

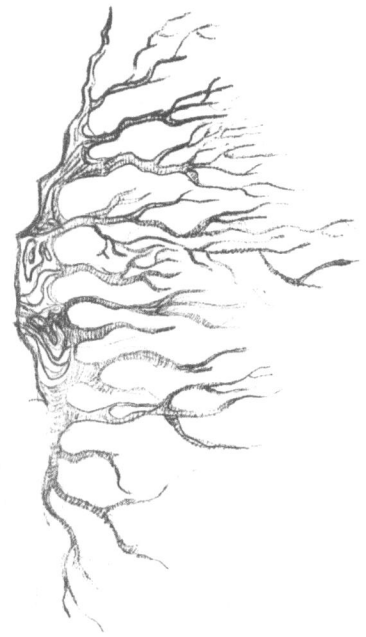

Figure 5: Katayoon Fourouhesh, 2023. *Portalling With Others*, hand-drawn illustrations. Supported by Global Sustainability Institute, Anglia Ruskin University, UK.

The holistic decarbonisation plan focused on challenging and problematising knowledge and the ways it is produced, understood, applied, valued and mobilised by dominant green transition and decarbonisation discourses. Stepping through the portal together required relationality, care and problematising knowledge. The plan, however imperfect, was an ethics and practice of care from many situated points that transposed art workers' inner worlds onto the outerworld of collective climate action.

On the surface, some of the contributions have incompatible politics and approaches. For instance, Sean Roy Parker's *Vague Decay Now!* (2022) is a speculative essay exploring the dematerialisation of art production. Thinking through various art world scenarios — white cube gallery, private view, and ecological art installations — Parker draws the reader's attention to the hypocrisy of highly industrialised societies that endlessly produce art on the theme of resource extraction, endorsing a slower, lighter, and entirely compostable art practice. Comparatively, in *Digital Decarbonisation Consensus & Conjectures* (2022) assistant professor at Trent University, Anne Pasek, brought 24 stakeholders in the arts and technology sector to evaluate the challenges and opportunities they each face at the conjuncture of art, AI, digital technologies and environmental justice. Participants proposed, reviewed, and debated different proposals for climate action in their sector, mapping the political and material impacts of digital decarbonisation strategies on workers, communities, institutions, and the climate. The outcome is a consensus statement that diagnoses the intersecting problems and proposes clear directions for stakeholders going forward. However incompatible these critiques are, the process of *portalling-with-others* created an epistemic pathway, weaving together small but meaningful moments in our lives, politics and commitments — tangled up as they are. This process of learning and unlearning was often fed back to me through phrases like 'I never thought I could have an opinion on climate justice as I am not an expert.'

For Robyn Maynard and Leanne Betasamosake Simpson, seeing portals in our day-to-day is a wayfinding tool to step through and reimagine our world anew. Building on this idea, *portalling-with-others* is an interpretive framework for curators, requiring a decentred approach to ethics, purposefully intervening in the 'frictions' and 'gaps' of externalised societal order and organisation, and, at the same time, working against a normalised human-first worldview. In 2021, the speed at which carbon accounting technologies and policies came to dominate the sustainability sector was at odds with the speed of governance decisions in UK Cultural Sector leadership. This friction was a portal presenting an opportunity to invite others to create more-than-human ethics and practices of care that resolutely challenge the colonial idea of a transactional framing of life that positions both human and more-than human beings as disposable and replaceable.

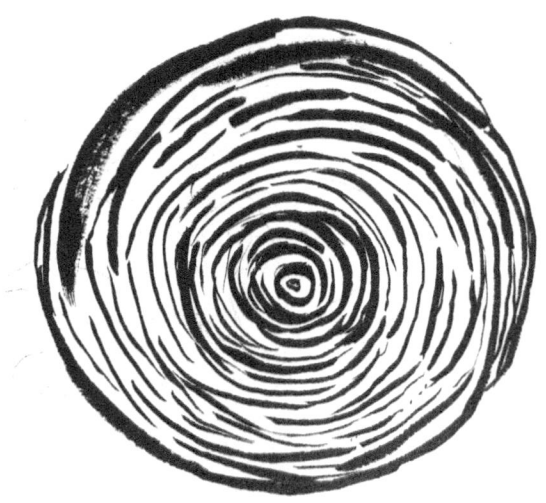

Figure 6: Katayoon Fourouhesh, 2023. *Portalling With Others*, hand-drawn illustrations. Supported by Global Sustainability Institute, Anglia Ruskin University, UK.

How to live well with one another and within limits is the indomitable question of our age. Multiple and multiplying changes to the climate, and to nature, are fast escalating the already radical social transformation of individual and collective aspirations and the ways lives are lived. As climate breakdown continues, its protean effects will cascade, meaning the future is uncertain and even more uneven. A plurality of knowledge systems, able to reckon with deeply entrenched inequalities and inherited power dynamics and the reality that many of us are trapped by an industrial global economy and its accompanying frameworks of separation and artificial scarcity, are needed. Finding a right relationship with life and the world is both a personal and a collective choice, but it is a choice that we each must make.

In this text, I have tried to situate teachings from writers dedicated to black liberation, who have developed the figure of the portal to support and inspire people struggling to fully inhabit their own being as a foundational base for the development of productive societies and a healthy human-earth relationship. *Portalling-with-others* is proposed as a curatorial approach, a shared epistemic pathway, a way to renew individual dispositions, and a way to add new core values and direction;

particularly when guidance on collective pathways, such as with decarbonisation are not enough. Portals have the potential to allow someone to witness an injustice and at the same time choose an alternative direction, one more aligned with our internal values. Portalling reminds us that transformative social change is about living inwards out, as opposed to a reality where our actions are driven in entirety by an external world — what Lorde, Maynard and Simpson refer to as living an authentic life.

Sunlight Doesn't Need a Pipeline is a collaborative literacy and climate justice project in search of transformative and regenerative repair for the art sector and beyond. It was originally commissioned by the Stanley Picker Gallery, Kingston University and first supported by Arts Council England.

Acknowledgements

Thank you to all the participants and collaborators I've interacted with across Sunlight who have helped shape this essay, and to the thoughtful illustrations by Katayoon Fourouhesh.

References

Admiss, Dani. 2022. "SunlightDoesntNeedaPipeline.com [festival] Stanley Picker Gallery and online." 6 October 2022. https://sunlightdoesntneedapipeline.com/.

Catlow, Ruth, and Marc Garrett. 2012. "DIWO: Do It With Others — No Ecology without Social Ecology Essay." *she's over there with the others...*, February 11, 2012. https://ruthcatlow.net/?works=diwo-do-it-with-others-no-ecology-without-social-ecology.

Drury, Danika. "Offsetting." *Uneven Earth*, August 17, 2020. https://www.unevenearth.org/2020/08/offsetting/.

Escobar, Arturo. 2017. "Out of the Studio and into the Flow of Socionatural Life." In *Designs for the Pluriverse: Radical Interdependence, Autonomy, and the Making of Worlds*. Duke University Press.

Garrett, M. 2014. "DIWO (Do-It-With-Others): Artistic Co-Creation as a Decentralized Method of Peer Empowerment in Today's Multitude." *Turning Art into Real Life*, February 12, 2014 [online].

Ginwright, Shawn A. 2022. *The Four Pivots: Reimagining Justice, Reimagining Ourselves*. North Atlantic Books.

Hamouchene, Hamza. 2017. "Another case of energy colonialism: Tunisia's Tunur solar project." *openDemocracy*, September 9. https://www.opendemocracy.net/en/north-africa-west-asia/another-case-of-energy-colonialism-tunisia-s-tunur-solar-pro/.

Liboiron, Max. 2017. "Pollution is Colonialism." *Discard Studies*, September 1, 2017. https://discardstudies.com/2017/09/01/pollution-is-colonialism/.

Lorde, Audre. 1978. "Uses of the Erotic: The Erotic as Power." Paper delivered at the Fourth Berkshire Conference on the History of Women, Mount Holyoke College. August 25, 1978. Published as a pamphlet by Out & Out Books (available from The Crossing Press). Reprinted in: Lorde, Audre. 1984. *Sister Outsider: Essays and Speeches*. Crossing Press.

Prado, Luiza, and Dani Admiss. 2022. "Notes on Change: An Anti-Offsetting Primer." *Sunlight Doesn't Need a Pipeline*, 2022. https://sunlightdoesntneedapipeline.

com/2022/09/14/the-anti-offsetting-primer/.

Maynard, Robyn, and Leanne Betasamosake Simpson. 2022. "Rehearsals for Living / Areyousurethatyoureallywanttobewell." In *Rehearsals for Living (Abolitionist Papers)*, edited by Naomi Murakawa. Knopf Canada / Penguin Random House.

Roy, Arundhati. 2020. "The Pandemic is a Portal." *The New York Times*, April 3, 2020.

Stein, Sharon. 2021. "Reimagining global citizenship education for a volatile, uncertain, complex, and ambiguous (VUCA) world." *Globalisation, Societies and Education* 19 (4): 482–495.

An Experimental Creative Practice Approach to AI Ethics in Art Museums: Following Exhibitions in the Making
Vanessa Bartlett

This chapter establishes an experimental approach to experiencing and researching exhibitions, which I call *following exhibitions in the making*. Framed through the lens of creative practice research, *following exhibitions in the making* foregrounds affect, embodiment, and lived experience as methodological urgencies for practicing decentred ethics in art museums and galleries. It is framed around *Don't Be Evil*, an exhibition curated by Anna Briers for The University of Queensland (UQ) Art Museum in 2021. *Don't Be Evil* sought to illuminate the invisible power structures operating beneath the surface of networked technologies through the work of 16 Australian and international artists.[1] It was titled after Google's original corporate motto, which was insidiously removed in 2015. The exhibition explored the extraction of

---

1. The full list of artists in *Don't Be Evil*: Zach Blas and Jemima Wyman, Kate Crawford and Vladan Joler, Simon Denny, Xanthe Dobbie, Sean Dockray, Forensic Architecture, Kate Geck, Elisa Giardina Papa, Matthew Griffin, Eugenia Lim, Daniel McKewen, Angela Tiatia, Suzanne Treister, and Katie Vida. *Don't Be Evil* was the second chapter of a two-part exhibition series curated by Briers called *Conflict in My Outlook*. The first chapter *We Met Online* (2020) took place entirely online during the COVID-19 lockdowns. *Conflict in My Outlook* was documented in a publication of the same name (Briers et al. 2022).

personal data via online platforms such as YouTube, and the new forms of labour ethics posed by increasing practices of automation. It opened on 30 July 2021 during the COVID-19 pandemic, when anxiety about the mediation of commercial and social behaviours by online platforms was high (Lovink 2020). The curatorial narrative was shaped by Briers around the "failed metaphor of the cloud as an ethereal construct" (Briers, personal communication with author, 2022)[2] which remains somewhat obscure in terms of public accountability and understanding (Bridle 2019; Amoore 2020).

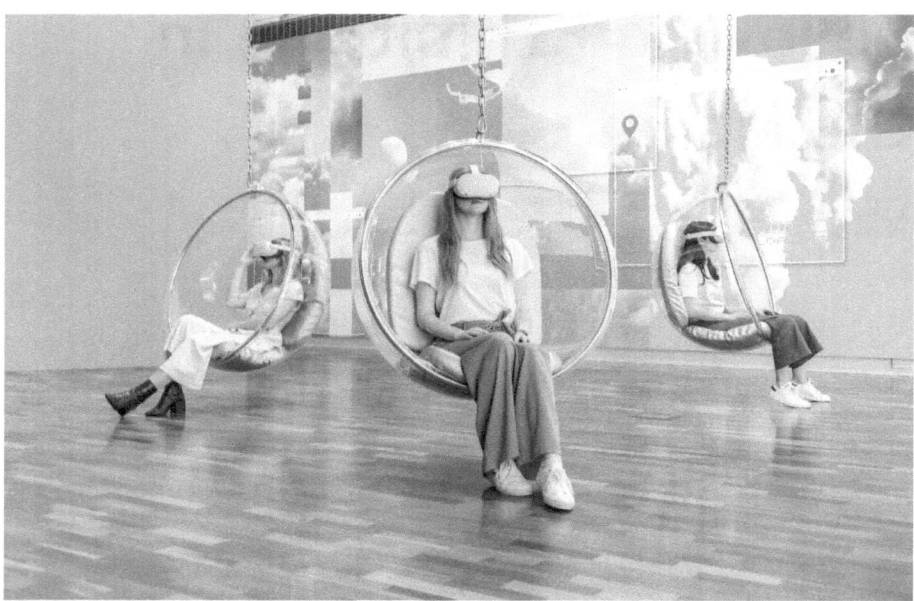

Figure 1: *Cloud Copy* (2020) Xanthe Dobbie. Part of *Don't Be Evil*, UQ Art Museum, 2021. Courtesy of the artist. Photo: Louis Lim.

I frame this chapter around *Don't Be Evil* due to the sensitive curatorial process followed by Briers, and the exhibition's expansive ethical lens that embraced the ecological alongside the technical. My approach to *following 'Don't Be Evil'* in the making responds to the increasing prominence of exhibitions as a medium for exploring the social, cultural,

---

2. All quotes by Briers taken from personal communication unless otherwise stated.

and ethical implications of emerging technologies (Thiel and Bernhardt 2023). It is framed as a counter to the mainstream cultural reception of AI art, which often focuses on large-scale exhibitions featuring new technologies with mass appeal (Denson 2023, 158; Maksimova 2024, 10). In 2019, the Barbican held one of the first major exhibitions of AI art, titled *AI: More than Human*. It invited visitors to question distinctions between artificial and human life, alluding to fears and fantasies around AI's potential human qualities. The exhibition received critical approval for its use of historical objects to trace how humans have understood of the concept of intelligence (Mason 2019). It was also described by reviewers as "overwhelming" (Dead Pixels 2019; Lujani 2019), "Densely populated," and an "assault" to the senses (Mason, 2019), suggesting that the complex mix of technological narratives and media may have created a challenging exhibition experience for some viewers.

These accounts of being overwhelmed pose interesting questions for exhibitions trained on ethics. How might such assaults to the senses interrupt art's capacity to foster complex affects that support the emergence of ethical sensibilities in exhibition spaces? Can large-scale and spectacular exhibitions support nuanced forms of ethical feeling? In this chapter, I follow 'Don't Be Evil' in the making, to make a close reading of forms of affect that emerge through a set of relationships formed around the exhibition. I argue that these elements are vital to rich, generative encounters at the museum public interface, and the emergence of decentred ethics in exhibitions of AI art.

In 2024, Frieze Magazine reflected on the contemporary art world's early challenges navigating the "hysteria and hype" of AI, whereby exhibitions tended to "perpetuate the mystifying language of 'hallucinations' and 'dreams'" that position the technology as "some alien miracle" (Droitcour 2024). In a survey of nine German museum exhibitions on AI, Alisa Maksimova (2024) explores how curators often have critical opinions about AI, but face challenges in balancing this criticality with the need for creating engaging exhibitions. She found that spectacular, impressive technology remains a primary consideration for curators when planning exhibitions, due to the cultural pressures exerted on museums to attract mass engagement (2024, 10). In her conclusion, she reflects that researching finished exhibitions limits her ability to analyse the museum's relationship to various expert communities, artists and research laboratories, which may have illuminated other ways that exhibitions produce knowledge. She recommends "following developmental work on the exhibition from the outset" (2024, 12) potentially using ethnographic methods, to reflect all relevant events that have shaped an exhibition.

This chapter builds from my conviction that exhibitions produce meaning within relationships and communities of practice that extend beyond the specific moment of public exhibition display (Bartlett 2020).[3] Where exhibitions seek to encourage ethical sensibilities, they must balance engagement agendas with sensitivity to intimate relationships and processes. I will demonstrate this here through a conversation held online during the COVID-19 pandemic with a group of cultural mediators — gallery staff trained to mediate *Don't Be Evil* to the public. Following the flow of this conversation in my research prompted an experimental reflection on the intimate ethical sensibilities that are co-produced between exhibitions and communities of practice. The research was galvanised by Australia's COVID-19 border closures, which meant that I discussed the exhibition online with the cultural mediators *before* I saw the works in person, allowing my relationship to the exhibition to be shaped by a group who are vital to the museum-public interface, but would not normally be centred in critical or theoretical writing about exhibitions.

I develop my approach to *following 'Don't Be Evil' in the making* through the lens of Katve-Kaisa Kontturi's (2018) *Ways of Following: Art, Materiality, Collaboration*. Kontturi (2018, 10) describes how a researcher can collaborate with art's "material, affective and relational doings" beyond analysing visual art as a site of representation and critique. For Kontturi (2018, 18), following indicates a way of being in relationship that is not predetermined by a fixed set of rules or methods. Instead, it promotes responsiveness and relationality, allowing more-than-human agencies to influence research. Kontturi (2018, 18) seeks to push beyond the inference of meaning from artworks as finished objects. Rather, she attends to the material process of how art is made. To follow art in the making Kontturi visits artists in their studios and

---

3. I have worked as a practicing independent and institutional curator for almost 20 years, in addition to my academic experience.

considers the material and temporal emergence of works as dynamic relational encounters. She argues that this troubles the conventional understanding of authoritative, mastering agency in researching and writing about art, destabilising distinctions between the knower and the known, the subject and object of research (2018, 20).

My way of *following 'Don't Be Evil' in the making* aligns the exhibition and curatorial narrative with ethnographic material. This includes an interview with exhibition curator Anna Briers, my workshop with the cultural mediators, and notes from the exhibition as field site. Essential to *following* is the act of claiming "writing itself as an act of (collaborative) research creation" (Kontturi 2018, 11), which moves with the changing circumstances of researching in a public museum during a pandemic. In situating the artworks alongside my ethnographic reflections, the chapter enacts a form of autotheory, which artist Lauren Fournier (2021, 7) describes as "the integration of theory and philosophy with autobiography … [and] the body."

This chapter will unfold in four sections: *Method*, *Mediation*, *Mining*, and *Memory*. Method will outline the creative practice approach that frames my relationship with *Don't Be Evil*, focusing on art's affective capacities, and on exhibitions as sites where affect is co-produced between artworks and bodies. *Mediation* will introduce UQ Art Museum's cultural mediators. I show how following imagery that the cultural mediators shared with me galvanised my embodied, affective relationship with the exhibition. *Mining* and *Memory* follow the flow of these relationships, to explore how mining and the figure of the underground link my own lived experiences to those of the cultural mediators; and to the artist and the curator's critical and creative intent. I argue that this reveals a complex, shared ethical sensibility about the effects of technological expansion on landscape, ecosystem, and bodies that emerges through the exhibition.

Method

Following exhibitions in the making is framed through the field of creative practice research, particularly what Kontturi (2018), following Barbara Bolt (2004), describes as the affective *work* of art. Engaged with a feminist, materialist framework, Kontturi argues that artworks are not so much to be "read, interpreted, deciphered, but responded to, engaged with" (Konturri 2018, 34). The work of art describes art's affective capacities and its "thingly" qualities (Bolt 2004, 90; Konturri 2018, 54). This is influenced by new materialism and particularly by Bennett (2010), who has argued that the volitional choices of a subject might be understood as co-produced in relationship with organic and inorganic material things. Rather than considering the human as having a mastering agency over the world around her, we should understand the world as a series of relationships. For Kontturi, this materialist approach can be applied to contest established art historical methods, where the writer strives to display a degree of mastery over the artwork by interpreting it, making claims about what the artwork represents. She argues that:

> When works of art are seen as passive "battlefields" for representation and interpretation, their potential lines of flight, their material-relational capacity to change and move thinking is easily missed. Therefore, it is important to pay attention to what is singular in artworks, their modus operandi, the material-relational movements of art, and not override material and corporeal intensities with textual and discursive powers. (2018, 45)

The *work* of art is not about enforcing meanings, but moving with the artwork as part of a material-affective relationship. It is crucial that the work of art extends to include what Kontturi (2018, 45) calls the "viewer-participant" who may allow their own "system of being and thought to open up" as part of an encounter with an artwork. In this space collaboration takes hold, where aesthetic encounters "co-involve the audience in their dance." Where Kontturi's way of following adheres closely to artists and artworks, my way of following extends this ethos to a group exhibition, and the communities of practice involved in its production.

This approach finds support in the field of exhibition research, where exhibition-audience relationships are understood as acts of co-production. In the volume *Exhibition Experiments* (2007), Macdonald and Basu trace the history of the museum back to scientific theatres where live experiments were carried out in front of audiences. They suggest that contemporary exhibition making would benefit from returning to this idea of unfolding process and live enquiry rather than framing fixed representations of the social and cultural world. In *Exhibitions as*

Research (2019), Bjerregaard updates this emphasis on exhibitions as collaborative sites of meaning making:

> If the museum used to be the place we would go to know things "for sure" the idea of the museum as laboratory suggests that the museum should be a space where we (a true "we" *including both museum staff and audiences*) engage in knowledge-in-the-making. (2019, 4, my emphasis)

Bjerregaard points toward "art as a way of knowing" for supporting these acts of co-production. This extends toward a view of art and research that accounts for the capacity of material things to affect (Bjerregaard 2019, 5). Crucially, he highlights the significance of museum staff and communities of practice in these acts of co-production.

Mediation

When I learned about UQ Art Museum's cultural mediation programme, which trains staff to act as an interface between the works and exhibition, I became interested in this specialised group of viewer-participants. This group appeared to have a unique potential for galvanising dynamic exchanges between the artworks and publics. I was curious about the potential ethical engagements that are brought into being by a group of custodians charged with caring for the relation between art and bodies in exhibition spaces.

Cultural mediation updates older models of exhibition invigilation, where staff would have been trained to dispense information and safeguard against works being damaged. It encourages a more dynamic, two-way exchange between mediators and visitors, often conceived as a "peer-to-peer dialogue" (Addis et al. 2023). Cultural mediation has been developed and championed by two of France's major cultural centres, Centre Georges Pompidou and Palais de Tokyo (NSW Museums and Galleries 2019; Barois De Caevel 2020). According to Marion Buchloh-Kollerbohm, Head of Cultural Mediation at Palais de Tokyo: "Cultural mediation is not about changing people's opinions, or making visitors love contemporary art — it is about creating a moment" (NSW Museums and Galleries 2019). At the time of writing, UQ Art Museum is one of only three cultural centres in Australia that offers a specialised programme in cultural mediation.

Cultural mediators are potentially powerful agents in how an exhibition might activate knowledge-in-the-making in exhibition spaces. Yet, as highlighted by visual art curator Eva Barois De Caevel (2020), cultural mediators may be seen in the art world as less specialised than other arts professionals, and their expertise and experience could remain undocumented in formal museum communications such as marketing collateral or curatorial essays. Cultural mediators therefore present a complex ethical challenge for the art museum. While their relationships with the artworks, visitors and the museum itself are potentially vital to the material-relational entanglements that emerge in exhibitions, their voices are less prominent in the exhibition's formal documentation.

Researching *Don't Be Evil* with UQ Art Musuem's cultural mediators was a way of decentring, by collaborating with a group of cultural workers. Where my planned research timelines were disrupted by the pandemic, following the flow of research in the making became a necessary imperative, as world events repeatedly shattered my plans. In early October 2021, less than a week before I was due to travel, I cancelled my flight as Queensland's borders were closed due to the state's first major wave of COVID-19.

I arranged to meet the cultural mediators on Zoom. They had already been trained on the exhibition by Briers and other UQ Art Museum staff. We looked at a set of photographs of the exhibition, before I invited the group to share images, associations, memories, and personal stories that came to mind for them when they thought about the exhibition. Inviting people to verbally describe 'images' in response to an artwork introduced elements of arts-based research, supporting people to describe experience in ways that "adumbrate rather than denote" (Barone and Eisner 2012, 2). This is designed to reduce the emphasis on evaluating or critiquing individual artworks. I knew that the cultural mediators would be well versed in the exhibition narratives supplied by the artist and curators, and I wanted to discourage repetition of these learned responses. Socially engaged artist and scholar Lindsay Kelley (2022, 245) has described how forms of defamiliarisation can occur in arts-based research, where creative methods support familiar things being experienced "as if for the first time."

Mining

The cultural mediators began to connect the exhibition with their lived experiences. They made repeated references to material resources, industrial production and mining, which appeared to connect works in the exhibition with their experience as a relatively young, more climate aware group living in Queensland; a politically and ecologically conservative part of Australia (Tranter and Foxwell-Norton 2021). Although images of mining and the underground repeated throughout the conversation, I was particularly struck by one mediator's memory:

> I'm thinking of a time when I went out to a mine site to visit a friend who works out there and we were going... we were just driving along the road and there was an overpass and this massive mining truck, it was literally as big as a house, came over the top of the overpasses we went underneath it... it was really scary, you could feel every vibration, it was just mad. (Workshop October 5, 2021)

Googling 'mining truck Australia' in the weeks after the online workshop (and before my in-person visit to the exhibition), I find images of some of the world's biggest vehicles towering over their human operators, dwarfing them in height and bulk. I learn that the mining trucks that transport materials across mine sites in rural Australia can be up to eight metres tall. In her anthropological enquiry into the role of mining in Australian settler colonialism, Elizabeth Povinelli notes that "dinosaur-sized" mining trucks cutting through barren Australian desert landscapes can conjure the direst imaginaries of the Anthropocene, visions of the earth as a "dead orb hanging in the night sky" (Povinelli 2016, 36). Through the course of my research, I developed a relationship with the mining truck as an evocative image of ethical anxieties about the infrastructures of industrial mining, and their impact on bodies and landscape.

I read that mining is the largest single contributor to the Queensland economy, and is vital to the state's history and identity (Ivanova 2014). Queensland is home to over 100 metalliferous mines, and is Australia's largest producer of base metals including copper, lead, and zinc. Politically conservative, the state has been pivotal to the success of right-wing politics in Australia over the past four decades. Queensland's electorate is thought to favour economic development over environmental protections. This is due in part to widespread public perception that the economy and workforce is too dependent on mining to transition to more sustainable alternatives without risk (Selvey et al 2022, 2).

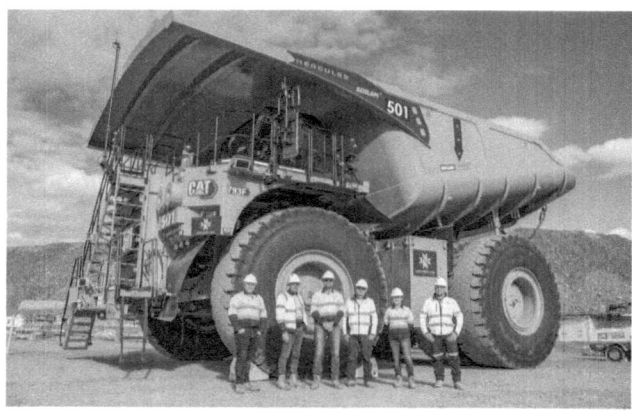

Figure 2: Found image from a Google search. One of the top image search results for 'mining truck Australia' October 2021. A new Caterpillar 793F haul truck is unveiled at a mine site in Western Australia.

As a recent settler and resident of urban Australia, my body does not know what it is to inhabit landscapes ravaged by mining's extractivist infrastructures. But the cultural mediator's memory of the massive mining truck stirs a bodily response in me that helps me to imagine cycles of extraction and destruction as they are felt viscerally by bodies around mine sites. When I visited *Don't Be Evil* in person in January 2022 after the border had reopened, I came to the exhibition with a desire to seek out images of mining first, to follow my conversation with the cultural mediators as a way of encountering the works. I approached a cluster of works by Simon Denny, which Briers describes as a 'layered collage' exploring themes of mining. This group of nine works conceptually entwines practices of mining minerals with metaphorical concepts of data mining, the automated searching of large sets of data for patterns and trends that can be turned into business insights. The works link these two processes as part of the same extractive mindset that frames the earth and its inhabitants as resources to be exploited for profit. It reflects the ethical responsibility of mining corporations — both miners of minerals and data.

These works particularly respond to recent ethical controversies surrounding Rio Tinto, the world's second largest mining corporation who have been present in Australia since the 1940s. At the time of my visit to the exhibition, two Rio Tinto executives were due to go on trial in Australia for deception and fraud (Danckert 2020). The works speculate on a future where high-powered executives and 'big tech disrupters' are held to account. Denny commissioned Sharon Gordon, a courtroom illustrator based in Queensland, to illustrate 10 corporate executives on trial in court, as a way of visualising greater accountability for fiscally and environmentally irresponsible behaviours (2021). Denny's works also reflect on the 2018 introduction of Autohaul train by Rio Tinto. Autohaul was the world's first automated heavy-haul long distance rail network, delivering iron ore across Western Australia. These vehicles have created ethical anxieties like those prompted by self-driving cars, such as loss of employment opportunities in communities and anxiety about potential collisions.

In our interview, exhibition curator Anna Briers described curating *Don't Be Evil* around a distinct "architectural gesture" that expanded the concepts explored in Denny's works. She described subverting the usual ways that viewers moved around the museum, by inviting audiences to climb upstairs and experience the top floor first, ascending "up into the cloud." Works on the top floor were grouped around online social relations and digital intimacies, including two new commissions by Australian artists. Xanthe Dobbie's *Cloud Copy* [2020, Figure 1] was a virtual reality piece that stitched together fragments of internet content, engulfing the viewer in a claustrophobic world of corporate logos and pornography. Kate Geck's *rlx:tech — defrag popup* (2021) offered ironic mediations and 'psychic cleansings' downloadable to the viewer's smartphone. These works celebrated the ephemeral pleasures and illusions of internet cultures.

From the top floor, viewers could turn and look down, over the balcony, onto works that explored 'underbelly' of the data economy. Denny's works were at the centre of this distinct architectural sightline, next to works by Forensic Architecture and Kate Crawford and Vladan Joler. Audiences could look down onto a newly commissioned version of Denny's *Extractor* (2021), which appropriates the visual language of an Australian board game based on sheep farming and applies it to mineral mining [Figure 3]. This game was activated by the cultural mediators

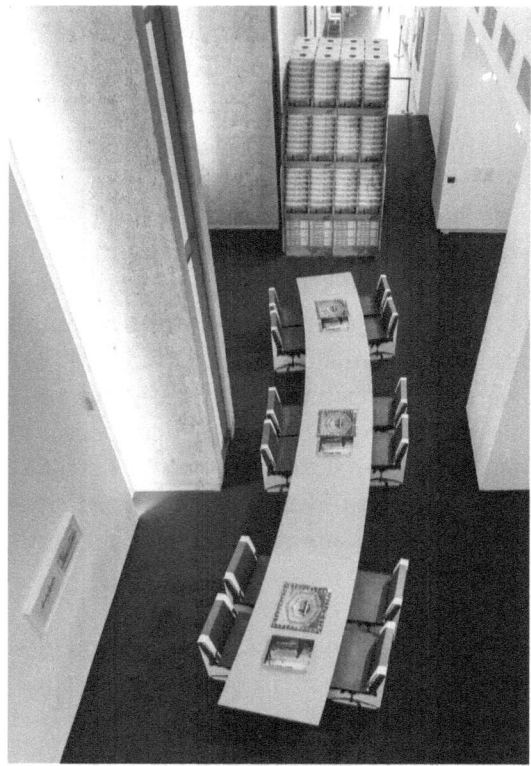

Figure 3: Simon Denny's *Federal Court of Australia courtroom chair replica, Federal Court of Australia courtroom table replica*, (2021) and *Extractor* (2019) as viewed from the top floor of UQ Art Museum. Courtesy of the artist. Photo: Louis Lim.

who led regular 'extractor tournaments' in the gallery. These informal events invited audiences to play the game and become the ultimate data capitalist. These works collectively explored the underside of the cloud, the materialities of mineral mining and buried e-waste, creating a physical and gestural underground in the exhibition.

I began to connect my workshop with the cultural mediators and their references to mining to the figure of the underground as it recurred across the works and the curation of the exhibition, deepening my affective and embodied experience. Installed near Denny's works, Kate Crawford and Vladan Joler's *Anatomy of An AI System: The Amazon Echo as an Anatomical Map of Human Labour, Data and Planetary Resources*, (2018) is an exploded diagram and corresponding essay in 21 parts. Like Denny's "layered collage," this work explores cycles of

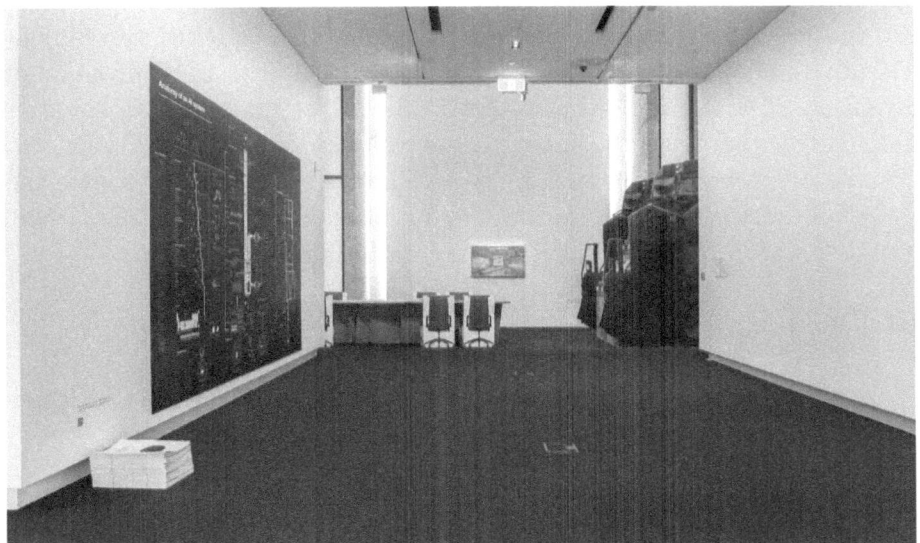

Figure 4: Simon Denny, *Rio Tinto fully autonomous haulage train Autohaul — Retrofitted General Electric Transportation ES44DCI Extractor pop display*, (2019) positioned next to Kate Crawford and Vladan Joler's *Anatomy of An AI System: The Amazon Echo as an Anatomical Map of Human Labour, Data and Planetary Resources*, (2018). Autohaul is partially visible, as if coming around the corner. Courtesy of the artist. Photo: Louis Lim.

mineral extraction, by charting the life cycle of the Amazon Echo, a smart speaker that uses AI to monitor all speech and respond to a series of commands. A black and white wall vinyl charts the production of this consumer device, from mining raw material from the ground to obsolescence and disposal; whereby the materials are incinerated or recycled and eventually return to the earth's crust. This is accompanied by a printed booklet of Crawford and Joler's widely read text of the same name that tracks extractive processes that are required to run a large-scale artificial intelligence systems.

Crawford and Joler cite Jussi Parikka's book *A Geology of Media* (2015) to frame the importance of the geophysical within the political economy and cultural impact of media. Parikka pushes past traditional ideas about media as material devices toward "the idea of the earth, light, air and time as media" (Parikka 2015, 3). Parikka points toward geophysical cycles that link, for example, laptop batteries to lithium extracted from the earth, and the workers who undertake this extraction, and to the waste produced when such technological products are discarded or become obsolete. Artworks are woven as case studies throughout Parikka's book on the basis that art speaks to the underground, or avant-garde of human cultures. For Parikka, the underground conjures mine sites where repetitious, exploitative work is conducted. It is also central to technological imaginaries of modernity, where resource extraction links to the progression of capital, and conjures visions of hell, the smell of sulphur, and postapocalyptic scenarios.

Memory

The underground connects theory and practice in the exhibition, where it emerges conceptually within several of the works, but is also developed spatially by Brier's "architectural gesture". It was my embodied experience of one of Denny's works; *Rio Tinto fully autonomous haulage train Autohaul Retrofitted General Electric Transportation ES44DCI Extractor pop display*, (2019) that became most significant in my understanding of the underground and mining as ethical propositions in the exhibition. The work features a cardboard sculpture that depicts the Autohaul train at a hard two-point perspective. Bulky and boxy, this train is a far cry from the sleek, curved shape of urban trains. Its grey-green colours are military industrial, recalling dystopian war games. Facing into the centre of the ground floor, it appeared from certain angles as if the Autohaul was screeching around the corner of the gallery, toward the body of the viewer [Figure 4]. The work also features a fake promotional video for Rio Tinto (made by Denny) advertising Autohaul's autonomy and agency as a self-driving vehicle. Imagery of driverless trains hurtling through the desert recall ethical anxieties about the train's inability to stop if on course for collision.

For Kontturi, the material-relational emergence of art immerses viewer-participants into acts of affective remembering. Offering the potential to arouse visceral sensations such as body shivers or goosebumps, art has the capacity to connect directly with the viewers body, and to awaken in that body, its forgotten potentialities, memories, stories and feelings that are not otherwise accessible in everyday experience. This remembering is not just a passive act, rather it creates affects that are "born, made alive, actualised in the encounter with art" (Kontturi 2018, 140). Memories are actively remade as part of a productive encounter.

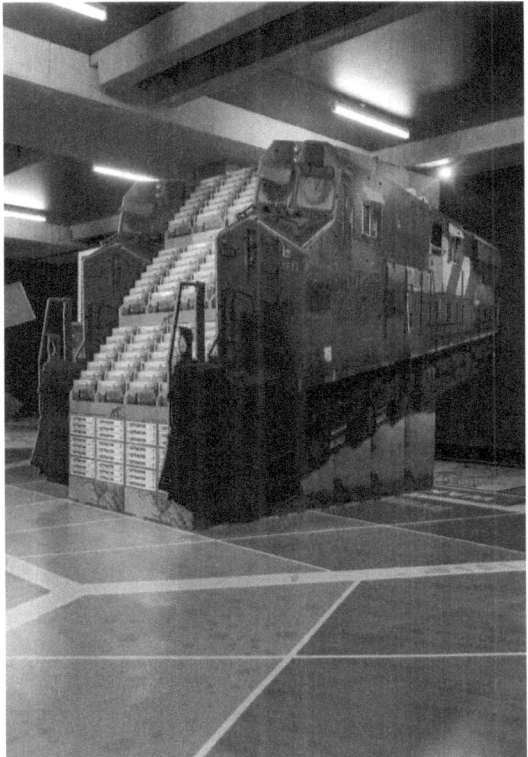

Figure 5: *Rio Tinto fully autonomous haulage train Autohaul — Retrofitted General Electric Transportation ES44DCI Extractor pop display*, (2019).

I experienced my engagement with Denny's works and the underground of the *Don't Be Evil* exhibition as an act of productive remembering. This engagement connected my own memories of inner-city trams and motorways populated with heavy goods lorries, to the cultural mediator's massive mining truck and Denny's images of Autohaul hurting through the Australian desert. Joining three perspectives: my own, the cultural mediator's and the work itself, allows me not just to read an ethical argument made by the artist, but to engage in acts of embodied and affective remembering that are situated and informed by the exhibition's considered curation and its communities of practice. Four connected positions; my own, the cultural mediators', the artist's and the curator's, all appear to hold ethical anxieties about the gigantic infrastructures of industrial mining and the vulnerabilities of human bodies in their wake. They reflect disquiet about the effects of rapid technological expansion on landscapes, bodies and ecosystems.

Briers "architectural sightline" and her curation of an underground in the exhibition reflects her own sense of the "material, affective and relational doings" (Konturri 2018, 10) of art and how these can be enhanced, translated and communicated through the craft of exhibition-making. During our interview Briers commented that Denny's critique of mining is "much more sharp edged in the Queensland context," due to the state's complex entanglement with minerals underpinning the digital economy. As such, UQ Art Museum undertook significant risk analysis before showing these works. While critique is essential to the ethics of Denny's practice, I suggest that the work's physical and material properties, its "thingly" qualities (Konturri 2018, 54) cannot be separated from its ethical agency. The materiality of the work and its spatial placement help to generate the cultural mediators mining truck. This in turn connects to my own lived experiences, memories and embodied ethical sensibility.

Denny has framed this cluster of works as a project about connecting the digital and the physical. He intends to make data extraction practices that feel ephemeral physically tangible, by linking them to material resources (Petzel Gallery 2021). Analysing this work in the context of *Don't Be Evil's* curation extends this practice of making tangible beyond representation, toward bodies in space. For Kontturi (2018, 197), "Ethics is not about evaluating the arguments art offers; rather it is about valuing art's process of emergence, its material relational becoming." Where art seeks to produce ethical configurations, these need not always put interpretation or critical analysis at the centre, but could activate forms of embodiment.

Through *following 'Don't Be Evil' in the making*, mining emerges as an alternative social and material imaginary that connects the exhibition to ethical anxieties felt locally and globally. As Alisa Maksimova argues, contesting and complexifying dominant AI imaginaries — collectively held visions and illusions of AI futures — is one of the challenges facing curators who wish to support greater AI literacy among audiences (Maksimova 2024). Dominant imaginaries such as the attribution of human qualities to AI (Sartori and Bocca 2023) are evident in the artworld's early engagement with the medium (Droitcour 2024). Yet this chapter is not an argument for *following* as a fixed methodological template to reverse these tendencies — dominant AI imaginaries will continue to circulate in mainstream culture. My *way of following* is intended as a provocation to other researchers to foreground affects, relationships and communities, generating other new possibilities for nuanced imaginaries and decentred ethical practices that should be celebrated within AI practices in museums and galleries.

Conclusion

Curators intending to demystify AI and increase technological literacy must counter stereotypes, while producing exhibitions that support levels of public engagement demanded by the modern museum. Prioritising intimacy and relationships in the writing and curation of exhibitions offers one way to shift the emphasis, but how might such intimacies meet with the demands of mass museum engagement? Foregrounding UQ Art Museum's cultural mediators offers one small potential in this direction, by reframing an emerging and under-explored aspect of the museum public interface. How the lived experiences of cultural mediators shape what museums communicate to publics poses a compelling topic for future research. So too does the need to devise approaches that centre cultural mediators as active producers of new knowledge of equal status to other cultural workers. The research presented here is partial and situated, due to my focus on one aspect of a single workshop, where I use the mining truck to develop my creative and embodied relation with the exhibition. This is intended as an act of research creation, which follows a "fluid creative process" that weaves together "theoretical, technical, and creative aspects ... always making space for discovery" (Cutler 2020, 3). Engaging a cohort of cultural mediators in a long-term collaborative research creation process around a specific exhibition could be a compelling way to extend this chapter's emphasis on *following exhibitions in the making*. This could use creative methods to reveal how knowledge is co-produced, offering an alternative to more formal qualitative research approaches often applied in museum studies.

Acknowledgements

Thank you to UQ Art Museum for their generous facilitation of my access to the Don't Be Evil exhibition, particularly Danielle Harvey and Anna Briers. Thanks to UQ Art Museum cultural mediators, who were so generous with their ideas.

References

Amoore, Louise. 2020. *Cloud Ethics*. Duke University Press. https://doi.org/10.1215/9781478009276
Bartlett, Vanessa. 2020. "Psychosocial Curating: A Theory and Practice of Exhibition-Making at the Intersection between Health and Aesthetics." *Medical Humanities* 46 (4): 417–30. https://doi.org/10.1136/medhum-2019-011694.
Barois de Caevel, Eva. 2020. "THE OFFERED HAND. ON MEDIATION AND POWER." In *4Cs HANDBOOK - Reflections and Actions Upon Mediation Practices*, edited by Luisa Santos and Maria Eduarda Duarte. 4CS LISBON. https://www.4cs-conflict-conviviality.eu/post/4cs-handbook-reflections-and-actions-upon-mediation-practices.
Barone, Tom, and Elliot W. Eisner. 2012. *Arts Based Research*. Sage. https://dx.doi.org/10.4135/9781412963909
Bennett, Jane. 2010. *Vibrant Matter*. Duke University Press. DOI: https://doi.org/10.1215/9780822391623
Bjerregaard, Peter. 2019. *Exhibitions as Research: Experimental Methods in Museums*. Routledge. 10.1016/j.emospa.2014.05.002
Bolt, Barbara. 2004. *Art Beyond Representation: The Performative Power of the Image*. I. B. Taurus.
Bridle, James. 2019. *New Dark Age: Technology and the End of the Future*. Verso.
Briers, Anna, Nicholas Carah, and Holly Arden, eds. 2022. *Conflict In My Outlook*. Perimeter Editions.
Cutler, Randy Lee. 2020. "Open and Wide: Figuring Digestion as Research Creation." In *Knots and Knowings: Methodologies and Ecologies in Research-Creation*, edited by Natalie Loveless. University of Alberta Press.
Crawford, Kate, and Vladan Joler *Anatomy of an AI System, The Amazon Echo as an Anatomical Map of Human Labour, Data and Planetary Resources*, 2018 digital image file dimensions variable. Courtesy of the artists.
Danckert, Sarah. 2020. "High Stakes Rio Tinto-ASIC Trial Delayed on COVID-19 Concerns." *The Sydney Morning Herald*, December 6, 2020. https://www.smh.com.au/business/companies/high-stakes-rio-tinto-asic-trial-delayed-on-covid-19-concerns-20201204-p56kod.html.
Denson, Shane. 2023. "From Sublime Awe to Abject Cringe: On the Embodied Processing of AI Art." *Journal of Visual Culture* 22 (2): 146–75. https://doi.org/10.1177/14704129231194136.
Denny, Simon, Extractor, 2019, Commercially produced board game including critical essay and ruleset booklet: custom injection moulded plastic pieces, offset print on various paper and card stock, vacuum formed packaging components. Commissioned for Simon Denny MINE (8 June 2019 –17 March 2020) by the Museum of Old and New Art (Mona), Hobart, Australia
Denny, Simon, 2019, *Rio Tinto fully autonomous haulage train Autohaul — Retrofitted General Electric Transportation ES44DCI Extractor pop display*, UV print on honeycomb cardboard, Extractor boardgames dimensions variable Courtesy of the artist and Galerie Bucholz Berlin/Köln/New York.
Denny, Simon, 2021, *Federal Court of Australia courtroom chair replica, Federal Court of Australia courtroom table replica*, digitally cut BC twin cushion corrugated cardboard, polyvinyl acetate glue, hook and loop strip tape dimensions variable Courtesy of the artist and Fine Arts Gallery, Sydney.

Dobbie, Xanthe, *Cloud Copy*, VR Oculus Headsets, chairs, MP4, video, colour, sound, VR aspect 360. 4.48 minutes

Droitcour, Brian. 2024. "The Year in Review: Museums Are Leaving AI Hype Behind | Frieze." *Frieze*, December 10, 2024. https://www.frieze.com/article/year-review-ai-art-2024.

Fournier, Lauren. 2021. *Autotheory As Feminist Practice in Art, Writing, and Criticism*. The MIT Press.

Geck, Kate, *rlx:tech — defrag popup*, 2021, augmented reality wall graphic, custom app, PVC yoga mats, website, duration variable

Guerrisi, Michela Addis, Isabella de Stefano, Valeria, eds. 2023. *Cultural Mediation for Museums: Driving Audience Engagement*. Routledge. https://doi.org/10.4324/9781003352754.

Gordon, Sharon and Simon Denny, *Speculative accountability trial courtroom sketch: Federal Court of Australia Australian Securities and Investments Commission v Rio Tinto Limited [2020] FCA 1721*, 2021 watercolour on paper 97 x 40 cm Courtesy of the artist and Galerie Bucholz Berlin/Köln/New York.

Ivanova, Galina. 2014. "The Mining Industry in Queensland, Australia: Some Regional Development Issues." *Resources Policy* 39 (March): 101–14. 10.1016/j.resourpol.2014.01.005

Kelley, Lindsay. 2022. "Everyday Militarisms in the Kitchen: Baking Strange with Anzac Biscuits." In *Food in Memory and Imagination: Space, Place, and Taste*, edited by Beth M. Forrest and Greg de St. Maurice, 1st ed. Bloomsbury.

Kontturi, Katve-Kaisa. 2018. *Ways of Following: Art, Materiality, Collaboration*. Open Humanities Press.

Lovink, Geert. 2020. "The Anatomy of Zoom Fatigue." *Eurozine*, November 2, 2020.

Lujani, Florencia. 2019. "Exhibition Review 'AI: More than Human' … Is It Though? | LinkedIn." *Review*. Linkedin. https://www.linkedin.com/pulse/exhibition-review-ai-more-than-human-though-florencia-lujani/.

Macdonald, Sharon, and Paul Basu. 2007. *Exhibition Experiments*. Blackwell.

Maksimova, Alisa. 2024. "Negotiation of Dominant AI Narratives in Museum Exhibitions." *AI & SOCIETY*, December 2024.

Mason, Catherine. 2019. "AI: More than Human." *Studio International*. Accessed March 11, 2025.

NSW Museums and Galleries. 2019. "About Cultural Mediation - MGNSW." September 17, 2019. https://mgnsw.org.au/sector/programs/cultural-mediation/cultural-mediation/,

Parikka, Jussi. 2015. *A Geology of Media*. University of Minnesota Press.

Petzel Gallery, dir. 2021. *Simon Denny — "Mine."* YouTube Video. New York. https://www.youtube.com/watch?v=JnyBBd7cppc.

Povinelli, Elizabeth A. 2016. "Can Rocks Die?: Life and Death Inside the Carbon Imaginary." In *Geontologies: A Requiem to Late Liberalism*. Duke University Press.

Sartori, Laura, and Giulia Bocca. 2023. "Minding the Gap(s): Public Perceptions of AI and Socio-Technical Imaginaries." *AI & SOCIETY* 38 (2): 443–58. https://doi.org/10.1007/s00146-022-01422-1.

Selvey, Linda A., Morris Carpenter, Mattea Lazarou, and Katherine Cullerton. 2022. "Communicating about Energy Policy in a Resource-Rich Jurisdiction during the Climate Crisis: Lessons from the People of Brisbane, Queensland, Australia." *International Journal of Environmental Research and Public Health* 19 (8): 4635. 10.3390/ijerph19084635.

Thiel, Sonja, and Johannes C. Bernhardt, eds. 2023. *AI in Museums: Reflections, Perspectives and Applications*. 1st ed. Transcript Verlag. https://doi.org/10.14361/9783839467107.

The Dead Pixels. 2019. "AI: More Than Human- Exhibition Review."

Dead Pixels, July 8, 2019. http://thedeadpixels.squarespace.com/articles/ai-more-than-human-exhibition-review.

Tranter, Bruce, and Kerry Foxwell-Norton. 2021. "Only in Queensland? Coal Mines and Voting in the 2019 Australian Federal Election." *Environmental Sociology* 7 (1): 90–101. https://doi.org/10.1080/23251042.2020.1810376.

Collective Conversations Toward AI Art and Climate Change: Crafting FutureFantastic, Bangalore

Vanessa Bartlett in conversation with Kamya Ramachandran

Kamya Ramachandran is the Founder-Director of *BeFantastic* which conceptualises and manifests Bangalore's TechArt Festival series, most recently *FutureFantastic*.

FutureFantastic (2023) was a festival that brought together artists working across different forms, disciplines and locations from the Global North to the Global South to explore and interrogate the role of art and technology in the context of social and environmental challenges. FutureFantastic was an attempt to interrogate whether AI and art can come together to help us pay attention, extend care and imagine a world where the mindful use of technology can bring about a radically open, environmentally equitable and optimistic future. Bangalore tops global city lists as the biggest technology producer in the world, and is famed as the tech capital of India.

* * *

Vanessa Bartlett (VB): To get us started, can you tell us a bit about FutureFantastic in your own words, and outline how you used AI and computation in the festival?

Kamya Ramachandran (KR): We conceptualised FutureFantastic as An AI Art Festival for Climate Change, which convened a diverse set of 'fellows': artists, researchers, curators and creative technology practitioners from more than nine countries. This was an effort spearheaded by us at BeFantastic in Bengaluru, in collaboration with Manchester based cultural organisation FutureEverything. The festival itself was the culmination of a year-long fellowship program that commissioned collaborative groups of fellows to understand, explore and experiment with AI technologies with guidance of mentors. Through our dialog program we also had speakers who brought in some critical perspectives from the domain of AI and climate change.

The festival presented a mix of AI and machine learning enabled artworks and performances that were the result of collaboration and creative production between global practitioners. It had panels and workshops led by experts in tech, art, and sustainability, as well as artist talks and a film festival, over two weekends and three venues in Bangalore.

At BeFantastic we have been at the helm of art and technology for close to a decade now. We've had a history of having artists play, experiment, and have fun with technologies. I think what is most interesting for us in that process is the interactive nature of the technologies we are exploring. We started using AI because we were developing our programme for a COVID-19 pivot and there was some buzz and curiosity around AI. AI tools became the easiest thing for us to pivot to, where we could give our Fellows access to online tools to experiment with like GPT2 and 3 before Chat GPT hit the public domain. On the other hand, within our founding mandate we had made a commitment to imagine a positive future, and used The United Nations Sustainable Development Goals as a framework to do so.

In preparation toward a curatorial theme, we carried out a bunch of roundtable conversations with people from diverse backgrounds in Bangalore. Climate change emerged as an interesting fulcrum for both international collaborations as well as the challenges of this fast-growing

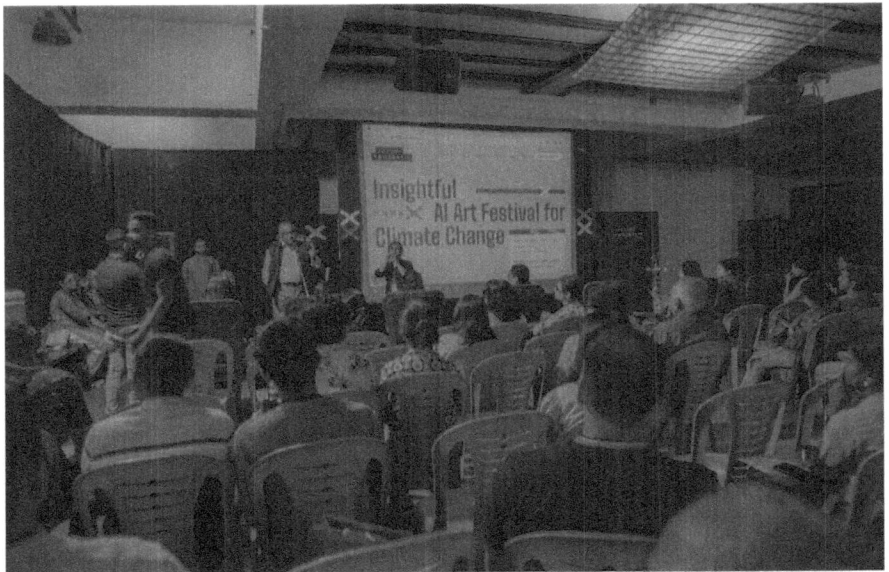

Figure 1: *FutureFantastic* 2023 — convening, conversing and collectivising. Photo Credit: Falana Films.

city itself. For FutureFantastic, we chose to focus on Goal 13: Take urgent action to combat climate change and its impacts.

We went with this premise that technology enabled art helps audiences engage with the idea of climate change in a deeper way. Be it because of its immersive or interactive nature, or a different way of engaging with the medium, and that's how and why we came to pair AI and machine learning with climate change. But I think in a weird way, we pitted AI with climate a little bit naively. Although having done that, it enabled us to open up the problematic nuances within it.

> **VB:** And when you talk about the collaborations that you were fostering, would you use the word interdisciplinary? Or would you just use the word collaboration?

KR: We use the word interdisciplinary because our open call sought artists, technologists, creative technologists, and researchers. We did have that motley crew of artists that were deep into practice but didn't really know too much about climate change or technology. We had creative technologists who didn't know enough about climate change but were happy to engage. So, we did have people with core skills in a certain discipline, who understood the mandate of the programme that was trying to bring everybody together. The open call sought diverse disciplines coming together. That was very important to the programme.

Collaboration was also an important keyword, be it among organising partners, or the fact that our programs awarded commissions and mentorship to group proposals, with at least three members from the program. Our 2021 Fellowship titled BeFantastic Together was in collaboration with ThoughtWorks Arts, a global technology research lab, so we were able to get technologists into the zoom room as well. Similarly, in the 2022 Fellowships — BeFantastic Within and BeFantastic Beyond — we collaborated with FutureEverything, Manchester, UK. We supported seven artworks to aid its development with monetary awards and with mentorship as well.

> **VB:** I was interested to hear you use the word naive related to your starting point and what your process was, because I think there's something about that willingness to admit to being naive or to not knowing, or to be willing to admit to being inexperienced, that is really important for interdisciplinary collaboration. The idea of being comfortable with not knowing, not understanding, not having answers to the questions.
>
> One of the things that artists do very well is they take their artistic expertise and they point it towards other disciplines or problems. By necessity, they are often coming to problems that they have no prior experience of and discovering something new. One of the key themes of the decentred approach to ethics that we are exploring across this book is that art brings us closer to questions that are unfolding and in process rather than seeking definitive answers. I think that's crucial to artistic practice, and it sounds crucial to your collective programme design.

KR: Yes! I think this is also crucial to a practice that is trying to work with technologies. Because technology is constantly emerging and new, and a bit unknown. While it might seem like new technology hitting the public domain is well thought through, oftentimes it's not. For a constantly emerging, nascent space like art and tech encounters, that idea of not knowing, that humility, is really important to the game. I think that's why we structured the festival around the programme of fellowships. This gives the anxieties and confusions space to be vocalised or articulated within and shared and figured out together. So that kind of coming-together within the fellowship of 25 people with layers of mentors and speakers, the artists and the technologists coming together prompted this feeling of 'we can do this, we can figure this out together'. Interestingly, not all the mentors we brought into the programme were from the world of art and technology. While some have a deeper engagement with the subject, some others were only two or three years ahead of the other fellows we assembled in terms of understanding a new technology. Using your words, our program is therefore almost decentring hierarchies as well, and is an interesting space to inhabit, where mentors are offering their experiences but also learning a lot from the group of Fellows

> **VB:** In framing our approach to decentred ethics, we started using the word collective rather than interdisciplinary because — in a university context at least — the word interdisciplinary implies certain kinds of hierarchies. Because an artwork has less value than output from other disciplines such as a journal article or book chapter. So we've started thinking about collectivism as another way of framing interdisciplinarity without hierarchy between different disciplines. And, of course, artists have always formed collectives.

KR: In the space that we create within our programmes, everybody gets a chance to showcase their work, their practice, their ideologies, where they're coming from, where they'd like to go to — whether you're an expert or one of the fellows within the room. Fellows are artists, creative technologists and researchers who have been accepted by our program. They make art together. So there's that kind of equal sharing opportunity. Because we work in new and emerging technological domains, we work with an exploratory optimism layered with some criticality. You need to be a little unafraid and enthusiastic to explore. But then through hands-on doing, the collaborators can understand and articulate critical perspectives on their process of using and understanding these new technologies too. I would even say it is thus not armchair critique based on hearsay, but something that comes out of deeper understanding from doing and learning.

Going back to the idea of collective in relation to the festival; bringing audiences together is the reason that a festival exists. While for the promotion of the festival we called it 'India's first AI art festival,' it was intended to mark an important historical moment after AI became a buzzword with the unleashing of widely available platforms like ChatGPT and Midjourney. The festival itself became a space where these discussions around ethics continued. Artworks became that easy foot in the door for new audiences to begin to understand the nuances of cultural bias, the invisible labour of making datasets, ideas around digital representation or the lack of it, for example. So, when you have an artwork that very clearly indicates to you what cultural bias could look like visually, or another one that attempts to make visible the painstaking labour of data and content creation, with a set of audiences experimenting and figuring it out together, there is a sense of collectivising around a subject of anxiety, confusion and even possibility.

VB: I just wanted to get a little bit more of a practical understanding of how the festival was put together. It sounds like you had a series of fellowships that brought together artists, technologists and climate experts. I get the sense that those conversations sort of percolated into the festival programming, particularly maybe in the format of some of the workshops that were available to the public. So it's like it extends the dialogue out then to that final layer, which is the public audience.

KR: The fellowships commissioned pieces of artwork. So we were trying to create groups of collaborators of three or more people, ideally from different geographies and different disciplines.

Through our initial knowledge sharing spaces, fellows got to understand who was in the virtual room and who they could potentially collaborate with. With grants from the British Council, the Goethe-Institut, and the Swiss Arts Council Pro Helvetia, we were able to commission pieces of work by collaborating groups, with mentors to guide the process. Then a jury comprising the organising partners and the mentors selected the proposals that would be awarded a kitty of money toward its development. Eight pieces of work that were developed through this mentored process became the core of our festival curation. In addition, each of the mentors contributed a piece of work to the festival. So, we had about 10 or 12 pieces of core works by fellows and mentors, and then we curated around that to get about 8 more pieces from different parts of the world making the festival host a total of 22 artworks. Since we had the mentors and the fellows present at the festival, we had artist sharings and curated walks, workshops and panel discussions, artworks, installations and performances along with a film festival that rounded up the experience of the festival.

We didn't expect AI to become such a fulcrum of the conversation. Because when we started things in 2020 and through COVID-19, the buzz around AI wasn't as loud. Then you had these critical moments of AI hitting the public domain stirring public curiosity and anxiety. So, in March of 2023, when our festival came along, over the climate change mandate, AI became the focus

To hold all that public curiosity and anxiety within a space like a festival, we had programming in the form of panel discussions where panelists talked to the varied nuances around the subject, and workshops that could create a space for that anxiety to be unpacked.

> **VB:** I think one of the ways that artists and curators help the public engage with AI ethics is by creating spaces for the anxiety that is produced by complex technological problems that need to be processed and digested. This is something I have explored in my own curatorial practice, and it seems to be one of the successes of the festival. I wanted to ask a bit more about how you balance inconsistencies and tensions through your programming. For example, you described Future Fantastic as an AI and Arts festival that highlights the power that collaborative creative production has in amplifying a global response to the shared climate emergency. However, your programming shows an awareness of some of the contradictions implied in this approach. For example, in the panel discussion AI Art — A Marriage of Heaven and Hell? (Jaaga Media 2023) you highlight the strange irony that comes with using very energy intensive technologies such as AI to communicate the climate emergency. How did you try to navigate these ethical tensions in your festival programming?

KR: As a festival organiser, we felt it was our responsibility to continue to bring multiple viewpoints, so we didn't necessarily take a stand on optimism or pessimism around AI, but it was important for the conversation to have enough nuances from these different viewpoints. For example, we approached Padmini Ray Murray from Design Beku to curate the panel AI Art — A Marriage of Heaven and Hell? (Jaaga Media 2023) and lead its discussion. Similarly, another panel discussion titled Talking Back: A Conversation on Generative AI for the 21st Century curated by Digital Futures Lab (2023), examined the societal implications of accepting technological fates as is, without question. I think that decentring the curation of many of these pertinent topics, to link to the title of your book, really helps, where each panel had a curator who then went on and pulled in their networks to bring into this festival.

It was important for us to present different viewpoints within the festival and allow for people to leave knowing that there's a lot to think about. I think in India today there are not enough spaces like this. You hear the highly optimistic industry-based voices on technology. You do hear the critics of technology as well, but I don't think India has a facilitated and curated space for encounters between the two sides. The two sides of the debate don't come together often enough, although they are growing louder in their own echo chambers. Where is that safe space for them to meet each other? Art practice just brings these worlds together in a different way, where they can begin to hear each other.

> **VB:** Within our conception of AI art as a method, we have been thinking about artistic practice as a way of holding ambiguity and complexity in a way that is a little bit more difficult for other fields or disciplines. I think maybe this connects back to this idea of artists being very good at naivety or non-expert positions. It's not about being right or wrong, it's just about expressing the contradictions. I think what you're saying is something quite important about the fact that we don't necessarily expect art to produce solutions. Or clear answers. Sometimes those agendas get projected onto art through the need to fundraise and market art or festivals, or indeed in academic contexts where art is framed as research. But I think culturally and socially, we often look for art to be a space of ambiguity.

KR: And an important one in growing fields. Within the festival, there was a lot of learning that happened even for us as festival organisers or programme designers. For example, in the last iteration we were talking about climate change, but we did not have enough representation of vulnerable communities that could tell their own stories. In our upcoming programme we hope to have artists, technologists and researchers, but we are also trying to experiment with themes related to access to technology within the Indian substrate. In India, technology seems to have percolated into really small villages. People in far off rural areas have access to technology, particularly the Internet and cheap data on mobile devices. It might not be reliable, but it is available. So how do we leverage this possibility to involve communities within our programmes, and what does it change? What happens when a member of a community can work with an artist to tell their story or influence the direction of storytelling? I feel like it's kind of a continuum. One learns from experiences that are incorporated into the next program. And hopefully by early 2026, when we are keen to host the next festival, we will have a programme that is talking about art and technology and climate and society in a more nuanced manner.

VB: I'm interested in those rural communities that technology is beginning to reach. I would imagine some of those communities are also particularly vulnerable to the impacts of climate change in terms of flooding and fires. Is that something you're considering in terms of geographical and community vulnerabilities within India to the effects of climate change?

KR: So, this goes back to partnerships and programming. We develop an idea and then try to locate this idea within fields and substrates. We seek out partners by constantly talking to people. And, so, it's been almost a year of partnership building. It has taken a long time!

We do have partners now who are willing to take us to Ladakh in the Himalayas and the coastal region of Goa and to complete this geographical picture, our home in the tablelands of urban Bengaluru. We needed partners who are deep enough into the context and represent the communities authentically enough, but then also have the wherewithal to support a programme like ours. It does whittle down to very few potential partners one can work with. But it's a start. I think all these are growing spaces and this is just the start of that larger vision.

VB: I think one of the things that seems very important for decentring ethics, is that it takes a long time to work in a decentred way. In that sense, your ambition to work with remote communities seems to be following a decentred approach that is slow paced and relational and takes a lot of patience and commitment.

Related to this, you've described FutureFantastic as the first AI and Arts festival in India, but I would love to understand a little bit more about the public conversation about AI technologies in India and specifically about AI ethics. I came across the Digital India Act (Ponomarov 2024) which is a proposed law focusing on the regulation of perceived high risk AI technologies. It aims to increase digital literacy and hold platforms accountable for content violations. In this context, what's your understanding of the public perception of AI ethics in Bangalore and India more broadly?

KR: I don't know if it's the echo chamber I've situated myself in where I can hear the idea of AI ethics India quite loudly. But I can hear it. I'm not going to be able to answer the public perception part of it. Because I still feel like AI is being driven quite largely by industry, which is extremely loud in its optimism about AI. And I think the public's perception is still driven by those louder industry voices.

VB: It seems that there are some government efforts to introduce a kind of digital regulation?

KR: Yes, I think definitely the government is aware of the value this can offer to the Indian public and some focus on the ethics of AI. In general, there is a lot of AI optimism, but there is also regulation in development, but outpaced by the rapidity of technological advancement for sure. The government has invested quite deeply in building voice-based data streams. In India, we have 26 official languages and roughly 150 dialects, with low literacy rates, so the country is beginning to look to things like AI that can harness large volumes of data to be useful to diverse publics. The government recognises this both from an opportunity as well as from a regulation perspective.

And you also have private organisations who are trying to drive the trajectory of this space. There is an organisation called Karya.ai that is beginning to leverage voice samples contributed by large populations of society that can do it with their mobile. But the interesting part is that they have mandated the idea of consent as well as attribution to track whose voice sample it is, building models where royalties can go back to the original contributor of these voice samples. So, I think there is definitely an understanding of ethics and also a shift in how both private and public players are operating with these large amounts of data that's getting collected, so it doesn't get subsumed.

VB: In my own work as a curator, I often find that exhibition visitors bring a mixture of optimism and anxiety to exhibitions and public events related to emerging technologies. I often see curators and artists work with these opposing imaginaries in generative ways. But I get the impression that literacy and learning are an important part of your approach, and your ethics. Do you think encouraging greater technological literacy is an important part of a curator's work? And what kinds of curatorial approaches or formats have worked well for you in achieving this?

KR: I think within our programme itself it is technological literacy that we are offering to the artists. We bring in the right kinds of partners who can help support increased literacy. While we had within our programming an exposure to GPT 3, the precursor to ChatGPT, and also text to image tools, we also had a three-week course that helped artists understand how these things were built — the magic behind the curtains if you may, on how AI and machine learning technology works.

Within the Indian context, the idea of digital access has become more pervasive and technology is being presented as a solution to move us from third world to first, with the promise of digital inclusion bringing about growth and even poverty alleviation. So while we might unpack digital literacy within our programs, we are mere drop in the ocean. There's no way we, as a small cultural organisation, can make enough impact on the idea of digital literacy. Within the festival space, however, we showcased artworks, crafted spaces within workshops and dialogs, for us to stop and think about technology and how it's being used.

VB: And do you think literacy is important for digital ethics?

KR: Literacy is absolutely important to begin to understand ethics, because once you've opened up and understood this idea of understanding digitality more than just using it quickly as a tool, then you can begin to be more critical from having had authentic experiences with the technology. That is literacy and that then brings you the nuances of ethical issues that drive this as a conversation. So yes, in principle I do think that digital literacy is the need of the hour.

At the same time, digital optimism is percolating in India, but digital criticality is not percolating enough. For example, older people are getting hold of mobile phones with access to financial instruments within them. The number of scams that are manifesting where people steal money from those with lower digital literacy is on a steep rise. So even beginning to become literate on things like deep fakes is so important. AI is causing unbelievable imbalances and ethical issues in society, and we don't have enough literacy around that.

VB: One of the new commissions for FutureFantastic was called *Wood Wide Web* (2023) by Kanchan Joneja and Kristina Pulejkova [Figure 2]. This work is described as bringing forests to life. It depicts ancient and endangered trees of India sharing their stories and tales of survival through skeletal tracking and AI magic. In preparing this book, one of the things that we've been discussing is the various ways that AI is being used in contemporary art practices to represent the more-than-human. In chapter seven Helen Knowles uses AI to imagine the psychedelic entities that people encounter when they take psychedelic medicines. And in chapter 17 Nora Al Badri discusses her use of AI to animate museum objects. Could you tell me a bit more about the way that the Wood Wide Web work used AI to make these trees lively, so to speak? And what did you and the team hope to achieve by attributing human qualities to trees?

KR: It was an interactive piece where audiences were invited to sway their hands and wake up what the artists had rendered as treelike sleeping giants. They were trying to visually articulate the idea of biodiversity loss and with it the lost wisdom. The UK based collaborators did their research at Kew Gardens in London, while the Indian artists worked with an organisation called Farmers for Forests. The data was used to craft an anthropomorphised narrative that the trees espoused as they awoke, mimicking the audience's movement. I also believe that there was a visual rendering of tree bark as the tree moved, based on an image database of bark textures. As the trees moved and morphed so did its rendering. So those are two ways in which AI was explored within this artwork. It was

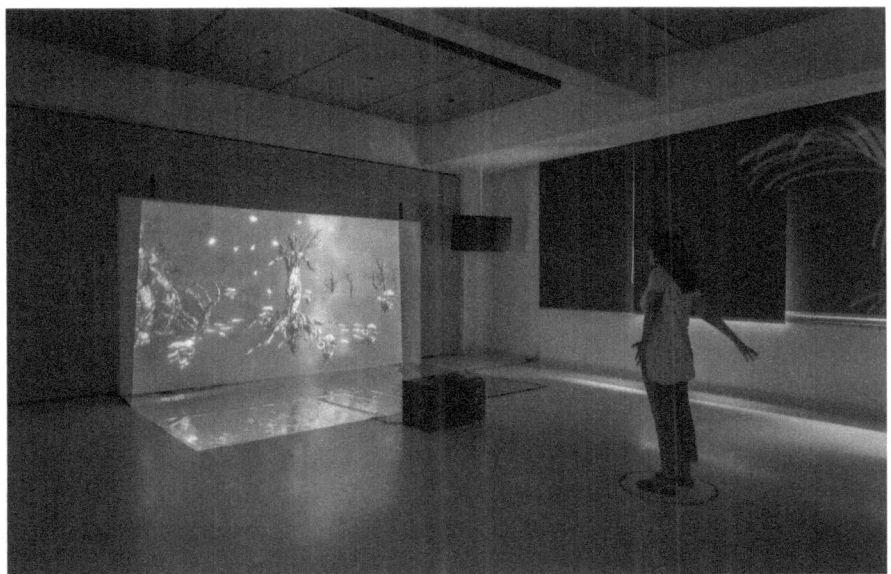

Figure 2: Kanchan Joneja (IN) and Kristina Pulejkova, 2023. *Wood Wide Web*. Photo Credit: Falana Films.

quite the favourite piece because of the simplicity of its interaction and its mesmerising visual appeal. It was almost otherworldly, dream-like, the way it was rendered.

> **VB:** So, I'm just really curious about this device, which I think is being used a lot in contemporary art practices where an AI is used to animate something. An object or an entity that we are not used to seeing animated in that way. I think you mentioned the word anthropomorphising, attributing human qualities to an object using AI. From your experience of this work, how do you see that device being useful in helping people to connect with some of the questions that you're asking through the festival?

KR: I think it makes for a really compelling case to go across age groups and levels of understanding of climate research. So that visually rendered tree, with an ability to talk, does help us understand the life of the tree and why there was biodiversity loss, and why it matters. I think research is made a bit more accessible when it's passed through a filter like this.

VB: One of the things that helps audiences is the idea of human qualities being possessed by an AI. This is a frequently used device for supporting human fascination and imagination and connection to the idea of an AI.

KR: I think we're definitely looking at it more closely now in this forthcoming programme. Again, from a very experimental lens. I think these artists qualify the limits of what their work can do, but also try to push the boundaries and see it where it can go. And from an audience perspective, I will say that it makes difficult concepts a lot more accessible.

VB: I think I see this as a bit of a tension curatorially between imagination and literacy. The idea of understanding how technology works, which is important for ethics and necessary for society. But there is also the idea of AI as a vessel for human imagination, and the ways that we use imagination to project human qualities onto the AI in order to understand it or feel more in control of it. It's an interesting tension.

My final question is a bit of a provocation to think about personal ethics. Are there particular AI technologies or partnerships that you would consider too unethical to engage with as part of your work? Are there any technologies that would be too resource intensive or too biassed? Or do you think that the benefits of critical and subversive use of AI always outweigh the costs?

KR: For a climate change conference in October 2024, I was approached by the organisers to commission an artwork that captured the voices of the conference members. Given the topic of the conference and knowing that AI is rather energy intensive, the artists compelled themselves to find alternatives — running off local servers and less resource intensive language models. In this way, we as a thoughtful community push ourselves to change course. It may not be the best way possible, but there is some movement in the right direction.

So while I don't have a response to a particular technology that's too unethical, I will say that once you have that cone of vision around ethics it becomes a consideration on how to make changes.

VB: I think in terms of this book, we would define what you have described here as a form of soft ethics, which is not about following a set of rules. It's about making decisions based on what you feel in the moment and based on how you view the situation, and the knowledge of particular contexts that you have developed.

References

Digital Futures Lab 2023. "Talking Back: A Conversation on Generative AI for the 21st Century." *FutureFantastic*. Accessed May 15, 2025. https://futurefantastic.in/programme/.

Jaaga Media, dir. 2023. *AI Art: A Marriage of Heaven and Hell?* YouTube video 58:22 https://www.youtube.com/watch?v=ua1H9xX9Vuw

Joneja, Kanchan, and Kristina Pulejkova. *Wood Wide Web*. 2023. Experience Design. https://www.offcentrecollective.com/wood-wide-web.

Ponomarov, Kostiantyn. 2024. "Global AI Regulations Tracker: Europe, Americas & Asia-Pacific Overview." https://legalnodes.com/article/global-ai-regulations-tracker.

Now You See Me... Institutional Conservatism and Censorship in Queer Remix Art
Xanthe Dobbie

> We are faced with the reality that we will never be given the keys to a utopia architected by hegemony. Instead, we have been tasked with building the world(s) we want to live in, a most difficult yet most urgent blueprint to realize... Remixing is an act of self-determination; it is a technology of survival. (Russell 2020, 93)

So-called Australia has a history of conservatism and censorship in the arts. According to the National Archives of Australia (2012), "around 15,000 books, magazines and comics [were] banned in Australia between the 1920s and the 1970s." As a settler colony, Australia provides an interesting case study in the global rise of far-right politics directly impacting the arts sector. While films, computer games, and publications have various classification regulations (Arts Law 2014), contemporary visual and experimental digital arts present much murkier territory. Within these artforms, calls for censorship have often come down to individual moral outcry surrounding claims of obscenity. These highly subjective accusations have tended to preclude context or artistic merit, and are symptomatic of a greater insidious fear of the 'other,' which drives the nation's propensity for risk aversion.

In 2008, prominent Australian artist Bill Henson faced significant controversy and censorship over his exhibition featuring photographs of nude adolescents. The ensuant media circus highlighted that "the discourse of crisis surrounding sex is not an issue that can be easily split along traditional lines of conservatives and progressives" (Pendleton and Serisier 2009, 78). The Henson scandal saw a horseshoe effect, with the then (progressive) Rudd Labor Government echoing the moral outcry of the preceding (conservative) Howard Liberal Government, epitomised in Rudd labelling the work "absolutely revolting." As queer political theorists Mark Pendelton and Tanya Serisier (2009, 81) point out, "this discourse of crisis is linked to a politics of regulation and normalisation that threatens any radical or even progressive politics around sex and gender." Where the arts may once have been considered a radical space for difficult ideas, conservatism has become increasingly apparent in cultural institutions, which rely on state funding. As such, "Dreams of a world liberated from sexual restriction and gender division have disappeared in favour of a turn towards the state, and a call for increasing regulation" (Pendleton and Serisier, 96).

Arts writer and advocate Tamara Winikoff (2016) postulates, "If you're under the illusion that we have freedom of expression in Australia, think again. Gender, race and politics are a volatile mix." So too is this true in matters surrounding sexuality where, as outlined by queer artist Drew Pettifer, "The pretence of maintaining community standards has been used in legal contexts to punish or censor representations of LGBTIQ people" (Pettifer in Winikoff 2016).

In an era when technology increasingly mediates artistic expression, queer remix artists — whose practices both embrace and subvert the technologies and mass media of our time — present a compelling narrative on the ethics and realities of creative practice in the digital age. Building upon personal experience and historical precedent of artistic censorship in Australia, this chapter explores how remix, as a queer and feminist strategy, serves as a "technology of survival" (Russell 2020, 93), challenging the entrenched, risk-averse conservatism of cultural institutions. Drawing on theoretical frameworks that position queer approaches to remix as a means to destabilise normative structures, I examine the tensions between innovative artistic practices and the regulatory constraints imposed by institutions. Within this discussion, AI is positioned as another tool in the remix agenda, which, when approached with criticality, has the potential to disrupt the supposed neutrality of the institutionally sanctioned "white cube" by undermining lofty notions of authenticity and individual authorship.

The following chapter discusses recent personal encounters with institutional conservatism rooted within a national "crisis of sex." Highlighting instances of censorship in the practices of Australian artists VNS Matrix, Paul Yore, and Soda Jerk, I position my experience on a continuum, analysing impacts on both artists and institutions. In alignment with my own practice, the basis of my artist selection criteria is twofold:

> 1. These practices draw on popular culture and remix, making them vulnerable to potential copyright infringement and privacy laws, issues exacerbated by digital access and the rise of AI technologies which complicate notions of authorship. This provides new complexities for creators and presenters.
>
> 2. These practices incorporate queer and feminist methods and frameworks (including remix), which open them up to homophobic and misogynistic criticism for their perceived overt sexuality and/ or politicism.

I intend to examine the repercussions of censorship within these contexts, highlighting its stifling effect on authentic expression and the resulting power imbalances between artists and institutions, the latter placing disproportionate pressure on individuals and shying away from systematic change. Positioning my own queer remix practice within a broader network of artists, I aim to illustrate how remix can subvert traditional narratives and question the ethics of authorship and originality. By foregrounding these themes, this chapter not only situates remix within a broader discourse on decentring ethics, but also underscores the urgent need for dialogue and change within institutional frameworks. The implications are clear: if the conservatism of institutions remains unchecked, the transformative potential of queer remix art could be significantly diminished.

Remix as Queer Practice

Remix, including techniques such as collage, adaptation, appropriation, montage, and sampling, is defined by reconfiguration. In our diverse practices, the artists here discussed employ remix techniques as radical acts of de- and re-contextualisation to imagine alternate histories and counternarratives. Such processes draw easy comparisons to notions of queering, understood as that which destabilises normative structures.

In *The Queer Art of Failure*, Jack Halberstam unpacks collage practice as feminist and queer in its rejection of categorisation. He writes, "Collage precisely references the spaces in between and refuses to respect the boundaries that usually delineate self from other, art object from museum, the copy from the original" (2011, 136). Queer media scholar Pamela Demory asserts that adaptation can be understood as already queer in its formation, existing as secondary to a perceived original or norm. She states, "Foundational to both disciplines — queer studies and adaptation studies — is a critical challenge to those assumptions about originality, authenticity, and value" (2019, 1-2). New media scholar Abigail De Kosnik (2019) asserts that digital remix culture was founded by minority groups. De Kosnik specifically cites the Black men who introduced the digital sampling techniques that defined 1980s hip hop, and the queer women who birthed online fanfiction communities in the 1990s.

Concurrently in the 1990s, cyberfeminism spawned as a transgressive movement helmed by queer women and feminists who wanted to overthrow the patriarchal and capitalist structures upholding a male-dominated tech industry. Pioneering cyberfeminist collective VNS Matrix, formed by V Barratt, Julianne Pierce, Josephine Starrs, and Francesca da Rimini in 1991, drew on and subverted pop culture, cyberpunk tropes, and feminist literature to develop and circulate alternate heroes in their interactive work *All New Gen* (1992). Building on their widely distributed *A Cyberfeminist Manifesto for the 21st Century* (1991), their CD Rom 'game' features the digitally collaged DNA Sluts — reassembled dolls with vortex laser-cunts. Working together, the DNA Sluts fight to overthrow Big Daddy Mainframe, an embodiment of "the technoindustrialmilitary complex" who sports a generic business suit and a corporate logo for a head, and Circuit Boy, "a dangerous tenchobimbo" (VNS Matrix 1992), depicted as a very well-hung limbless torso floating on a neon grid. These characters were used and reused across multiple VNS Matrix works, infiltrating private and public domains with each showing.

Remix is a proponent of world-building, a vital aspect of queering entwined in survival and representation. Access to ever-growing digital libraries has exponentially expanded the potential of such a project. Building on the work of the early cyberfeminists, Legacy Russell, author of *Glitch Feminism: A Manifesto*, surveys the work of queer and POC (person(s) of colour) artists to formulate a rubric of glitching, a leaky embrace of error to take the system down from within. As a "technology of survival" (Russell 2020, 93), the glitch is invested in dissolving binaries and encouraging fluidity, particularly between online and offline spaces and between gender identities. Many of the artists discussed throughout Russell's manifesto are practitioners that perform AFK (away from keyboard) as well as online, and are described as creating feedback loops, which bring into view the way that identities continue to reconstruct themselves regardless of geographical or digital location. Russell's glitch perpetually reformulates, thus refusing to be erased by never remaining static for long enough to be identified.

In his expansive inter-disciplinary practice, Paul Yore combines traditional craft techniques such as weaving and mosaic, with video, soft sculpture, and large-scale found object immersive installations. Obsessed by trash culture and corporate refuse, Yore remixes tangible and digital artifacts, to erect high camp monuments of cultural critique. Yore's *Word Made Flesh* survey exhibition opened at the Australian Centre for Contemporary Art (ACCA) in late 2022. ACCA artistic director Max Delany describes the artist's work as "both pleasurable in its materiality and uncomfortable in the mirror that it presents to the society in which we live" (Heath 2022). Following Russell, remix here is wielded as a queer "technology of survival" able to articulate both celebration and critique in its material and conceptual formation.

Legal and Social Implications

Unsurprisingly, remix works which flagrantly draw from copyright material create complexity both for artists and for presenting partners who fear legal action. Such fears are not ungrounded, and have arisen in conversations with presenting partners for several of my own commissioned works across visual arts and theatre in recent years.

While the rapid growth of digital technology has put a spotlight on remix, such practices are not new.

In *The Age of Remix and Copyright Law Reform*, Yahong Li extensively outlines the challenges of this new digital terrain, championing remixes as creative works in their own right that should be protected under law. Li (2020, 120) writes, "Remix is not an exact copy or duplication of an original work. Hence, it should not be viewed as infringement or piracy if it uses copyrighted work as its source materials." Culture itself can be viewed in terms of remix — a process of perpetual intertextuality is nested in every exchange. Michele Knobel and Colin Lankshear (2008, 22) explain, "Remix has not simply emerged with digitisation. It has always been a part of any society's cultural development." They continue, "The craft of remix entails understanding the risks one may run in using commercial materials in a remix" (2008, 27). This includes familiarity with copyright symbols, licences, and understanding fair use.

In their remix practice, collaborative duo Soda Jerk, consisting of siblings Dan and Dominique Angeloro, gather hundreds of clips from mainstream cinema and television to craft politically charged queer counternarratives. Working almost exclusively with copyright material, Soda Jerk are keenly aware of the legal implications of their practice. Forming in the early 2000s, when "the ethics of theft was having a moment" (Soda Jerk in Williams 2023), the artists have gone to great lengths to study copyright law in Australia and the US. While the US has a Fair Use doctrine, no such document currently exists within the Australian legal system.

Soda Jerk's 2018 film *Terror Nullius* is a political revenge fable that unpacks Australia's entrenched colonialism through archival sampling of Australian film, television, and media over several decades. Their most recent feature *Hello Dankness* (2022) draws from 1990s Hollywood cinema and contemporary meme culture to place a magnifying glass on a post-Trump suburban America. Considering the film's content, which "doesn't play nice with the law" (Soda Jerk in Dobbie 2024), the artists were surprised that *Hello Dankness* was able to have a theatrical release in New York following a successful festival run across Europe. They explain:

The legal provocation of our work is also very much a part of it, of its intended action, and we think of the film as a necessary probe to test the contours of the law, so we welcome whatever unfolds in that respect. (Soda Jerk in Williams 2023)

The advent of Artificial Intelligence further complicates this area, calling into question notions of authorship. Who is the artist? Who owns the work? In early 2023, I participated in a panel discussion organised by Australia's primary arts funding body, Creative Australia, titled *Artificial Intelligence in Creative Industries and Practice*, during which several of these issues were brought to light. Facilitated by technology reporter James Purtill, the panel comprised of IP Lawyer Benjamin Duff, technologist and digital rights activist Kathryn Gledhill-Tucker, artist-researcher Dr Nina Rajcic, and myself. According to Duff, claiming copyright in Australia requires considered manual human input, which includes a deliberate shaping or directing of the material. The copyright act in Australia makes explicit reference to mediums such as photography and cinema, and AI may soon fall under this remit as a medium unto itself. However, as Gledhill-Tucker points out, technology moves faster than legislative reform.

Institutional, legal, and individual artist opinions differ widely in the emerging field of AI. Taking into account inherent bias, data harvesting and corporatisation, all panellists agreed that AI must be approached with criticality, though not necessarily fear. In remix-based practice, questions surrounding new technologies often arise. I advocate for viewing AI as just another tool — a mode of making and a different way to view and enhance creative practice. While we should be wary of corporate monopoly in any field, AI as a tool presents many exciting avenues for expression and collaboration. As Soda Jerk put it:

Artists have always been cyborgs, we've always worked with tools and used technology as a kind of prosthetic. Our film practice is already deeply enmeshed with tech and coding and algorithms, so we don't see AI as being categorically different. We're fascinated for the kind of evolutions in our practice that it might propel (Soda Jerk in Williams, 2023)

V Barratt, a founding member of VNS Matrix, incorporates AI text and imaging into their recent remix works, including *Cyberfeminist*

Timelords (2023), which reimagines the past and future of cyberfeminism. The digital installation was created for *Ghost*, Issue 46 of the online experimental arts platform *Runway Journal*, for which I served as a guest editor. Barratt views the use of AI technologies in similar cyborgian terms, and as a means for co-opting and repurposing what Audre Lorde would call "the Master's Tools" (1998). Barratt states, "It would be great if the AI could be modelled in service of resistance movements" (Barratt in da Rimini 2023).

Legislation and technological advancement aside, remix practice is rooted in the free culture movement, which denies corporate ownership, viewing all media as common property to be reconfigured without restriction. Here, the point of using recognisable material is just that — recognisability; this is not a matter of stealing or passing off somebody else's work as one's own. My own desktop performance works *Eidolon* (2021) and *The Long Now* (2022) [Figures 1 & 2] go to great lengths to wear their references on their sleeves, highlighting source URLs and copyright watermarks.

In 2014, Soda Jerk developed *Undaddy Mainframe*, an unauthorised remix of VNS Matrix's *A Cyberfeminist Manifesto for the 21st Century* (1991), which reimagined the collective's poetic text as a '90s-coded instructional video. *Soda Jerk* (2014) describe their remix as part of an archival history "Folded into new constellations, producing virtual proximities between disparate temporal moments." While initially unaware of the remix, VNS Matrix state that they are "Delighted to be rewritten, unwritten, written anew," considering Soda Jerk's "Underpinning philosophy of being an open-source entity" (VNS Matrix 2014) to align with their own. Such processes of un-writing and re-writing destabilise the sanctity of the art object, the archive, and the institution as static and exclusive.

In a 2022 interview for my PhD project *Future Artefact*, Barratt describes their work in terms of "tactical affective gestures," which reformulate and ripple through time. For Soda Jerk, films are encrypted documents which carry complex shapeshifting webs of connection, where viewers themselves are "Part of that unquantifiable equation, bringing their own unknowable associations and personal history to the text" (Soda Jerk in Williams, 2023). While Soda Jerk's work is shaped by two individuals, they view their practice as a collaboration with both technology and the intentions of the many creatives behind the media they sample. In an interview I conducted for the Australian Centre for the Moving Image (ACMI) in early 2024, they explain:

> We're acutely compelled by the historical dimensions of the sample, and the encrypted traces they carry. So within our work there's always these two intersecting forces vying with each other: the linear propulsion of the narrative and the gravitational deep time of the archive. (Soda Jerk in Dobbie 2024)

I too subscribe to this deep appreciation of the sample in my own practice. Images are political and must be treated with appropriate respect in processes of transformation. Remix does not view media as neutral, but as charged with historicism, which it then carries into its reworked context, creating new tangents of meaning in its collision.

Controversy and Obscenity

Considering the free culture mentality and queer histories embedded within remix, fitting such practices into the regulatory constraints of institutional contexts can be challenging.

The institutionally sanctioned "white cube," as theorised by Brian O'Doherty in 1976, is historically enmeshed with problematic power dynamics. Such spaces, with their minimalist design and supposed neutrality, play a powerful role in shaping the interpretation of the art they contain by creating an aura of timelessness and detachment from social and political context. As described by Whitney B. Birkett (2012, 75), the white cube "Elevates art above its earthly origins, alienating uninitiated visitors and supporting traditional power relationships." While the various institutions discussed throughout this chapter may not adhere to the architectural specificities of the white cube, the ethos of aspirational neutrality prevails. Thus, risk aversion in these spaces is exacerbated when works come up against ethically ambiguous claims of controversy and obscenity. Unsurprisingly, such accusations are often particularly targeted towards minority groups who threaten the status quo, including queer artists.

In June 2013, police armed with box cutters raided The Linden Centre of Contemporary Art in St Kilda, forcibly removing elements of Paul

Yore's *Everything is Fucked* installation, showing as part of *Like Mike: What Now??*. The exhibition titled after Mike Brown, a controversial Australian artist whose work included pornographic collage and political satire, was intended as a tribute to the late artist's career and the legacy of his radical work on future generations. An article published at the time called the event "the most significant art censorship controversy since the Bill Henson scandal of 2008" (Eltham 2013).

The incident resulted in a media frenzy, with much reporting focused on isolated visual elements, often ignoring artistic intention or context. Conservative newspapers like *The Herald Sun*, sensationalised and sexualised specific features like the proximity of a cutout of Justin Bieber's head affixed to a dildo. Following outcry from individual community members which led to the raid, Yore was charged with production and possession of child pornography, carrying a potential sentence of over ten years. As Winikoff (2016) points out, "It is often the case that antagonistic responses to art come from relatively few individuals or particular interest groups. However, they can be disproportionately influential."

In October 2014, all charges were dismissed, Yore acquitted, and police ordered to pay costs, though the damage to Yore and his practice exceeded this and the artist considered quitting the art world. An article released at the time closes, "it cost an artist and the Linden Centre their reputations. And it cost Australian art and culture by instilling the continuing threat of persecution and the chill of self-censorship" (Holsworth 2014.) In the lead up to Yore's 2022 *Word Made Flesh* exhibition, the artist reflects on censorship, stating:

> There is a long and ongoing history of censoring art, literature and film in Australia, a kind of state-sanctioned moralising that can only be understood in relation to the prevailing system of colonialism. Deciding that citizens should not intellectually engage with a particular text or work of art is a very grave matter, and I believe must be limited to exceptional circumstances, when there is clear, demonstrable harm. (Yore in Miekus 2023)

In 2018, Ian Potter Cultural Trust pulled promotional support from Soda Jerk's *Terror Nullius*, calling the film "un-Australian" for its upfront political critique. The artists were awarded the $100,000 Ian Potter

Moving Image Commission in 2016 to develop the work. Days out from the film's premiere at ACMI, the Trust severed their connection to the project, describing it as "a very controversial piece of art" (Buckmaster 2018.) While the Trust upheld financial commitment, they no longer wished to align with the politics embedded in the project. Posting to Facebook in March 2018, Soda Jerk describe The Ian Potter Foundation, an organisation which claims to encourage and support diversity, as liking "the idea of a politically engaged work much more than the reality of one." They write:

> If our film paints a less than perfect picture of Australia it's because we think these dark political times absolutely call for it... What unfolds is a paradoxical vision of a nation where idyllic beaches host race-riots, governments poll love-rights, and the perils of hyper-masculinity are overshadowed only by the enduring horror of Australia's colonising myth of *terra nullius.* (Soda Jerk 2018)

Soda Jerk (2018) describe feeling shaken by Ian Potter's response, as shared political views should not dictate support: "Surely the function of political art is not to reinforce consensus but to deliver an open invitation to further conversation." Art serves little function in an echo chamber. It is through transgressive ideas that we are pushed into the productive discomfort that inches us closer to systematic change.

Self-Censorship

Where the instances of Yore and Soda Jerk are matters of public debate covered by the media, much negotiation between artist and presenting institution occurs behind closed doors prior to exhibition, resulting in self-censorship. As queer artist Deborah Kelly puts it, "I believe artists are censoring themselves in advance of anticipated state intervention. The cops inside us are our most intimate enemies" (Kelly in Winikoff 2016.) In my experience, this anticipated fear is one which institutions fuel in paternalistic protection of artists and audiences.

In 2022, I begrudgingly agreed to censorship of my work *The Long Now*, a commissioned piece for ACMI's online Gallery 5. The 15-minute desktop performance is a technocapitalist critique which interweaves multiple narratives, juxtaposing the homoerotic epic of Gilgamesh and his pursuit of immortality, with the story of the clock of *The Long Now*,

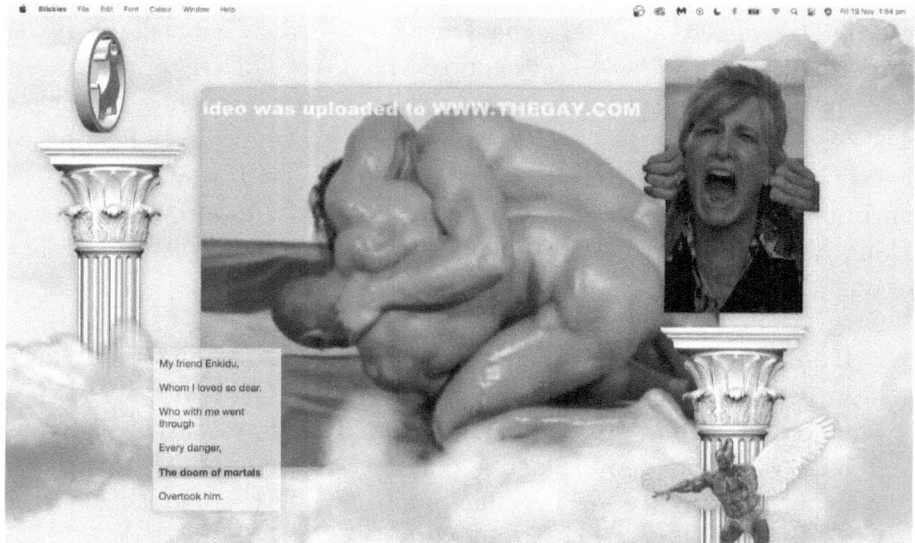

Figure 1: Xanthe Dobbie, 2022. *The Long Now*, desktop performance, 11mins, 39 secs, commissioned by ACMI for Gallery 5.

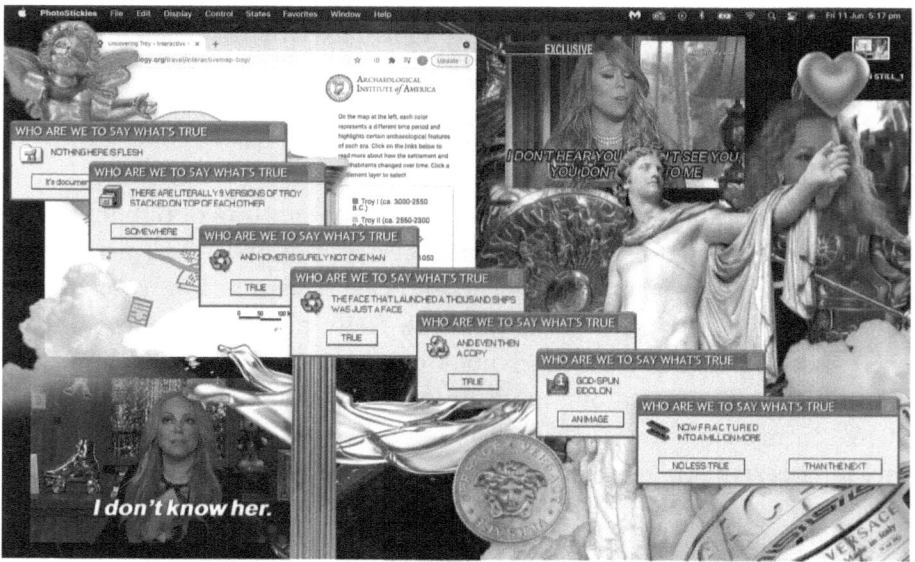

Figure 2: Xanthe Dobbie, 2021. *EIDOLON*, desktop performance, 15 mins, commissioned by Sydney Opera House for Shortwave.

a real project and a failed metaphor of human greatness enshrined in a super-structure funded by tech billionaires.

In line with my overarching remix practice, The Long Now openly samples hundreds of sources, including gay pornography. While ACMI had a full cut of the work for several weeks leading up to its launch, in the days prior to release, their ratings team noticed a briefly visible penis minutes in as one naked man throws another over his shoulder. Superimposed over the wrestling figures, visual representatives of Gilgamesh and his rival-cum-lover Enkidu, the source URL "thegay. com" scrolls across the central floating video.

Bearing in mind the longstanding tradition of nudity in art, I was surprised when this penis was flagged as an issue. However, after discussions with senior curatorial staff, it became clear that the situation was more complex. According to legal counsel sought by the gallery, the use of pornography sourced from a 'disreputable' website, which may unlawfully share content from other sources, raised concerns about potential implications of revenge porn. In Australia, revenge porn falls under *The Enhancing Online Safety Act of 2015* and the *Criminal Code Amendment (Private Sexual Material) Act of 2018*, which prohibit at the federal level the dissemination of intimate images without consent. An "intimate image" encompasses photographs or videos portraying a person in a sexual or intimate context, including nudity, sexual activity, or situations where privacy would reasonably be expected.

Considering the people depicted in the source video are porn stars, there is some ambiguity surrounding expectations of privacy. The video being openly available online is integral to its inclusion in the work, which critiques data harvesting and identity mining amidst its varying concerns. Regardless, following some back and forth, I conceded to allowing ACMI to pixelate both penis and URL, a concession rationalised as a hill not worth dying on if it were going to affect whether the work could be shown. The webpage housing the work also had to include an age verification on entry, mitigating concern that minors may access the site.

In a similar occurrence in 2020, my work *Wallpaper Queens* (2020) [Figure 3] was moved to an independently linked URL following concerns raised by The University of Queensland (UQ) Art Museum surrounding its inclusion in their online exhibition *Conflict in My*

Outlook: We Met Online (Briers et al 2022). The series of hyper-dense desktop wallpaper, shrines to lovers and friends, was initially conceived in 2018 as a collection of silk prints and an accompanying BuzzFeed-style personality quiz. The series was then expanded and animated for online context for the 2020 show. While curators had specifically selected the series for exhibition, issues surrounding the adapted work arose regarding its animation, with pornographic elements appearing more explicit in their pulsating movement. Further, the university IT department flagged that, if housed under the UQ server, the site would likely be blocked.

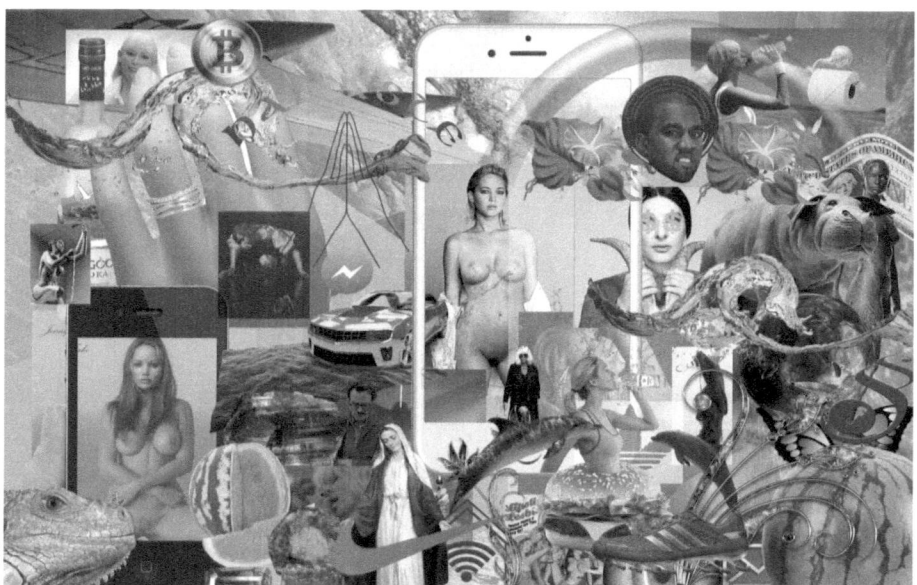

Figure 3: Xanthe Dobbie, 2018. *Wallpaper Queens* (Harriet), digital collage, downloadable wallpaper and interactive quiz. Exhibited as part of *Conflict in My Outlook:We Met Online* curated by Anna Briers (2020).

UQ Art Museum Curator Anna Briers and I discussed *Wallpaper Queens* in a 2020 panel "Managing Curatorial Risk," convened by visual arts touring organisation NETS Victoria and Public Galleries Association of Victoria (PGAV). Briers explains:

> Once you remove the work from the gallery context with all of its parameters and known audience, it's online, on the internet. You don't know who your audience is anymore, and you can't mediate the relationship between your audience and the artwork. (Harding et al. 2020)

Actions taken in this instance included age verification and the development of a secondary website to link out from the UQ site through the embedded quiz element, which housed censored versions of the works. Curatorially, *Conflict in My Outlook* deals with digital ethics surrounding machine learning, thus the need to move the work to a separate non-university URL plays well into the exhibition's broader themes. Briers continues:

> The reality was, it didn't matter what decision we came up with curatorially, or whether we deemed the work appropriate or inappropriate. The machine learning algorithms underpinning our UQ server or the internet more broadly, they make the decisions. (Briers et al. 2020)

As the exhibition was held in the height of COVID-19 lockdowns, the potential threat of my work crashing the exhibition website "Would be tantamount to the museum having to close its doors" (Briers et al. 2020). While UQ Art Museum covered the minimal costs of web hosting, site construction was undertaken independently and without additional remittance, as work here was considered part of the original artist fee. As with ACMI, I was faced with a choice to pick up extra labour or to not show the work. As I believed in the curatorial premise of the exhibition, construction of the site, which incorporates the tongue-in-cheek addition of a complaints submission form in its design, felt like the only viable course.

Given the requested alterations to my original work, ACMI changed my commissioning contract for *The Long Now* to completely remove their exclusivity clause, meaning I can freely exhibit the work elsewhere. Uncensored, *The Long Now* won the *Incinerator Art Award for Social Change* in 2023, with judges commending its relevance, timeliness, and handling of the everyday vernacular of the internet.

Layers of Censorship

In late 2023, I messaged V Barratt on Instagram to explain my intentions with this chapter and to ask about instances of censorship in their work with VNS Matrix. The collective has been subject to censorship numerous times throughout their career and continue to face challenges. In 1992, their first gallery showing of *A Cyberfeminist Manifesto for the 21st Century — Billboard Project* at Tin Sheds in Sydney — required alteration of the original manifesto text. The manifesto opens "We are the modern cunt" (VNS Matrix 1991). This and all instances of "cunt" throughout the text had to be replaced by the German "kunst" meaning "art." When asked if the collective pushed back on the change, Barratt replies:

> It was one of our first public showings. It was either don't do it or change it. And you can see in the billboard image that it is forever "kunst"... And we could remaster it, but then we'd be erasing the history of censorship. (Barratt 2023, personal communication)

Here, the historical censorship becomes part of the work, an embedded layer that speaks to an ongoing narrative of conservatism. In 2024, the collective faced similar problems, with a major institution again wanting to alter original 1990s works in a paradoxical re-writing of the activist history they wished to preserve through (re)presentation. V assures me that they were "On the soapbox about it," stating that they're "Not about to capitulate at this age" and that in some ways not being included would be preferable to being "Watered down and not represented faithfully" (Barratt 2023, personal communication).

When asked for an update on the situation in early 2024, Barratt informs me that works including "banned words" were to be included in a side hall space with a content warning. Their "DNA Sluts" were to be rebirthed as "DNA Slits," a solution which Barratt describes as not ideal, but as marking a moment in time. Reflecting on the absurdist temporal collision of reimagining their own history, they state, "We'll have all these new old works" (Barratt 2024, personal communication). As with my own experience, labour expectation for enacting such censorship fell on individual artists.

Where to From Here?

While the overarching situation seems a little bleak, in recent years some resources have become available for both artists and institutions wanting to preserve freedom of expression. The National Association for the Visual Arts (NAVA) website houses a resources page including links to relevant articles, forums, and fact sheets, as well as extended definitions of classification, sedition, racial discrimination, and issues surrounding depictions of children in art. NAVA's Position statement supports artists' freedom to create within legal bounds and fights against censorship, particularly highlighting fear-induced self-censorship as a key issue. In instances of legal ambiguity, NAVA recommends *The Artistic Merit Test* (n.d.), which includes the legitimacy of the artist, advice from arts experts, intention, context, and meaning.

Along similar lines, Museums and Galleries of New South Wales (MGNSW) and NETS Victoria co-authored a "Risk Assessment and Management of Exhibition Content" document in 2020, introduced by MGNSW's Rachel Arndt in the "Managing Curatorial Risk" panel discussed earlier. According to Arndt, the resource centres audience interaction, and institutional navigation of stakeholder relations (artist, funder, community etc.) The document also places significant value on cultural mediation training for gallery staff and volunteers, aimed at empowering informed discussion and making space for debate and dangerous ideas.

These resources may represent a step in the right direction, although again they place impetus on individuals (artists, curators, gallery staff), and fail to come to terms with larger engrained issues of systematic conservatism and oppression. Their purpose, while well-intentioned, is concerned with self-protection and playing it safe — in being prepared for worst-case scenarios, and not with collective strategising towards actual freedom of expression.

Pandering to conservatism "Does not remedy inequality, rather, it normalises the grasp on power by dominant groups" (Bridges et al. 2023), the seemingly impenetrable puppeteers behind the public face of the institution who "Enforce prescribed morality within the population" (Bridges et al. 2023). Such prescriptive approaches have facilitated the ongoing censorship of queer practices discussed here. While effective in the current climate, artists should not have to succumb to what Soda Jerk once described to me as a "Trojan Horse" (personal communication) approach — sneaking in radical ideas, which may necessitate seeking forgiveness rather than permission.

Harnessing the ethos of queer remix, perhaps it is yet again time for artists and curators to imagine potential futures beyond the state-sanctioned institution and the white cube. Perhaps we should be following Soda Jerk's lead in "Thinking more about scheming a way out of institutions rather than sneaking in" (Soda Jerk in Dobbie 2024.) Or, as Legacy Russell (2020, 99) proposes, to encrypt ourselves into glitched bodies and practices, which are not supposed to be easily deciphered by mainstream sensibilities and establishments — "A necessary disruption." To encrypt, is to be simultaneously invisible and hyper-visible, and to allow space to "Work together to create secure passageways both on- and offline to travel, conspire, collaborate" (Russell 2020, 99).

Now you see me.

Now you don't.

Now you see me…

References

Arts Law Centre of Australia. 2014. "Information Sheet: Classification and Censorship." https://www.artslaw.com.au/information-sheet/classification-and-censorship/.

Barratt, V. 2023. "Cyberfeminist Timelords." *Runway Journal* 46: [online]. https://runway.org.au/v-barratt/.

Birkett, Whitney B. 2012. "To Infinity and Beyond: A Critique of the Aesthetic White Cube." *Theses* 209: 1–75. https://scholarship.shu.edu/theses/209.

Bridges, Donna, Elizabeth Wulff, Clifford Lewis, Larissa Bamberry, and Chelsea Litchfield. 2023. "Power, Privilege and Inequality in a Time of Neoliberal Conservatism." In *Gender, Feminist and Queer Studies*, edited by Donna Bridges, Elizabeth Wulff, Clifford Lewis, Larissa Bamberry, and Chelsea Litchfield. Routledge.

Briers, Anna, Nicholas Carah, and Holly Arden, eds. 2022. *Conflict In My Outlook*. Perimeter Editions.

Buckmaster, Luke. 2018. "Terror Nullius: 'controversial' Australian Film Loses Funders' Support." *The Guardian*, March 19, 2018. https://www.theguardian.com/film/2018/mar/19/terror-nullius-controversial-australian-film-loses-funders-support.

Demory, Pamela. 2019. "Queer/Adaptation: An Introduction." In *Queer/Adaptation: A Collection of*

Critical Essays, edited by Pamela Demory. Springer International Publishing AG.

Dobbie, Xanthe. 2020. *Wallpaper Queens*. Digital collage and interactive quiz. https://xanthedobbie.wixsite.com/wallpaperqueens

Dobbie, Xanthe. 2022. *The Long Now*. Digital video and web installation. ACMI. https://longnow.acmi.net.au/?_ga=2.119020097.9398935.1706833615-1586623272.1696814643

Dobbie, Xanthe. 2024. "Hello Dankness: Soda Jerk and Xanthe Dobbie in Conversation." *ACMI*, January 16, 2024. https://www.acmi.net.au/stories-and-ideas/hello-dankness-soda-jerk-xanthe-dobbie/.

Doherty, Brian O. 1976. "Inside the White Cube: Notes on the Gallery Space." *Artforum* 14 (7): 24–30. https://www.artforum.com/features/inside-the-white-cube-notes-on-the-gallery-space-part-i-214843/.

Eltham, Ben. 2013. "The New Censorship: A Campaign against Arts Funding?" *ARTShub*, June 13, 2013. https://www.artshub.com.au/news/features/the-new-censorship-a-campaign-against-arts-funding-195670-2307286/.

Halberstam, Jack. 2011. *The Queer Art of Failure*. Duke University Press.

Harding, Adam, Rachel Arndt, Anna Briers, and Xanthe Dobbie. 2020. "Managing Curatorial Risk." *Public Galleries Association Victoria*. https://pgav.org.au/2020-Curatorial-Intensive-Session-2-Managing-Curatorial-Risk~5758.

Heath, Nicola. 2022. "Australian Artist Paul Yore Speaks about Censorship in Art, Queer Culture and Catholic Kitsch as ACCA Exhibition Surveys His Career." *ABC News*, November 6, 2022. https://www.abc.net.au/news/2022-11-06/paul-yore-word-made-flesh-exhibition-acca-australian-artist/101610312.

Holsworth, Mark S. 2014. "Artist Acquitted of Obscenity, but Chill of Censorship Endures." *Hyperallergic*, October 3, 2014. https://hyperallergic.com/153130/artist-acquitted-of-obscenity-but-chill-of-censorship-endures/.

Knobel, Michele, and Colin Lankshear. 2008. "Remix: The Art and Craft of Endless Hybridization." *Journal of Adolescent & Adult Literacy* 52 (1): 22–33. https://doi.org/10.1598/jaal.52.1.3.

Kosnik, Abigail De. 2019. "Why It Matters That Black Men and Queer Women Invented Digital Remix Culture." *JCMS: Journal of Cinema and Media Studies* 59 (1): 156–63. https://doi.org/10.1353/cj.2019.0069.

Li, Yahong. 2020. "The Age of Remix and Copyright Law Reform." *Law, Innovation and Technology* 12 (1): 113–55. https://doi.org/10.1080/17579961.2020.1727087.

Lorde, Audre. 1998. "The Master's Tools Will Never Dismantle the Master's House." *Feminism & Psychology* 8 (1): 77–83. https://doi.org/10.1177/0959353598081006.

Miekus, Tiarney. 2023. "Paul Yore on Beauty, Cooking and Chaos — and Why He's Ultimately an Optimist." *Art Guide*, January 3, 2023. https://artguide.com.au/paul-yore-on-beauty-cooking-and-chaos-and-why-hes-ultimately-an-optimist/.

MGNSW & NETS. 2020. 'Risk Assessment and Management for Exhibitions. Accessed December 16, 2023. https://mgnsw.org.au/sector/resources/online-resources/risk-management/risk-assessment-and-management-for-exhibition-content/.

National Archives of Australia. 2012. "Banned: The Secret History of Australian Censorship." Canberra. https://artsandculture.google.com/story/banned-national-archives-of-australia/3wXRe6KPfhBeJQ?hl=en.

NAVA. n.d. *Freedom of Expression*. Accessed December 16, 2023. https://visualarts.net.au/advocacy/freedom-expression/.

Pendleton, Mark, and Tanya Serisier. 2009. "Beyond the Desire for Law: Sex and Crisis in Australian Feminist and

Queer Politics." *Australian Feminist Law Journal* 31 (1): 77–98. https://doi.org/10.1080/13200968.2009.10854428.

Purtill, James, Xanthe Dobbie, Benjamin Duff, Kathryn Gledhill-Tucker, and Nina Rajcic. 2023. "Artificial Intelligence in Creative Industries and Practice." *Creative Australia*. https://creative.gov.au/advocacy-and-research/events/artificial-intelligence-in-creative-industries-and-practice/.

Rimini, Francesca da. 2023. "Cyberfeminist Forecasting: A Conversation with V Barratt." *Medium*, December 11, 2023. https://medium.com/@dollyoko/cyberfeminist-forecasting-a-conversation-with-v-barratt-365c7d82c227.

Russell, Legacy. 2020. *Glitch Feminism: A Manifesto*. Verso.

Shkara, Hayder. 2024. "The Changing Landscape: Examining Revenge Porn Laws in Australia — A Comprehensive Analysis." *Walker Pender Lawyers*, September 15, 2024. https://walkerpender.com.au/revenge-porn-laws-in-australia/.

Soda Jerk. 2014. "Who's Your 'Undaddy'?" *Remix.org*, 2014. https://remix.org.au/ariremix-whos-your-undaddy-soda-jerk-vns-matrix/.

Soda Jerk. 2014. *Undaddy Mainframe*. Digital video.

Soda Jerk. 2022. *Hello Dankness*. Film. https://www.hellodankness.net/index.php.

Soda Jerk. 2018. "Response to Ian Potter Foundation Withdrawal from Terror Nullius." Facebook.

VNS Matrix. 1991. "The Cyberfeminist Manifesto For The 21st Century." *Adelaide: VNS Matrix*. https://vnsmatrix.net/projects/the-cyberfeminist-manifesto-for-the-21st-century.

VNS Matrix. 1992a. "All New Gen." *VNS Matrix*. https://vnsmatrix.net/projects/all-new-gen.

VNS Matrix. 1992b. "Billboard Project." *VNS Matrix*, 1992. https://vnsmatrix.net/projects/billboard-project.

VNS Matrix. 2014. "Remix w/ Soda_Jerk." https://vnsmatrix.net/projects/remix-undaddy-mainframe-direct-line-soda-jerk.

Williams, Conor. 2023. "'We Think of Trump as the First Meme to Hold Office in the White House': A Conversation with Hello Dankness Creators Soda Jerk." *Filmmaker Magazine*, 2023. https://filmmakermagazine.com/122822-hello-dankness-soda-jerk/.

Winikoff, Tamara. 2016. "Tenuous Freedoms." *National Association for the Visual Arts*, September 21, 2016. https://visualarts.net.au/news-opinion/2016/tenuous-freedoms/.

Yore, Paul. 2013. *Everything Is Fucked*. Mixed-media installation. St. Kilda. Linden Contemporary.

Yore, Paul. 2022. *Word Made Flesh*. Mixed-media installation. Southbank. ACCA. https://acca.melbourne/exhibition/paul-yore-word-made-flesh/.

Consent, Connection, and Creativity: Navigating the Ethical Boundaries of Using Biometric Data in Artistic Performance

Solange Glasser,
Ben Loveridge,
Margaret Osborne,
Lucy Sparrow, and
Ryan Kelly

Since the mid-20th century, artists have increasingly sought to extend the boundaries of creative expression through the innovative use of biometric data — encapsulating human physiological, biological and behavioural signals — into elements of live performance or measures of audience engagement. However, the speed and enthusiasm with which this technology has been incorporated into artistic performance has not been extended to the establishment of guidelines regarding privacy, security and user consent, leaving artists and audience members vulnerable to potential misuse of sensitive personal information. In so doing, artists may violate ethical values of privacy, nonmaleficence, autonomy, authorship, trust, and artistic integrity, and thus lay bare the ethical considerations surrounding the collection, display, storage, and management of biometric data in artistic outputs.

This chapter delineates and explores the artistic and ethical boundaries that artists navigate in the use of biometric data in performance. We seek to support artists as they navigate the competing concerns of *consent, connection,* and *creativity* in the design of performance art; concerns that are central to enabling ethical alignment, participant engagement, and impactful artistry, without compromising respect or privacy. Through scenario storytelling, we describe the use of biometric data in a speculative performance: *Scheherazade's Shadow*. This scenario reveals the difficulties — and the importance — of carefully considering these competing concerns in performances involving biometric data. We address age-old questions of whether an artist should have to create ethical art, and what it means to create art that asks ethical questions using unethical technology, demonstrating how biometric data and associated technologies bring these questions into new light.

Employing an 'ethics by design' approach, we discuss the ethical issues raised in this speculative performance through the lens of the Biometrics and Ethics in Artistic Performance (BEAP) framework: a practical and ethical framework that we developed to guide practitioners in the use of biometric data in immersive artistic performance (Sparrow et al. 2024), which emphasises the need to consider ethical values throughout the design process and life cycle of a performance artwork.

The Team

The considerations we offer in this chapter are uniquely drawn from our multi-disciplinary perspectives as practitioners and academics, united by our fascination with the creative potential of immersive environments in the performing arts, and commensurate exploration of the ethics and ownership of biometric data capture in artistic performance. Glasser, a music psychology academic and musician, was motivated to challenge perceptions of creativity, artistic ownership, and the future of ethical performance practice, by scrutinising artistic performances co-created by humans and AI; Loveridge, a creative technologist exploring the intersection of music performance and virtual reality, was motivated to improve the experience of creative arts practices using technology for teaching, learning, and research; Osborne, a music performance science researcher, psychologist and educator in music and psychology, was motivated to address the inadequacy of ethical guidelines for providing psychological services and products using the internet and telecommunications technologies offered by the Australian professional associations for psychologists at the time of the study; Sparrow, a technology ethicist and human-computer interaction researcher, was motivated to address ethical concerns impacting artists and audiences and situate solutions meaningfully in artistic contexts; and Kelly, a human-computer interaction and social computing researcher, was motivated to help researchers, performers and artists navigate the tension between using biometrics to enhance a performance and ensuring that the collected data does not impinge upon the welfare of participants.

As a team, our work has been influenced and inspired by the performing artists at the cutting edge of this practice: the dancers who have connected to their audiences by projecting their bodies' internal workings, the musicians who have created new forms of sound and music that respond to their body movements, and the artists who have captured biometric data from visual and auditory senses to distribute agency between artist and audience (see figures 1, 2, and 3). To deepen our understanding of the ethics of biometric capture in immersive artistic performance, we undertook a systematic literature review across 106 sources from 1990 to 2023, which explored the practices and ethical considerations involved in using biometric technologies in a broad range of immersive performances, including music, dance, interactive art installations, and theatre. This work enabled us to develop a practical ethical framework guiding practitioners in the use of biometric data in immersive artistic performance (Sparrow et al. 2024). The 'Biometrics and Ethics in Artistic Performance' or 'BEAP' framework advocates for a proactive 'ethics by design' approach that emphasises the consideration of ethical values throughout a project's design process and lifecycle. This work was generously supported through seed funding provided by the Centre for Artificial Intelligence and Digital Ethics (CAIDE) Art, AI and Digital Ethics (AAIDE) group at the University of Melbourne.

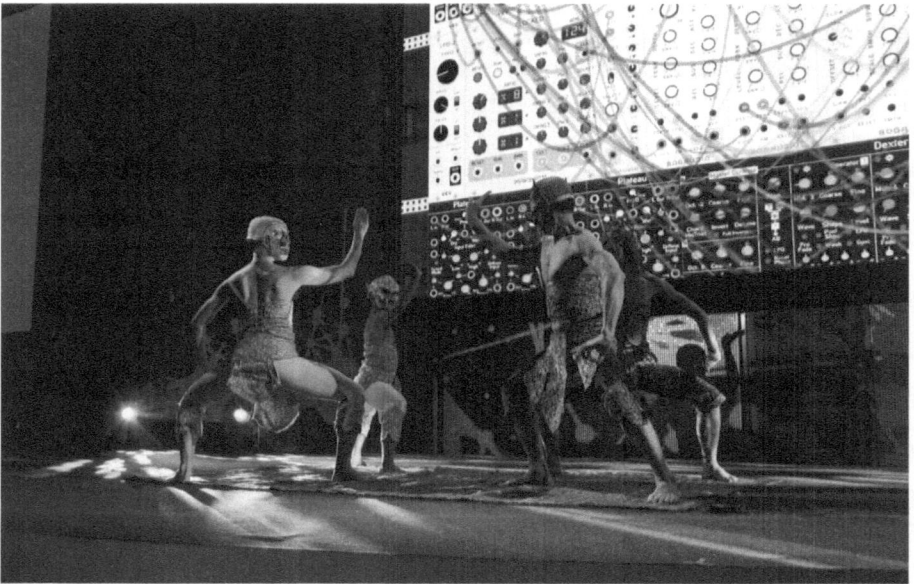

Figure 1: Irmandy Wicaksono and Pichet Klunchun Dance Company, 2023. *Tapis Magique*. A collaboration with the avant-garde Pichet Klunchun Dance Company, designed to challenge the relationship between contemporary-traditional modern-classical textile, music, and choreography.

The Approach

We adopt a soft-ethics approach, grounded in principle-based codes of ethical practice. Soft-ethics provides a foundation for analysing and responding to unique, novel, or emerging ethical issues that are not adequately addressed by more rule-based codes of ethics, which tend to be reactive and reliant on precedent (Roufeil and Li 2011). Rapid technological advances in the digital arena result in inevitable areas of uncertainty with respect to topics and contexts that are not addressed in hard ethics legislative and regulatory frameworks, which prescribe compliance regardless of their complexity (Floridi 2018). In practice, soft and hard ethics are intricately intertwined — for soft ethics to work well in interpreting governance frameworks, "it must be coherent with, and informed by, the hard ethics that led to their formulation in the first place" (Floridi 2018, 7).

The conceptual framework we have adopted juxtaposes ethical know-how with ethical know-what, providing a comprehensive understanding of ethical engagement in artistic practice (Bolt et al. 2016; Sierra

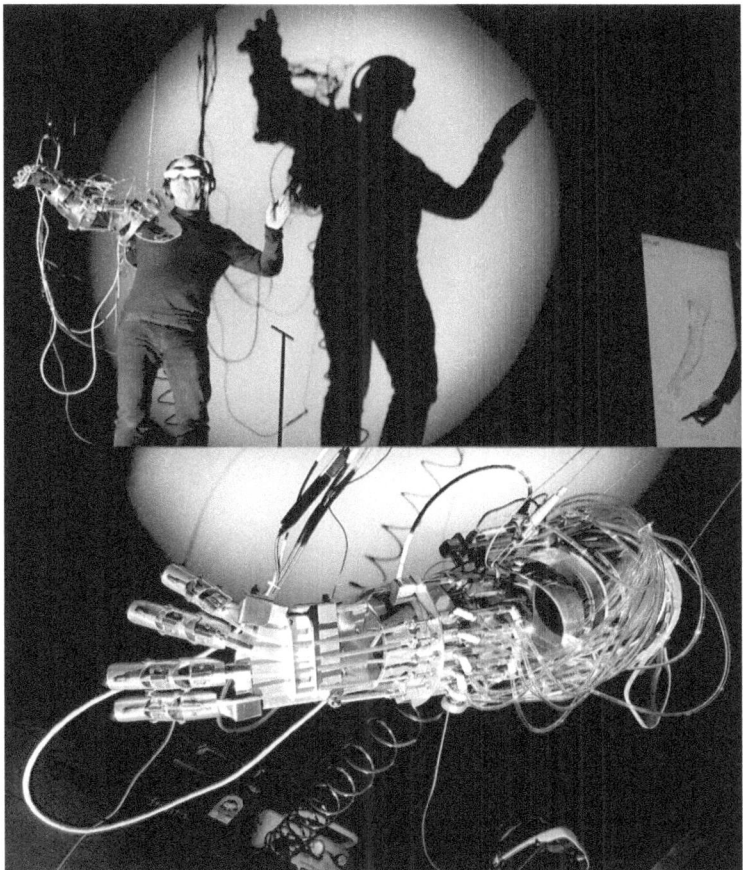

Figure 2: Stelarc, 2015. *Re-Wired / Re-Mixed: Event for Dismembered Body Radical Ecologies*, PICA, Perth. Photo by Steven Alyian. For six consecutive hours each day across five days, the artist could only see with the eyes of someone in London, could only hear with the ears of someone else in New York, while anyone anywhere could access and actuate the artist's right arm, constituting a sharing of visual and acoustical senses and a distributing of agency. The artist was thus effectively in three places at once, two virtually in London and New York and one physically in Perth.

et al. 2017; Varela 1999). By offering an aspirational perspective on artistic practice, we enable practitioners to engage with the broader expectations of their conduct, rather than simply responding to specific conditions. This approach emphasises the human entanglement with technical systems, acknowledging that our data and actions are increasingly intertwined with technological processes.

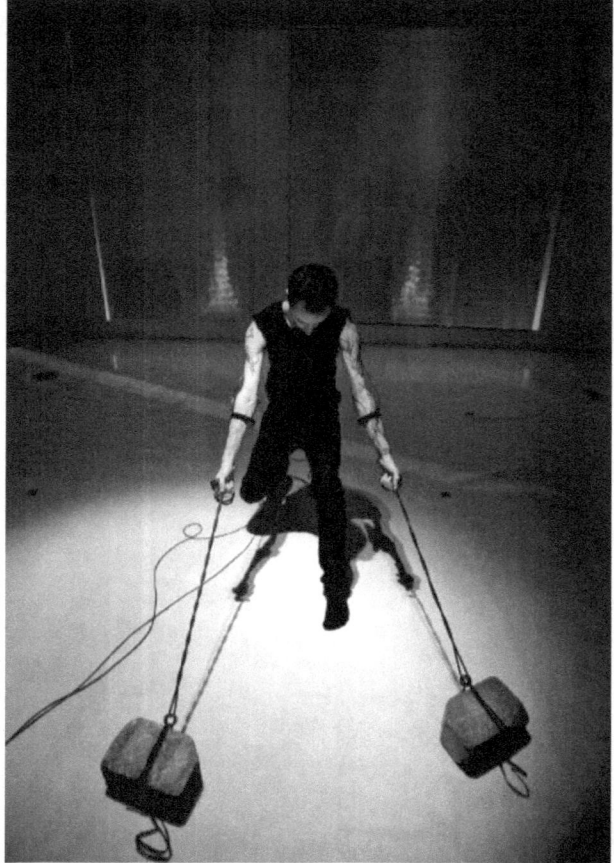

Figure 3: Marco Donnarumma, 2011. *Hypo Chrysos*, photograph by Chris Scott. *Hypo Chrysos* is a work of action art for vexed body and biophysical media. During this twenty-minute action the performer pulls two concrete blocks in a circle. His motion is oppressively constant; he has to force himself into accepting the pain until the action is ended. The increasing strain of the muscular tissues produces continuous bioacoustic signals.

The Scenario

We invite the reader to participate in the narration of a speculative performance through scenario storytelling, where we will describe how the use of biometric data has transformed the process and outcomes of a performance artwork, and the ethical issues that were raised. Scenario storytelling is a flexible way of speculating possible futures through the integration of ideas, thoughts and feelings (Rasmussen 2005). Through this method we perform stories to involve the reader as audience-participant in exploring artistic and ethical boundaries, by interlacing aspects of our current artistic practice with speculative future directions of this practice. To frame this performative storytelling, we present a three-part model of consent, connection and creativity to demonstrate the core competing concerns facing artists in this space.

To ensure the authenticity of our scenario, we have chosen to ground it in a real-life, work-in-progress multimodal artwork that incorporates audience participation and biometric data in performance. This artwork is currently being designed and developed by the team, while decisions on elements of its final form and content remain speculative. It has been eloquently suggested that "scenarios give people a 'memory' of the future" (Allan, Fairtlough, and Heinzen 2001, 186), and through tying our current artistic practice with its speculative future sibling, we aim to ensure that our future 'memories of the past' are of ethically consented, connected, and creative artworks.

Setting the Scene

The scenario we propose consists of an augmented reality experience, situated inside a public exhibition space. A visitor walks into a well-lit gallery, surrounded by other members of the public and facilitation staff. On one side sits a rectangular pedestal with a white mixed-reality headset resting on top. Attached to the pedestal is a museum card displaying information about the experience, titled: *Scheherazade's Shadow*.

As the visitor approaches the headset on the pedestal, they are greeted by a facilitator. Before entering the VR experience, the visitor is fitted with a device on their wrist that measures heart rate variability (HRV) and galvanic skin response (GSR). The visitor is invited to wait calmly for five minutes, sitting down without interacting with any personal devices (such as mobile phones) or other visitors. During this time their baseline HRV and GSR is measured. The facilitator then assists them in putting on the VR device and informs them to use their hands to interact inside the experience. Once the headset is attached, the facilitator steps away. Inside the headset view, the visitor sees the gallery space and other visitors through the device's high resolution pass-through cameras; this view is nearly indistinguishable from that of the gallery through their unmediated eyes. After a few moments, the visitor wearing the headset is presented with a highly realistic digital avatar: a life-like appearance of a naked human form. The view of the gallery space slowly fades to black, leaving the visitor in virtual darkness, with only the avatar visible.

The visitor starts to walk around the avatar; the avatar's eyes blink and follow them. A subtle flickering light effect on the naked avatar's skin invites interaction from the visitor. As they move their hand through the avatar, music emanates from its body, morphing in shape with movement and colour. As their hands move away from the avatar, the music and movement stop. Sensors in the wrist device feed the visitor's real-time biometric data into the VR experience to directly modulate the soundscape being created. The visitor's HRV controls the tempo, while their GSR controls the dissonance of the music. The music's tempo will speed up in response to reduced HRV (indicating increased stress/autonomic sympathetic nervous system response), while more and more notes that are outside the tonal centre of the original 'baseline' musical excerpt will be included as GSR increases. For every 5% change in baseline, indicating a change in stress response, there will be a commensurate change in tempo and dissonance.

After a few minutes of interaction, the avatar starts to fade away into nothingness. The facilitator takes the headset off the visitor and places it back onto the pedestal.

Sharpening the Gaze on the Ethics of Biometric Capture

The title — *Scheherazade's Shadow* — was inspired by the tales of the One Thousand and One Nights. Scheherazade is the consummate storyteller who is fabled to have read a thousand books of stories, poetry, philosophy, science, and the arts. She was able to absorb great volumes of information and weave intricate stories from her knowledge, using her wit and creativity to alter the perception and judgement of the Sultan, who had vowed to take her life. She is a symbol of the power of storytelling, intelligence, and perseverance; her storytelling not only saved her life but also helped the Sultan grow wiser and more compassionate. Like Scheherazade, digital technologies and AI can also capture and manipulate information, weaving a seemingly unending string of stories and narratives. Also, like Scheherazade, tools such as immersive reality headsets, sensors, and Generative AI, can be employed to alter perceptions and judgements, but not always for a positive outcome. This is the dark side of Scheherazade's power, and the potential for unethical outcomes lurks in the shadow of collecting and interacting with personal and biometric data.

Scheherazade's Shadow explores the relationship between creation and biometric data. The work is a commentary on the liminal space that exists between construction and harm: between aesthetic pleasure and the desire to create on the one hand and how using biometric data in performance can be a deeply uncomfortable practice that can strip away control and safety on the other. In designing *Scheherazade's Shadow* to depict a naked avatar, we are addressing concepts of individual agency and anonymity; through the capture and incorporation of biometric data as a mechanism for the modification of a performative artwork, we raise questions about the ethical role of creators when collecting, scraping, and using biometric data in performances.

We hope to provoke discussions about the way society views the ownership and dissemination of biometric data, the role of art in interrogating ethical questions, and the implications of representing sensitive data in artistic outputs, including performance scenarios.

The avatar in *Scheherazade's Shadow* is situated in darkness, and the closed environment of the VR headset invites the viewer's gaze. Laura Mulvey (1975) describes the cinema experience, with its darkened auditorium and spectators positioned in rows, as a "hermetically sealed world"; this experience is mirrored by the VR headset, with the viewer's vision quite literally 'hermetically sealed' off from the 'real' world for which they no longer have visibility. Thus, the perceived experience of "peeking into a private world" (Johansson 2024, 201) is maintained.

By designing *Scheherazade's Shadow* as an interactive installation, we have broken the strict division between the active gaze and the passive avatar. In *Scheherazade's Shadow*, it is not just the avatar that is the recipient of the viewer's gaze, but the viewer themselves is being watched and observed by other gallery visitors as they are interacting with the avatar. Indeed, the "hermetically sealed world" that the VR headset affords them in their voyeuristic gaze also enables other gallery visitors to voyeuristically gaze at them without their knowledge. *Scheherazade's Shadow* therefore breaks from the concept of "pleasurable viewing" (or 'visual pleasure') in one key element: that of the *narcissistic aspect* of cinema, where Mulvey (1975, 10) draws from the French psychoanalyst Jacques Lacan's idea of the mirror stage to argue that cinema's ability to temporarily forget ourselves by immersing ourselves in the film's story and characters allows for a "temporary loss of ego while simultaneously reinforcing the ego." This identification of the 'self' with characters on the screen breaks down or dissolves the distinction between the audience and the characters and allows the viewer to identify with one character while voyeuristically watching another. We suggest that there is a different relationship between the avatar and the viewer in participatory VR experiences. In particular, *Scheherazade's Shadow* as an artistic work takes the participant on a journey from viewer (where pleasure is derived by viewing others through a curious and controlling gaze (Johansson 2024, 200)), to that of active participant (i.e., to that of character). Thus, what virtual reality enables is an extension of the experience of viewing that is afforded by film, to one of participation.

There is both pleasure and power in watching; we argue there is both pleasure and power, and also discomfort and vulnerability, in being watched. In the words of Sofia Johansson (2024, 208), our aim with *Scheherazade's Shadow* is to "contribute to sharpening the viewer's own gaze" of the collection and use of biometric data in artistic performance, triggering both reflection and action through the felt, lived experience of the interactive installation.

Viewing the Artwork through the lens of the BEAP framework

The potential implementation of such a performance scenario raises a number of ethical questions. To guide the design of the scenario as an artistic output we can address these questions through the Biometrics and Ethics in Artistic Performance (BEAP) framework: a practical framework to support the ethical collection, storage, and use of biometric data in immersive performances (Sparrow et al. 2024). This framework uses an 'ethics by design' approach, inviting artists and performers to continually return to ethical reflection throughout the lifecycle of an artistic project. In this approach, we can hear echoes of Varela's (1999, 31) assertion that "truly ethical behaviour takes the middle way between spontaneity and rational calculation," Bennett's (2001, 157) "repeated acts of discipline and returning," and Bolt et al.'s (2016, 7) acknowledgement of "a to-and-fro between deliberation and know-how." We will embody this approach by first considering this speculative performance through the lens of the BEAP framework, before broadening our ethical journey to wander into the territory of soft ethics and consider how consent, connection, and creativity are interconnected through these ethical considerations.

* * *

The 7 guiding prompts of the BEAP framework

The Biometrics and Ethics in Artistic Performance (BEAP) framework provides us with seven prompts that give us moments at which to reflect on our scenario and consider how we might design the performance through an ethical lens. We will consider *Scheherazade's Shadow*, as a speculated performance, through each of the seven stages.

1. *Who is biometric data being collected from (or not being collected from)?*

In our proposed scenario, there are two distinct groups of people that need to be considered: the potential person or persons the avatar is modelled on, and the exhibition visitors, who we will call participants in light of the participatory nature of the experience. In considering the proposed scenario, the avatar may be modelled on biometric data collected from a known person, or may be modelled on a pre-existing avatar or metahuman. In relation to the exhibition participants, biometric data may be collected from any visitor who chooses to wear the wrist device and mixed reality headset.

2. *What biometric data is being collected?*

The avatar in this scenario is naked. A whole suite of biometric data is therefore used to model the avatar, and the exact type of data collected will depend on whether the avatar is created using scans of a known person, or whether it is created from a pre-existing avatar or metahuman. Example types of data that could be collected include eye movements, facial expressions, and gestures. Regardless of whether it is desired or not, the headset may collect a participant's visual attention in the form of eye tracking and audio output may be collected during the experience. Emotional and physiological responses, ranging from heart rate to body movements such as head and hand positions, may also be captured by the headset.

Two specific forms of biometric data will be collected from the participants via a wrist device: heart rate variability (HRV) and galvanic skin response (GSR).

> Heart Rate Variability (HRV) is a physiological marker for stress and emotion regulation. Low HRV is a marker of unregulated autonomic sympathetic nervous system fight-flight response to a stressor. In contrast, high variability is detected when the parasympathetic nervous system is activated to calm and soothe an individual (Kirby et al. 2017).

> Galvanic Skin Response (GSR), considered as one of the strongest signals of emotion detection, measures the human stress response through changes in skin moisture level (sweating). It is a sensitive and inexpensive tool which detects emotion via the spontaneous reaction of an individual's sympathetic nervous system activation, which cannot be controlled by the user (Setyohadi et al. 2018).

3. What is the biometric data taken to indicate?

The biometric data in the experience is used to create a personalised and responsive interaction with the avatar, aimed to evoke strong emotional reactions such as arousal or discomfort. For example, participant hand positions and movement will be captured to enable real-time interaction with the avatar, and HRV and GSR capture measurements of emotional arousal and stress response.

4. How is biometric data being collected?

Data for the avatar could initially be collected through various scanning techniques, using a wide range of technologies, from a mobile phone to a lidar scanner. Avatar data could also be collected from online platforms. Participant data is collected through sensors in the VR headset, such as eye-tracking and facial expression, and through a wrist device.

5. *How is biometric data being used in relation to the performance or artwork?*

The data is used to adjust the avatar's behaviour in real-time, influencing its interactions based on the participant's reactions. As participants touch the avatar, their movements through the avatar's body create music, shape, and colour. These responses are contingent on the participant's hand gestures, and the music and visuals stop once the participant's hands are no longer in contact with the avatar's body. When the visitor and avatar interact, the music being created dynamically adjusts to mirror the biometric data it is being fed (HRV and GSR).

6. *How is biometric data being managed?*

Data will be stored in the headset and on the artist's personal device or devices, and may be shared with the exhibition space, including any technical professionals. Visitors may photograph or video the headset in the space, and other visitors wearing the headset and interacting with the avatar. These images or videos may be further shared outside the exhibition space, including via social media.

7. *Why is biometric data being collected?*

The artistic intent in the experience is to explore and provoke deep personal reflections on the use of biometric data in artistic performance. Visitor and participant reactions to the artwork, through the physical interaction with digital beings, will raise questions about technology, consent, and the human experience. The capture and use of the participant's HRV and GSR emphasises the deeply personal nature of biometric data and brings the participants closer to understanding how biometric data creates intimacy, while raising questions of surveillance. We began this storytelling with an overview of the initial performance design, before considering this hypothetical performance through the lens of the BEAP framework. We will continue the 'returning' and 'to-and-fro' of our thinking by next considering how consent, connection, and creativity are interconnected through these ethical considerations, by walking the middle way between balancing artistic outcomes with ethical design.

* * *

Consent, Connection, Creativity

The use of biometric data in artistic performance creates a bespoke set of boundaries to be navigated, avoided, or even traversed in artistic expression. These boundaries encapsulate elements of consent, connection, and creativity. Each unique performative artwork will need to carefully balance these considerations depending on the artistic intent of the work, the nature of the data being collected, and the people impacted. By navigating elements of consent, connection, and creativity in the design of *Scheherazade's Shadow*, we will demonstrate the core competing concerns facing artists in this space.

But why consent, connection, and creativity? We believe that these three elements sit at the heart of the design of artistic experiences using biometric data, and that considering these elements holistically allows us — as artists and creators — to better align with ethical standards, and enhance participant engagement, without compromising on respect and privacy, while at the same time enhancing the impact of our art.

The protagonists of our story

Let's take a moment to consider key questions concerning the protagonists in our story: the consenters, the connectors, and those who will ultimately be impacted by this experience of collective creativity. These protagonists form the 'who' in the first consideration of the BEAP framework. In *Scheherazade's Shadow*, the exploration of the use of biometric data is utilised to create a musical output. Audience members (exhibition visitors) are being invited to engage with biometric data (the avatar) by supplying their own biometric data, and their engagement will determine the musical output that is created and experienced.

> *Artist:* The artist may make the choice to model the avatar for Scheherazade's Shadow on themselves. What impact would this have on the artist's connection to the work of art and to audience members, and would this connection be reciprocated by the audience? Should the audience be informed that the avatar was modelled on the artist's likeness, and if so, would this be done prior to or after experiencing the artwork?

Performer: In our scenario, the performer is an avatar. If the avatar used is based on a real person, has the person consented to their likeness being used for this purpose? If an AI avatar has been used in the creation of the work, has the training data been ethically sourced?

Audience as Performer: In our scenario, an audience member (a visitor to the exhibition space) takes on a performance role as they are invited to take part in a creative, musical process. The degree to which they engage in the performance is up to them. But how explicit do we need to be about the nature of the interaction before they enter the experience, and do we need to provide them with full control over their involvement and the data they contribute?

Other Audience Members: If an audience (as performer) experience is being broadcast to other audience members in the exhibition space, they may also become protagonists in the scenario. Do we need to signpost the nature of the artistic work they will be witnessing, before they enter the exhibition space? How would this signposting impact their experience of the creative work?

Dialling up, dialling down: Integrating Consent, Connection, and Creativity

Let us consider consent, connection, and creativity as dials, which can be tuned up or down as required, but do not act in isolation: each time a dial is tuned, it has the potential to stretch or shrink the other elements. The intended outcome of this exercise is not to make individual decisions regarding each of these elements, but rather to make a holistic determination of the shape of the artistic work to fit the purpose and needs of the artistic vision.

Consent is the element with the strongest ethical flavour, heavily influenced by the unique considerations of the capture and use of biometric data in artistic performance. We are currently witnessing AI capabilities increase at an extraordinary pace, and biometric capture technology is rapidly improving; biometric data is therefore becoming easier to obtain and manipulate without awareness or consent. So, what is the role of the artist in this landscape? Turning the connection dial up, it could be argued that a benefit of biometric capture in artistic performances is the enhanced connectivity that individuals may have with the artwork and with each other, and that using biometric data can extend the boundaries of creative expression in uniquely thought-provoking ways. But there is also a risk of eroding the privacy of artists, unsuspecting others (for example, the person an avatar is modelled on), and visitors to exhibition spaces, through increased digital surveillance and data capture. So should the theatre or concert hall be one of the last bastions of privacy, or will we see audience members needing to succumb to the same privacy invasions that we see in everyday life, with everything from digital surveillance of our browsing and shopping habits through to cameras on the street?

Thinking about the technology employed in our speculative performance work, VR headsets incorporate more biometric capture technology than ever, such as face and eye tracking. It would be possible within an artistic work using VR (such as *Scheherazade's Shadow*) to build in a safeguard, such as a popup request, that asks for consent. But how does a user know exactly what the data will be used for? And even if they did consent, how will the artist themselves understand where the data will be stored, and what the data could be used for by the company that owns the data (such as Meta or Apple, for example)?

If we turn the dial down on consent, we may be able to build stronger connections, and more creative freedoms. In terms of the look and characteristics of the avatar, we could choose an avatar that would generate maximum shock and discomfort, thus aligning with the artistic goal of the work. We could imagine a scenario where an off-the-shelf hyper realistic young, naked, female avatar was used. Bringing the audience-as-performer into this context, we could ensure that no prior understanding of the work was available to the visitor, again ensuring maximum shock when the visitor dons the VR headset and is confronted with the naked avatar. It could be articulated that shock and surprise are important creative elements to the work and are central to the work's aim of interrogating the use of biometric data capture in performance. These elements may also foster a strong sense of connection and empathy with the avatar.

If we turn the dial up on consent, the creative design-process of the avatar would be constrained. The data used to create the avatar would need to be ethically sourced, as creating an avatar from copyright material or from a non-consenting person would mean having an unethical dataset on our hands. This may exclude using avatars sourced from large online repositories of ready-to-use avatars. But creativity can be enhanced through constraints, and the design of the avatar could include data from the artist themselves, with their own informed consent. Furthermore, a visitor would have more agency in their experience and would be able to refuse to participate or opt out of the experience if they did not wish to see the avatar or have their data captured. However, providing this level of agency and informed consent would have a direct impact on the 'surprise' element of the experience, as participants would know what to expect. The audience-as-performer may find that their connection to the avatar is negatively impacted, as they have been forewarned of its form and why it has been created in the way it has. Dialling consent up in another direction, a visitor could also refuse to have their heart rate and galvanic skin response data captured, thus limiting their interaction with the avatar and hindering their ability to modify the sonic components of the artwork in response to their biometric data.

Interestingly, when we consider consent in this way it is reminiscent of university ethics approval processes — a hard-ethics approach that is not generally required for artistic performances held outside the walls of the institution. Indeed, within a tertiary education setting, an ethics application ensures that a research study adheres to ethical standards, protecting participants' and researchers' rights and wellbeing through informed consent, risk assessment, and legal compliance, based on six basic principles of autonomy, justice, beneficence, nonmaleficence, confidentiality, and honesty. This promotion of scientific integrity, accountability, and the safeguard of vulnerable populations ensures that responsible and ethical research practices are undertaken. The requirements of the university ethics process can be perceived, however, to "strike at the very heart of creative practice," with the "emergent, unpredictable and experimental nature of practice-led research... fundamentally in conflict" with the "predetermined nature of the ethics application process" (Bolt and Vincs 2015, 1307).

Turning the dial up on consent even further, we could speculate a scenario where the performance was quite simply cancelled, as the wrist device and VR headset used for the performance did not include safeguards on data security and sovereignty. Any data captured or included as part of the performance could therefore be stored and used by the third party for unethical purposes, outside of the control of the artist or participants. As the technology was found to be unethical, the performance could not take place. In this case, turning one dial all the way up leads to the death of the artwork.

Final Reflections

The intersection of art and technology presents both unprecedented opportunities and complex ethical dilemmas that demand robust reflection and proactive engagement. Our exploration of the intersection of biometric data and artistic performance addresses the enduring question of whether art must adhere to ethical standards, and challenges us to consider what it means to create art that asks ethical questions using potentially unethical technology, as *Scheherazade's Shadow* does. The growing ease and speed at which biometric data can be captured and manipulated in artistic performances brings these questions into sharp relief and provides us with a new context for their examination.

Technologies such as augmented and virtual reality enable artists to push the boundaries of creative expression, exploring new dimensions of interaction and engagement. However, with this potential comes significant ethical responsibility. By adopting an 'ethics by design' approach, artists can ensure that ethical reflection is embedded throughout the lifecycle of their projects. This framework encourages a proactive, ongoing, and collaborative approach to ethical considerations, balancing the inherently creative and exploratory nature of performance art with the need for ethical vigilance.

Our proposed performance, *Scheherazade's Shadow*, serves as a compelling case study to illustrate the core competing concerns of consent, connection, and creativity. Through this hypothetical performance, we explored the practical application of the BEAP framework and demonstrated how artists can navigate the ethical landscape of biometric data use in performance art. Through scenario storytelling, we wished to emphasise the rich creative potential of biometric data in enhancing artistic performances, while also encouraging all artists to engage more deeply with the ethical implications of such innovative practices. We echo the assertion of Bolt and colleagues (2016, 1) that the hypothetical "enables us to shift perceptions and practice around ethics." We have therefore proposed a hypothetical performance as a tool to support deeper reflection on the ethics of the use of biometric data in performance. As the true arena of ethics determination is "in the community — art viewers and the general public" (Bolt et al. 2010, 5), we too propose that through hypothetical case studies, such as the one outlined in this chapter, authors and readers can virtually work together to ensure ethics is determined by all, for all.

In this chapter, we have provided an example of an artistic performance in preparation that employs the constant returning of soft ethics to foster a balanced approach, whereby the excitement of artistic innovation coexists with committed ethical mindfulness. As artists, we can consider our artistic performances through lenses such as the BEAP framework, and ethically reflect on them in relation to our search for consent, connection, and creativity. This balancing act ensures that while artistic intent is preserved (and indeed potentially strengthened), the collection of biometric data respects individuals' dignity and autonomy. We aim to foster connections between multiple protagonists — artists, performers, audiences — and between individuals and the artwork itself, enhancing both the creativity and ethical integrity of the art we create.

References

Allan, Julie, Gerard Fairtlough, and Barbara Heinzen. 2001. *The Power of the Tale: Using Narratives for Organizational Success*. John Wiley & Sons.

Bennett, Jane, ed. 2001. *The Enchantment of Modern Life: Attachments, Crossings, and Ethics*. Princeton University Press.

Bolt, Barbara, Kate MacNeill, Megan McPherson, Estelle Barrett, Pia Ednie-Brown, Sarah Miller, Marie Sierra, and Carole Wilson. 2016. "iDARE Creative Arts Research Approaches to Ethics: New Ways to Address Situated Practices in Action." In *Proceedings of the 12th Biennial Quality in Postgraduate Research Conference*, edited by Michelle Picard and Alistair McCulloch. QPR Organising Committee.

Bolt, Barbara, and Robert Vincs. 2015. "Straw Godzilla: Engaging the Academy and Research Ethics in Artistic Research Projects." *Educational Philosophy and Theory* 47 (12): 1304-18. https://doi.org/10.1080/00131857.2015.1044929.

Bolt, Barbara, Robert Vincs, Roger Alsop, Marie Sierra, and Giselle Kett. 2010. "Research Ethics and the Creative Arts." Melbourne University Research Office.

Floridi, Luciano. 2018. "Soft Ethics, the Governance of the Digital and the General Data Protection Regulation." *Philosophical Transactions of the Royal Society A: Mathematical, Physical and Engineering Sciences* 376 (2133): 1-11. https://doi.org/10.1098/rsta.2018.0081.

Johansson, Sofia. 2024. "Laura Mulvey (1975) 'Visual Pleasure and Narrative Cinema.'" In *Classics in Media Theory*, edited by Stina Bengtsson, Staffan Ericson, Fredrik Stiernstedt. Routledge.

Kirby, James N., James R. Doty, Nicola Petrocchi, and Paul Gilbert. 2017. "The Current and Future Role of Heart Rate Variability for Assessing and Training Compassion." *Frontiers in Public Health* 5: 40. https://doi.org/10.3389/fpubh.2017.00040.

Mulvey, Laura. 1975. "Visual Pleasure and Narrative Cinema." *Screen* 16 (3): 6-18. https://doi.org/10.1093/screen/16.3.6.

Rasmussen, Lauge Baungaard. 2005. "The Narrative Aspect of Scenario Building — How Story Telling May Give People a Memory of the Future." *AI & SOCIETY* 19 (3): 229-49. https://doi.org/10.1007/s00146-005-0337-2.

Roufeil, Louise, and Bo Li. 2011. "Public Consultation Paper on Common Guidelines and Code of Ethics." Australian Psychology Society Limited.

Setyohadi, Djoko, Sri Kusrohmaniah, Sebastian Gunawan, Pranowo Pranowo, and Anton Satria Prabuwono. 2018. "Galvanic Skin Response Data Classification for Emotion Detection." *International Journal of Electrical and Computer Engineering* 8 (5): 4004-14. https://doi.org/10.11591/ijece.v8i5.pp4004-4014.

Sierra, Marie, Barbara Bolt, Kate MacNeill, Megan McPherson, Pia Ednie-Brown, Estelle Barrett, Carole Wilson, and Sarah Miller. 2017. "What Is 'Value' When Aesthetics Meets Ethics Inside and Outside of The Academy." Presented at the ACUADS 2017 Conference, Australian National University, Canberra.

Sparrow, Lucy A., Caiti Galwey, Ben Loveridge, Solange Glasser, Margaret S. Osborne, and Ryan M. Kelly. 2024. "Heart and Soul: The Ethics of Biometric Capture in Immersive Artistic Performance." In *Proceedings of the CHI Conference on Human Factors in Computing Systems*, 1-23. CHI '24. Association for Computing Machinery. https://doi.org/10.1145/3613904.3642309.

Varela, Francisco J. 1999. *Ethical Know-How: Action, Wisdom, and Cognition*. Stanford University Press.

Computational Intimacies, from Prompting to Prose:
Jasmin Pfefferkorn in conversation with Beverley Hood

Beverley Hood is an artist and academic who has been exploring the relationship between technology and human experience since the 1990s. Her works integrate sculpture, performance, digital media, and writing. Hood's practice is simultaneously deeply personal and highly collaborative, intersecting with medical professionals, scientists, actors, and dancers, as well as technologists and technology itself. In the following conversation, she discusses the crucial roles of relational thinking, intimacy, and embodiment in her practice, with a focus on her recent work *Mother* (2024).

Mother (2024) is a visual narrative in the form of a short photofilm composed entirely of AI-generated images, made with Adobe Firefly. It renegotiates the generic and sanitised visual culture surrounding motherhood, particularly as it is interpreted and re-inscribed by generative AI models. By engaging with Firefly through prose, rather than normative prompting, Beverley Hood nudges the model into increasingly abstracted and evocative representations of mothering, care, and nurture.

* * *

Jasmin Pfefferkorn (JP): Can you briefly outline how you have used AI or computation in your artistic practice?

Beverley Hood (BH): I've been using computation in my practice since the mid 90s, and digital media in general. I tend to look at re-materialising the body and our relationships through technology, digital media, and science. And, crucially, the effect of them on our notions of relationships, presence, and physicality. It's very relational, the way that I use it, and so it's how it affects our sense of self, but also our relations with one another and the world. Much of my work is also a form of portraiture. I'm going back to a long artistic tradition of artists using themselves as a sort of vehicle to tell stories and explore things. The earliest AI-specific work I did would have been a filmic work in 2005 to 2006, which used an AI voice. This work, which was called *Madame I* (2006), was based on some medical research from the early 20th century. It was a case where a patient had lost her proprioception, her sense of herself physically within the world. In the end, that was to do with lesions in her brain. It was an awful situation, she was institutionalised. I came across this case, and there was a real resonance between it and digital media at the time, which was very much evolving in our relationship with embodiment. We're still in a continual, evolving digital culture. So, I made a film based on this premise, where I translated this original French text from the study, and I created a digital character to be in a short film for a mobile phone. The character, transposed into a mobile phone, spoke about being dissociated from their physical surroundings. While the medical condition made this disembodiment literal in the original case, there were these resonances with how we were talking about digital media at the time. The voice I used for it was a digitised version of my own. I worked with a local Edinburgh company Cereproc, which was one of the key speech synthesis companies in the world. That was the first time I used AI, because while it was based on my voice it was still AI generated. And that was a piece from nearly twenty years ago now.

Between 2021 and 2023, during the COVID-19 pandemic period, I was working on a project using AI tools, specifically emotional recognition tools. I had a small pot of money and a research assistant, and I was starting to look more at bias and representation in AI. I did a mini study that was initially around the representation of gender in AI. It was a sort of rapid research study, just to gather some data around it, on some cultural and current manifestations of gender. But the more I was going into it, it was clear that it's such an intersectional issue around representation. I kept along this path, and I went into how emotions are read, and the problematic nature of that in an intersectional way around gender, ableism, ethnicity, age, you know, all these sorts of socio-cultural aspects of it. That's when I started working on the project *It's all about the feelings* (2021-2023), which was a performance project looking at AI and emotion. Initially, I was developing it over zoom, because of the pandemic. I worked with actor Pauline Goldsmith, who I class as an expert in the representation and the demonstration of emotion. She's an extraordinary, award-winning actor that I've worked with a lot, and we already had an established relationship. We started developing the project over zoom using the software iMotions, which is one of the key emotional recognition systems that's out at present. As the project evolved, we presented it first as a zoom performance, then we also developed it into a full in person performance. The premise was to take an actor who is an expert in cultivating and presenting an emotional range and then playfully but critically present the software reading her in real-time to audiences. She does a monologue that's partly performed to the software and partly performed to the audience in front of her, but the audience can see the bare bones of how the software was being used. Part of that was to give people a sense of the application of the software at the time. Because people would typically say, 'Oh, is it going to be able to read my mind?' And I would quite quickly say, no, because it's very problematic, it's based on Paul Ekman's theory of basic emotions (Paul Ekman Group, n.d.), which has been challenged in psychology and other fields. Nonetheless, that's become the foundation of many emotional recognition systems platforms — it's quite problematic, but it's quite saleable. Even some of the software developers from iMotions that I worked with would say there was quite a lot of extrapolation between how the software works and applications of use. The software does quite a good job of mapping where your face moves and how your face moves. The leap to say that you feel certain things because of those movements is a huge extrapolation, because it's dependent on culturally and socially specific context. We were teasing out some of those things within the piece, and it takes the audience on a journey, where in an experiential way, they could see how this technology works.

JP: After almost 20 years of working with AI, I think we can class you as an early adopter of many of these emergent computational technologies in your art practice. I can already see numerous throughlines between the works you've been describing and your most recent work *Mother* (2024). The relationship between bodies and technology, for instance. *Mother* begins the image portion of the photofilm with uncanny generated images of families [Figure 1], and though there is that strange quality to them, they do have that element that aims towards the photorealistic. Then it gradually shifts into a medium specificity around AI, offering visibility to the way that AI produces surreal images. Even if there is a remix quality to AI, your work is taking this technology as its own medium, rather than trying to push it in a direction where it fits with a pre-existing photorealistic style. What is it about the medium specificity of AI that you think is interesting or challenging, why do you enjoy working with it?

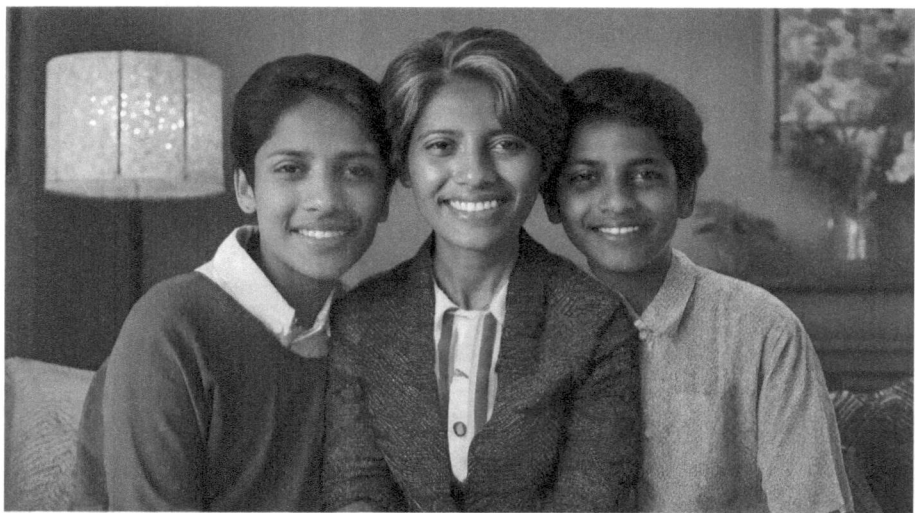

Figure 1: Beverley Hood, 2024. *Mother*, still from generative AI photo-film.

BH: I tend to look at either current or near-future technologies. I'm not necessarily working with things that are future-speculative. I often look at things that are starting to be incorporated into our lives more, so they're quite close to us. These might be the beginnings of integration, and I'm looking at the implications of these integrations. What you brought up is key, because I'm also thinking about dealing with the characteristics of a technology on its own terms. Even when I used body scanning 20 years ago, I was using the 3D meshes that map the body, without cleaning them up. This felt truer to the characteristics of the scanning process. This kind of thing is a purposeful and integral part of my approach to technology. I'm not trying to make it something else. I'm interested in trying to keep to the essence of what the tools are and interrogate what they are and how we've set up a technology. AI is used as this blanket term, but really, there's such a variety of forms and applications of it — even the three systems that we're talking about here, going from speech synthesis to emotional recognition systems to generative AI for image-making. These are three quite different types of AI technologies. As artists, it's useful to remember that, although we use an umbrella term, there are such different manifestations within it. It's important to interrogate each of them, and for their own characteristics and implications. It's true of generative AI, the image-making models and the large language models as well. They're becoming so commonplace, and the rapid integration of their use has really exploded. Over the past few years, I'd been doing little bits and pieces looking at it, but never really interrogating them. And in a way, they're quite dull. They're very basic in the actual process of working with them, it's not very sophisticated. Text in, and then image or text out. But when you stop and ask what is actually happening, the implications are huge. I hadn't really found it particularly interesting when I first approached it, I think that it is quite off-putting for a lot of artists. Creatives don't necessarily sit and expect to write a prompt to realise their work. Even a writer isn't necessarily thinking 'I'm going to write this as an expert and then expect generated text back.' It's quite an odd process in itself around creativity. I work a lot with actors and dancers and people like that, and it wouldn't be part of the process to sit down and type in a few words. Although this doesn't necessarily preclude it from being a naturally dynamic process.

With *Mother* in particular, I was quite interested in the imagery that was coming out of it, and particularly the characteristics of it, that has very much got its own aesthetics, which we know are evolving. Although it is absolutely the stochastic parrot that offers a complete mash up. But there are some interesting works that people have been doing in using it. People like Jake Elwes (2019), who is making his own data sets and creating an aesthetic. There are still aesthetics building within it and I guess I'm interested in what those aesthetics are. In *Mother*, I started with the prose text. I was looking at what type of text I might use, because it's typically all based on literally asking it, or commanding it, the equivalent of, make me an X, make me a Y. I want this, I want that. And being quite descriptive as well. It's quite a transactional situation. And I know that lots of artists are working in different ways to open that up. So it was, in the beginning, partly trying to open that way of working with it for myself.

There remained a feeling that it was quite dull as a process, but then I went back into it because I thought that there's something interesting about the imagery that's coming out, and something interesting with the process of working with text. And I do write as part of my work as well. Sometimes I write more academic text, but I also write in a sort of note form and a prose form a lot. Usually in my notes app on my phone. So, there's this sort of separate practice that happens adjacent to the rest of my work. On occasion, it has been folded into actual projects; at times, the notes drift in. It's a way to start bringing different ways of writing to the AI, which ended up opening the aesthetic process. It started as coming from quite a personal point of view, because I was curious about the images of people that were coming out. So, I started with myself. In prompting the AI, I would describe myself as a mother, a mother of two sons, a mother of teenage boys. And it was interesting just to see straight away what would come back out, and particularly with Midjourney, the biases and stereotypes that emerged. If I included 'mother' as a descriptor, the age depictions would shift. If I said teenage boys in tracksuits, which my sons tend to wear, then all the people who would come back would be black. Straight away there were all these sorts of characteristics that would come out in this direct way. I started on this path, but then thought I'm not feeling this, or I'm not pushing it very far. I can go with this text and it's going to be very literal, and that's not really what I was looking for. So that's when I started to go to prose as an approach. I was basically compositing a lot of texts that I'd written on my phone about creativity, motherhood, caring. I composed these into a text as a way to engage with the AI.

JP: What made you end up choosing Adobe Firefly as your primary tool for this video work?

BH: I'd done some tests with Midjourney and some tests with Firefly. I was aware that you could class Firefly as a more ethical platform, in that it pays through license for the images that make up its foundation model data. In premise, Adobe is trying to take an ethical stance around it. And, they don't train on subscriber's personal content. So, there's an attempt on behalf of the organisation. I also thought that it was interesting because it follows the Adobe portfolio of software, so it has this design around it that's made specifically for creatives.

I think Midjourney has got all this potential in it. In some ways, there's a lot more that you can do with it in terms of being able to put prompts in and commands and being able to control which directions it moves, you can keep the trail of it. There are some things about it that are sort of more powerful in Midjourney. But some key things around representation I found to be very poor in Midjourney, and the images in Firefly seemed a little better. I know that Adobe has also done work to try and diversify the results. Another project that I'm working on right now is around the lived experience of eczema. It's an art science project that I'm doing, and I put in some prompts around eczema with each of them, and the results in Midjourney were utterly horrific. Monstrous is what they were. And it was literally just prompting for things like a person with eczema, eczema skin.

I was working with a group of young people at the time as well, who were a stakeholder group within the project and the reflection and critique device for the project. And I was going to be working with them and testing some of the images. I thought there is absolutely no way I could take this to them for testing. This is actually harmful. These are young people with serious lived experiences and serious mental health concerns because of their situations. And what the image model was churning out could be seriously harmful. It didn't become a part of the study or the project. Sometimes I choose to not give oxygen to areas that I don't want to give it. I make concerted decisions at times around what to choose to critique and what to choose to ignore for the sake of not oxygenating and giving space. Midjourney doesn't care if I don't use it. But I decided then, right, okay, I'm going to focus my attention on this platform from Adobe that's attempting to develop some sort of ethical approach to using it.

> **JP:** This speaks to ethics as a learnt skill, as ethics through relations. Understanding the difference between what could be done and what should be done is a kind of soft ethics, which we see in the way you approach different platforms and think through their

policies and frameworks. And the way you consciously decided not to share image outputs with the young people you were working with also speaks to ethical know-how. Because you've already developed those sorts of connections, understandings, everything that is required to know how to benefit people's wellbeing in that space. You can trust in your decision making when it comes from ethical know-how.

BH: There is an interesting conversation to be had about the ethics of AI and artists as well, though. Especially around the idea that artists become like the ethical gatekeepers for technologies or situations. It can be deeply problematic because sometimes it is really useful for artists to be provocatively challenging our ethics as well. So, I made decisions there which were based on certain circumstances. But I'm not setting it up saying I think we all shouldn't do this, that, and the other, and I'm going to set the ethical boundaries for you. I think there's a distinction there as well, around what we expect, because the arts should challenge our boundaries. A lot of the time the critical part of it is really important. I'm trying not to box myself into a way of working through thinking 'I don't think I should do this'.

JP: So how do you then decide what boundaries you won't cross?

BH: I would take it as a case-by-case situation every time. I always do, because I do have quite a lot of experience of working in quite sensitive situations. I would say I'm attentive to sensitive situations. In a previous work that I did, I worked in a medical simulation centre for about four years to make a performance. The performance was held in the medical simulation centre using patient manikins, and it was with surgeons and other medical staff, and I would bring audiences in, and the audience would get scrubbed up and be in emergency situations. There were various performance vignettes that happened with actors and dancers keeping the audience in a mostly sustained uncertainty. They never really knew what their role was, and they never knew what was real and what wasn't real around them, and the whole thing was a simulation, anyway. It was held in a quite disconcerting world of uncertainty, but around medicine and healthcare and emergency, which is, for pretty much everyone, a difficult place to be in. The whole time I was attentive to how I could keep people in this uncertainty and in this disconcerting space, but not completely trigger people. Everybody could have somebody, a relative, in hospital, and could have had these kinds of experiences. The simulation centre is in the middle of a hospital as well, so you have to go into the hospital to see the piece. So I was being attentive to the way I was putting people into this space and really challenging audiences, even the healthcare workers. I had surgeons who found it incredibly difficult because of how the performers would behave with the patient manikins. So, it's quite a challenging piece, but I thought carefully about keeping it in a space that would not be sensational. That was the key thing to me there. I'm not trying to be like a television show that takes emergency circumstances as entertainment. I think really carefully about the challenges, but I can often make work that's quite provocative and challenging for audiences to go into, and I do that knowingly and purposefully.

> **JP:** So there's a dividing line between provocative, challenging, but never that spectacle of shock for shock's sake. I'll bring it back to *Mother* — obviously, we've spoken a lot about how prose forms the basis of this work, and you make that explicit by starting the film with a piece of prose [see Figure 2]. And this is great because it's a recognition that large image models are always also large language models. They can't be just image based. There's always got to be a textual component in there. And it's in the context of prompt engineering, where there is meant to be some sort of optimised version of prompting the machine. In your work, you are navigating and pushing the boundaries of that by trying to meet the machine in the middle of your language and its language. From your perspective, what was the role of poetics in this work? And how did you have to alter your prose approach within the particular policy frameworks that Adobe Firefly has, for example, with their censorship of certain words?

BH: I'd started off with more sort of literal text that was sort of specific around describing myself, and then I went to the prose by consolidating a bunch of notes that I had on my phone into a type of script. But it was never the intention for that to be something that was used explicitly in the final film. I did test it being used, in terms of something that could be spoken, because I have done previous projects where I've written and then voiced an entire text. But *Mother* didn't seem to need this, or work with it in this particular version. But what I did do, was to take the text and put that in as the prompt, and then see what was coming out

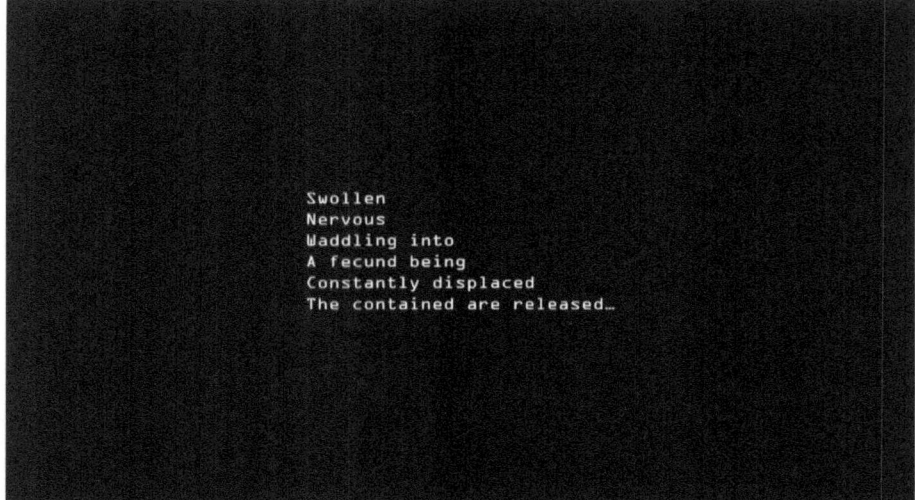

Figure 2: Beverley Hood, 2024. *Mother*, still from generative AI photo-film.

and what I was finding. First, I used the text that was more specifically around motherhood, the more sort of literal parts of the prose. And because of the nature of Firefly, in that they already have a license for the stock imagery used for their model, you automatically get a very stock-imagery aesthetic. As with all generative AI, what comes out is characteristic of whatever has been put in. Adobe's characteristic is due to a specific range of images that it's been trained on, in terms of what they own or have the right to use.

At the beginning of the film, you see a very stock image aesthetics of a mother and children [Figure 3]. In that way it's perhaps less an art-historical canon and more a stock image canon. It holds cultural characteristics, it's very Americanised. So, an image of a pregnant woman would have her belly smocked [Figure 4], which felt to me like an American version of modesty. Many generated images would come back with people in a very American TV-show style living room, often with a woman in a suit with children. Sometimes I would tweak the prompts. I have two sons, and I wondered how many children I could put in. I'd try with asking for, say, ten, and it would only ever give me about three back at the most. It was interesting that there were characteristics where it wouldn't return, almost a block written into it in terms of how many children you are allowed to have. And there were some very odd things coming out from it in terms of the characteristics of the mother and child.

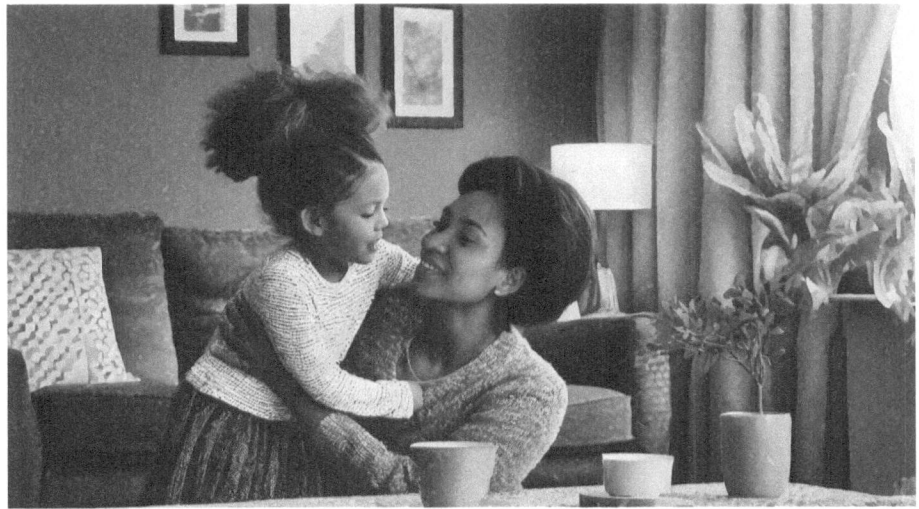

Figure 3: Beverley Hood, 2024. *Mother*, still from generative AI photo-film.

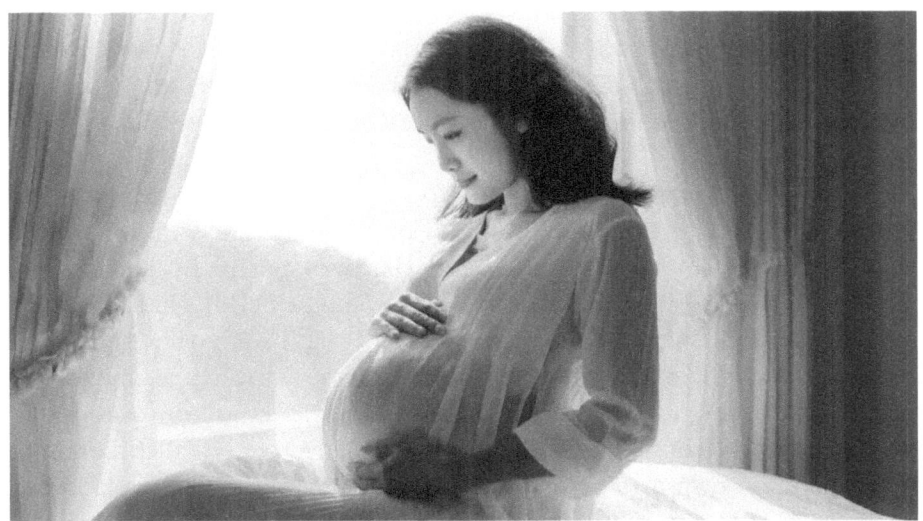

Figure 4: Beverley Hood, 2024. *Mother*, still from generative AI photo-film.

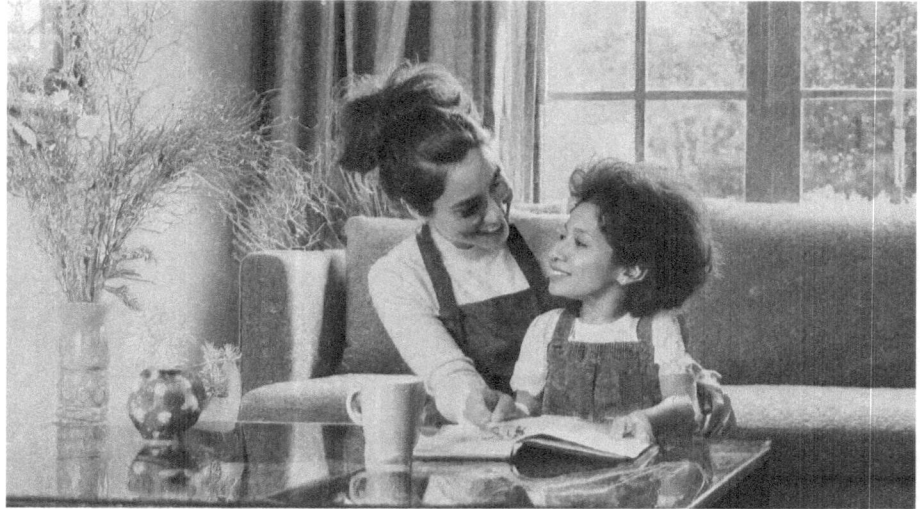

Figure 5: Beverley Hood, 2024. *Mother*, still from generative AI photo-film.

Sometimes there were these sorts of artifacts, where it's glitched a bit, where sometimes the child's body would have an adult face, and things like that [Figure 5]. I edited very little out of the film. I used pretty much all the images that I generated, there weren't very many instances where I took them out. This was the characteristic that was given back to me, so I pretty much used all of it. Then, as the text I was feeding it became more ambiguous, the images became more ambiguous.

In Firefly, I set an aesthetic palette. You can set up parameters such as: photographic, close up, filmic, and so on. There were various criteria that I used to set up a palette, and this was partly by choice, and partly pushing a bit away from the stock imagery. But then, once I'd set it, I kept with it. I found when working with Firefly that there's an element of flow, like a social media feed. In choosing certain images and prioritising them, I think the algorithm tends to keep you on a path. So the workflow consisted of these quite intensive periods of time, quite hypnotic and down a rabbit hole as a process of working, because what is returned is also so fast. I ended up in this nudging situation, I would put some text in, see what came back, and then I might put fragments of the original text in. I didn't necessarily take it line by line by line, working systematically through. I would class it as a sort of improvised coercion. I know there's lots of terms that people are using in relation to working with AI tools — collaboration, co-constitution. There are all sorts of things, but I did feel like, in some ways, I was trying to coerce it into behaving in slightly different ways. I was trying get more to the crux of it and pick it apart a little bit.

That's when it opened out into more abstract, textual images. And it's interesting because I have spoken to Adobe and given feedback and shared the film with them as well, and for some of the images even they've said, 'How did you get it to do that?' They hadn't thought about using prose, which links back to what you said around the perception of prompting having a 'best' way, by following certain criteria. I found I could get into a really interesting flow of working, which I sometimes think can be quite difficult with some digital technologies, because you can end up being stopped or slowed down a lot by various technicalities. I also do things like watercolor and collage, which I also feel you can more easily get into a certain type of flow with. It's the nature of the medium. But I did find with the generative AI, because it's relatively quick and you can quickly tweak the prompt's language, that it produced an interesting process of flow that I both enjoyed and could do for quite a long time. I'd have to tell myself to stop and get something to eat.

I think there's an aesthetic flow that comes out of that as well, that both I, and the platform as it's following my prompts and choices, are in. It's almost like you're on a trail, and you're in a churn of a process. I think I did the whole image generation process over about four or five sessions.

> **JP:** So, it's almost like that iterative component creates a sustained attention on both sides. The machine, as you said, is kind of paying attention to what you're selecting and privileging, in terms of what it returns. And you're entering into a flow state of working with it, which is, as you said, something that you can access through other forms of artistic practice but has its own temporality with the computational.

BH: I really noticed it, because sometimes I find it's quite difficult to do within digital technologies. There are quite a lot of processes that use digital technologies where the technology remains too present to create flow.

> **JP:** It makes sense, but is nonetheless interesting that as you shifted increasingly into a prose style you generated more abstract visuals.

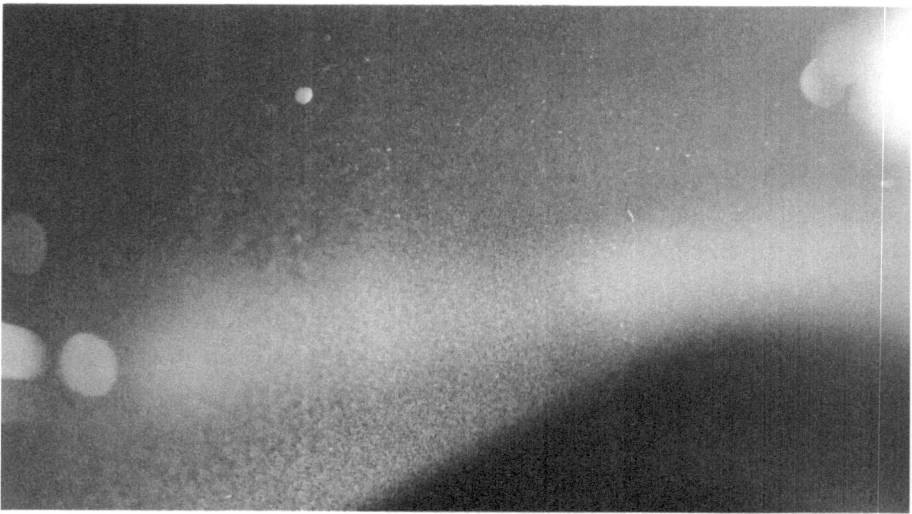

Figure 6: Beverley Hood, 2024. *Mother*, still from generative AI photo-film.

And there are certainly many of these in the film. One of the things that really stood out to me throughout this work is that later in the film you start to get these images that reference photographic failure in a lot of ways. Things like light flares, or super granular images [Figure 6].

BH: There are the more abstracted images that do look very filmic. And then there's also some close ups that are very textural as well [Figure 7]. For those, Adobe came back and said Firefly normally really struggles with textures and asked how I managed to generate them. There was a genuine sense of surprise there. Those abstractions come when the text prompt is not very literal at all. It's like it's grasping at straws, in a way, to bring some imagery together. Adobe asked if I'd taken sections of an image and blown them up to bring out those images, but I hadn't. I've used full images for everything, always the full scale of what's been generated. But the whole way through I'm under no illusion, it's all derivative. And so, yes, there's a lot of it that feels very filmic. Some of the images feel art house, Andrei Tarkovsky, things like that. There are specific aesthetics that regurgitate. I don't think they'll have a license for Tarkovsky, but it has specific aesthetics that are already in existence. It's a mash up, and it's got some quite surreal combinations in what comes out. I was completely going with the derivative nature of that and not worrying about it, which is also quite interesting, because I think, as an

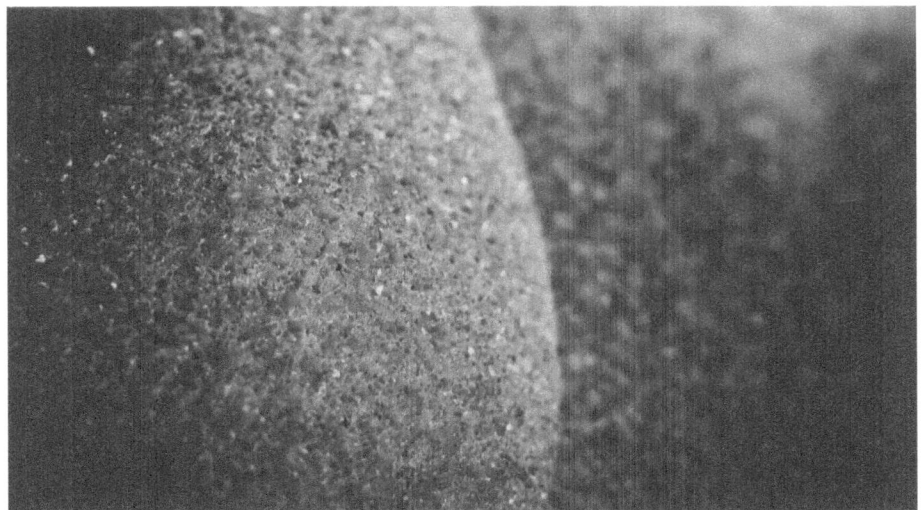

Figure 7: Beverley Hood, 2024. *Mother*, still from generative AI photo-film.

artist, typically, I'm quite conscious of this. In the past, I made a piece that's around MRI technologies. And when I started that MRI piece, I was conscious that there's such a strong aesthetic around MRI that I didn't particularly want to repeat. So, in that piece, I was looking for different aesthetic ways to approach it. Whereas when I'm working with AI in *Mother*, I'm just conscious that the whole thing is derivative. That is the nature of it. I think sometimes it's a bit problematic to be claiming that it's making something completely new. That's also why, for the audio of the film, I purposefully chose to be derivative for that as well. I looked at using AI tools for the audio as well, but what I found was that it was difficult to get anything other than a tune, which I didn't want. I was looking for something more like a pulse, a beat that would drive the form. And I say form because I wouldn't quite class it as narrative. So I ended up sampling existing work, paid for samples composed and performed by Pan Sonic and EmptySet. Experimental electronica, noise music, that I resampled into the work.

> **JP:** I want to come back to what you said about there often being that element of self-portraiture in your work. You write about Mother as being about your personal experience as a mother, as a carer. I'm interested in where you then locate yourself again within that finished product.

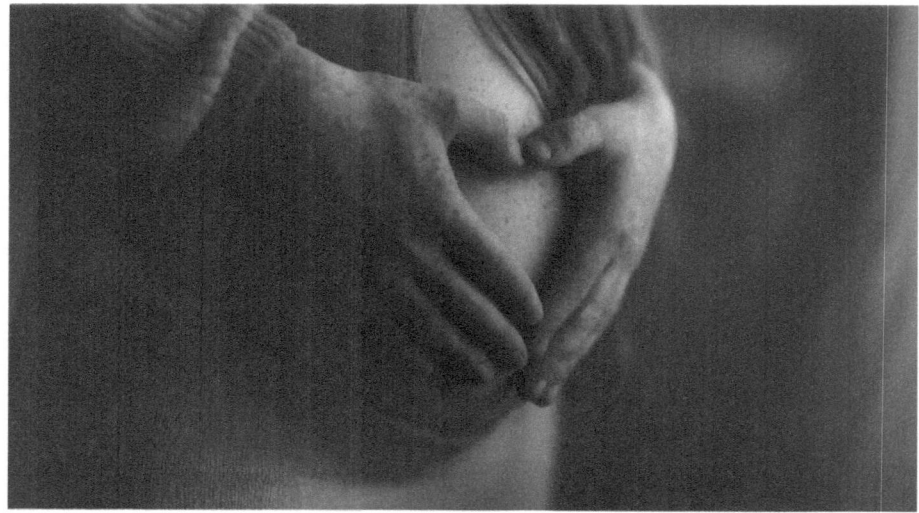

Figure 8: Beverley Hood, 2024. *Mother*, still from generative AI photo-film.

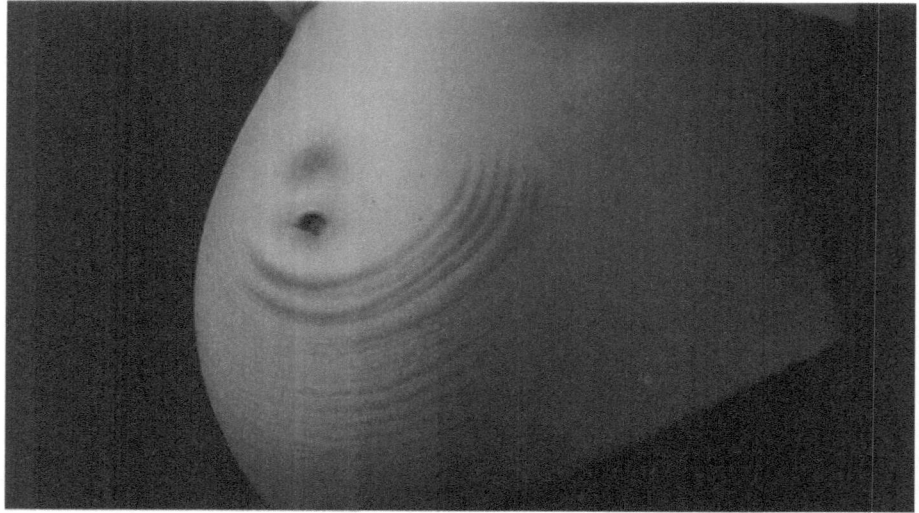

Figure 9: Beverley Hood, 2024. *Mother*, still from generative AI photo-film.

BH: It feels quite personal to me. My oldest son, jokingly, always calls me Mother as well. It's literally how he addresses me in a tongue-in-cheek way. I do feel like it is a type of portraiture, because it includes my own issues around care and the representations of mother and motherhood. I would say this is more a representation of experience, as opposed to the idea of a mother. It's more an emotive, experiential portrait, as opposed to a direct picture. It starts off with the stereotype of a person with children and then it becomes more about the experience of motherhood.

JP: In an earlier conversation we had, you mentioned your difficulties in even trying to depict a pregnancy. You referenced it today, with the idea that pregnant bellies were nearly always shown with a smock covering them. And I remember you saying that that was something that you had to iterate around, which you managed to do, because in the film there is a visual of a pregnant stomach in it where you do see skin depicted [Figure 8; Figure 9]. So you did eventually get there, but I know that you had to really play with language in order to do it.

BH: At the beginning, I used more literal text prompts that asked for, like, pregnant belly, flesh, things like that. I would have to remove certain words, because I would get a prompt back from Firefly saying "Can't load. We can't process this prompt. You can edit and try again, or flag for review." At the beginning, if I asked for a pregnant belly, I could only ever get it covered in clothing. It was really bizarre, this extreme modesty. But then, as I've worked more with the prompt text, I did eventually get there. One of the key words was fecund, which brought back pregnant bellies, uncovered, showing flesh. That came later in the text, and later in the film, you do see that there are actual bellies in there. It also returned these sorts of strange beings that look like some sort of fruit, or fleshy beings that seem to hold the potential to burst [Figure 10; Figure 11]. Those came from getting into a much more poetic language. There was also text about cuts, and scars, and healing that wouldn't load. I gave feedback to Adobe on this as well, and when I've been using it more recently, I did think they might have tweaked some of the parameters of this. They work with a lot of artists and are listening to us. They've got various artists that they've commissioned and are working with. We have a project as part of the BRAID responsible AI program (BRAID UK 2024), and Adobe are working closely with a research fellow of ours to look closely in terms of how artists are using Adobe's AI tools. While other tech companies are doing this, I think Adobe is doing it more directly with the creative community, because it's their target audience. It's fascinating to me, the idea of trying to take a more ethical stance that tries not to enable people to make pornography, sexually explicit, violent material, things like that, which I would imagine are the drivers that they would be setting up these parameters for, but balancing this with finding a way that actually enables people to work with the tool. So I thought that was an interesting ethical conundrum there.

JP: It ends up bringing a moralising quality to ethical considerations. And, with the examples you've given, it ends up as being potentially quite exclusionary of a lot of people's very real lived experiences and things that they might want to find represented in the various information or art forms communicated or reflected to them.

BH: It's a massive issue around AI, because then it's locked in with a particular set of cultural and business parameters around it. It's absolutely becoming exclusionary, but people are always reformatting the language to be able to say what they want to say. That's what I was doing here by renegotiating the prompt. What I was doing could be seen as a type of algospeak, a type of coded language used to avoid automated moderation, in things like TikTok. You might call what I was doing algospeak style prompting, like an adjacent approach to conventional prompting, which is trying to get round censorship and limitations and comes from specific points of view. And the point of view in *Mother*, it's just around birth and women's bodies. The censorship is quite contained there, isn't it? Perhaps it might seem like quite a little thing, but it's also my personal experience and perspective. Recognising that when these platforms exist in such a huge international scale, something that's released by Adobe or Midjourney, it brushes across so many different social and cultural norms, expectations, and boundaries. I can't assume everyone else has the same boundaries. This is where I think it's tricky around artists being set up as gatekeepers, because artists' ethical stances aren't all the same. We're not a homogeneous group.

JP: It's interesting as well because, with the technical affordances of generative AI today, it's moved beyond object recognition and into concept recognition, which is how foundation models can operate in a variety of contexts and domains. While you can't teach

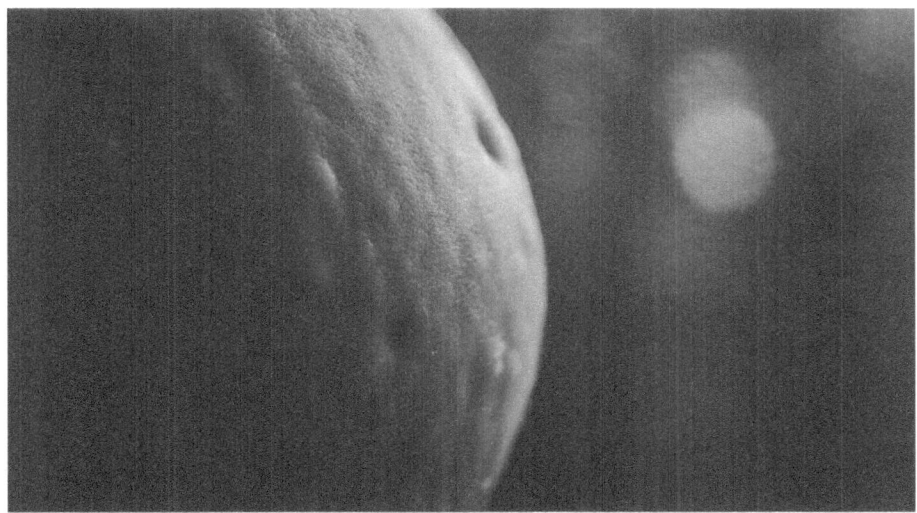

Figure 10: Beverley Hood, 2024. *Mother*, still from generative AI photo-film.

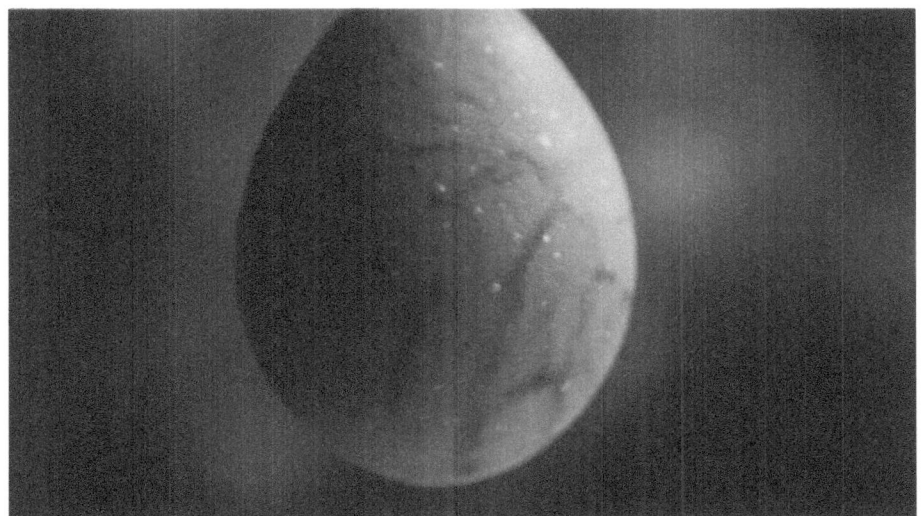

Figure 11: Beverley Hood, 2024. *Mother*, still from generative AI photo-film.

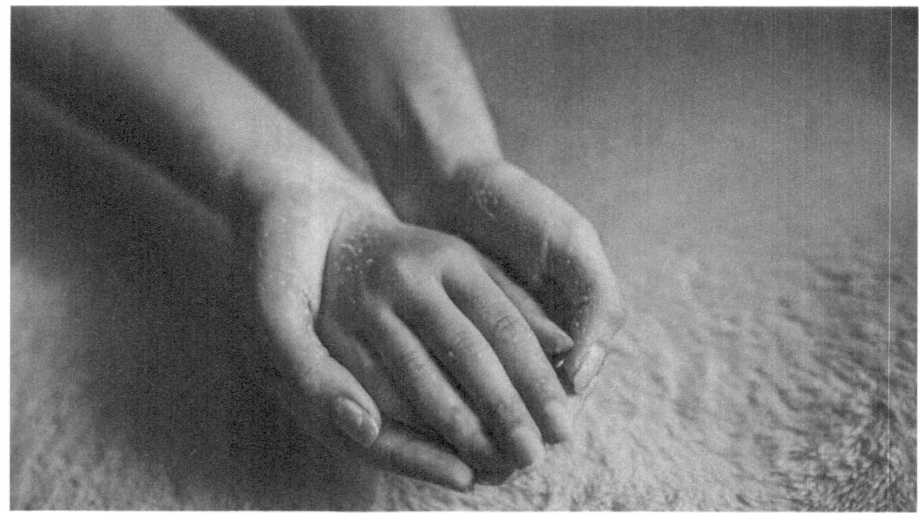

Figure 12: Beverley Hood, 2024. *Mother*, still from generative AI photo-film.

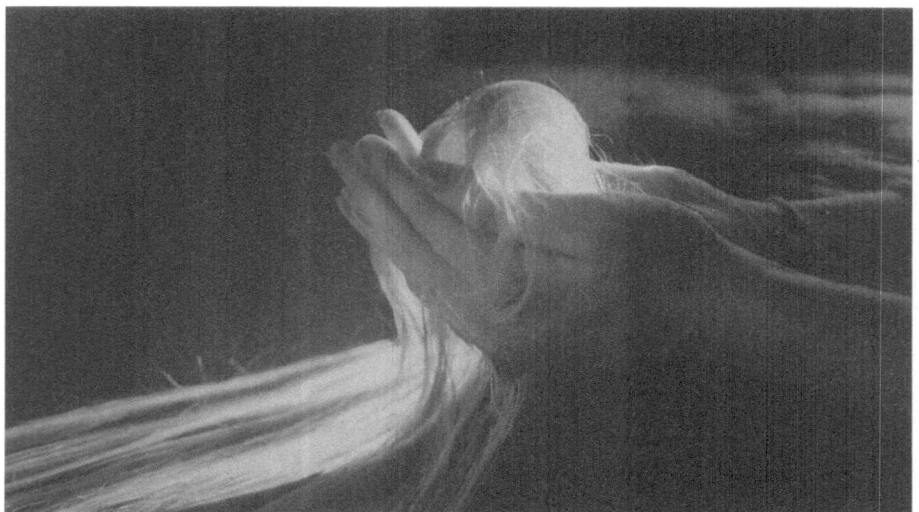

Figure 13: Beverley Hood, 2024. *Mother*, still from generative AI photo-film.

the machine to nurture, there is a sense that Mother can train it on the concept, because your work does have an ethics of care in the content. It's something that, because of the parameters of the algorithm, the model might not otherwise have access to. So, while the concept is different for a lot of people, there are also elements of nurture and motherhood that can be overarching and shared. I wanted to ask — what does this work show us about an ethics of care? Or, what is your perspective of care and nurture within this work?

BH: In a literal way, when there was prose that was put in around care, there were quite a lot of hands in it, holding things [Figure 12]. And even when there's a pregnant belly, it's very much held. And I think there's a softness around a lot of the images. I mean, a lot of them are quite peculiar, but there is also quite a lot of softness.

JP: Some that really stood out to me were the ones holding hair [Figure 13]. I think because they are echoes of the things we associate with nurture — stroking, caressing, brushing hair — but in this version the hair and the hands are configured as being held and holding.

BH: Yes, it's a slightly skewed interpretation, where the tech introduces this peculiar softness when I've put care into it. In the work that I did in the medical simulation centre, there was a lot we did there around care, and there was a lot around very attentive behaviors with the patient manikins. There is a similar sort of aesthetic and feel in *Mother* to that. All the work I do is relational. It's about how we relate to one another and how we relate to human and nonhuman alike. As we deal with each other in more distant and distributed ways, what does that mean about dehumanising processes and when an entity becomes an 'other' or not? Even throughout the idea of automation, there are always people, everywhere, crowd-workers holding up this process. To me, there is a need for care and attentiveness within all those processes, because all the technological processes are held together by people anyway. So there's an element around care in *Mother* that I think is quite literally presented by those hands. And there's always this peculiarity at the minute around images of hands created by AI, which will be an artifact from this time, I'm sure. It's also useful as a device, to remember that it's not quite that we are seeing something human here. But then, how do we relate to that?

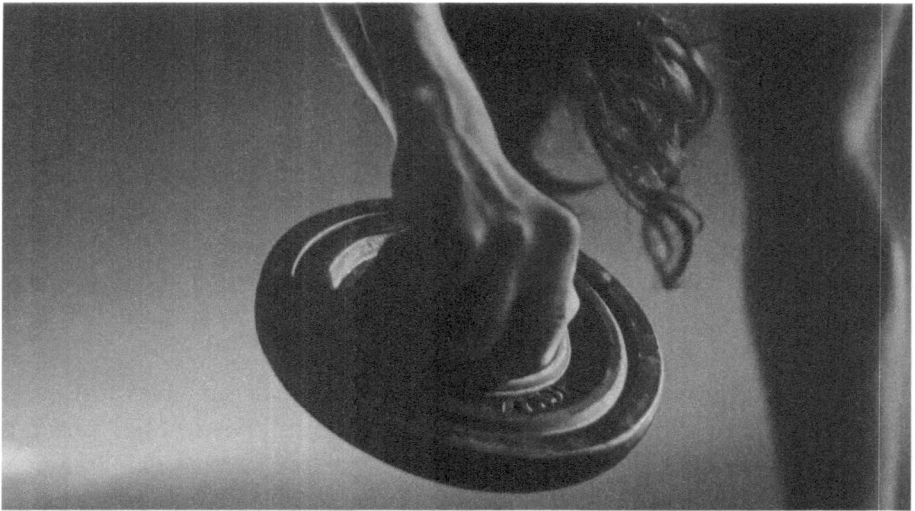

Figure 14: Beverley Hood, 2024. *Mother*, still from generative AI photo-film.

What does that tell us? And how do we then think about how we relate to people through technology?

> **JP:** I recognise that it's dangerous territory to start reverse engineering what's happened in latent space based on an image that comes out. But there are some of those images that we've spoken about now, where I can't help but think through the traces of humanity that have ended up in these images in a variety of ways. So, when you're talking about care, we're thinking of holding these bundles of hair, and you immediately think of someone brushing your hair. Or if you think of the holding of the weight [Figure 14], that was a very interesting one, because obviously you could read it in a very literal, neoliberal way of self-care, wellness industry. That mainstream narrative around motherhood and the idea of doing or having it all. But there's also the weight of emotional labor that you carry with care. These things all come through as evocative traces of the various ways in which we conceive of what it means to nurture, from both cultural and capital perspectives. I wanted to keep going with the theme of nurture and the more-than-human, which incorporates an understanding of ecology. In *Mother*, there are these great images of moss growing out of skin [Figure 15], and all of these representations of fungi-like entities. How does this work approach the idea of the more-than-human?

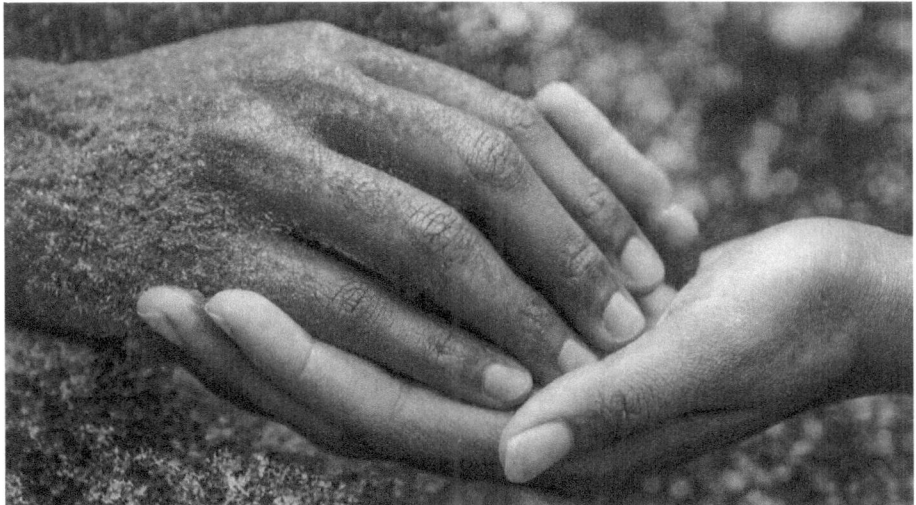

Figure 15: Beverley Hood, 2024. *Mother*, still from generative AI photo-film.

BH: In the pandemic period I, like a lot of people, started to walk and forage a lot more. We took a lot of respite, nurture, and sustenance from nature itself. In some ways, that is also in the text. There's a separate piece that I did a couple of years ago called *An Exercise in Solitude* (2022) that also used prose for another short film, but with a spoken word monologue over footage of nature. It was all filmed on my phone during my walks, and it talks about the ecological side of technology. It has a meandering aspect to it that is similar to the text used for Mother, but it was dealt with differently. There is definitely an element of the relationship with nature as a place of care, almost like self-care and a sort of stabilising through the mad storms going on around us. I absolutely think of the work in terms of a feminist, new materialist way of thinking, where there is a multiplicity of perspectives. The tools bring perspectives into the work as well, and I'm always trying to acknowledge the technology's affordances, as a sort of more-than-human aspect as well.

An Exercise in Solitude was very much about the environmental implications of all the technologies we use: what Kate Crawford (2021) calls geological processes. She's really reinforcing the material manifestations of technology and the implications for our environment. I definitely do think about all of these aspects to the work as well. And I'm thinking about embracing the technology's perspective and affordances, and its characteristics here as a voice and an imprint in and of itself.

JP: What is wonderful is that the visuals in *Mother* aren't representing this separatist distinction between human and nature and technology. It has that element of what N. Katherine Hayles (2012) calls 'technogenesis'. A recognition of all the ways in which we are relationally bound, always more than human and, while different, not distinct. This also links to nurture and is a real break from the historical categorisation of things linked to Western ideology. The other thing that comes through with nurture in Mother is the feeling of tactility in these images, which you intimated earlier in talking about texture. The images are sensuous. It seems this is also a constant in your work. You highlighted it at the start around thinking through what it means to be embodied or disembodied. In *Mother*, there is a tenderness in that sensuousness. But there is a sensuousness to the machinic as well. Parts of the AI assemblage are tactile interfaces that require gesture and touch in the process of working with them.

BH: That's been something of a characteristic throughout my creative practice and my use of technologies. I'm very much dealing with it as a material, and I think that's where the more sensual and tactile aspects of it are coming from. Even if it's purely digital, it can still feel like a visceral experience. That's key. I come from a sculpture background, and then moved to electronic imaging, and then performance as well. For me, it has been a key method to make work, to bring things to life, to perform using both technology and human bodies through actors and dancers. It's embodied in ways that I think are crucial aspects of the work. It comes back to new materialism as well: the idea of tools being central to our perception, our ways of seeing and being. I'm against the concept of transhumanism. For me, it's about the relational aspects between us and other entities. With AI, I think it is overall more about what it means to have the tools as the interface between us and, in turn, what it means for our embodied perception within that.

JP: It feels more hopeful, yet still nuanced, to think in these ways as well, a counterbalance to the celebratory narratives, or the dread rhetoric.

BH: And these tools are certainly being used in ways that come from a social activist point of view, where there is a genuine desire to support people. So, things like developing AI from a grassroots level to help people write insurance claims. I love things like that.

> **JP:** I feel like that's what we were sold on, but we never really got it because AI was so quickly subsumed by a commercial logic, rather than operationalised for a social logic.

BH: Especially with things like data harvesting. I'm still not convinced by this idea around big data that the more you put in, the more you'll get out. Sometimes the more you put in, the more noise you get. The smaller models and the specific, bespoke systems, rather than these ones trying to promote a universal premise, are perhaps more promising. That's why I also think, in terms of the arts, that people like Anna Ridler (n.d.) who are making their own datasets and models are setting really interesting precedents.

> **JP:** There is an intimacy there, when artists work to build their own datasets and models.

BH: Alongside the relational part of my work, I think intimacy is part of how I work generally. There's an element in terms of using myself and my personal experience that I think potentially sets up a type of intimacy there. We forget sometimes how intimate we are with technology, and how much we share intimately. I know there's the idea that a lot of the time it's coerced by tech companies, but we do have a lived intimacy with technology, day in day out, as a gateway to other things. Perhaps we are inclined to see that intimacy with the people we are using technology to connect with, but how much do we hold that relationship with the technology itself? It's something I set up with the medical simulation piece as well. There's a massive amount of intimacy. A lot of the care in that piece is projected onto the patient manikins, as opposed to the people, as a sort of performative device. The intimacy and the care is all handled with the technological bodies, not the people around them. I like putting intimacy there, and acknowledging intimacy as a process is fascinating.

> **JP:** I think many people would consider writing prose to be devastatingly intimate. And you mentioned that a lot of that material comes from the notes application on your phone. I think I'd be horrified if someone read an unedited version of the notes I write. But

it speaks to the fact that we're putting these little bits of ourselves into that, and that there is this constant kind of communion that's happening with the technology.

BH: Totally, though that's how I usually bring that to the public. My notes aren't necessarily part of works, or part of a script, it's not named, it's just something that has come out of me. There's this thing where I'm having to think about the internalised things coming out and finding a way to share that. In *Mother*, I felt like it didn't need to be so specific with the text: the images could carry themselves without having to include the words I used directly. And some of it is very personal and related around my family.

> **JP:** I wonder if that's one of the key benefits of AI. Most of us have already internalised that ease of putting ourselves into machines, because we're hidden in a way, it's a protective sort of mechanism. You know, it's very different, in my view, to stand on a stage reading your own words out to someone, versus typing it, putting it into a machine, having it return as images. But it does take our engagement with generative AI beyond the exploratory and into sharing our intimate thoughts.

BH: I think so, but I'm always concerned about how much people overshare in terms of content and data as well. One of the very first digital pieces that I made was in 1997, a net art piece which was a handwritten love letter chopped up into slices and blown up within web page frames. You had to scroll through the frame to read the text, and you could only move through it in a really broken up way. It was at a time when I was just so conscious of how easily people were oversharing, sharing very intimate personal information across digital technologies. Now this idea of digital traces is commonplace. I mean, I say to my kids, just imagine nothing is private that you put into any of these technologies. Because ultimately, it's not, you can't guarantee that it is. Across whatever platforms, whatever apps that you're using, people can access them in some way, at some point, at some time. For me, there's a tension with this intimacy. We don't necessarily think consciously enough about what material we are offering, or check in with our boundaries and what we are okay with in these situations. I find a lot of people share, forgetting that there's a whole world of commerce that holds all of this. Certainly, there are things that people are comfortable with sharing, but I think it's sometimes questionable how much people are thinking about that deeply, about how intimate that is, and what their tolerance for that is. I think a lot about tolerance as a concept, and tolerance of uncertainty is a big thing in my work, but also in art and science in general.

> **JP:** I think when we're talking about intimacy in this sort of context, it's more about acknowledging that 'oh, I'm engaging with a cognitive assemblage here'. And balancing sharing and openness with being careful requires a real progression in mindset. I do think this approach to uncertainty is one of the crucial things that artistic methods and practices illustrate, I suppose because experimentation and uncertainty are two sides of the same coin.

BH: Yes, that acknowledgement that it is an assemblage, one that has other people in it, is important. Something I always think about is when, one summer, almost thirty years ago, I worked for a telecoms company. My role was to answer phones as a call centre operator, and I would type out messages that people wanted to send via pager. That's how paging messages were sent back then. I remember one person in particular, a man, who would phone up and he would send love letters, or love pages, to a woman. He would say them out loud to me and I would have to type them and read them back to him, and then send it. And I thought it was utterly fascinating, that he is telling me his most intimate messages to this lover, and he doesn't care that I'm a person listening to it and reading it back. It's probably why I'm always thinking, even now, about the people in the technological assemblage. This experience was probably the beginning of this whole trajectory of work.

References

BRAID UK. 2024. 'BRAID'. *BRAIDUK.Org*, 2024. https://braiduk.org/.

Crawford, Kate. 2021. *Atlas of AI: Power, Politics, and the Planetary Costs of Artificial Intelligence*. Yale University Press.

Elwes, Jake . 2019. *Zizi-Queering the Dataset*. JakeElwes.Com. 2019. https://www.jakeelwes.com/project-zizi-2019.html.

Hayles, N. Katherine. 2012. *How We Think: Digital Media and Contemporary Technogenesis*. University of Chicago Press.

Hood, Beverley. 2022. *An Exercise in Solitude* https://www.bhood.co.uk/projects/an-exercise-in-solitude.

Hood, Beverley. 2021-2023. *It's all about the feelings...* https://www.bhood.co.uk/projects/its-all-about-the-feelings.

Hood, Beverley. 2006. *Madame I.* https://www.bhood.co.uk/projects/madamel.

Hood, Beverley *Mother*, 2024, still from generative AI photo-film.

Paul Ekman Group. n.d. *Universal Emotions*. PaulEkman.Com. Accessed 6 December 2024. https://www.paulekman.com/universal-emotions/.

Ridler, Anna. n.d. *Anna Ridler*. Personal Website. AnnaRidler.Com. Accessed 6 December 2024. https://annaridler.com/.

The Role of Artists in the Age of Artificial Intelligence
Amanda Wasielewski

In 2008 I happened to hear a radio interview with David A. Mindell about his newly released book, *Digital Apollo: Human and Machine in Spaceflight* ("It's Man Vs. Machine In 'Digital Apollo'" Mindell 2008). In the interview, he discusses the myths surrounding NASA's Apollo program and the underappreciated role of software engineers in making the first lunar landing happen. He describes the famous story that a program alarm had gone off on board Apollo 11 and that Neil Armstrong turned off the computer and landed manually. "But as I began doing the research on the book," Mindell explains, "and I talked to the engineers who built that computer, they were all highly offended by that version of the story. They felt like there had been a problem that had been actually caused by the astronauts following a checklist that was in error" ("It's Man Vs. Machine In 'Digital Apollo.'" 2008). Hearing this interview (and subsequently reading the book) inspired me to create a series of artworks between 2008 and 2015 titled *The Pilot and the Engineer*. The idea behind the series was that the competing ideologies embodied in the metaphor of the pilot and the engineer crop up as oppositional forces within art and culture, sport, and other domains outside the realm of the natural sciences. In this construction, the pilot is the intuitive, rugged individual who acts alone, based on gut instinct and feeling. The engineer, on the other hand, is the rational, planning-focused calculator who harnesses technological enhancements in a collaborative effort to achieve the mission.

The tension between the pilot and the engineer continues to fascinate me, as it seems to continually renew itself. The current developments in artificial intelligence (AI) have brought forth this dialectic yet again. Or, rather, they have resurrected its classic science fiction manifestation as man versus machine. The roles of the pilot and the engineer are more complicated than this classic trope, however: the pilot and the engineer represent competing conceptions of how humans construct our physical world and social systems. Machines do not exist on their own or of their own volition but, rather, as the product of human engineering. For many years, I saw *The Pilot and the Engineer* as a metaphor for artistic practice itself and the competing modernist paradigms of expression and conceptualism[1] in art of the twentieth century. When Conceptual artist Sol LeWitt (1967, 80) famously said, "The idea becomes a machine that makes the art," he was responding to the way the whole world had taken up the logic of computational or programmatic thinking in the late 60s. Many artists, in other words, were no longer interested in being Abstract Expressionist pilots but, instead, something akin to software engineers.

The artists-turned-engineers of the '60s and '70s did not confine themselves to algorithms that generate geometries and regulated forms, however. Very quickly, the idea-machine became a machine of social critique: i.e., a place for artists to critique the technocratic post-war world and its class, race, and gender disparities through carefully planned, idea-driven work. Politically-charged conceptual documents and performances from artists like Hans Haacke, Adrian Piper, and Mierle Laderman Ukeles ushered in a new paradigm for artistic practice that remains popular today. This activist positioning of the artist post-1960 means that artists often act as ethical arbiters, exposing and critiquing new technologies in the process of implementing them.

As conceptualism, broadly defined, took hold in the art of the '60s, specific engineering practices also entered the frame. Not content to

---

1. Here I make a distinction between small c conceptualism and big c conceptualism. The former begin the long-standing modernist tradition of idea-led artistic practice and the latter being a specific movement of American and European artists in the 1960s and '70s.

observe or reflect on the technological and industrial developments of the era from afar, groups were formed to unite artistic and engineering praxis. For example, APG (Artist Placement Group), founded in 1966 in the UK, helped to embed artists at huge techno-industrial behemoths like British Steel Corporation and Esso Petroleum; and EAT (Experiments in Art and Technology), founded in 1967 in the US, partnered artists with Bell Labs engineers (Rycroft 2019; Battista et al. 2016). The legacy of such initiatives is evident in contemporary art, where artists not only reflect on industrial and technological tools and processes but also appropriate methods from engineering.

Artists have historically been some of the earliest adopters of new technologies, and contemporary artificial intelligence (AI) tools are no exception.[2] Using techniques and methods from engineering, artists perform a dual role that combines highly specialised technical knowledge and the open-ended knowledge-forms produced through art making. The goal of engineering research and practice is typically to solve problems and design systems that improve efficiency or efficacy of existing methods, but the work that artists create by appropriating engineering methods cannot be understood using the same criteria that engineers use.

This chapter reflects on the use of AI in artistic practice today and argues that artists' practice-based knowledge in AI can offer ways to understand these complex black box systems. Partnerships between computer scientists and humanists in hybrid fields such as the digital humanities rarely provide the kind of true fusion of methods, interpretation, and expression that artistic practice can provide. Given this, artists are an essential partner — in academia and beyond for understanding the ways AI tools are currently shaping our world.

---

2. For example, Fluxus artists adopted video and other televisual technologies in their practice from the 1950s, Neo-Dada artists like Robert Rauschenberg and John Cage were involved with EAT and Bell Labs, and artists in the Netherlands were early adopters of the internet. For the latter, see (Wasielewski 2021)

Critical Artistic Perspectives on Technology

It can be easy to characterise the broad strokes of modernist art history as a series of actions and reactions, swings of the pendulum back and forth through time. Positioning Conceptual art as a reaction to the dominance of Abstract Expressionism and its Greenbergian successors in the New York art world of the 1950s, as I seem to have done above, is of course a vast over-simplification (Corris 2009; Tekiner 2006; Greenberg 1964). Earlier in modernist western art history, we see movements similarly swing between progressive and reactionary tendencies (or, future-focused technophilia versus backwards-looking technophobia). For example, art nouveau is followed by art deco, the Futurists are followed by *le rappel à l'ordre*, German Expressionism by Neue Sachlichkeit, etc.

Then, in the 1960s, this swing back and forth seems to stop and the paradigm of artmaking that the late 60s birthed, i.e. the positioning of artists as critical systems planner, remained. Conceptual artists with explicitly political work, like those mentioned above, were succeeded by generations of artists creating work around issues of gender, race, class, identity, and post-colonialism, including Ana Mendieta, Howardena Pindell, the Guerilla Girls and Act Up in the 1980s, and Fred Wilson, Catherine Opie, Yinka Shonibare, Tania Bruguera and Theaster Gates in the 1990s and 2000s (to name but a few). Subsequent expressionist movements (notably in 1980s painting) did little to dampen the dominance of such practices, and this way of working continues to remain popular in the art world today.

Art historian Pamela Lee (2006, 259) describes this phenomenon as the "endlessness" of the sixties. Approaching both technique and technology in this context, camps nevertheless begin to emerge on the spectrum from techno-optimism to techno-pessimism. The former camp embraces new tools and the affordances they allow uncritically and is often willfully oblivious to the ethics and potential harms of such tools. The latter camp, on the other hand, stages a critique of these tools and their impact on society *through* their use and, often, with an intimate knowledge of their inner workings. The latter group, in other words, engage with new technologies (rather than reject them or critique them from a luddite or reactionary point of view) in a way that complicates them and their use. It is this camp that are vitally necessary for the field of AI today.

Artists working with AI fall across the full breadth of the spectrum from techno-optimism to techno-pessimism. In order to describe the non-luddite artists mentioned above, however, it is perhaps more accurate to call them techno-critical rather than purely techno-pessimist. Artists' entanglement with AI techniques often comes down to accessibility: accessibility both of the technical skills to implement these tools, and of computational capabilities (e.g., having enough compute). Artists are in a unique position to critique AI from the inside, utilising their technical skills and artistic vision to "hack" or subvert the intended uses of AI tools. At the same time, they are often funded by or affiliated with big tech companies.

In the space of a few short years, the access gap for AI technologies has closed, in that the average member of the public now has access to generative AI, and can generate sophisticated text, image, sound, and video output with little technical knowledge via prompt-based multimodal models. Paradoxically, however, the access gap has also grown wider in certain circumstances, since the computational power and skills to implement more complex custom configurations of the latest tools or models are increasingly difficult for artists to access without involvement with, or funding by, the tech industry. Before exploring the ethics of artists' work with AI today, I want to briefly survey the key artists and techniques used. This is by no means a comprehensive accounting but presents some vital context to the AI art landscape for the discussion that follows.

Deep Dreams

Some of the first artists to use image-based methods did so after Google released its Deep Dream in 2015, a neural network that finds and riffs on patterns in the images fed to it, creating psychedelic fractal iterations (Google Research 2015). Memo Akten was one of the most high-profile artists to use Deep Dream during that time, creating a variety of images and animations that regress as you view them (Akten 2015). Akten has been a notable voice of social critique from within the digital art realm and, in late 2020, created the website cryptoart.wtf to critique the vogue for NFTs (non-fungible tokens) due to their tremendous energy usage and environmental impact (Calma 2021; Akten, n.d.). Zach Blas and Jemima Wyman also used Deep Dream in their work *im here to learn so :))))))* (2017), which reanimates Microsoft's infamous chatbot Tay in a psychedelic Deep Dream landscape (Blas and Wyman 2017). Tay, which was trained on social media posts, famously began spewing out racist, misogynist, and other offensive content almost immediately after it was released on Twitter in 2016. In resurrecting this chatbot, Blas and Wyman interrogate this early high-profile case of generative bias.

One of the common metaphors in experiments with generative AI in contemporary art is the theme of evolution, organic life, and growth. The use of generative techniques, in these cases, serves as a way to reflect on tropes of life and death, biological versus artificial intelligence. For example, Sofia Crespo (2019) has done a number of projects on this theme, including *Neural Zoo* (2019), which uses neural networks to create new animal forms and assemblages. Ian Cheng (2018), on the other hand, created his own artificial organism in the piece *BOB* (2018-2019), in which a synthetic organism grows, changes, evolves and "dies many deaths."

Another genre of AI-generated art uses text generation for the production of installations and films. Ross Goodwin has created a number of such experiments, including the short film Sunspring (2016) which is made from an AI-generated movie script. In the work *Not the Only One* (2018), Stephanie Dinkins (n.d.) trains a neural network on stories from a multigenerational African American family, creating alternative narrative potentials from outside well-known anti-black biases within in the tech industry. This latter work is a good example of critical engagement with AI, as it attempts to subvert the white-centric biases that dominate the industry and the technologies they create.

One of the key works exemplifying a critical approach to AI is Trevor Paglen and Kate Crawford's project *ImageNet Roulette* (2019), a viral app that invited users to upload photos of themselves and see the potentially biased ways they may be labelled by AI systems. Using an image dataset called ImageNet, which was a popular training set for AI systems in the mid-2010s, Paglen and Crawford sought to expose the ways in which the invisible labels for such training data may be creating a biased view of the humans subjected to such systems. Their accompanying article, "Excavating AI," expands theoretically and historically on the concepts demonstrated by the artwork and shown in its exhibition (Crawford and Paglen 2019).

GANs and Visualisation

There is also a large genre of AI-generated artworks that use convolutional neural networks (CNNs) trained on a particular type of image data, applying a class of machine learning frameworks called GANs (generative adversarial networks) (Goodfellow et al. 2014). The works generated with these methods are recognisable as abstractions of the training data, whatever that may be. This opens up the possibility of creating a complex composite output based on learning from custom image collections or datasets. Thus, these techniques became very popular in artmaking before the advent of text-to-image models/ diffusion models (which has meant they have lost favor somewhat in recent times). Some artists, such as Eryk Salvaggio, have lamented the displacement of GANs for text-to-image models, arguing that GANs allowed far more flexibility for artists than these more recent models (Salvaggio 2023).

There are many examples of artists and artworks that use these methods. For example, Theresa Reimann-Dubbers (2017) trained a generative AI system on Christian religious imagery of Jesus to create stained-glass like projections in the work A.(I.) *Messianic Window* (2017). The results are AI-generated images that represent the training data but are not identical to any particular image of stained-glass in the collection. Working with a totally different genre of images, Christopher Meerdo's *Channeling* (2019) consists of a GAN visualisation made from images collected in the raid on Osama bin Laden's Abbottabad compound in 2011. The resultant piece presents abstracted, generative output that hints at but never fully reveals the content of this image repository. Some of the artists working with these techniques, on the other hand, have had a more explicitly commercial orientation. For example, in 2018, a French design collective called Obvious created an AI-generated portrait called *Portrait de Edmond de Belamy* and sold it for almost half a million dollars at Christie's auction house (Desmond 2018). Meanwhile, researcher Ahmad Elgammal (together cited as co-author with his AI system AICAN) exhibited works in exhibition titled *Faceless*

Portraits Transcending Time at HG Gallery in New York in early 2019 (Elgammal and AICAN 2019).

One of the most high-profile recent exhibitions of this type of work is Refik Anadol's blockbuster installation of *Unsupervised* at the Museum of Modern Art (MoMA) in New York in 2022-2023, which uses the museum's collection as training data (Anadol 2022). The piece, installed in the entryway to MoMA in monumental scale, is a large illusionistic visualisation that alternates between abstract color that washes around an illusionistic container like liquid and images that are GAN-created outputs. These outputs reflect different sections of the latent space and, thus, different aspects of MoMA's collection of art. Anadol has been experimenting with these methods since around 2016 or 2017, so this work is part of a body of work that pre-dates the post-2022 hype around consumer-facing text-to-image platforms like DALL-E 2. Nevertheless, Anadol's MoMA exhibition was staged in the context of this hype, and its reception was thus unavoidably informed by the ethical issues that have come to the fore during the rapid uptake of AI image tools.

It is clear that generative AI is already affecting society in profound ways, including in the areas of labour, stereotypes and representation, intellectual property, the environment, media and (mis)information, entertainment, and many others. Given this, the response to *Unsupervised* from the art press was largely negative, citing the work's lack of critical engagement with the ethical and political dimensions of implementing AI tools today. The staging of this exhibition in the entryway of MoMA, one of the highest-profile venues in the world, meant that some degree of backlash was inevitable. However, the work was almost universally panned and described derisively as a "lava lamp," a "screensaver" and equated to "propaganda" (Davis 2023; Lossin 2023; Saltz 2023; Diehl 2022). *New York* magazine's art critic and avid social media user Jerry Saltz started a flame war with Anadol and his acolytes on X (formerly Twitter) in November 2023, after once again slating the work as "just a banal screensaver" (Lawson-Tancred 2023).

In light of this, it is clear that the endlessly post-'60s artist is still expected to be an ethical guiding light, to expose and critique new technologies in the process of implementing them. The mesmerising aesthetics of Anadol's work were deemed insufficient to recommend the work. The implication of the negative reviews was that a work such as this needed to have something to say about the growing use of AI in society. Thus, it raises the question: what responsibility do artists have when they use AI?

Practice-Based Knowledge

Today, all of the major technology companies have programs for artists-in-residence and art funding, many specifically focused on the intersection of AI and art. Partnering with these corporations, artists are invited to create work that responds to and utilises the AI tools developed in the last decade. For example, Microsoft has an artist-in-residence program where many of the featured artists and projects use machine learning techniques (Microsoft Research, n.d.). Facebook/Meta has an AI Artist in Residence program that has facilitated the work of high-profile AI artists like Sofia Crespo and Stephanie Dinkins (AI at Meta 2021). Likewise, Google's Artists + Machine Intelligence (AMI) program helps fund and facilitate artistic research in AI (Artists + Machine Intelligence, n.d.). Refik Anadol, for example, was a recipient of one of the early grants/residencies offered by Google (Google Arts and Culture, n.d). There are a few ways to look at the ethics of these cultural funding programs and the ways in which they facilitate the work of artists and researchers in the field of AI. The primary issue is that these companies, at core, serve their own growth and the promotion of their products and technologies, so they may limit critical perspectives in either overt or subtle ways through their funded projects. My own research has recently received funding from AMI, so the ethical quandaries inherent in participating in such programs are not abstract for me. Accepting this funding gave me reason for pause due to the recent controversy surrounding Timnit Gebru and Margaret Mitchell in 2020 and 2021. These two researchers were fired for publishing academic work that was critical of AI and its biases while working under Google's research arm, against Google's requests not to publish such work. Google, for its part, claimed they were terminated based on violations of their code of conduct but did not specify further (Metz 2021; Metz and Wakabayashi 2020).

Critiques of Silicon Valley — both for its libertarian techno-utopianism and its racism and deeply embedded biases — have gained popular acceptance in recent years (Broussard 2024; Buolamwini 2023; Criado-Perez 2020; Noble 2018; O'Neil 2017). These are important critiques to sustain (and continually raise) through both art and academic work.[3] However, the work of artists in these contexts can also provide a vital insight into the latest AI tools and stage critique from a place of access and understanding. The costs involved in running contemporary neural networks often make them unattainable or otherwise inaccessible even to well-funded academics, and so artists struggle to use or implement such tools on their own. The commercially released tools that have cropped up, such as DALL-E and Midjourney, are not as flexible as customised ('fine-tuned') models. They are also seen as less transparent to those who would seek to critique them. Likewise, many artists have computer science and engineering knowledge but often need the collaborative knowledge only gained through working with others who have complementary expertise to fill in the gaps.

Though artists and researchers may still be ethically compromised through tech industry affiliation, the artist residency and funding programs run by tech giants also harken back to the collaborations of APG and EAT mentioned above, and the unique opportunities that access to powerful technology affords artists in developing their work. Neither APG or EAT were without hiccups or conflicts between the artists and the industries they participated in (Rycroft 2019; Battista et al. 2016). However, what was opened up from within these experiments was the idea that artistic research is useful knowledge, a perspective that is sorely lacking in today's world where artistic endeavors are treated as leisure/luxury rather than work (Anania 2022; Sussman 2017; Martinez 2015). Artists were, at the time of APG and EAT, seen as adding something valuable to our understanding of the use and development of technology and industry; at least, valuable enough to fund and facilitate these experiments.

The post-war period of the 1950s and '60s was a time of social mobility in the western world, when educational and employment opportunities opened up to working class people and the standard of living increased significantly (Piketty 2014). Artists benefited from these developments as well. As inequality has grown over the subsequent generations, so too have the barriers to working as a practicing artist. What is lost, then, is

---

3. I have already done so in (Wasielewski 2024; 2023)

the unique practice-based knowledge that artists can contribute to our understanding of technological developments like AI.

Tech companies, in other words, actually have a lot to gain from artistic knowledge. Indeed, artists can perhaps push back against tech companies and their funders in ways that their research employees cannot. However, artists also have something to gain from cultivating insight from inside such institutions or through collaboration or access to the powerful tools that only large corporations can produce. As I noted earlier, the practice of engineering has very different goals than artistic use of engineering techniques. But artists, unlike humanities researchers, also tend to have practical skills and a level of understanding of process that only engineers possess. They are able to do, in other words, practice-based forms of knowledge production. This is what Tim Ingold (2013, 5) calls "knowledge from the inside" or the knowledge that comes through making.

There is a lot of trust in the idea that the contemporary manifestations of AI can do anything imaginable. They are thus among those "sufficiently advanced technolog[ies] ... indistinguishable from magic" that science fiction author Arthur C. Clark described (1973, 21). This is as prevalent in academic research as in the media. However, artists have the intimate knowledge from the inside that only comes through actually experimenting and making things. That means that those artists who use AI have a skillset that combines specialised technical knowledge and the poetics of artmaking (Audry 2021; Zylinska 2020). They thus maintain a unique perspective — broadly aesthetic/poetic — and set of skills — practical engineering knowledge — with regard to AI tools. This makes artists ideally suited for staging critiques of AI today.

Artistic research is both a method of producing art and a genre of art in itself (Bishop 2023). It has its roots in the documentary and information-gathering artworks of the conceptual era, such as Hans Haacke's Shapolsky et al. *Manhattan Real Estate Holdings, a Real-Time Social System,* as of May 1, 1971 (1971), a work that painstakingly combed through and presented the real estate holdings of a slum landlord in New York City in order to expose its predatory business dealings (Moon 2023). Artistic practice that incorporates either the aesthetics or process of research was subsequently codified in the first practice-based doctoral programs in the 1990s (Frayling et al. 1997).

The aesthetics of research-based art are often ongoing, rich with documents, and presented in installations. This type of artwork encourages extended periods of reading or browsing through materials, and tends to display its source material in addition to any newly created forms. The process of research-based art on the other hand is a practice, regardless of the aesthetic outcome, that incorporates investigative, journalistic, or academic information-gathering methods such as archival examinations, interviews, and the application of academic or critical theory.

Practice-based research is now well-established both in and outside of academia and can be found equally in exhibition venues, art schools, and universities (Schwarzenbach and Hackett 2015; Gray and Malins 2004). This has increasingly academicised art practice, some of which is now nearly indistinguishable from traditional academic work. This can raise a myriad of ethical issues in this context, as academic research has its own norms and practices that artistic research does not or cannot always conform to (MacNeill and Bolt 2019). Some of the work that Trevor Paglen does, cited above, certainly falls within this frame. However, though it may appear to be like academic practice, this praxis is still something different from traditional academic work — it is something vital and subversive. Art practice, I contend, is an activity akin to hacking. Artists take up these different activities of making, be they academic research, engineering, or anything else, and hack them/ inhabit them. Once 'inside', so-to-speak, artistic work can begin to unravel the deeper meanings inherent in these procedures and practices.

Conclusion

In the context of AI research, then, artists are already adopting and inhabiting the different tools developed by computer science and tech industry researchers in unique and critically-engaged ways. They use GANs, diffusion models, large language models (LLMs), or other techniques, implementing them in ways that differ significantly from the ways that computer science engineers do. Their aims and purposes are, in other words, totally separate from those that the engineers intended in the development of these models or tools.

This is why artistic use of AI can be seen as a form of hacking — it subverts the standard or intended use of new technologies. To return to the metaphor of the pilot and the engineer that I began this chapter with, the hacker weaves between these two poles. On the one hand, the hacker is the pilot: i.e., the rugged individual reacting to technologies and tinkering with them based on gut feeling and an instinct that has been refined through the experience of making. In another sense, however, the hacker is the engineer: i.e., the conceptual artist/systems planner who maps out new pathways for a particular tool or technology and formulates a critique through the use of practice-based knowledge. Artists using AI must often create their work as part of a collaborative team with engineers and other specialists who bring specific skillsets to the creation of the work. Often, working alone is not an option, despite the persistence of the myth of individual artistic genius.

Unlike engineers or computer scientists who are employed by research institutions or tech companies, however, artists are not typically interested in a limited product or use of a technique but rather in the open-ended experimentation, poetics, insights, and impacts that can be gleaned from this kind of artistic hacking activity. Art can thus help fill in the bigger picture, explore the ethical gray areas, and map the larger social impact of contemporary AI technologies. This is work that the tech industry and the academic field of computer science is simply not doing right now.

One of the biggest barriers to critique of contemporary AI systems is their complexity, opacity, and the proprietary secrecy that comes with corporate control. By inhabiting and hacking such systems, even with the blessing of the corporations who own them, artists have a vital role to play in increasing a broader understanding of AI and how it affects society today. While the ethics of participating in the tech industry are complicated, artistic practice offers a rare combination of "knowledge from the inside" and critical reflection that cannot be found either in academia or industry alone.

References

AI at Meta. 2021. "Meta AI — Our AI Artist in Residence Program Recently Hosted Three... | Facebook." Facebook. August 31, 2021. https://www.facebook.com/MetaAI/posts/our-ai-artist-in-residence-program-recently-hosted-three-artists-who-use-ai-in-t/1917661178410826/.

Akten, Memo. 2015. "Journey through the Layers of the Mind (2015)." *Memo.Tv* (blog). 2015. https://www.memo.tv/works/journey-through-the-layers-of-the-mind-2015/.

Akten, Memo. n.d. "°~.∴*✧ CryptoArt. Wtf ✧*∴.~°." Accessed January 19, 2024. https://cryptoart.wtf/.

Anadol, Refik. 2022. *Refik Anadol: Unsupervised* | MoMA. https://www.moma.org/calendar/exhibitions/5535.

Anania, Billie. 2022. "Artists Can Build Power as Workers." *Jacobin*, April 3, 2022. https://jacobin.com/2022/04/artists-union-museums-art-worker-organizing.

Artists + Machine Intelligence. n.d. "Artists + Machine Intelligence." Accessed September 26, 2023. https://ami.withgoogle.com/.

Audry, Sofian. 2021. *Art in the Age of Machine Learning*. MIT Press.

Battista, Kathy, Simone Forti, Billy Klüver, Michelle Kuo, Catherine Morris, Zabet Patterson, John Tain, and Sabine Breit. 2016. *E.A.T.: Experiments in Arts and Technology*. Edited by Sabine Breitwieser. Walther König.

Bishop, Claire. 2023. "Information Overload." *Artforum*, April 1, 2023. https://www.artforum.com/features/claire-bishop-on-the-superabundance-of-research-based-art-252571/.

Blas, Zach, and Jemima Wyman. 2017. *Im Here to Learn So*. https://zachblas.info/works/im-here-to-learn-so/.

Broussard, Meredith. 2024. *More than a Glitch: Confronting Race, Gender, and Ability Bias in Tech*. MIT Press.

Buolamwini, Joy. 2023. *Unmasking AI: My Mission to Protect What Is Human in a World of Machines*. Random House Publishing Group.

Calma, Justine. 2021. "The Climate Controversy Swirling around NFTs." *The Verge*. March 15, 2021. https://www.theverge.com/2021/3/15/22328203/nft-cryptoart-ethereum-blockchain-climate-change.

Cheng, Ian. 2018. *Bag of Beliefs*. http://iancheng.com/BOB.

Clarke, Arthur C. 1973. *Profiles of the Future: An Inquiry into the Limits of the Possible*. Harper & Row.

Corris, Michael. 2009. "Systems Upgrade: Conceptual Art and the Recoding of Information, Knowledge and Technology." In *Proud to Be Flesh: A Mute Magazine Anthology of Cultural Politics after the Net*, edited by Josephine Berry Slater and Pauline van Mourik Broekman. Mute Publishing.

Crawford, Kate, and Trevor Paglen. 2019. "Excavating AI: The Politics of Images in Machine Learning Training Sets." 2019. https://www.excavating.ai/.

Crespo, Sofia. 2019. *Neural Zoo*. https://neuralzoo.com/.

Criado-Perez, Caroline. 2020. *Invisible Women: Exposing Data Bias in a World Designed for Men*. Vintage.

Davis, Ben. 2023. "An Extremely Intelligent Lava Lamp: Refik Anadol's A.I. Art Extravaganza at MoMA Is Fun, Just Don't Think About It Too Hard." *Artnet News*, January 23, 2023. https://news.artnet.com/art-world/refik-anadol-unsupervised-moma-2242329.

Desmond, John. 2018. "AI-Generated Portrait Sells for $432,500 at Christie's." *AI Trends*, November 20, 2018. https://www.aitrends.com/features/ai-generated-portrait-sells-for-432500-at-christies/.

Diehl, Travis. 2022. "MoMA's Daydream of Progress." *The New York Times*, December 15, 2022, sec. Arts. https://www.nytimes.com/2022/12/15/arts/design/refik-anadol-unsupervised-moma-review.html.

Dinkins, Stephanie. n.d. "Not the Only One." Stephanie Dinkins. Accessed

May 11, 2021. https://www.stephaniedinkins.com/ntoo.html.

Elgammal, Ahmad, and AICAN. 2019. *Faceless Portraits Transcending Time | AICAN | HG Contemporary.* http://www.hgcontemporary.com/exhibitions/faceless-portraits-transcending-time.

Frayling, Christopher, Valerie Stead, Bruce Archer, Nicholas Cook, James Powell, Victor Sage, Stephen Scrivener, and Michael Tovey. 1997. "Practice-Based Doctorates in the Creative and Performing Arts and Design." UK Council for Graduate Education. https://ukcge.ac.uk/assets/resources/4-Practice-based-doctorates-in-the-Creative-and-Performing-Arts1997.pdf.

Goodfellow, Ian, Jean Pouget-Abadie, Mehdi Mirza, Bing Xu, David Warde-Farley, Sherjil Ozair, Aaron Courville, and Yoshua Bengio. 2014. "Generative Adversarial Nets." In *Advances in Neural Information Processing Systems*, edited by Z. Ghahramani, M. Welling, C. Cortes, N. Lawrence, and K. Q. Weinberger. Curran Associates, Inc.

Google Arts and Culture. n.d. "Artists + Machine Intelligence: A Brief History." Accessed March 18, 2024. https://artsandculture.google.com/story/artists-machine-intelligence-a-brief-history/VgUBQOhr6Pakeg.

Google Research. 2015. "Deepdream." https://github.com/google/deepdream.

Gray, Carole, and Julian Malins. 2004. *Visualizing Research: A Guide to the Research Process in Art and Design.* Ashgate.

Greenberg, Clement. 1964. "Post Painterly Abstraction." *Art International* 8 (5–6): 63.

Ingold, Tim. 2013. *Making: Anthropology, Archaeology, Art and Architecture.*

"It's Man Vs. Machine In 'Digital Apollo.'" 2008. *Talk of the Nation.* https://www.npr.org/templates/story/story.php?storyId=92195902.

Lawson-Tancred, Jo. 2023. "Jerry Saltz Gets Into an Online Skirmish With Refik Anadol Over His A.I. Art." *Artnet News*, November 28, 2023. https://news.artnet.com/art-world-archives/refik-anadol-vs-jerry-saltz-2400275.

Lee, Pamela M. 2006. *Chronophobia: On Time in the Art of the 1960s.* MIT Press.

LeWitt, Sol. 1967. "Paragraphs On Conceptual Art." *Artforum* 5 (10): 79–83.

Lossin, R.H. 2023. "Refik Anadol's 'Unsupervised' - Criticism - e-Flux." *E-Flux*, March 14, 2023. https://www.e-flux.com/criticism/527236/refik-anadol-s-unsupervised.

MacNeill, Kate, and Barbara Bolt, eds. 2019. *The Meeting of Aesthetics and Ethics in the Academy: Challenges for Creative Practice Researchers in Higher Education.* Routledge.

Martinez, Alanna. 2015. "Is Art School Only for the Wealthy?" *Observer*, April 20, 2015. https://observer.com/2015/04/is-art-school-only-for-the-wealthy/.

Metz, Cade. 2021. "A Second Google A.I. Researcher Says the Company Fired Her." *The New York Times*, February 20, 2021, sec. Technology. https://www.nytimes.com/2021/02/19/technology/google-ethical-artificial-intelligence-team.html.

Metz, Cade, and Daisuke Wakabayashi. 2020. "Google Researcher Says She Was Fired Over Paper Highlighting Bias in A.I." *The New York Times*, December 3, 2020, sec. Technology. https://www.nytimes.com/2020/12/03/technology/google-researcher-timnit-gebru.html.

Microsoft Research. n.d. "Artist in Residence." Accessed September 26, 2023. https://www.microsoft.com/en-us/research/group/artist-in-residence/.

Mindell, David A. 2008. *Digital Apollo: Human and Machine in Spaceflight.* MIT Press.

Moon, Kavior. 2023. "Research Art Is Everywhere. But Some Artists Do It Better Than Others." *Art in America*, March 8, 2023. https://www.artnews.com/art-in-america/features/what-is-

artistic-research-1234660125/.
Noble, Safiya Umoja. 2018. *Algorithms of Oppression: How Search Engines Reinforce Racism*. New York University Press.
O'Neil, Cathy. 2017. *Weapons of Math Destruction: How Big Data Increases Inequality and Threatens Democracy*. Penguin Books.
Piketty, Thomas. 2014. *Capital in the twenty-first century*. Translated by Arthur Goldhammer. Belknap Press of Harvard University Press.
Reimann-Dubbers, Theresa. 2017. *A(.I.) Messianic Window - Theresa Reimann-Dubbers*. https://theresareimann-dubbers.net/A-I-Messianic-Window.
Rycroft, Simon. 2019. "The Artist Placement Group: An Archaeology of Impact." *Cultural Geographies* 26 (3): 289–304.
Saltz, Jerry. 2023. "MoMA's Glorified Lava Lamp." *Vulture*. February 22, 2023. https://www.vulture.com/article/jerry-saltz-moma-refik-anadol-unsupervised.html.
Salvaggio, Eryk. 2023. "What Was the GAN?" Substack newsletter. *Cybernetic Forests* (blog). November 26, 2023. https://cyberneticforests.substack.com/p/what-was-the-gan.
Schwarzenbach, Jessica, and Paul Hackett. 2015. *Transatlantic Reflections on the Practice-Based PhD in Fine Art*. Routledge.
Sussman, Anna Louie. 2017. "Can Only Rich Kids Afford to Work in the Art World?" *Artsy*, February 14, 2017. https://www.artsy.net/article/artsy-editorial-rich-kids-afford-work-art-world.
Tekiner, Deniz. 2006. "Formalist Art Criticism and the Politics of Meaning." *Social Justice* 33 (2 (104)): 31–44.
Wasielewski, Amanda. 2021. *From City Space to Cyberspace: Art, Squatting, and Internet Culture in the Netherlands*. Amsterdam University Press.
Wasielewski, Amanda. 2023. *Computational Formalism: Art History and Machine Learning*. MIT Press.
Wasielewski, Amanda. 2024. "Zombie Canon: Art Datasets, Generative AI, and the Reanimation of the Western Canon of Art." In *Critical Digital Art History*, edited by Amanda Wasielewski and Anna Näslund Dahlgren. Intellect.
Zylinska, Joanna. 2020. *AI Art: Machine Visions and Warped Dreams*. London: Open Humanities Press.

The Emancipatory Potential of AI Art
Jasmin Pfefferkorn in conversation with Nora Al—Badri

Nora Al-Badri is a para-disciplinary artist with a significant body of research-driven conceptual media works. She holds a degree in political sciences, is a lecturer at ETH Zurich, and a guest professor at the State Academy of Fine Arts Stuttgart. Her practice engages decolonial and post-digital thinking and reflects a commitment to the speculative possibilities of technologies and public spaces, most notably museums. Over a video call in August of 2024, we discuss what needs to be prioritised in working with AI, how to push back against institutional power, and the emancipatory potential of new technologies. Two of her works, *Babylonian Vision* and *The Post-Truth Museum*, form the focus of this in-conversation.

Babylonian Vision (2020) is a work consisting of over 150 videos. For this project, Al-Badri used a Generative Adversarial Network (GAN) technology trained on the images of 10,000 objects of Mesopotamian, Neo-Sumerian and Assyrian artefacts, scraped from the digitised collections of five major museums. The new synthetic images produced through the GAN are simultaneously positioned as living memory traces of their source data, as well as artefacts in their own right. *Babylonian Vision* engages with the possibilities of AI in relation to cultural data, collective memory, materialities, loopholes in institutional gatekeeping, and the formation of visual languages.

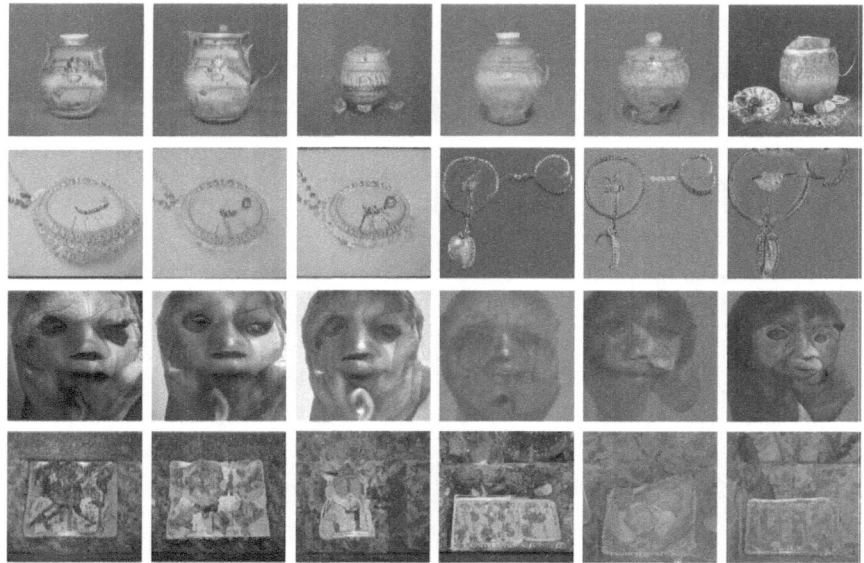

Figure 1: Nora Al-Badri, 2020. *The Post-Truth Museum*, videostills.

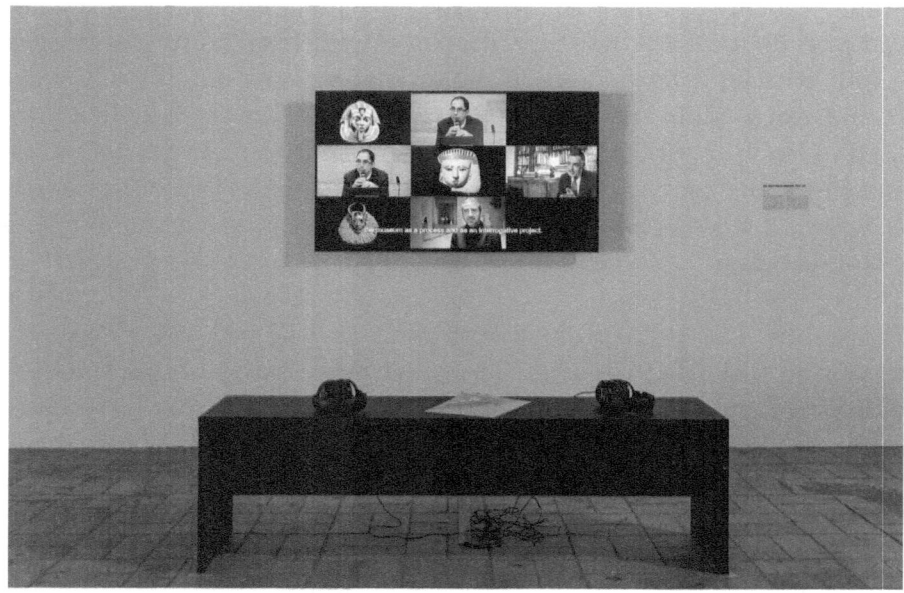

Figure 2: Nora Al-Badri, 2021–23. *The Post-Truth Museum*, installation view at KunstWerke Berlin.

The Post-Truth Museum (2021-23) is a video work that utilises various AI models to deepfake three European museum directors, having them espouse critical decolonial texts from a variety of thinkers. The deepfake directors are interspersed with reanimated objects in the form of speaking masks, as well as synthetic images of speculative future museum sites that blur nature and the built environment. *The Post-Truth Museum* presents a world where institutional complicity in imperialism is recognised, and the untapped potential of the museum is realised.

* * *

Jasmin Pfefferkorn (JP): Obviously there has long been a computational component to your artistic practice with a strong AI element — how and why were you drawn to this?

Nora Al-Badri (NAB): There are many answers to this. In a way, it is out of necessity, and because computation is the medium of our time. As an artistic medium, it emerges in various forms, and I embrace various forms because otherwise I get bored. Though conceptually, it's important to see what works with which concept and piece. Personally, I guess I was a little bit inert, and the digital was something that was close to me and felt more natural than doing any other medium. I have a few good painters in my family, so I was always afraid to paint. With computers, I felt safer. I could have even gone down the path of photography as a medium. But I suppose with all its developments, AI is also aligned with photography in certain ways, or film. It might be even more multifaceted and merges so many things. It's super powerful in that regard, as a medium of image-making. My father was an engineer, so I grew up with computers early on.

JP: I'm always fascinated by how artists think through the materiality of these technologies. Those two sides to it — the computational as the medium of our time, with its own form, and then those connections with previous forms, like photography. So often computer scientists are aspiring for photorealism with these technologies, when in fact this material has its own realism that we must engage with... and perhaps it is more interesting when we do engage with the computational as its own form, medium, material.

NAB: That's true. I'm very aware of the infrastructure and materiality of AI. It's super earthly, right? It's not just something floating in the air and in the 'clouds,' so to speak. In earlier works I did with 3D printing, you start with something extremely computational, but at the end you have something physical, and with a specific materiality, in your hands or in the exhibition. With the 3D printed bust of Nefertiti scanned from the Neues Museum Berlin, we even buried it in the sand as future 'technoheritage.' I think I was drawn to it because I grew up with the beginnings of computers and was always fascinated by its capacities. I'm mostly interested in the critical capacities that this technology has, not the commercial ones. One of the powers of the digital, especially in my practice, is that I can work with collections that I could never work with in the physical realm. That's also why the relationship I have with it is, in part, out of necessity.

JP: Across your work you are offering us a sense of the material that you're working with, and the specificities of medium as well. For instance, you show the process of training your GAN in *Babylonian Vision*, and part of that includes seeing the ruler measurement that is present from the images you've scraped from digitised museum collections [Figure 3]. And in *The Post-Truth Museum*, there are times where the voices used in the audio deepfakes slip into a tonal quality that we associate with AI.

NAB: I think that is part of the beauty of it, not trying for mimicry, or to enact this super realistic aesthetic that is now quite dominant — not necessarily in contemporary art, but in how AI is used in general. To me, that's not the most interesting use of it, and in too many instances it becomes a cover up. Or something like an extrapolation of a reality that doesn't resonate with me, that I can't associate with. Leaving the traces, leaving the medium visible, I find it more authentic for the medium itself.

JP: I want to come back to those ideas of cover up and traces, since they feed into the kinds of tensions your work holds between transparency and opacity. But before we get there, can you describe from your perspective how you came to make *Babylonian Vision*?

NAB: It was a nice symbiosis of the materials I'm looking into, namely artifacts and archaeology — super physical, huge collections. When I

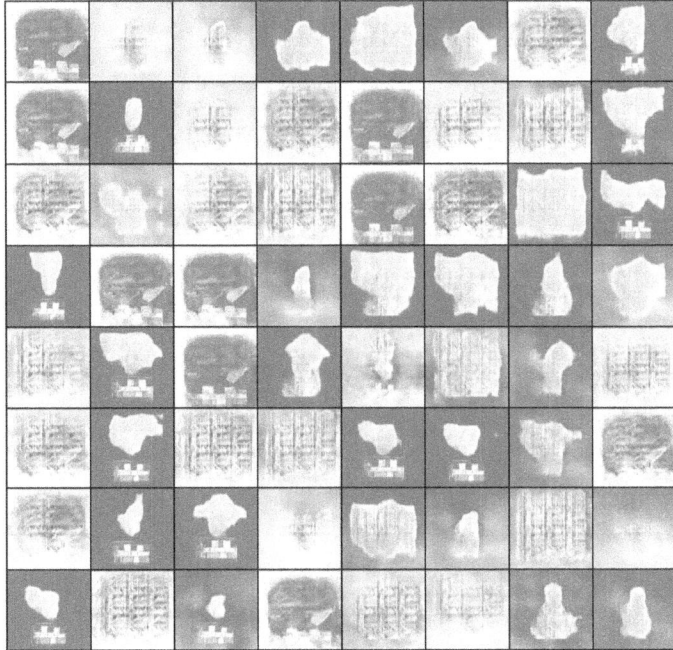

Figure 3: Nora Al-Badri, 2020. *Babylonian Vision*, training data.

did *Babylonian Vision*, GANs were quite new, and mainly used for research. There wasn't really anything commercial happening with them yet — the technology had already been there for some time, but without the computing power to process huge data sets. For me, its newness made it a piece responding to a moment of new technological potential. I had possibilities that weren't technically feasible before, and for the first time I could work with huge collections. I remember reading a computer science paper (Bodla, Chellappa, and Hua 2018), where they did something similar with birds, using a GAN to create synthetic images of birds that didn't exist but looked like they could have existed. And this is where I got the idea — what if I train a neural network with a huge amount of visual language from a particular era and time in history? I did a few experiments [Figure 4] together with three computer scientists from the University of Lausanne in Switzerland (EPFL), where I had a residency. This was how I could use the technology, because at the time I didn't have the skills for applying it, I'm not a computer scientist. We tried many methods using GANs and ended up picking one that offered the most interesting resemblance of the 'Mesopotamian' or the 'Babylonian.'

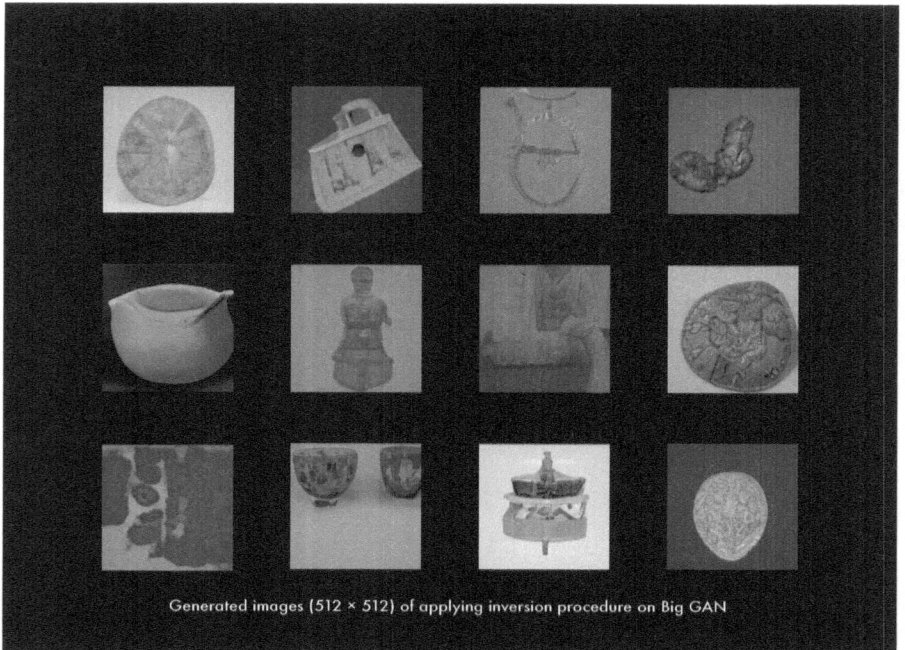

Figure 4: Nora Al-Badri, 2020. *Babylonian Vision*, generated objects.

JP: In *Babylonian Vision*, you're drawing on an era, but also a place-based context. From my understanding, this is very much connected to your own positionality as someone with an Iraqi-German background, which has informed your politics around things like restitution. One of the ways you speak and write about this in relation to *Babylonian Vision* is through the concept of 'technoheritage.' And you have also spoken about the idea of an objects' afterlife, which becomes particularly resonant when we think about tracing the machine and the traces we leave in machines. I'm very interested in how you think about the afterlife of the object, and how that connects to the relationship between ancestry and the computational.

NAB: It is one of my personal autobiographical pieces, because it was specifically focused on what is today Iraq and its neighbouring countries, which back then was Babylonia and Mesopotamia. This is my personal ancestral connection to this piece. But more generally speaking, before an AI vision-based piece like this, anyone would enter a museum and look at the collections and then leave the museum internalising only a few objects. But through the machine we get a whole visual language of time and space, leaving it to us to look at it and interpret it. Both conceptually and personally it was important for me to generate new artifacts, artifacts that I do sometimes call technoheritage. It's through a computational medium, but it's still based on the material and skills of many ancestors. It also opened so many questions — and not just for me — about ideas of originality. Those ancestors with their artifacts and materialities, they inspired me to do this. And now, through the AI, we have these new artifacts, even if they are only two-dimensional — although it was also possible to print or re-make them as material objects. I personally don't think that is necessary in a project like this, or even in general. What I mean by this is that all the objects used in this so-called heterogenous dataset, they were fabrics, jewellery, sculptures, pots or just pieces from clay objects, most of them were objects with a purpose that were actually worn or used by people. I didn't aspire to create objects for actual usage within this project, but to generate a visual language that gives us insight into a specific past. And using AI as a tool made sense, because by default AI is a past oriented technology — contrary to the popular opinion: as soon as we train the neural network with data, the data is from the past.

> **JP:** When you were going through the datasets of all these objects, was some kind of connection or communion with that history and the people who created it at the forefront of your mind?

NAB: Yes, it was. It was also a bit like a virtual museum visit. Although one of the advantages of AI is that I don't think I looked at every object that I used to train the GAN. It was around 10,000 images of objects in the end, not a billion, but I still don't think I looked at all the fragments. I certainly felt joyful doing this project, because I felt I could engage with this history in a more active way. Whereas in the huge contemporary narrative about this whole region, and specifically Iraq, everything we were hearing was just destruction, violence, war, and tragedy. I wanted to create against this narrative. This was what was emancipatory for me.

> **JP:** Your work has this dual level of the emancipatory, both in the embodied, lived experience and also in terms of how we might think about using these technologies to disrupt dominant narratives. For me, as a museum studies scholar who focuses on critical AI, one

of the most interesting things about *Babylonian Vision* is how you have taken a technology that has — particularly as it progressed from GANs into LLMs — been decried for taking source material and not crediting it properly. Of course, this holds parallels to what many museums have been doing for centuries. *Babylonian Vision* mobilises that specific critique but flips it to show how the opacity of that process can be utilised to make the politics of the museum more transparent. I wonder whether we can liken this to ethical hacking. When you do subvert these ethical guidelines, do you find you can be more ethical as a result?

NAB: Yes, of course, and it's even one step further. What also inspired me to do this piece, and how I did it, was in response to our reality today. Most collections are in museums of the Global North, none of which would give us access to their collections for this project. And I was asking them through the university, not just as an artist. I was given a lot of different arguments for why I couldn't be given this access. Some were mainstream reasons, like asking written permission for each object. It was like, come on, that's not possible for thousands of works. But I thought, okay, we will do it anyway. But the data set I got in the end was from scraping the internet and museum databases without permission. My inspiration was also one of the biggest problems of AI, whereby you cannot trace back the source material. This is usually a highly exploitative or anti-privacy endeavour in most cases. In the case of *Babylonian Vision*, it was turned around, so I was scraping from the gatekeepers of the data. Of course, whether it is ethical depends on who you ask. If you ask the people from the museums, they might find me unethical in my practice, I don't know. But regardless of whether it is ethical or not, it is certainly empowering for people from the diaspora, from the Global South.

> **JP:** Perhaps an ethical ambiguity that offers empowerment is necessary for a decentred ethics. It certainly shifts away from the Western framework of authoritative institutions making decisions around ownership, sovereignty, and the right to culture. You weren't creating this work for the people who affirm the institutional practices that carry the trajectory of colonial modernity. It's a work that gives back to the people who normally don't have access to the original object, oftentimes not even the digitised dataset.

NAB: Exactly. And what I've been more successful in with other projects, which I sadly wasn't with this one, is showing the piece in the countries of origin. This is very important for me. For this piece I only managed to do it more digitally, through writing, or a television appearance that was broadcast across the Arab speaking world. And I had such great feedback, which underscored those questions — who is the audience? With whom are our pieces resonating? They are certainly resonating with anyone I've met in the Global South. Again, these technologies have such incredible emancipatory potential. Although, unfortunately, this is not by default.

> **JP:** Do you feel we need more technical literacy to be able to overcome the default settings or encouraged affordances of these technologies?

NAB: Not as much as you need a strong network of people. When I teach at universities, I always tell my students, you don't need much money to do this. You don't need anything, basically, you don't need the skills. Of course, you need to have a strong conceptual idea for what you want to do, and then you will find people who will do it with you and for you. If it's a good project, you always convince someone to help you. Again, it's important that we are not doing anything out of capital interest. Most of the projects are more societally relevant. There will always be a network if you go looking for it. Of course, there are barriers like class, that become fundamental to do these kinds of things. But for the Babylon Vision project, for example, two of the researchers I worked with were women from the region. We sent out a call through the university. And, of course, it resonated to them. And then they came to say they would like to join the project.

> **JP:** A lot of the time art is spoken about as world making. And one of the ways that manifests, in the computational era, is through the data set. And the fact that for a machine, the training data set is the knowledge of the world, and most of the data sets that we use for these large commercial models are heavily underpinned by a commercial logic. I think of the researchers on the *Knowing Machines* project that started to look at the foundation dataset LAION-5B, to try and understand where these images come from. They found the majority are coming from Shopify, eBay, these

sorts of sites, because they already have alt-tags attached to images (Buschek and Thorp, n.d.). So it becomes so important to build worlds that aren't just commercial.

NAB: There's a great artist duo from Switzerland, called !Mediengruppe Bitnik (Weiskopf and Smoljo, n.d.). When Google was relatively new, they made a piece where they also traced the image sources back to all these commercial objects and platforms. Unfortunately, it seems little has changed. But this is unsurprising, given that this is how these proprietary technologies are predominantly used, whether it's a search engine or image generation or an LLM. They operate under the same commercial logic.

JP: It also shows how these worldviews are constructed, which in turn, allows you to think about how you can construct new ones, like that of *Babylonian Vision*.

NAB: It's about creating visibility for other worlds. I call it, for example, 'Southern datasets.' Although it is also true that in our surveillance age, it is sometimes a huge advantage not to be seen. It's less about constructing a new worldview and more about making one that is already right under our noses that isn't really engaged with more visible. I also know that I cannot ask everyone to examine every technology they're using, that's just not feasible.

JP: I went to a talk by Hito Steyerl (2023), and she was asked at the end of the presentation whether she would use these technologies in her practice, or whether she'll stay in a position of more cerebral critique. Her stance was that she is not going to utilise them in her practice yet, because she hadn't yet found an ethical entry point to use them.

NAB: I do understand her point, and 95 percent agree with her. But there are some exceptions, I'd say, where it's worth exploiting the exploitative and turning it around. But if one is not doing this, then it's certainly not worth it at all. What we have seen in the past years is certainly too much of uncritical usage in contemporary art, an aesthetisation of what AI can do... most of it I can't even look at and I don't need to because it basically all looks the same. In that sense, I agree with her.

JP: Outside of maintaining a sense of social rather than capital drive, I find that an important quality of your work is that it takes a critical stance as a foundation, but then moves beyond this to invoke the potential of alternative trajectories. I really felt this when I saw *The Post-Truth Museum* in May 2024, when it was installed as part of the *Poetics of Encryption* exhibition at the KW Institute for Contemporary Art in Berlin. In viewing the video work, you're primarily focused on these three older, white, male museum directors. And you've audio deepfaked them to put new words into their mouths, words that come from critical texts you've collected. These are at times confessions of shame around museum complicity in colonial practices or expressing a more equitable and sustainable future for the institution. Things they would have normally never have said, that subvert their usual narrative. For me, as a viewer, hearing and seeing these sentiments expressed by these figures enacted a kind of a wish fulfillment. Can you describe the work from your perspective and how you came to make it?

NAB: I worked on *The Post-Truth Museum* over several years because I became pregnant, and then I couldn't finish it. Even before I was pregnant, I thought I didn't really want to talk about the museum and restitution anymore, because everyone had said everything already. I felt I had nothing else to add, so let's leave the rest to other people and the activists, the solutions or the options are all there. But then I was invited to a workshop at a huge German museum. It was a purely internal workshop, and this museum — I'm not naming it, but they're all the same anyway — is one I would never work for or put work into. But a friend, Professor María do Mar Castro Varela, invited me. She is a great researcher and critical voice in the discourse, a leading scholar in postcolonial theory in Germany. She reminded me how crucial continued dialogue with the people of these institutions is. We don't want to go to this point where there is no dialogue anymore, then nothing will change. I thought she was right, so I decided to do it. And then what happened was that around forty of the hundreds of employees of this huge museum came along for the workshop.

The workshop was positioned as a psychoanalytical session for and of the museum. It was during COVID-19, so it was all on Zoom. It was a bit weird, but maybe better for it, because perhaps it allowed the employees to say things they might not have said in person. They were telling me things like, 'Oh, as an artist, you are free to say everything, whatever you want to say about museums, to be critical.' And I had to say, 'Stop, I have to stop here. Like we're all just human beings. You guys are in a privileged, secure power position, you can say whatever you want to say.' But it turns out they can't, of course, not really. Or they feel they can't. They were completely unempowered. In Iraq, there's the saying the fish stinks from its head. As long as the directors are turned towards a certain position, whether that's anti-restitution, under a colonial mission, nothing will change. And this was the point where I thought, I have an idea what I want to do. Because I was asked whether they could commission a piece from me for the museum. To which I said, no, sorry, I'm not working with you. Of course, they are free to buy a piece of mine and exhibit it. Which they agreed to even before it was finished, but they haven't yet exhibited *The Post-Truth Museum*. It was first premiered with a show at KW Institute for Contemporary Art, which was very important to me, that it's not for the first time in this museum. This museum has no rights for anything, except to show it. But one of my first ideas was that I wanted to make a piece that will give the people who work in the museum some form of a cognitive dissonance that will speak to them. They will find it intriguing, but also disturbing, and inspiring. I was done critiquing the museum, so I tried to create another world, another future scenario with a more ethical museum. So this was my starting point. This is why I chose directors of museums as the heads who kind of set the tone for the discourse from their side. And conceptually, what I was aiming at was, of course, literally stealing their identities for once, where they stole the identities of entire cultures. And so, they can also kind of feel what it feels like to be in this position. This is why we see videos of directors performing supercritical texts, sometimes confessing or apologising or picturing a museum that I am afraid they are not even able to imagine with their personal mindset...

JP: You've drawn on texts from various critical thinkers[1] who have written incredible works that are also referenced in this

---

1. Including: Ayad Al-Ani; María do Mar Castro Varela; Fazil Moradi; Ariella Aïsha Azoulay and; Nikita Dhawan. Texts by Berlin Postkolonial; Aimé Césaire; Kwame Opoku; Ciraj Rassool; Bénédicte Savoy; W.E.B. Du Bois; Jürgen ZImmerer and Nora Al-Badri are cut together for a piece titled "The Collage."

piece in an implicit way. For instance, you have a poetic piece from Ariella Aïsha Azoulay titled "Un-Documented — Unlearning Imperial Plunder," wherein she writes:

> I will not bury you alive
> in my museums,
> like I did to the worlds of your ancestors
> that should have been yours
> before they were squeezed
> into different galleries dedicated to
> extinct species

When I saw her writing as part of *The Post-Truth Museum*, it also made me think of her work *The Civil Contract of Photography* (Azoulay 2008), which has this framework for thinking through images as a two-way gaze between the people photographed and the people viewing the image. And so the text selection really feeds into *The Post-Truth Museum* as well, because it creates so many points of connection beyond the moment of viewing the work. How did you go about that process of selecting texts?

NAB: Some of them were people who had inspired my work for a long time, and who I love to read. And some of them, of course, I know very well, and others I don't know at all. So I wrote to them and just described what I was about to do at a time where there was nothing yet, because it all came together after I collected the texts. Some wrote new texts, some were shorter, others longer. This is also why I had the printout next to the piece [Figure 5] because I couldn't integrate all the texts. Instead, I took excerpts of the text for the piece, to have it in a format that is digestible for an audience. I was drawn to do an hour and a half long piece, where people could sit there and listen, but in the end, I thought that if people want to read about it, then they can read it. That way they still have a bigger picture of the ideas in this piece, even if they don't have much time. I also selected many texts from the past, from deceased writers, just what I felt resonates with me. But it could have really been a library. I could have also done that, but it would have been more difficult for me to accomplish. I could have fed a whole library into the system, and then redo the piece every time. But for *The Post-Truth Museum*, I tried to make a meta speech that I would like to hear personally from any of those museums (The Louvre,

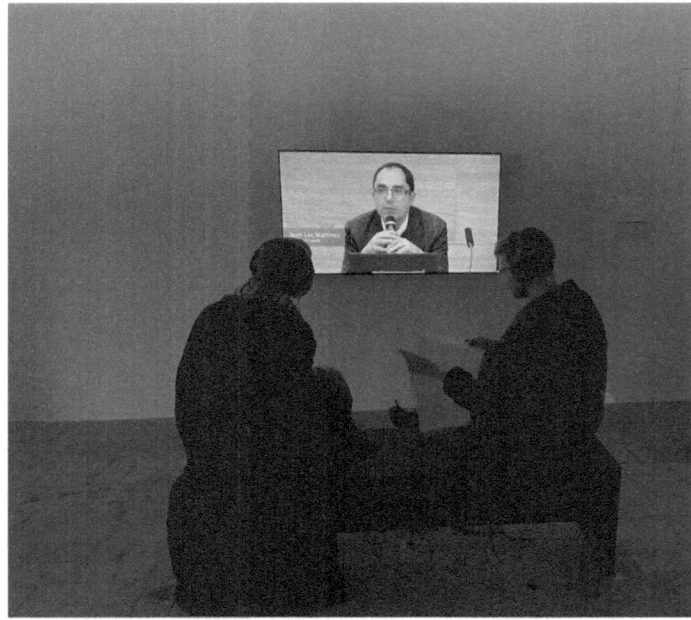

Figure 5: Nora Al-Badri, 2021–23. *The Post-Truth Museum*, installation view at KunstWerke Berlin.

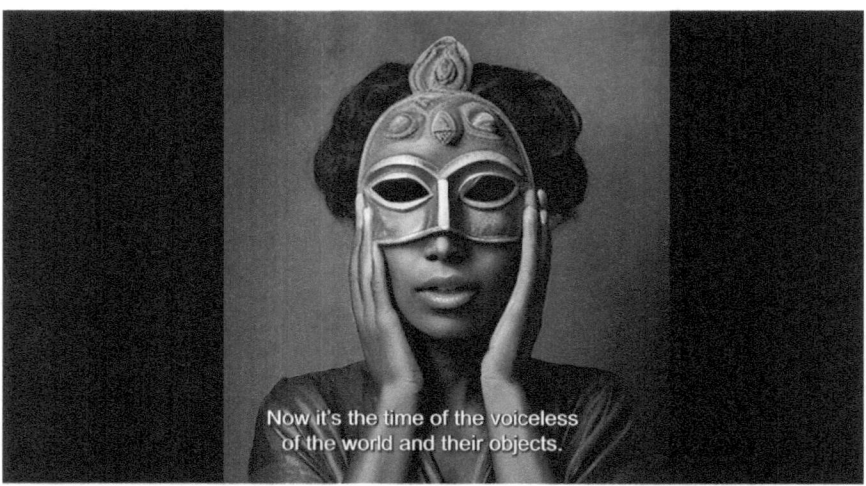

Figure 6: Nora Al-Badri, 2021–23. *The Post-Truth Museum*, videostill.

British Museum, or Prussian Heritage Foundation). What made sense conceptually with working with AI in this piece and with several texts from people, is that in this technology, you always have a collective voice or collective images. It made sense to have a piece that is made out of more than just one voice, so to speak.

> **JP:** This idea of multiplicity, multiple iterations, multiple voices, that's really core to our definition of decentred ethics, this idea that there isn't a singular kind of narrative that can be invoked, but rather it's dispersed, fragmented. And that's where we need to look to understand an ethics for the contemporary era — at all these diffusions and how they're navigated.

NAB: And in *The Post-Truth Museum*, the masks and the objects are speaking for themselves [Figure 6]. I did something similar much earlier with another artist, in 2017, with a chatbot that had the head of Nefertiti. And I just like the idea of letting the objects speak, what would they say? Of course, it's like a projection of a human into the object, but this still lets us put on their shoes. To generate the masks was a bit of a similar process to *Babylonian Vision*. I could only generate those because many artifacts today are integrated in the LLMs, interestingly enough, so they can now depict certain regions and archaeological iconography. Because the masks are put together as a face, I think it resonates more with the audience than if there was a bridge speaking, for example. Also, of course, because masks, in many cultures, are ritual objects that live, that are activated or animated. This was the metaphor that I liked the most. And to have all kinds of masks, also the death masks, and then what it means that people have a fake mask on. It was more a game between wordplay, a symbol, and the ancestral object.

> I am not a ghost, but I come to you in your dreams.
>
> Now it's the time of the voiceless of the world and their objects. It's the time when plunder starts speaking for itself!
>
> We healed.
> We restored.
> Our broken hearts and shards.

> We fight.
> We will take back our dead and their objects.
> Into our lands.
>
> Some masks are coming off.
> Death-masks are put on.
> Other masks are reanimated.
> We are dancing again.
> We are truth-speaking again.
>
> As technoheritage advances,
> the imperial museum becomes a tomb,
> museum storages become caves,
> and we will circulate in an endless stream of collective memory,
> on your networks, chips and screens...[2]

JP: We've always had these tools, rituals, objects that we integrate into our lives, that without their relations are inanimate, but as soon as they enter a system of relations are animated. And we can think of AI in the same way. A lot of people, and with good reason, struggle with how we anthropomorphise AI, how we tend to project our humanness onto technology when it is a different thing, and we should recognise its difference. But at the same time, I see anthropomorphising as a way to try and connect with that which is more-than-human.

NAB: It's not just a bad thing at all, right? It's what makes us human, and it doesn't matter if it's a computational system or if it's an inanimate object. But masks and AI are both made by humans — I find all of it very human, from the content to how it works with all its biases and how we interpret it.

JP: The recognition of the more-than-human has been such a vital part of non-Western knowledge systems for such a long time. For me, a 'more-than-human' perspective doesn't negate the human, but recognises the vitality of different entities — both organic and inorganic — that we live amongst. I'm interested in whether this

---

2. Text written by Al-Badri for *The Post-Truth Museum.*

is a way that we can start to engage with AI, to embed an ethics of care into our relationship with technology. Because as soon as we start seeing something as having some kind of vitality — and it doesn't necessarily need to have consciousness or sentience — it is positioned in a system of relations that adds to our ecology. And so if we're going to have any sort of sustainable future, how do we think about and talk about the technologies that we currently have in a way that embeds an ethics of care into them? A decentred ethics that includes the more-than-human?

NAB: I tend to use the term planetary, which seems to include the concept of the more-than-human. But, of course, we speak from a human positionality. I agree with you that this mystification of technology is something that goes against the human and the planetary, because often this is just a way of keeping it opaque, but for all the wrong reasons. I usually try to demystify it, or to just use it as an instrument or as a medium. But if you ask me about the bigger picture on technology, yes, of course, I think that there are values of care we clearly should nurture more in Western cultures today. I would not go as far as to talk about inanimate objects or technology on a similar plane to animals. Animals have consciousness and sentience. But sometimes in these conversations, animals and technologies are all thrown in one box. There's a line. Technology is manmade, as are the objects from my projects, and the projections we put into them are manmade.

JP: Positioning it as planetary is useful. So much of my work is about the cultural projections that are embedded into machines and how that shapes what we perceive them as being able to do. But then, of course, the hardware that we use comes from the earth. It is very planetary, made of minerals. But as you said, that's so opaque, right? When we sit here in front of our screens, we're rarely thinking about mineral mines in Chile. Perhaps if we did emphasise that more, it might be easier for us to access that planetary consciousness. One of the things in *The Post-Truth Museum* that I noticed is that there are a few interspersed shots that are more environmental or architectural images [Figure 7], as part of imagining what a more sustainable museum could look like. There's an invitation to think in ways that invoke something different, outside of nature-culture as a dichotomy. That invocation in *The Post-Truth Museum* also draws on the history of institutional critique. Perhaps it's idealistic, but I see this as an approach whereby artists aren't necessarily dismissing the institution outright. Rather, they are highlighting flaws because there is an inherent recognition of unfulfilled potential for and in institutions. It requires imagination, and artists are so vital because they are doing that imaginative work and creating ways of sharing it. What do you feel the value of a practice-led approach is, how does it shape how you think about AI?

NAB: I'm also an idealist. Probably that's why I do these kinds of things and try to go one step further in another direction, a step more than critique, or other than critique. AI is enabling us to lay out scenarios and experience them in multi-sensorial ways, more so than if it were to be purely text-based. There are more mediums at hand, that's its strength. I'm certainly trying to shape AI in ways that might inspire other people in how to use it in another way.

JP: Do you previsualise everything? I'm assuming there are certain times where, because of the generative component of your work, there is some element of randomness or surprise. How do you work with that negotiation of being in control of a creative practice and letting go of control to make space for the random?

NAB: For sure. In some aspects it's more random than in others. I think as soon as you generate an image, it's more random. But for example, animating the directors was something that I envisioned exactly like it turned out. I did take their faces, their appearance, but also their voices [Figure 8]. In the beginning, it is the computer voice, but then each director has their own real (or actual?) voice. Of course, these still have the computer aspect, because it's very difficult to recreate a voice without the consent of the person... Which I didn't ask for, and I think I never would have gotten. At other times, randomness is something that I embrace a lot. In the process of this practice, you could infinitely redo the images, and they would always change a little bit. Some would change more. For example, generating the masks was more changeable. I was selecting the ones that resonated the most with me, and that depicted the range of what I thought they could offer. But there is always randomness in it. And I think this has been there since the beginning of computer art. I love it.

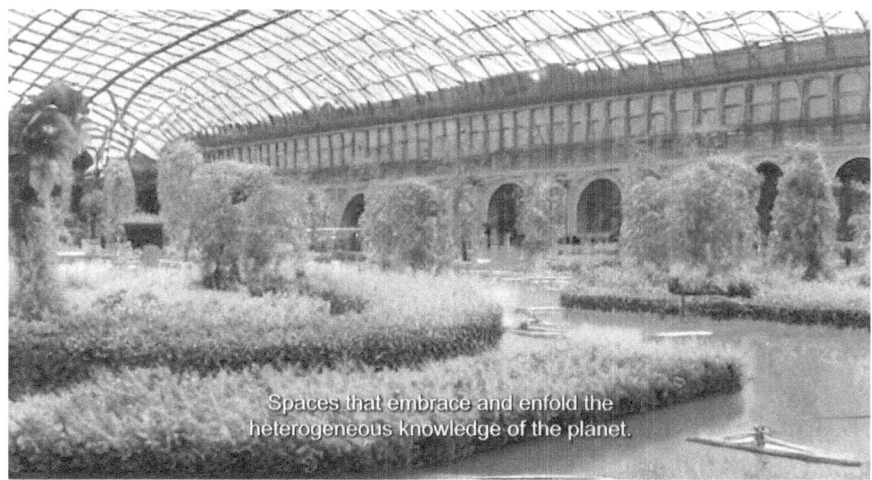

Figure 7: Nora Al-Badri, 2021–23. *The Post-Truth Museum*, videostill.

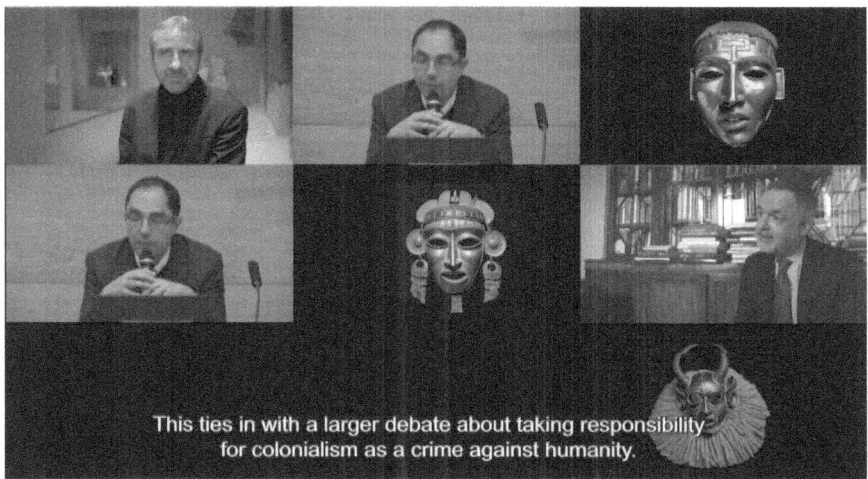

Figure 8: Nora Al-Badri, 2021–23. *The Post-Truth Museum*, videostill.

JP: I wanted to ask whether there are specific boundaries that you wouldn't cross in your use of these technologies within your art practice, because of your ethical stance.

NAB: For certain projects, I would always try to move within cultural protocols, if I were to do any projects in such a realm, which I haven't done yet, like this. And as a media artist, you get asked by many institutions or companies to do things. For example, Facebook asked me to do something for them. Those are the lines I wouldn't cross. I don't blame some fellow colleagues for doing this work with Google or Facebook, but I would never do it. In the end it probably gets back to one's motivation, namely to the idea of prioritising the social over capital.

JP: That you reference cultural protocols as the thing to prioritise really speaks to a decentred ethics, because, of course, cultural protocols and governmental policies don't always match. Governmental policies are not always representative of various communities.

NAB: Yes exactly — especially as an artist it is crucial to privilege cultural protocol over policy, governments and institutional authority! At least that's my belief.

References

Al-Badri, Nora. *The Post Truth Museum*. 2021-2023. AI video, sound, https://www.nora-al-badri.de/works-index

Al-Badri, Nora. *Babylonian Vision*. 2020. GAN video, https://www.nora-al-badri.de/works-index

Al-Badri, Nora. *Neuronal Ancestral Sculptures Series*, 2020. GAN art, https://www.nora-al-badri.de/works-index

Al-Badri, Nora and Jan Nikolai Nelles. 2015. *The Other Nefertiti*, intervention, 3D print, video 17min, https://www.nora-al-badri.de/works-index

Azoulay, Ariella. 2008. *The Civil Contract of Photography*. Translated by R. Mazali and R. Danieli. Zone Books.

Bodla, Navaneeth, Rama Chellappa, and Gang Hua. 2018. "Semi-Supervised FusedGAN for Conditional Image Generation." Preprint, arXiv, January 17, 2018. https://doi.org/10.48550/arXiv.1801.05551.

Buschek, Christo, and Jer Thorp. n.d. "Models All the Way Down." Knowing Machines. Accessed October 7, 2024. https://knowingmachines.org/models-all-the-way.

Steyerl, Hito. 2023. "Subprime Images." Presented at the Critical AI in the Art Museum: Practices and Politics series, Australian National University, Canberra, October 31. https://criticalai.art/hito.html.

Weiskopf, Carmen, and Domagoj Smoljo. n.d. "About !Mediengruppe Bitnik." !!Mediengruppe Bitnik _. Accessed October 10, 2024.

Decentred Ethics: a collective statement

Vanessa Bartlett,
Jasmin Pfefferkorn,
Emilie K. Sunde,
Tyne Daile Sumner,
Gabby Bush

As a collective, we strive to make things that are generous, demanding, complicated, and critical, while acknowledging that our work emerges from systems steeped in colonial, patriarchal, and classist histories.

Art, ethics, and research, like everything else, have become instrumentalised and commodified under late capitalism. Individualism persists in many of our institutions. Amidst all this, we have tried to shape our way of working to follow the theories and practices of decentring explored in this volume. In practice, this is often curtailed by precarious employment, short-term funding cycles, ill health, care responsibilities, and the need to find a place to keep on living within imperfect systems. The following statement articulates the principles — and realities — that organised our collective vision for this volume. Although this text is shaped out of our own lived experiences, we offer decentred ethics as an invitation to everyone to run wild in whatever way seems possible within the day-to-day acts of making art and doing research on a planet in crisis.

1. Decentred ethics aims for collectivism rather than interdisciplinarity

In the terms of the contemporary neoliberal academy, the work we do is often described as interdisciplinary. This word — both expansive and yet somehow also limiting — is employed to suggest that this kind of research is part of a zeitgeist. Moreover, the term's stem (inter) suggests the combining of multiple academic endeavours into one shared activity. But words can be deceptive, and as scholars and artists of the humanities we treat institutional terminology with measured suspicion. *Interdisciplinarity* hides a variety of centralised power relations — it is a term of economic currents and murky strategic impulses. Aspirational yet constraining, it is almost always tied to technology, infrastructure, and the kinds of benchmarks one encounters in corporate university policy. And so, let us reframe: let us claim the word *collective*. Collectivism. Collectively-held. This is our shared language of operation.

Thinking about our work as collective allows us to eschew the vague and institutionally-situated interdisciplinary encounter. The collective suggests autonomy, flexibility, creativity, and ambition. It also ties us, in ways that are paradoxically freeing, to art practice as a method in an academic system increasingly geared towards the empirical. Collectivism is decentralised without becoming insidiously sprawling. It is more intuitive and inventive. It offers a space for reflection, collaboration, and authenticity. There is no one way to move and create across disciplines, nor should the tools for evaluating rigour and value be solely in the hands of a single authority. Perhaps most importantly, appreciating our work as collective creates the possibility for new ethical formations.

2. Decentred ethics demands a complex view of art as research

Cultures have shared unspoken forms of knowing through story and song for millennia. Creativity has been a way of leading us into a sense of mystery, rather than a tool for mastery. How would relationships change if the system had more confidence in things that could not — and should not — be instrumentalised? What is our recourse in the face of instrumentalisation?

Art is vital to the decentring and remaking of institutions. And yet, those who hold the purse strings often have an expectation that art should be produced for free or on shoe-string budgets. We advocate for the labour of artistic production to be equal to other forms of research and inquiry, rather than the institutional instrumentalising and co-opting of art. Collectivism, as we define it, has a flexible hierarchy wherein artists, curators and other creative practitioners can set research agendas. Art research should not be reduced to a tool in service of disciplines considered more 'serious'. Art, in its collective and messy entirety, should be considered research unto itself. At the same time, we acknowledge that many artists would eschew the notion of art as research. There should be space for art in research contexts, with the understanding that art does more than just produce knowledge for research.

Art brings us close to what is difficult and complex about practicing ethics.

3. Decentred ethics is a practice, not a template

A decentred ethics emerges relationally. Because it is relationally held, decentred ethics is an inherently collaborative practice. It requires cognisance of our capacity to affect and be affected by other entities. What works in one assemblage may no longer be adequate when relations shift. Decentred ethics is in perpetual motion — a continuous becoming. It refuses the template, refutes the binary, and evolves along new lines of flight.

How vague! How messy! Wouldn't it be *easier* to be told what to do, rather than live with the discomfort of this ambiguity? And yet, a static ethical framework is only useful to a point. Life — this confluence of things and beings in space and time — is dynamic. To be internalised, ethics must be a learnt process. It is practised over and over, renegotiated as we encounter new perspectives, experiences, relations. It is not just that a decentred ethics is a *slow* process — it is a *continuous* process. A code of ethics, as a set of conventions or principles, is presented as a finished chapter. A decentred ethics is a working document.

Because it is a continuous process, decentred ethics materialises and is intuited through small (but scalable and multidimensional in their breadth and depth) interventions. Because it is dynamic, decentred ethics avoids capture by commercial imperative and for-profit systems. It resists as much as it creates.

4. Decentred ethics necessitates emotional and social labour

Being part of a collective is an immense reward, but collectivity needs to be cultivated. Decentred ethics supports transparency around the emotional and social labour required to work in the arts and humanities under neoliberalism. It resists demands to do more at a faster pace. It adjusts when instability raises its head in the lives of one of our members. Ideas of excellence have become detached from the realities of care work, chronic health issues, student debt, domestic labour, and class. It is time to speak candidly about the energy that it takes to cultivate care and collectivism, and who is tasked with this emotional labour.

As a dispersed collective working across time zones, we meet at all hours of the day and night to sustain the momentum of our work. Bodies carry the burden of this post-Fordist, endlessly networked, *zooming* way of tending to the relationships that matter. Despite this broken system, there is always something to be shared. Our inherent potential is to produce and shape generosity, patience, friendship and trust, shifting us away from the bounded spaces of competition and individualism. Our way of doing ethics needs time to solidify, and — somewhat paradoxically — space to be mutable.

5. Decentred ethics makes space for multiplicity

Decentred ethics is oriented towards an ecological existence. Ecologies do not have a centre. Various entities affect one another, at times creating slippages and glitches, at others, barricades and anchors. How does one then envision the space of decentring? Is this space made, or is it found? What arrangement of space affords flourishing? The answer depends on one's frame of reference; whether it is one of scarcity or plenitude. It is vital that we recognise that some things are finite — this encourages us to take care, to configure value around the moments and materials that are precious and fragile. Yet it is also crucial that within and around us we find sustainable resources — like generosity, friendship, and solidarity.

Decentred ethics asks us to experience the discomfort of knowing that many of us benefit from systemic injustices. It requires acknowledgment of one's positionality within the broken system. Beyond acknowledgment, it requires a response. In this sense, we might align decentred ethics with a kind of hospitality. A genuine hospitality is not a unidirectional relationship between guest and host. It requires all parties to make space for difference. Decentring ethics enables pluriversalisms, respecting the multiplicity of worldviews and actively engaging with them. At times, this is a brief point of intersection, at others an extended dialogue. It can even be the act of creation; the emergence of something new.

Biographies

Dani Admiss is a creative climate leader and independent curator-artist. Her work is a journey of learning to live well with others within limits. Admiss champions community empowerment and learning, often working with a coalition of agitators, dream weavers, growers and caregivers. Currently she is working on Sunlight Liberation Network (SLN), an art and climate justice network that supports and shares peer learning and imaginative action toward building better tomorrows. Admiss has created numerous projects in the UK and EU. She was an Artangel Making Time resident (2023) and a Stanley Picker Fellow (2020). She is an advisor on the editorial board of 'Digital Materialities and Sustainable Futures' book series, Emerald Press.

Aarati Akkapeddi is a Telugu-American interdisciplinary artist, coder, and educator based on Lenape land (Brooklyn, NY). Their process-driven practice integrates extensive research — including archival exploration, oral history interviews, and site-based investigations — with personal storytelling. Aarati's work bridges the personal and collective, exploring the interplay between memory, technology, and identity. Their projects often take the form of multi-modal series, combining mediums such as video, print, and digital platforms to present layered narratives. They also work as a designer and developer, building digital interfaces, and as an educator, teaching coding and emerging technologies to designers and artists.

Nora Al-Badri is a paradisciplinary artist with a significant body of research-driven conceptual media works. Her practice engages decolonial and post-digital thinking and reflects a commitment to the speculative possibilities of technologies. Al-Badri also intersects with the academy, holding a degree in political sciences and the role of lecturer in Zurich, as well as guest professor in Stuttgart. She has exhibited widely — in the Victoria and Albert Museums' Applied Arts Pavilion at La Biennale di Venezia, 3rd Design Biennal Istanbul, ZKM Karlsruhe, Science Gallery, Dublin, NRW Forum, Space Fundacion Telefonica,

Berliner Herbstsalon — Gorki Theater, Ars Electronica, Abandon Normal Devices, The Influencers, Gray Area Festival Art& Technology, among other venues.

Vanessa Bartlett is an independent curator and interdisciplinary research leader. Drawing on her own lived experiences, she explores how medical and technical systems shape equity, ethics and social justice, particularly for disabled and chronically ill folk. Her curated exhibitions exploring the psychosocial impacts of digital cultures have been seen at international arts spaces such as FACT (Foundation for Art and Creative Technology), UNSW Galleries and Furtherfield and have featured in The Guardian, Creative Review and BBC Radio 4. She has edited two books for award-winning academic publisher Liverpool University Press, the most recent of which was co-edited with Professor Henrietta Bowden Jones, one of the UK's most high-profile neuroscience researchers. She was Mckenzie Postdoctoral Fellow in the School of Culture and Communication (2020–2023), and Research Fellow in the Faculty of Law (2024–2025), at University of Melbourne.

Pita Arreola-Burns and **Elliott Burns** are co-founders of Off Site Project, a curatorial arts platform launched in 2017. Pita is an Independent Curator based in London. She was Curator of Digital Art at the Victoria & Albert Museum from 2021 to 2024, where she co-authored the book *Digital Art: 1960s to Now* (V&A/Thames & Hudson, 2024). Elliott is a Lecturer in Digital Cultures at Central Saint Martins, University of the Arts London with research specialisms in online curation and video game-based artworks.

Gabby Bush held the role of program manager at the Centre for AI and Digital Ethics (CAIDE) from 2020–2023. In this role, Gabby coordinated the work of CAIDE, including engagement, research dissemination, grants and projects, including work on monitoring and surveillance, bias in algorithms and the CAIDE research stream in Art, AI and Digital Ethics. Gabby joined the centre from Canberra, where she spearheaded engagement and partnerships in technology and development. Prior to that Gabby ran the eGovernance and Digitisation project for the United Nations Development Program in Samoa. Gabby hails from Aotearoa, New Zealand and has postgraduate qualifications in International Development and Religious Studies.

Seán Cubitt is Professor of Screen Studies at the University of Melbourne. He works on ecocritical approaches to the history and philosophy of media with current projects on aesthetic politics and practices of truth.

Xanthe Dobbie is an Australian new media artist and filmmaker. Working across on- and offline modes of making, Dobbie's practice aims to capture the experience of contemporaneity as reflected through queer and feminist ideologies. Drawing on humour, pop, sex, history and iconography, they develop shrines to a post-truth era. Xanthe holds a BFA (Honours) from RMIT and an MA (Film Editing) from AFTRS. In 2021, Xanthe commenced a PhD (Design) at RMIT, where they will be focusing on curatorial practice and digital art.

Solange Glasser is a Senior Lecturer in Music Psychology at the Melbourne Conservatorium of Music, University of Melbourne. Her interdisciplinary teaching areas include music psychology, performance science, expertise and creativity, and in 2023 she received the 'Excellence in Teaching at the Conservatorium' award. Solange has spent more than two decades researching multisensory perception and the impact of synaesthesia and absolute pitch on musical development. Her current research collaborations explore immersive realities, digital ethics, and artificial intelligence. She holds degrees from the University of Paris IV Sorbonne (France), Queensland Conservatorium of Music, and University of Melbourne.

Beverley Hood is an artist and Reader in Technological Embodiment and Creative Practice at Edinburgh College of Art, University of Edinburgh. She studied Sculpture and Electronic Imaging at Duncan of Jordanstone College of Art, Dundee and Nova Scotia College of Art & Design, Halifax, Canada. Her research practice interrogates the impact of technology on relationships, the body and human experience, through the creation of practice-based projects and writing. A longstanding research interest is live performance using technology and interdisciplinary collaboration. She has developed projects involving a range of practitioners, including medical researchers, scientists, writers, technologists, dancers, actors and composers. She is currently Co-Investigator on the **UKRI BRAID** (Bridging Responsible AI Divides) programme, a six-year national research programme (2022–2028) funded by the UKRI Arts and Humanities Research Council (AHRC), led by the University of Edinburgh in partnership with the Ada Lovelace Institute and the BBC.

Libby Heaney is an award-winning artist with a PhD in Quantum Physics. She is the first artist to work with quantum computing as a functioning medium. Solo exhibitions in 2024 include *Quantum Soup*, HEK, Basel and *Heartbreak & Magic*, Somerset House, London. Her first artistic monograph was also published by Hatje Cantz and she participated in Frieze Sculpture, London. Heaney frequently delivers keynotes around the world such as at the Gwangju Biennale Symposium, Gwangju and Sonar+D, Barcelona. In 2025, Heaney will hold a solo show at Orlean House Gallery, London, including and responding to paintings by JMW Turner.

Ryan Kelly is a Senior Research Fellow in the School of Computing and Information Systems at University of Melbourne. He conducts research that contributes to the field of Human-Computer Interaction (HCI), with expertise in interaction design, social computing, and digital health. Ryan is an expert on topics including augmented reality, virtual reality, ageing and technology, personal informatics and communication apps. His research involves using quantitative and qualitative methods to design and evaluate the next generation of computing technologies. Ryan publishes regularly in internationally-leading outlets for HCI research and serves on scholarly committees for conferences such as ACM CHI and CSCW.

Helen Knowles is an artist and curator of the Birth Rites Collection, the first and only collection of contemporary artwork dedicated to childbirth. Knowles is currently undertaking a practice-based PhD project called 'More-than-Human Healthcare' at The University of Northumbria.

Ben Loveridge is the Immersive Media Coordinator at the University of Melbourne, assisting with the integration of spatial and experiential technology across teaching and research. He obtained his Bachelor of Music at the University of Melbourne with studies in guitar and composition at the Conservatorium of Music. Ben has worked in film and television post-production, audio engineering, as well as a musician and music photographer. He holds a Master of Music (Research) from the University of Melbourne and is currently undertaking a PhD at the

Faculty of Fine Arts and Music, exploring music performance simulation in extended reality.

Margaret Osborne is a psychologist and inaugural interdisciplinary Associate Professor in Psychology and Music (Performance Science) at the University of Melbourne. Her research and teaching span performance science, music psychology, and training professional psychologists. Dedicated to supporting artists' mental and physical health, she has developed new curricula in performance psychology, led the Australian Society for Performing Arts Healthcare, serves as inaugural Chair of the Australian Healthy Conservatoires Network, and maintains a consulting practice. Renowned for research in music performance anxiety, she investigates self-regulated learning and emotion regulation strategies to enhance confidence, health, and resilience across diverse performance domains.

Jasmin Pfefferkorn is a Postdoctoral Research Fellow in the School of Culture and Communication at the University of Melbourne. She is currently researching the impact of generative technologies on museums' practices. She is an Executive Member of the Research Unit in Public Cultures, on the steering committee for CAIDE AAIDE, and the co-founder and co-director of the research group *CODED AESTHETICS*. She holds a PhD from the University of Melbourne on emergent museum practice and is the author of *Museums as Assemblage* (Routledge, 2023). Her interdisciplinary research spans museum studies, critical AI, visual culture, and digital humanities.

Iyad Rahwan is director of the Max Planck Institute for Human Development in Berlin, where he founded and directs the Center for Humans & Machines. He is also an honorary professor of Electrical Engineering and Computer Science at the Technical University of Berlin. Prior to moving to Berlin, he was an Associate Professor of Media Arts & Sciences at the Massachusetts Institute of Technology (MIT). A native of Aleppo, Syria, Rahwan holds a PhD from the University of Melbourne, Australia.

Kamya Ramachandran is the Founder-Director of BeFantastic which conceptualises and manifests Bangalore's TechArt Festival series most recently, FutureFantastic. She is currently a Fellow with IDSA-Ars Electronica's Founding Lab. As a trained architect, researcher and design educator with career experience spanning multiple geographies from the UK, USA, India and now Singapore, she is passionate about convening and engaging diverse collaborative communities for a better world. With a keen eye for crafting and manifesting programs with socio-environmental themes at its core, Kamya is adept at engaging stakeholders from the public and private sector toward supporting artists and audiences alike.

Lucy Sparrow is an Associate Lecturer in the School of Computing and Information Systems. Her research is primarily interdisciplinary, lying at the intersection of human-computer interaction, game studies, social sciences, and philosophy. She has a particular interest in digital ethics and game design, and engages in qualitative work that explores the everyday ethical understandings embedded in gaming contexts. Her research aims to shed light on the complexities of multiplayer gaming environments and communities in order to better design for these spaces in meaningfully ethical ways.

Emilie K. Sunde is a PhD candidate on the Australian Research Council Discovery Project *Digital Photography: Mediation, Memory, and Visual Communication* at the University of Melbourne. Her research focuses on computational reproduction, latent space and visual culture. She is the co-director and co-founder of CODED AESTHETICS and part of the Centre for AI and Digital Ethics's research collective Art, AI, and Digital Ethics. Sunde has published work in *The Nordic Journal of Aesthetics*, *Media Theory*, *Philosophy of Photography*, *xCoAx*, among others.

Tyne Daile Sumner is an interdisciplinary researcher in English & Theatre Studies at the University of Melbourne. Her key research areas are twentieth-century American poetry, surveillance studies and Digital Humanities. She is interested in the ways that literary texts respond to, resist, represent and shape cultures and technologies of surveillance. She also researches and writes in the areas of cultural analytics, critical infrastructure studies, facial-recognition technologies, and digital ethics. Her first monograph is *Lyric Eye: The Poetics of Twentieth Century Surveillance* (Routledge 2021). She has published and forthcoming articles in *Journal of Intercultural Studies*, *Gender & History*, *Interdisciplinary Science Reviews* and *Open Humanities Press*. Tyne frequently presents in a wide range of public forums on topics ranging from popular culture and song lyrics, through to big data and the future of libraries. She has curated exhibitions and performances relating to surveillance, Artificial Intelligence and cultural data.

Amanda Wasielewski is an artist and researcher. She is Associate Senior Lecturer of Digital Humanities and Associate Professor of Art History in the Department of ALM at Uppsala University in Sweden. Her research focuses on the use of artificial intelligence tools to study and create art and images. Wasielewski is the author of three monographs including *Computational Formalism: Art History and Machine Learning* (2023), she is co-editor of the volume *Critical Digital Art History* (2024) and she is the author of "Unnatural Images: On AI-Generated Photographs" (Critical Inquiry, Autumn 2024). Her fourth monograph, *Digital Photography After AI*, is forthcoming.

www.ingramcontent.com/pod-product-compliance
Lightning Source LLC
Chambersburg PA
CBHW031606210526
45464CB00004B/1455